Air Raid:
Pearl Harbor!

Air Raid: Pearl Harbor!

RECOLLECTIONS OF A DAY OF INFAMY

Edited by Paul Stillwell

Naval Institute Press
Annapolis, Maryland

The following articles are reprinted by permission of The Trustees of Columbia University in the City of New York:

"The President Faces War," by Frances Perkins, © 1976 by Columbia University.

"Worse Than Dante's Inferno," by Vice Admiral Walter Stratton Anderson, © 1972 by Columbia University

The following articles are reprinted by permission of the U.S. Naval Academy Alumni Association, Inc.:

"Call Out the Marines," by Brigadier General Samuel R. Shaw, © 1973 by the U.S. Naval Academy Alumni Association, Inc.

"A Navy Bride Learns to Cope," by Peggy Hughes Ryan, © 1974 by the U.S. Naval Academy Alumni Association, Inc.

"Did the Japs Win?" by Evelyn W. Guthrie, © 1975 by the U.S. Naval Academy Alumni Association, Inc.

Library of Congress Cataloging in Publication Data
Main entry under title:
Air raid, Pearl Harbor!
    Includes index.
    1. Pearl Harbor, Attack on, 1941—Personal narratives. I. Stillwell, Paul, 1944–
D767.92.A67   940.54'28   81–81670
ISBN 0–87021–086–6   AACR2

Printed in the United States of America

Contents

Preface

"Remember Pearl Harbor!" That exhortation helped spur the United States to victory in World War II. Yet, the two generations of Americans born since 1941—mine and my sons'—cannot respond to the admonition, because they didn't experience the event in the first place. This collection of memories of that "date which will live in infamy" has two principal aims: first, to rekindle the feelings of the time in those who lived through that watershed day in American history; second, to acquaint younger Americans, in vivid, personal terms, with the happenings that so stirred their forebears. This compendium of individual recollections doesn't aim to be a definitive story of the events at Pearl Harbor; it seeks to provide a sampling of the many diverse viewpoints available, and to cover the broad spectrum of those events rather than to concentrate on a specific aspect.

My active naval service began in 1966 when I reported to a ship whose home port was Yokosuka, Japan. During the following two and one-half years, despite frequent forays southward to Vietnam and other places, I spent much time in Japan and developed considerable regard and affection for its people. Not so one of my shipmates, a chief quartermaster, who on 7 December 1941 was a seaman on board the battleship *West Virginia*. By the mid-1960s, his hatred for the Japanese had not abated. It was therefore a cruel irony that his assignment to our ship forced him to make his home ashore in Japan. On the long, slow evenings of standing watch at sea, he and I often chatted about that and many other matters. While I could sympathize with his feelings, I could not share his hatred. In our case, the "generation gap" encompassed the fact that I did not experience the events that gave rise to his bitterness.

During the course of my active service, I became a reader of the U.S. Naval Institute *Proceedings*. My reading continued after I returned to civilian life, and thus I became acquainted with many stories about the attack on Pearl Harbor. One such story—an article in this book by Commander Lawrence R. Schmieder—prompted me to write a letter to the editor of the *Proceedings*. Commander Schmieder had, I wrote, "fondly recreated the flavor of a time and place for those of us who were then only a gleam in the eyes of wartime fathers."

The Naval Institute celebrated its centennial in 1973, and shortly thereafter I joined the staff of the *Proceedings*. The job gave me the opportunity—indeed, the obligation—to see what had been published during the magazine's first one hundred years. In looking back, I found dozens of articles about the attack on Pearl Harbor and came to the realization that they constituted a treasure waiting to be mined. A few people probably read each article as it was published, but it did not seem likely that anyone had had a chance to read them all in such juxtaposition that the connections between them could be seen and the different viewpoints could be compared.

To publish all the *Proceedings* articles, book reviews, and comments about Pearl Harbor would require a far larger volume than this one. Consequently, I decided to include only those articles that dealt with the firsthand experiences of individuals, either on the American or the Japanese side, who had a connection with the attack. This first-person criterion provided the chance to use another Naval Institute resource, its oral history collection.

During the past dozen years, Dr. John T. Mason, Jr., has been interviewing people who made naval history. Bound volumes of those transcribed memories have been building up, but their contents have not yet enjoyed wide circulation. I hope that the value of the collection will come to be more and more appreciated. Dr. Mason's wife, Mrs. Elizabeth B. Mason, who is acting director of the Columbia University Oral History Research Office, provided valuable assistance by recalling that the university's interviews with Frances Perkins, a former Secretary of Labor, contained vivid descriptions of the weekend Pearl Harbor was attacked. She also arranged for me to use Vice Admiral Walter Stratton Anderson's oral history, which was recorded by her husband before he joined the Naval Institute. The efforts of the two Masons have certainly enhanced the quality of this book, particularly because almost all of the descriptions of events in Washington, D.C., contained herein are drawn from oral histories. I also want to acknowledge Captain Paul B. Ryan and Commander Etta Belle Kitchen, who conducted oral history interviews on the West Coast for the Naval Institute.

For the most part, the articles comprising this anthology are presented as they were written. They have been edited to varying degrees in the interests of accuracy, brevity, clarity, and consistency of style. All the authors who are still alive have had the opportunity to ensure that the editing has not violated accuracy. A few articles, particularly those written right after the attack, appear in virtually the form in which they were written. The oral histories have been converted from the interview format to first-person narratives—also with the concurrence of the subjects who are still alive.

Letting nearly four dozen individuals have their say brings out the fact that people don't always see or remember things in the same way. So be it. The expression of a diversity of views characterizes the forum principle which the *Proceedings* seeks to foster—the concept that the truth is arrived at by having a variety of views presented in the marketplace of ideas.

In the process of drawing together the various elements of the book, I have been accorded a great deal of cooperation by many individuals, and for that I am most grateful. The authors have shown remarkable patience in the face of my nitpicking questions and requests for information, for biographical data, and for photographs resurrected from their places of storage. Finding portrait photos of forty-seven people as they appeared around 1941 turned out to be much more of a challenge than I expected it to be. I particularly want to extend my thanks to the relatives of the authors who are no longer living. The following have given of their time: Mrs. Eleanor Ansel, Mrs. Evelyn L. Lee (daughter of Tai Sing Loo), Commander Arthur H. McCollum, Jr., Mrs. Marianna Radford, Mr. John Drake, Miss Mary Ann Ramsey, and Mrs. Jane Smith-Hutton.

Captain Roy C. Smith III, editor of the Naval Academy Alumni Association's *Shipmate*, very kindly made available memoirs that have appeared in that magazine. I thank him for those, Dr. Clark G. Reynolds, author of *The Fast Carriers*, for the article by General Minoru Genda, and Commander William Pettyjohn, editor of the *Naval War College Review*, for the article by Admiral Robert B. Carney. Thanks also go to Admiral James L. Holloway, Jr., Vice Admiral John L. McCrea, Commander Paul H. Backus, and Mr. Joseph C. Harsch for responding to my requests that they set down their recollections for inclusion in this book.

For their considerable help in rounding up illustrations, I want to thank Mrs. Patty Maddocks of the Naval Institute and Mrs. Agnes Hoover of the Naval Historical Center. Credit for the fine painting on the dust jacket goes to Mr. R. G. Smith and his assistant, Ms. Norma Bert, both of McDonnell Douglas Corporation. Others who assisted in my wide-ranging quest for pictures are Lieutenant Commander S. E. Becker of the Pearl Harbor Naval Base; Commander Thomas B. Buell, author of *Master of Sea Power*; Mrs. William P. Burford, whose husband was commanding officer of the USS *Monaghan*; Mrs. Billie-Viers Clatchey of the Naval Academy Alumni Association; Mr. Robert Cressman of Marine Corps History; Mr. John Harbron; Mr. Kohji Ishiwata, editor of *Ships of the World*; Captain Richard Knott, editor of *Naval Aviation News*; Mrs. Helen Knowles; Mr. John W. Leslie of the Department of Labor; Mr. Walter Lord, author of *Day of Infamy*; Mrs. Wilma Miles; Mr. Anthony S. Nicolosi, curator of the Naval War College Museum; Captain Roger Pineau, Captain Mitsuo Fuchida's coauthor; Mr. John Toland, author of *The Rising Sun*; Mr. Jim Trimble of the National Archives; Ms. Ann Whyte, Pan American World Airways; and Mr. Norman Polmar, author of *Aircraft Carriers*.

Dr. Dean Allard, head of the Naval Historical Center's Operational Archives, provided biographies of some of the authors, and Mrs. Gerald E. Foreman, widow of the USS *Oklahoma* historian, supplied the names of that ship's crew members at the time of the attack on Pearl Harbor.

The excellent design and layout of the book are the result of the efforts of Beverly S. Baum and Cynthia Taylor. For putting the finishing touches on this production with her customary professional skill, I thank Mary Veronica Amoss—truly an editor's editor. And, for putting up with my many absences while I was working on the book, I owe much to my wife Karen and sons Joseph and Robert.

Air Raid: Pearl Harbor!

I Led the Air Attack on Pearl Harbor

By Captain Mitsuo Fuchida, former Imperial Japanese Navy
Edited by Captain Roger Pineau, U.S. Naval Reserve (Retired)

In September 1941, I was transferred from the staff of the Third Carrier Division to the aircraft carrier *Akagi*, a position I had left just one year earlier. Shortly after joining my old comrades in the *Akagi*, I was given additional duty as commander of all air groups of the First Air Fleet. This was an assignment beyond all my dreams. I felt that something big must be afoot.

It was at Kagoshima on the southern tip of Kyushu that I first learned the magnitude of events in store for me. My good friend Commander Minoru Genda, air operations officer on the staff of the First Air Fleet, came to see me at the air base and said, "Now don't be alarmed, Fuchida, but we want you to lead our air force in the event that we attack Pearl Harbor!"

Don't be alarmed? It was all I could do to catch my breath, and almost before I had done so we were on our way out to board the *Akagi*, then anchored in Ariake Bay, for a conference with the Commander First Air Fleet, Vice Admiral Chuichi Nagumo, and his staff, including the chief of staff, Rear Admiral Ryunosuke Kusaka.

The more I heard about the plan, the more astonishing it seemed. Genda kept urging that torpedoes be used against ships in Pearl Harbor, a feat that seemed next to impossible in view of the water depth of only 12 meters and the harbor being not more than 500 meters in width. When I pointed this out, Genda merely grew more aggressive, insisting that if we could launch torpedoes, which would not be expected, it would add to the surprise of the attack and multiply its effectiveness. This line of argument won me over, and, despite the technical difficulties that would have to be overcome, I agreed to include torpedoes in our attack plans.

Shallow-water torpedo launching was not the only difficult problem I had to cope with. From ordinary fleet practice we had to shift our energies to specific training for this all-important mission calling for vast and intensive preparations; and, what is more, everything had to be done in haste. It was already late September, and the attack plan called for execution in December!

There was no time to lose. Our fliers had to work at the hardest kind of training. An added handicap to our efforts lay in the fact that, for security reasons, the pilots could not be told about the plans. Our progress was slow, especially with the problem of launching torpedoes in shallow water. Against my will, I had to demand more and more of every man, yet none complained. They seemed to sense the intensification of the international situation and gave of themselves unquestioningly.

It was not until early November that the torpedo problem was finally solved by fixing additional fins to the torpedoes, and then my greatest worry was over. I was indeed proud of my men and felt honored to be their commander and participate in this great attack.

In mid-November, First Air Fleet planes were taken on board their respective carriers which then headed for the Kuriles, traveling singly and taking separate courses to avoid attention. By the twenty-second, the entire force had assembled in isolated Tankan Bay (also known as Hitokappu Bay) on Etorofu, second island from the southern end of the chain extending northeast from Hokkaido. This force consisted of the carriers *Akagi*, *Kaga*, *Soryu*, *Hiryu*, *Shokaku*, and *Zuikaku*; the battleships *Hiei* and *Kirishima*; the heavy cruisers *Tone* and *Chikuma*; the light cruiser *Abukuma*; the destroyers *Urakaze*, *Isokaze*, *Tanikaze*, *Hamakaze*, *Kasumi*, *Arare*, *Kagero*, *Shiranuhi*, and *Akigumo*; the submarines *I-19*, *I-21*, and *I-23*; and the tankers *Kyokuto Maru*, *Kenyo Maru*, *Kokuyo Maru*, *Shinkoku Maru*, *Akebono Maru*, *Toho Maru*, *Toei Maru*, and *Nihon Maru*.

The following order was issued from Tokyo on the day that the *Akagi* sailed into Tankan Bay:

Imperial General Headquarters
Navy Order No. 5

21 November 1941
To: Commander in Chief Combined Fleet Isoroku Yamamoto
Via: Chief of Naval General Staff Osami Nagano
By Imperial Order

1. Commander in Chief Combined Fleet will, at an appropriate time, dispatch to standby points necessary forces for execution of operations.

2. Commander in Chief Combined Fleet is empowered to use force in self-defense in case his fleet is challenged by American, British or Dutch forces during the process of carrying out military preparations.

3. Detailed instructions will be given by the Chief of the Naval General Staff.

Four days later, Admiral Yamamoto accordingly issued an operation order from his flagship *Nagato* at Hiroshima to Vice Admiral Nagumo, in command of the Pearl Harbor Attack Force:

The Task Force will leave Tankan Bay on 26 November and, making every effort to conceal its movement, advance to the standby point, where fueling will be quickly completed.

The designated standby point was 42 degrees north 170 degrees west, more than 1,000 miles to the north of the Hawaiian island chain.

At six o'clock* on the dark and cloudy morning of 26 November, our twenty-eight-ship task force weighed anchor and sailed out into the waters of the North Pacific Ocean. The sortie was cloaked in complete secrecy. A patrol boat guarding the bay entrance flashed a message, "Good luck on your mission." But even that boat was unaware of our assignment. The *Akagi* signalled, "Thanks," and passed by, her ensign fluttering in the morning breeze. It would not be long before this ensign was replaced by a combat flag.

But this did not mean that the arrow had already gone from the bow. "In case negotiations with the U. S. reach a successful conclusion," Nagumo had been instructed, "the task force will put about immediately and return to the homeland." Unaware of this, however, the crews shouted "Banzai!" as they took what might be their last look at Japan.

On the *Akagi*'s bridge Commander Gishiro Miura, the navigation officer, was concentrating all his energies on control of the ship. Whether we reached the scheduled launching point successfully rested entirely upon his shoulders. So tense was his appearance that it made us feel he was a completely different man. His usual jovial attitude had dis-

*East longitude dates, Tokyo time (Zone minus 9) used primarily here; with west longitude dates, Hawaiian time (Zone plus 10½) given in parentheses, where helpful.

In his capacity as Commander First Air Fleet, Vice Admiral Chuichi Nagumo, who flew his flag in the carrier *Akagi*, was the operational commander of the Pearl Harbor Attack Force. Commander Fuchida, who was in command of the air groups of the First Air Fleet, tried in vain to persuade the cautious Nagumo to authorize a second strike on an already devastated Pearl Harbor. (Naval Historical Center: NH 63423, and *Ships of the World* magazine, Tokyo.)

This frame, taken from a Japanese newsreel, shows pilots being briefed on the upcoming strike while their carrier is en route to Pearl Harbor. (Courtesy of Captain Roger Pineau, USNR, Ret.)

appeared. He now wore shoes instead of his usual slippers, and he was neatly dressed, a decided change from his customary dirty, worn-out uniform. Captain Kiichi Hasegawa, the skipper of the ship, stood beside him. Sitting at the flight deck control post under the bridge, I watched the gradually receding mountains of the Kuriles.

The young men of the flying crews were boiling over with fighting spirit. Hard nights and days of training had been followed by hasty preparations, and now the sortie, which meant that they were going to war.

I felt their keen enthusiasm and was reassured. Still I could not help doubting whether Japan had the proper confidence for carrying out a war. At the same time, however, I fully realized my duty as a warrior to fight and win victory for my country.

Personally I was opposed to the operational policy. The idea of an attack on Pearl Harbor was a good one, but I thought the plan should have called for complete destruction of the U. S. Pacific Fleet at the outset, followed by an invasion of the Hawaiian Islands to push America entirely out of the Central Pacific. The plan covered expansion to the south—the Philippines, Malaya, Hong Kong, Guam, and other such vulnerable positions. It was my opinion that if Pacific operations to the east

proved successful, there would be no need for military operations in the south.

Since the United States was the main foe, I could not understand why operations were not aimed directly toward the east. Admiral Yamamoto was quoted as having said that he had no confidence in the outcome of war after the first year. Why, then, did he not press and press the enemy in the first year to force an early conclusion to the war? Anyway, the immediate mission was to strike a telling blow, and my assignment carried a grave responsibility. At the time, I thought, "Who could be luckier than I?"

My thoughts continued: What if the fleet is not in Pearl Harbor? In such a case we would seek out the enemy en route to the attack. If we should meet the enemy tomorrow, would Nagumo withdraw? No, we should attack and destroy him, I thought, and if the admiral showed any hesitation, I would volunteer my views on these matters.

Such thoughts came one after another, but one remained uppermost. I was determined to do my utmost for victory.

In the meantime, the fleet had assumed formation. The carriers sailed in parallel columns of three, followed by the tankers. On the outside, two battleships and two heavy cruisers took positions, the whole group encircled by a screen of the light cruiser and destroyers. The submarines patrolled about 200 miles ahead of our force. The course was direct to the standby point, speed was 14 knots. The first fueling at sea was carried out five days after our sortie, on 30 November.

Since our departure from Tankan Bay, a strict alert had been kept against U. S. submarines. Our course was chosen to pass between the Aleutians and Midway Island so as to keep out of range of air patrols, some of which were supposed to extend 600 miles. Another concern during the cruise was how to avoid a chance meeting with foreign merchant ships. The three submarines sent ahead of the fleet were to report any ships sighted to the fleet, which would then alter course to avoid them.

If an enemy fleet was sighted before X − 2 day, our force was to reverse course immediately and abandon the operation. On the other hand, if it was one day before X day, whether to reverse course or launch the attack was left to the discretion of the task force commander.

Meanwhile, deceptive measures were being taken elsewhere to cover up our movements. On 5, 6, and 7 December, sailors of the Yokosuka Naval Barracks were sent to Tokyo on a sight-seeing tour. In early December, the *Tatsuta Maru* of the N.Y.K. Line had even left Yokohama heading for Honolulu, and she reversed course only upon receipt of the news that hostilities had begun.

Since leaving Tankan Bay, we had maintained our eastward course in complete secrecy, thanks to thick, low-hanging clouds. Moreover, on 30 November and 6 and 7 December, the sea, which we feared might be rough, was calm enough for easy fueling. The not-too-rough sea also made it easy to maintain and prepare planes and gave the men, especially the flying crews, a much-needed chance to relax.

The fleet observed strict radio silence, but concentrated on listening for broadcasts from Tokyo or Honolulu. Our predominant concern was to catch any word about the outbreak of war.

In Tokyo a liaison conference between the government and the high command was held every day from 27 to 30 November to discuss the U. S. proposal of the twenty-sixth. It was concluded that the proposal was an ultimatum tending to subjugate Japan and making war inevitable. At the liaison conference of the thirtieth, the decision was made to go to war. This conference also concluded that a message declaring the end of negotiations be sent to the United States, but that efforts be continued to the last moment. The final decision for war was made at an Imperial Conference on 1 December.

The next day, the General Staff issued the long-awaited order, and our task force received the Combined Fleet dispatch of 5:30 p.m. which said, "X day will be 8 December."

Now the die was cast and our duty was clear. The fleet drove headlong to the east.

Why was 8 December chosen as X day? That was 7 December and Sunday, a day of rest, in Hawaii. Was this merely a bright idea to hit the U. S. Fleet off duty? No, it was not so simple as that. This day for the opening of hostilities had been coordinated with the time of air raids and landings in Malaya, which were scheduled for dawn. Favorable moonlight was a major consideration, three or four days after the full moon being the most desirable time, and on 8 December the moon would be nineteen days old.

There was another reason for choosing 8 December. Our information indicated that the fleet returned to harbor on weekends after training periods at sea, so there was great likelihood that it would be in Pearl Harbor on Sunday morning. All things considered, 8 December was the logical day for the attack.

Long before the planning of the Pearl Harbor attack, we had been interested in fleet activities in the Hawaiian area. Our information showed:

1. The fleet either went out on Tuesday and returned on Friday, or went out on Friday and returned on Saturday of the next week. In either case, it stayed in harbor about a week. When it went out for two weeks, it would usually return by Sunday.

2. The fleet trained to the southeast of Pearl Harbor. Intercepted radio messages from planes flying between this training area and Pearl Harbor showed that these planes were in flight for forty to sixty minutes. Accordingly, the training area was estimated to be near Maui, and probably north of 19 degrees north latitude.

3. It was hard to determine whether the fleet put in to any other port during training periods, and if so, where. There were some indications that it might go to Lahaina or Maalaea for a short while.

After Japan's decision to go to war had been sent to the attack force, intelligence reports on U. S. Fleet activities continued to be relayed to us from Tokyo. The information was thorough, but the news was often delayed two or three days in reaching Tokyo. These reports from the Imperial General Staff were generally as follows:

Issued 10:00 p.m., 2 December; received 12:17 a.m., 3 December

Activities in Pearl Harbor as of 8:00 a.m./28 November:
Departed: 2 BB (*Oklahoma* and *Nevada*), 1 CV (*Enterprise*), 2 CA, 12 DD.

Arrived: 5 BB, 3 CA, 3 CL, 12 DD, 1 tanker.
Ships making port today are those which departed 22 November.
Ships in port on afternoon of 28 November estimated as follows:
6 BB (2 *Maryland* class, 2 *California* class, 2 *Pennsylvania* class)
1 CV (*Lexington*)
9 CA (5 *San Francisco* class, 3 *Chicago* class, and *Salt Lake City*)
5 CL (4 *Honolulu* class and *Omaha*)

Issued 11:00 p.m., 3 December; received 12:35 a.m. 4 December

Ships present Pearl Harbor on afternoon of 29 November:
District A (between Naval Yard and Ford Island)
 KT (docks northwest of Naval Yard): *Pennsylvania* and *Arizona*
 FV (mooring pillars): *California, Tennessee, Maryland,* and *West Virginia*
 KS (naval yard repair dock): *Portland*
 In docks: 2 CA, 1 DD
 Elsewhere: 4 SS, 1 DD tender, 2 patrol ships, 2 tankers, 2 repair ships, 1 minesweeper
District B (sea area northwest of Ford Island)
 FV (mooring pillars): *Lexington*
 Elsewhere: *Utah,* 1 CA (*San Francisco* class), 2 CL (*Omaha* class), 3 gunboats

District C (East Loch)
 3 CA, 2 CL (*Honolulu* class), 17 DD, 2 DD tenders
District D (Middle Loch)
 12 minesweepers
District E (West Loch)
 No ships
No changes observed by afternoon of 2 December. So far they do not seem to have been alerted. Shore leaves as usual.

Issued 8:30 p.m., 4 December; received 4:20 a.m., 5 December

So far no indications of sea patrol flights being conducted. It seems that occasional patrols are being made to Palmyra, Johnston, and Midway Islands. Pearl Harbor patrols unknown.

Issued 10:00 p.m., 6 December; received 10:36 a.m., 7 December

Activities in Pearl Harbor on the morning of 5 December:
 Arrived: *Oklahoma* and *Nevada* (having been out for eight days)
 Departed: *Lexington* and five heavy cruisers
Ships in harbor as of 6:00 p.m., 5 December:
8 BB, 3 CL, 16 DD
In docks: 4 CL (*Honolulu* class), 5 DD

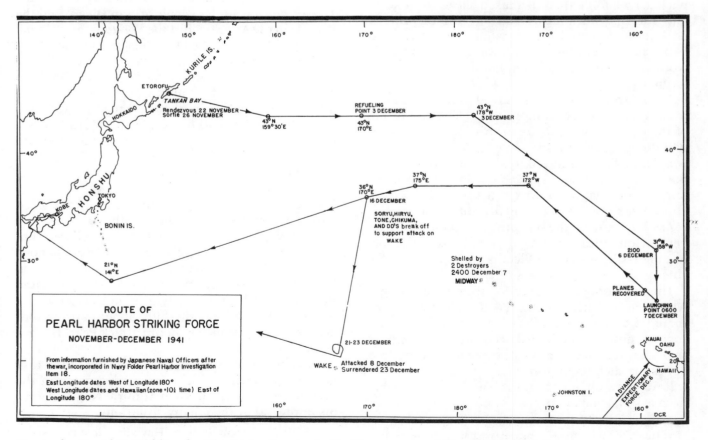

Drawn by David C. Redding for *The Rising Sun in the Pacific,* courtesy of Naval Historical Center.

Issued 5:00 p.m., 7 December; received 7:00 p.m., 7 December

No balloons, no torpedo-defense nets deployed around battleships. No indications observed from enemy radio activity that ocean patrol flights are being made in Hawaiian area. *Lexington* left harbor yesterday (5 December, local time) and recovered planes. *Enterprise* is also thought to be operating at sea with her planes on board.

Issued 6:00 p.m., 7 December; received 8:50 p.m., 7 December

Utah and a seaplane tender entered harbor in the evening of 5 December. (They had left harbor on 4 December.)
Ships in harbor as of 6 December:
  9 BB, 3 CL, 3 seaplane tenders, 17 DD
  In docks: 4 CL, 3 DD
All carriers and heavy cruisers are at sea. No special reports on the fleet. Oahu is quiet and Imperial General Staff is fully convinced of success.

These reports presumably had been sent from Honolulu, but I do not know the details.*

On 6 December, after fueling Carrier Division 2 and the screening force, the Second Tanker Train broke off from the task force. On the next day, the First Tanker Train fueled the screen again and departed. Our force then increased speed to 24 knots and raced toward Pearl Harbor. On the carrier decks, planes were lined up wing to wing for their final check. Maintenance crews and flying crews worked assiduously to complete final preparation of their planes.

About this time, we received Admiral Yamamoto's message for going to war: "The rise or fall of the Empire depends upon this battle; everyone will do his duty with utmost efforts." The message was immediately relayed to all hands, and the "Z" flag was hoisted on the *Akagi*'s mast. This was the same signal flag that was run up in the *Mikasa* almost thirty years before in Tsushima Strait.

At 12:25 p.m. on the seventh (4:55 p.m., 6 December in Honolulu), a message came in from the submarine *I-72*: "American Fleet is not in Lahaina Anchorage."

This anchorage was used for training because it was open and deep. If the Pacific Fleet had been there, it would have offered our best chance for success, and we had hoped accordingly. Receipt of the negative information, however, blasted our hopes for such an opportunity.

It was now obvious that the warships were either in Pearl Harbor or at sea. Admiral Nagumo was

*The times noted for these messages are based on Tokyo time, on which the Japanese ships' clocks remained.

thumbing through the message log to check on battleships reported to be in Pearl Harbor. Completing the count, he looked up and said to the staff members, "All of their battleships are now in. Will any of them leave today?"

The intelligence officer, Lieutenant Commander Kanjiro Ono, was first to reply: "Since five of their eight battleships reached port on the twenty-ninth, and two others left that day returning on the sixth, there is one more which has remained in harbor all this time, supposedly under repair, or perhaps in dry dock. The five ships which arrived on the twenty-ninth have been there eight days, and it is time for them to leave. I suspect they may go out today."

"Today is Saturday, 6 December," said Chief of Staff Kusaka. "Their general practice is to leave on Tuesday, which would be the ninth."

"It is most regrettable," said Genda, the operations officer, "that no carriers are in."

"On 29 November," Ono explained, "the *Enterprise* left harbor accompanied by two battleships, two heavy cruisers, and twelve destroyers. The two battleships returned on the sixth, but the rest have not yet come back. The *Lexington* came in on the twenty-ninth and left with five heavy cruisers on the sixth. Thus, the *Enterprise* ought to return today. The *Saratoga* is under repair at San Diego, and the *Wasp* is in the Atlantic. But the *Yorktown* and *Hornet* belonging to the Pacific Fleet must be out here. They may have arrived with the *Enterprise* today."

"If that happens," said Genda, "I don't care if all eight of the battleships are away."

"As an airman," remarked Commander Tamotsu Oishi, the senior staff officer, "you naturally place much importance on carriers. Of course, it would be good if we could get three of them, but I think it would be better if we got all eight of the battleships."

Chief of Staff Kusaka, who had always been strong for statistical studies of the U. S. Pacific Fleet, now spoke, "There is only a slight chance that carriers may enter the harbor on Saturday, and it seems unlikely that the battleships would leave on Saturday or Sunday. We may take it for granted that all eight battleships will be in the harbor tomorrow. We can't do anything about carriers that are not there. I think we should attack Pearl Harbor tomorrow."

Thus he set the stage for the decision of the task force commander, which was made known in the evening of the seventh when Admiral Nagumo gave his appraisal of the enemy situation:

1. Enemy strength in the Hawaiian area consists of eight battleships, two carriers, about ten heavy

Mitsubishi ("Val") dive-bombers warm up on the deck of a carrier just before being launched to attack Pearl Harbor. The one about to take off is given a waving farewell by members of the carrier's crew. (National Archives: 80-G-71198 and 80-G-30549.)

and six light cruisers. The carriers and heavy cruisers seem to be at sea, but the others are in the harbor. Those operating at sea are most likely in the training area south of Maui; they are not in Lahaina.

2. Unless an unforeseen situation develops tonight, our attack will be launched upon Pearl Harbor.

3. So far there is no indication that the enemy has been alerted, but that is no reason to relax our security.

At 5:30 a.m., 7 December,* the cruisers *Chikuma* and *Tone* each catapulted a "Zero" floatplane for a pre-attack reconnaissance of Pearl Harbor. On carrier flight decks, readied fighter and attack planes were lined up. The flying crews, also primed for the operation, were gathered in the briefing room. The ships pitched and rolled in the rough sea, kicking up white surf from the predawn blackness of the water. At times waves came over the flight deck, and crews clung desperately to their planes to keep them from going into the sea.

In my flying togs, I entered the operation room and reported to the commander in chief, "I am ready for the mission." Nagumo stood up, grasped my hand firmly, and said, "I have confidence in you." He followed me to the dimly lit briefing room where the *Akagi*'s captain was waiting with the pilots. The room was not large enough for all of the men, some of whom had to stand out in the passageway. On a blackboard were written the positions of ships in Pearl Harbor as of 6:00 a.m., 7 December. We were 230 miles due north of Oahu.

Calling the men to attention, I saluted Captain Hasegawa, who spoke a brief final order, "Take off according to plan."

The crews went out hurriedly to their waiting planes. Last to leave, I climbed to the flight deck command post where Genda put his hand on my shoulder. We smiled without speaking, knowing well each other's thoughts.

Turning to me, Commander Shogo Masuda, the *Akagi*'s air officer, said, "There is a heavy pitch and roll. What do you think about taking off in the dark?" The sea was rough, and there was a strong wind blowing. The sky was completely dark, and as yet the horizon was not visible.

"The pitch is greater than the roll," I replied. "Were this a training flight, the takeoff would be delayed until dawn. But if we coordinate the takeoffs with the pitching we can launch successfully." I saluted the officers and went to my plane, the tail of which was striped with red and yellow to distinguish it as the commander's.

*West longitude date and Hawaiian (Zone plus 10½) time used hereinafter.

The senior petty officer of the maintenance gang handed me a white *hachimaki* (cloth headband) saying, "This is a present from the maintenance crews. May I ask that you take it along to Pearl Harbor?" I nodded and fastened the gift to my flying cap.

The carrier turned to port and headed into the northerly wind. The battle flag was now added to the "Z" flag flying at the masthead. Lighted flying lamps shivered with the vibration of engines as planes completed their warm-up.

On the flight deck a green lamp was waved in a circle to signal "Take off!" The engine of the foremost fighter plane began to roar. With the ship still pitching and rolling, the plane started its run, slowly at first but with steadily increasing speed. Men lining the flight deck held their breath as the first plane took off successfully just before the ship took a downward pitch. The next plane was already moving forward. There were loud cheers as each plane rose into the air.

Thus did the first wave of 183 fighters, bombers, and torpedo planes take off from the six carriers. Within fifteen minutes, they had all been launched and were forming up in the still-dark sky, guided only by the signal lights of the lead planes. After one great circling over the fleet formation, the planes set course due south for Oahu Island and Pearl Harbor. It was 6:15.

Under my direct command were forty-nine level bombers. About 500 meters to my right and slightly below me were forty torpedo planes. The same distance to my left, but about 200 meters above me, were fifty-one dive-bombers, and flying cover for the formation there were forty-three fighters. These other three groups were led by Lieutenant Commanders Shigeharu Murata, Kakuichi Takahashi, and Shigeru Itaya, respectively.

We flew through and over the thick clouds which were at 2,000 meters, up to where day was ready to dawn. And the clouds began gradually to brighten below us after the brilliant sun burst into the eastern sky. I opened the cockpit canopy and looked back at the large formation of planes. The wings glittered in the bright morning sunlight.

The speedometer indicated 125 knots and we were favored by a tail wind. At seven o'clock, I figured that we should reach Oahu in less than an hour. But flying over the clouds we could not see the surface of the water, and, consequently, had no check on our drift. I switched on the radio direction finder to tune in the Honolulu radio station and soon picked up some light music. By turning the antenna, I found the exact direction from which the broadcast was coming and corrected our course, which had been five degrees off.

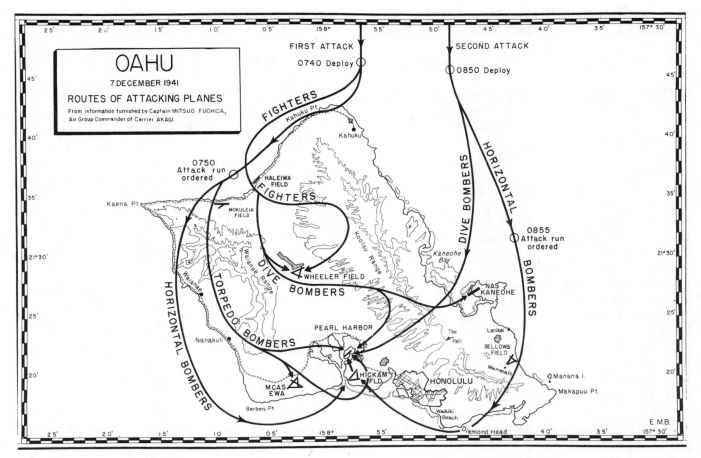

Drawn by Robert M. Berish for *The Rising Sun in the Pacific*, courtesy of Naval Historical Center.

Continuing to listen to the program, I was wondering how to get below the clouds after reaching Oahu. If the island was covered by thick clouds like those below us, the level bombing would be difficult; and we had not yet had reports from the reconnaissance planes.

In tuning the radio a little finer, I heard, along with the music, what seemed to be a weather report. Holding my breath, I adjusted the dial and listened intently. Then I heard it come through a second time, slowly and distinctly: "Averaging partly cloudy, with clouds mostly over the mountains. Cloud base at 3,500 feet. Visibility good. Wind north, 10 knots."

What a windfall for us! No matter how careful the planning, a more favorable situation could not have been imagined. Weather conditions over Pearl Harbor had been worrying me greatly, but now with this information I could turn my attention to other problems. Since Honolulu was only partly cloudy, there must be breaks in the clouds over the island. But since the clouds over the mountains were at 1,000 meters altitude, it would not be wise to attack from the northeast, flying over the eastern mountains, as previously planned. The wind was north and visibility good. It would be better to pass

to the west of the island and make our approach from the south.

At 7:30, we had been in the air for about an hour and a half. It was time that we were seeing land, but there was only a solid layer of clouds below. All of a sudden, the clouds broke, and a long white line of coast appeared. We were over Kahuku Point, the northern tip of the island, and now it was time for our deployment.

There were alternate plans for the attack: If we had surprise, the torpedo planes were to strike first, followed by the level bombers and then the dive-bombers, which were to attack the air bases, including Hickam Field and Ford Island, near the anchorage. If these bases were first hit by the dive-bombers, it was feared that the resultant smoke might hinder torpedo and level-bombing attacks on the ships.

On the other hand, if enemy resistance was expected, the dive-bombers would attack first to cause confusion and attract enemy fire. Level bombers, coming next, were to bomb and destroy enemy antiaircraft guns, followed by the torpedo planes which would attack the ships.

The selection of attack method was for my decision, to be indicated by signal pistol: one "black dragon" for a surprise attack, two "black dragons" if it appeared that surprise was lost. Upon either order the fighters were immediately to dash in as cover.

There was still no news from the reconnaissance planes, but I had made up my mind that we could make a surprise attack, and thereupon ordered the deployment by raising my signal pistol outside the canopy and firing one "black dragon." The time was 7:40.

With this order, the dive-bombers rose to 4,000 meters, the torpedo bombers went down almost to sea level, and the level bombers came down just under the clouds. The only group that failed to deploy was the fighters. Flying above the rest of the formation, they seemed to have missed the signal because of the clouds. Realizing this, I fired another shot toward the fighter group. This time they noticed the signal immediately and sped toward Oahu.

This second shot, however, was taken by the commander of the dive-bomber group as the second of two "black dragons," signifying a non-surprise attack which would mean that his group should attack first, and this error served to confuse some of the pilots who had understood the original signal.

Meanwhile a reconnaissance report came in from the *Chikuma*'s plane giving the locations of ten battleships, one heavy cruiser, and ten light cruisers in the harbor. It also reported a wind of 14 meters per second from bearing 080, and clouds over the U. S. Fleet at 1,700 meters with a scale seven density. The *Tone* plane also reported that "the enemy fleet is not in Lahaina Anchorage." Now I knew for sure that there were no carriers in the harbor. The sky cleared as we moved in on the target, and Pearl Harbor was plainly visible from the northwest valley of the island. I studied our objective through binoculars. They were there all right, all eight of them. "Notify all planes to launch attacks," I ordered my radioman, who immediately began tapping the key. The order went in plain code: "*To, to, to, to. . . .*" The time was 7:49.

When Lieutenant Commander Takahashi and his dive-bombing group mistook my signal and thought we were making a non-surprise attack, his fifty-three planes lost no time in dashing forward. His command was divided into two groups: one led by himself which headed for Ford Island and Hickam Field, the other, led by Lieutenant Akira Sakamoto, headed for Wheeler Field.

The dive-bombers over Hickam Field saw heavy bombers lined up on the apron. Takahashi rolled

Fighter planes were parked in rows at the Army Air Forces's Wheeler Field. While the arrangement made it easy to guard them against sabotage, it also made them easy prey for the Japanese aerial attack. (National Archives: 80-G-30555.)

his plane sharply and went into a dive, followed immediately by the rest of his planes, and the first bombs fell at Hickam. The next places hit were Ford Island and Wheeler Field. In a very short time, huge billows of black smoke were rising from these bases. The lead torpedo planes were to have started their run to the navy yard from over Hickam, coming from south of the bay entrance. But the sudden burst of bombs at Hickam surprised Lieutenant Commander Murata, who had understood that his torpedo planes were to have attacked first. Hence, he took a shortcut lest the smoke from those bases cover up his targets. Thus, the first torpedo was actually launched some five minutes ahead of the scheduled eight o'clock. The time of each attack was as follows:

7:55 Dive-bombers at Hickam and Wheeler
7:57 Torpedo planes at battleships
8:00 Fighters strafing air bases
8:05 Level bombers at battleships

After issuance of the attack order, my level bomber group kept east of Oahu, going past the southern tip of the island. On our left was the Barbers Point airfield, but, as we had been informed, there were no planes. Our information indicated that a powerful antiaircraft battery was stationed there, but we saw no evidence of it.

I continued to watch the sky over the harbor and activities on the ground. None but Japanese planes were in the air, and there were no indications of air combat. Ships in the harbor still appeared to be asleep, and the Honolulu radio broadcast continued normally. I felt that surprise was now assured, and that my men would succeed in their missions.

Knowing that Admirals Nagumo and Yamamoto and the General Staff were anxious about the attack, I decided that they should be informed. I ordered the following message sent to the fleet: "We have succeeded in making a surprise attack. Request you relay this report to Tokyo." The radioman reported shortly that the message had been received by the *Akagi*.

The code for a successful surprise attack was "*Tora, tora, tora....*" Before the *Akagi*'s relay of this message reached Japan, it was received by the *Nagato* in Hiroshima Bay and the General Staff in Tokyo, directly from my plane! This was surely a long-distance record for such a low-powered transmission from an airplane, and might be attributed to the use of the word "*Tora*" as our code. There is a Japanese saying, "A tiger (*tora*) goes out 1,000 *ri* (2,000 miles) and returns without fail."

I saw clouds of black smoke rising from Hickam and soon thereafter from Ford Island. This bothered me, and I wondered what had happened. It was not long before I saw waterspouts rising alongside the battleships, followed by more and more waterspouts. It was time to launch our level bombing attacks, so I ordered my pilot to bank sharply, which was the attack signal for the planes following us. All ten of my squadrons then formed into a single column with intervals of 200 meters. It was indeed a gorgeous formation.

The lead plane in each squadron was manned by a specially trained pilot and bombardier. The pilot and bombardier of my squadron had won numerous fleet contests and were considered the best in the Japanese Navy. I approved when my pilot, Lieutenant Mitsuo Matsuzaki, asked if the lead plane should trade positions with us, and he lifted our plane a little as a signal. The new leader came forward quickly, and I could see the smiling round face of the bombardier when he saluted. In returning the salute I entrusted the command to them for the bombing mission.

As my group made its bomb run, enemy antiaircraft suddenly came to life. Dark gray bursts blossomed here and there until the sky was clouded with shattering near-misses which made our plane tremble. Shipboard guns seemed to open fire before the shore batteries. I was startled by the rapidity of the counterattack which came less than five minutes after the first bomb had fallen. Were it the Japanese Fleet, the reaction would not have been so quick, because although the Japanese character is suitable for offensives, it does not readily adjust to the defensive.

Suddenly the plane bounced as if struck by a huge club. "The fuselage is holed to port," reported the radioman behind me, "and a steering-control wire is damaged." I asked hurriedly if the plane was under control, and the pilot assured me that it was.

No sooner were we feeling relieved than another burst shook the plane. My squadron was headed for the *Nevada*'s mooring at the northern end of Battleship Row, on the east side of Ford Island. We were just passing over the bay entrance, and it was almost time to release our bombs. It was not easy to pass through the concentrated antiaircraft fire. Flying at only 3,000 meters, it seemed that this might well be a date with eternity.

I further saw that it was not wise to have deployed in this long single-column formation. The whole level bomber group could be destroyed like ducks in a shooting gallery. It would also have been better if we had approached the targets from the direction of Diamond Head. But here we were at our targets and there was a job to be done.

It was now a matter of utmost importance to stay on course, and the lead plane kept to its line of flight

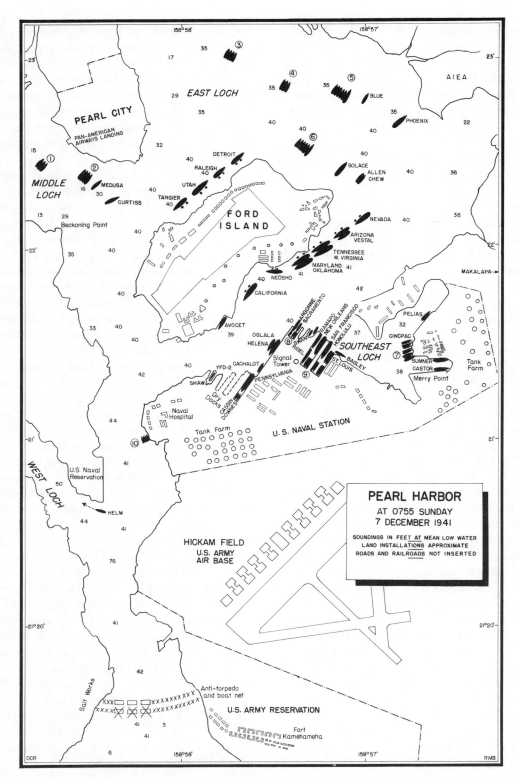

Key to chart of Pearl Harbor (Reading NW to SE in nests of ships): 1. Destroyer-minecraft *Ramsay, Gamble, Montgomery;* 2. Destroyer-minecraft *Trever, Breese, Zane, Perry, Wasmuth;* 3. Destroyers *Monaghan, Farragut, Dale, Aylwin;* 4. Destroyers *Henley, Patterson, Ralph Talbot;* 5. Destroyers *Selfridge, Case, Tucker, Reid, Conyngham;* tender *Whitney;* 6. Destroyers *Phelps, Macdonough, Worden, Dewey, Hull;* tender *Dobbin;* 7. Submarines *Narwhal, Dolphin, Tautog;* seaplane tenders *Thornton, Hulbert;* 8. Destroyers *Jarvis* and *Mugford* (inside *Argonne* and *Sacramento*); 9. Destroyer *Cummings;* destroyer-minelayers *Preble, Tracy, Pruitt, Sicard;* destroyer *Schley;* minesweeper *Grebe;* 10. Minesweepers *Bobolink, Vireo, Turkey, Rail, Tern.* Other auxiliaries, not shown, were moored up West Loch. There were also several tugs and yard craft, not shown, in the area of the chart.

Drawn by Robert M. Berish for *The Rising Sun in the Pacific,* courtesy of Naval Historical Center.

like a homing pigeon. Ignoring the barrage of shells bursting around us, I concentrated on the bomb loaded under the lead plane, pulled the safety bolt from the bomb-release lever and grasped the handle. It seemed as if time was standing still.

Again we were shaken terrifically and our planes were buffeted about. When I looked out, the third plane of my group was abeam of us, and I saw its bomb fall! That pilot had a reputation for being careless. In training his bomb releases were poorly timed, and he had often been cautioned.

I thought, "That damn fellow has done it again!" and shook my fist in his direction. But I soon realized that there was something wrong with his plane and he was losing gasoline. I wrote on a small blackboard, "What happened?" and held it toward his plane. He explained, "Underside of fuselage hit."

Now I saw his bomb-cinch lines fluttering wildly and, sorry for having scolded him, I ordered that he return to the carrier. He answered, "Fuel tank destroyed, will follow you," asking permission to stay with the group. Knowing the feelings of the pilot and crew, I gave the permission, although I knew it was useless to try taking that crippled and bombless plane through the enemy fire. It was nearly time for bomb release when we ran into clouds which obscured the target, and I made out the round face of the lead bombardier who was waving his hands back and forth to indicate that we had passed the release point. Banking slightly we turned right toward Honolulu, and I studied the antiaircraft fire, knowing that we would have to run through it again. It was now concentrated on the second squadron.

While circling for another try, I looked toward the area in which the bomb from the third plane had fallen. Just outside the bay entrance I saw a large water ring close by what looked like a destroyer. The ship seemed to be standing in a floating dock, attached to both sides of the entrance like a gate boat. I was suddenly reminded of the midget submarines which were to have entered the bay for a special attack.

At the time of our sortie I was aware of these midget submarines, but knew nothing of their characteristics, operational objectives, force organization, or the reason for their participation in the attack. In the *Akagi*, Commander Shibuya, a staff officer in charge of submarine operations, had explained that they were to penetrate the harbor the night before our attack; but, no matter how good an opportunity might arise, they were not to strike until after the planes had done so.

Even now the submarines were probably concealed in the bay, awaiting the air attack. Had the entrance been left open, there would have been some opportunity for them to get out of the harbor. But in light of what I had just seen there seemed little chance of that, and, feeling now the bitterness of war, I vowed to do my best in the assigned mission.

While my group was circling over Honolulu for another bombing attempt, other groups made their runs, some making three tries before succeeding. Suddenly a colossal explosion occurred in Battleship Row. A huge column of dark red smoke rose to 1,000 feet and a stiff shock wave reached our plane. I called the pilot's attention to the spectacle, and he observed, "Yes, Commander, the powder magazine must have exploded. Terrible indeed!" The attack was in full swing, and smoke from fires and explosions filled most of the sky over Pearl Harbor.

My group now entered on a bombing course again. Studying Battleship Row through binoculars, I saw that the big explosion had been on the *Arizona*. She was still flaming fiercely and her smoke was covering the *Nevada*, the target of my group. Since the heavy smoke would hinder our bomber accuracy, I looked for some other ship to attack. The *Tennessee*, third in the left row, was already on fire; but next in the row was the *Maryland*, which had not yet been attacked. I gave an order changing our target to this ship, and once again we headed into the antiaircraft fire. Then came the "ready" signal and I took a firm grip on the bomb release handle, holding my breath and staring at the bomb of the lead plane.

Pilots, observers, and radiomen all shouted, "Release!" on seeing the bomb drop from the lead plane, and all the others let go their bombs. I immediately lay flat on the floor to watch the fall of bombs through a peephole. Four bombs in perfect pattern plummeted like devils of doom. The target was so far away that I wondered for a moment if they would reach it. The bombs grew smaller and smaller until I was holding my breath for fear of losing them. I forgot everything in the thrill of watching the fall toward the target. They became small as poppy seeds and finally disappeared just as tiny white flashes of smoke appeared on and near the ship.

From a great altitude, near-misses are much more obvious than direct hits because they create wave rings in the water which are plain to see. Observing only two such rings plus two tiny flashes, I shouted, "Two hits!" and rose from the floor of the plane. These minute flashes were the only evidence we had of hits at that time, but I felt sure that they had done considerable damage. I ordered the bombers which had completed their runs to

Within minutes after the attack began, the effects of Japanese aerial torpedoes were apparent. Fuel oil spreads outward from the port side of the *Oklahoma* (which has not yet capsized) and the *West Virginia*. Astern of them is the repair ship *Vestal*. Moored inboard to the Ford Island quays are, right to left, the oiler *Neosho* (only her stern is visible), the *Maryland*, the *Tennessee*, the *Arizona* (whose magazine has not yet exploded), and the barely visible *Nevada*. (Naval Historical Center: NH 50472.)

return to the carriers, but my own plane remained over Pearl Harbor to observe our successes and conduct operations still in progress.

After our bomb run, I ordered my pilot to fly over each of the air bases, where our fighters were strafing, before returning over Pearl Harbor to observe the result of our attacks on the warships. Pearl Harbor and vicinity had been turned into complete chaos in a very short time.

The target ship *Utah*, on the western side of Ford Island, had already capsized. On the other side of the island, the *West Virginia* and *Oklahoma* had received concentrated torpedo attacks as a result of their exposed positions in the outer row. Their sides were almost blasted off, and they listed steeply in a flood of heavy oil. The *Arizona* was in miserable shape; her magazine apparently having blown up, she was listing badly and burning furiously.

Two other battleships, the *Maryland* and *Tennessee*, were on fire; especially the latter whose smoke emerged in a heavy black column which towered into the sky. The *Pennsylvania*, unscathed in the dry dock, seemed to be the only battleship that had not been attacked.

Most of our torpedo planes, under Lieutenant Commander Murata, flew around the navy yard area and concentrated their attacks on the ships moored east of Ford Island. A summary of their reports, made upon return to our carriers, indicated the following hits: one on the *Nevada*, nine on the *West Virginia*, twelve on the *Oklahoma*, and three on the *California*.

Elements of the torpedo bombers attacked ships west of the island, but they found only the *Utah* and attacked her, claiming six hits. Other torpedo planes headed for the *Pennsylvania*, but seeing that she was in dry dock they shifted their attack to a cruiser and destroyer tied up at Ten Ten Dock. Five torpedo hits were claimed on these targets, which were the *Helena* and *Oglala*.

As I observed the damage done by the first attack wave, the effectiveness of the torpedoes seemed remarkable, and I was struck with the shortsightedness of the United States in being so generally unprepared and in not using torpedo nets. I also thought of our long hard training in Kagoshima Bay and the efforts of those who had labored to accomplish a seemingly impossible task. A warm

A "Kate" high-level bomber flies above Hickam Field as smoke billows up. Ford Island is visible below the plane's left wing. Commander Fuchida, who was in command of the air attack, was a passenger in a "Kate" and sent the famous radio message, "Tora, tora, tora," to signal that surprise had been achieved. (National Archives: 80-G-178985.)

feeling came with the realization that the reward of those efforts was unfolded here before my eyes.

During the attack, many of our pilots noted the brave efforts of the American fliers able to take off who, though greatly outnumbered, flew straight in to engage our planes. Their effect was negligible, but their courage commanded the admiration and respect of our pilots.

It took the planes of the first attack wave about one hour to complete their mission. By the time they were headed back to our carriers, having lost three fighters, one dive-bomber, and five torpedo planes, the second wave of 171 planes commanded by Lieutenant Commander Shigekazu Shimazaki was over the target area. Arriving off Kahuku Point

at 8:40 a.m., the attack run was ordered fourteen minutes later and they swept in, making every effort to avoid the billowing clouds of smoke as well as the now-intensified antiaircraft fire.

In this second wave there were thirty-six fighters to control the air over Pearl Harbor, fifty-four high-level bombers led by Shimazaki to attack Hickam Field and the naval air station at Kaneohe, while eighty-one dive-bombers led by Lieutenant Commander Takashige Egusa flew over the mountains to the east and dashed in to hit the warships.

By the time these last arrived, the sky was so covered with clouds and smoke that planes had difficulty in locating their targets. To further complicate the problems of this attack, the ship and ground antiaircraft fire was now very heavy. But Egusa was undaunted in leading his dive-bombers through the fierce barrage. The planes chose as their targets the ships which were putting up the stiffest repelling fire. This choice proved effective, since these ships had suffered least from the first attack. Thus, the second attack achieved a nice spread, hitting the least-damaged battleships as well as previously undamaged cruisers and destroyers. This attack also lasted about one hour, but due to the increased return fire, it suffered higher casualties, six fighters and fourteen dive-bombers being lost.

After the second wave was headed back to the carriers, I circled Pearl Harbor once more to observe and photograph the results. I counted four battleships definitely sunk and three severely damaged. Still another battleship appeared to be slightly damaged and extensive damage had also been inflicted upon other types of ships. The seaplane base at Ford Island was all in flames, as were the airfields, especially Wheeler Field.

A detailed survey of damage was impossible because of the dense pall of black smoke. Damage to the airfields was not determinable, but it was readily apparent that no planes on the fields were operational. In the three hours that my plane was in the area, we did not encounter a single enemy plane. It seemed that at least half the island's air strength must have been destroyed. Several hangars remained untouched, however, and it was possible that some of them held planes which were still operational.

Such were my conclusions as I prepared to return to our carrier. I was startled from these thoughts by the sudden approach of a fighter plane banking from side to side. We were greatly relieved to see the Rising Sun on its wings. As it came closer, we saw that it was a *Zuikaku* fighter which must have been here since the first attack wave. I wondered if any other fighters had been left behind, and ordered my pilot to go to the rendezvous point for a final check. Sure enough, there we found a second fighter plane which also followed joyfully after us.

It was extremely difficult for fighter planes to fly long distances at sea. They were not equipped with homing devices and radar, as were the larger planes. It was therefore planned to have the bombers, upon completion of their missions, rendezvous with the fighters at a designated point and lead them back to the carriers. Some of the fighters, however, such as these two, must have missed the time of rendezvous, and they were indeed fortunate to find our plane which could lead them safely back to the task force and their carriers.

My plane was just about the last one to get back to the *Akagi*, where refueled and rearmed planes were being lined up on the busy flight deck in preparation for yet another attack. I was called to the bridge as soon as the plane stopped, and could tell on arriving there that Admiral Nagumo's staff had been engaged in heated discussions about the advisability of launching the next attack. They were waiting for my account of the battle.

"Four battleships definitely sunk," I reported. "One sank instantly, another capsized, the other two settled to the bottom of the bay and may have capsized." This seemed to please Admiral Nagumo who observed, "We may then conclude that anticipated results have been achieved."

Discussion next centered upon the extent of damage inflicted at airfields and air bases; and I expressed my views saying, "All things considered, we have achieved a great amount of destruction, but it would be unwise to assume that we have destroyed everything. There are still many targets remaining which should be hit. Therefore, I recommend that another attack be launched."

The factors which influenced Admiral Nagumo's decision—the target of much criticism by naval experts, and an interesting subject for naval historians—have long been unknown, since the man who made it died in the summer of 1944 when U.S. forces invaded the Marianas. I know of only one document in which Admiral Nagumo's reasons are set forth, and there they are given as follows:

1. The first attack had inflicted all the damage we had hoped for, and another attack could not be expected to greatly increase the extent of that damage.

2. Enemy return fire had been surprisingly prompt even though we took them by surprise; another attack would meet stronger opposition and our losses would certainly be disproportionate to the additional destruction which might be inflicted.

3. Intercepted enemy messages indicated at least fifty large planes still operational; and we did not know the whereabouts of the enemy's carriers, cruisers, and submarines.

4. To remain within range of enemy land-based planes was distinctly to our disadvantage, especially since the effectiveness of our air reconnaissance was extremely limited.

I had done all I could to urge another attack, but the decision rested entirely with Admiral Nagumo, and he chose to retire without launching the next attack. Immediately flag signals were hoisted ordering the course change, and our ships headed northward at high speed.

Mitsuo Fuchida (1902–1976) served twenty-five years in the Imperial Japanese Navy and was a captain at the end of World War II. An aviator with 3,000 hours of flight time, he served as commander of the air groups of the First Air Fleet from September 1941 to July 1942. He was wounded in the Battle of Midway and hospitalized for about a year thereafter. In June 1943, he became senior staff officer of the First Air Fleet, serving at Kanoya and at Tinian. From April 1944 to the end of the war, he was air operations officer of the Combined Fleet. Later, he was interviewed about the war by U.S. occupation officers in Japan. That experience eventually led to his conversion to Christianity. He subsequently toured the United States, lecturing at religious gatherings. He was coauthor of *Midway—The Battle That Doomed Japan: The Japanese Navy's Story*, published by the Naval Institute in 1955. (John Toland Collection, Franklin D. Roosevelt Library.)

Captain Fuchida's narrative is perhaps the classic first-person account of the attack on Pearl Harbor—a bird's-eye view by the man in command. It has been widely reprinted and frequently used as a source for others writing about Pearl Harbor. By contrast, Admiral Radford's story, which follows, has not appeared previously. It, too, tells of an attack on Pearl Harbor on a Sunday morning on the seventh day of the month. It also tells of defending forces being utterly surprised by the presence of carrier planes. The difference is that the carriers of which Admiral Radford writes were American and their planes dropped no bombs or torpedoes. The mock attack took place on 7 February 1932, nearly ten years before the Japanese acted out the roles assigned to them by a similar script.

Aircraft Battle Force

By Admiral Arthur W. Radford, U.S. Navy (Retired)

It was almost impossible to keep an aircraft squadron command for more than a year in the early 1930s. The Navy had relatively few squadrons for the group of lieutenant commanders, of which I was one. So after my pleasant year in command of Fighting 1B, I stayed on board the USS *Saratoga* to become aide and flag secretary on the staff of Commander Aircraft Battle Force. The commander himself was Rear Admiral Harry E. Yarnell; Captain John H. Towers was chief of staff.

Admiral Yarnell was a rather short man and generally very quiet. He seldom raised his voice above a conversational tone, but he could be as hard as steel if the occasion demanded. Captain Towers was another brilliant officer, as well as one of the Navy's first fliers. He was a tremendous worker and very ambitious. He and Admiral Yarnell were a good team. The admiral, while new to naval aviation, was intensely interested in its capabilities and future prospects. He was constantly talking to young pilots and enlisted mechanics. In a remarkably short time, he had a broad background of understanding, better in some respects than many of his staff.

The *Saratoga* and *Lexington* were at that time commanded respectively by Captain Frank R. McCrary and Captain Ernest J. King. There was always great rivalry between the two ships and particularly during the year when those two were in command. Captain King was tremendously competitive. He tried hard to lead in every way. Because the *Saratoga* was normally the flagship, King got the idea that the staff was partial to that ship. He let us know, directly and indirectly, that he was

Admiral Harry E. Yarnell (center), Commander Aircraft Battle Force, and his staff on 19 February 1932. Captain John H. Towers is fourth from left, and Lieutenant Commander Radford is between him and Yarnell. Lieutenant Commander Forrest P. Sherman is the officer at far right. (Naval Historical Center: NH 51859.)

alert to the problem and would not hesitate to bring the matter to Admiral Yarnell's attention, should he have good evidence of favoritism. I don't remember any showdown on the subject during the year, but I do remember that the staff was, on the whole, very careful not to favor the *Saratoga*. If, however, the *Lexington* did err, we took more than routine pleasure in preparing critical dispatches and letters to her commanding officer.

Grand Joint Exercise Number Four took place during February 1932 and received a great deal of publicity at the time. It was, as its title implies, a large-scale exercise between the Army and Navy. It involved an attack on the Hawaiian Islands by the U.S. Fleet. The islands were defended by the Army, particularly by units of the Air Corps. Admiral Yarnell, Captain Towers, and the staff appreciated what an opportunity this exercise was to dramatize the fleet's carrier aviation. Carrier aviation was essentially an offensive weapon, and in the design of Grand Joint Exercise Number Four, we would have the chance to use that capability.

The exercise took place from 1 to 14 February. Ships of the Battle Force sailed from the West Coast on 1 February and exercised together en route until zero hour for the start of the joint exercise, which was midnight, the beginning of Friday, 5 February. At that time, the carriers and their supporting destroyers left the battleships and cruisers and commenced their 25-knot run-in toward Oahu. Our initial launching point was about 100 miles north northeast of Oahu, which we planned to reach about one hour before sunrise on Sunday, 7 February. Radio intercept watches were set at zero hour on all aircraft frequencies used by the U.S. Army and Navy in Hawaii. In a remarkably short time, because of lax communication discipline in Hawaii-based units, we had a very clear picture of the location and activities of all Army Air Corps units. Officers and men in nearly all units which had been dispersed to outlying fields were very frank in telling loved ones when they expected to be home. They were also providing other useful information which we, the enemy, were glad to get. Navy patrol planes were almost nonexistent at that time. Even so, we had to make some provision for such planes. Our run-in at high speed placed us approximately 400 miles from Oahu on Saturday. It was a distance we did not feel patrol planes of that time could cover during daylight hours. At about three o'clock on Sunday morning, we were ready to launch carrier air groups from the *Lexington* and *Saratoga*. Aircraft units and fields on all the islands were targeted, and everything went beautifully and according to plan. Our squadrons struck

their targets shortly after it got light, taking them all by complete surprise. Within a few minutes, the strikes were over, and the planes returned to the carriers, which in the meantime had steamed toward the recovery point at high speed.

The complete surprise prevented Army Air Corps planes from following our aircraft back, a contingency we had expected and planned to counter with fighters ready to intercept. By about 6:00 a.m., we had recovered all the aircraft in the first strike and rapidly made ready for a second. We had decided that, as a result of the first attack, all the Army planes would take to the air and try to find us. We expected that their search would take about two or three hours and that by about seven o'clock all their planes would be back on the ground refueling and their crews getting breakfast. Our planning was perfect. About 7:15, our second strike caught nearly all of them on the ground again. This time, however, some planes were able to follow ours back to the vicinity of the carriers. For another hour or so, we were attacked, but by then we were convinced that we had won a tremendous surprise victory.

Grand Joint Exercise Number Four had a later part in which amphibious landings were made on some of the islands by the Fleet Marine Force, but the initial aircraft phase was called off about ten o'clock Sunday morning. By that time, some of the dogfights were getting too realistic. The critique for the joint exercise was held after the completion of all phases, during the third week in February. As in most critiques of peacetime war games, there were great differences of opinion. Army Air Corps units claimed little or no damage had been inflicted during the early surprise attacks. And, of course, they felt that they had later damaged the carriers severely.

The general nature of the exercise was pretty well publicized, and it was common knowledge that the Army considered that the attacks at daybreak on a *Sunday* morning, while permitted under the rules, were on the dirty side. Apparently, the Japanese read all this publicity in great detail. Their attack on Pearl Harbor, which came within two months of being exactly ten years later, was almost a perfect duplicate. The damage done by their surprise attack, however, was very real and very serious.

The second incident which I remember vividly from my year with Admiral Yarnell concerned Captain Ernie King of the *Lexington*. Shortly after the fleet returned to the West Coast home ports, San Diego and San Pedro, the *Saratoga* left for an overhaul at the Puget Sound Navy Yard in Bremerton, Washington. That meant our staff shifted to the

An amazing precursor to the Japanese surprise attack on Pearl Harbor was launched in a war game on 7 February 1932, almost ten years before the Japanese arrived. One of the two U.S. carriers in the mock attack was the *Saratoga*, shown from the air in March 1932 and with Curtiss F8C fighter planes lined up on her flight deck in April 1932. (National Archives: 80-G-466400 and 80-G-189164.)

Lexington for participation in a fleet exercise held en route to San Francisco.

I have mentioned the tension that existed between Captain King and the admiral's staff. On this trip, it was very real at times. Admiral Yarnell was not involved, but Captain King and Captain Towers—both ambitious, both meticulous as to detail, and both very energetic—drew sparks from each other on almost every contact. There was a rather frigid politeness evident whenever they had occasion to do business together. The staff, loyal to a man, supported Captain Towers in the feeling that Captain King was difficult to get along with.

Captain King, for his part, suffered no inferiority complex and certainly held his own in conflict with the staff. As a group, we had to be careful, extremely careful, not to give Captain King opportunities to question our abilities. It kept us on our toes. Consider, then, the contretemps which took place when the *Lexington* entered San Francisco Bay on com-

pletion of the exercises. Because the staff had only one major ship to take care of rather than a formation, it took no part in handling the details beyond seeing that a certain berth was assigned to the *Lexington*. Admiral Yarnell and most of us were on the flag bridge as we entered the Golden Gate. Most naval officers will not miss an opportunity to witness an entrance to San Francisco Bay from a good vantage point, and we were no exceptions.

It was a beautiful morning, and the fleet was an impressive sight. We had plenty to hold our interest without paying attention to the navigation of the *Lexington*, now in Captain King's hands. Suddenly, King manned a large megaphone and hailed a fleet submarine which had her anchor almost under the *Lexington*'s starboard bow, "You are anchored in my berth, Sir, please clear it at once." One can imagine the row of staff heads, and Admiral Yarnell, looking over the rail of the flag bridge which was just above the navigating bridge. Captain King

Captain Ernest J. King, commanding officer of the carrier *Lexington*, on the bridge of his ship. His well-known temper got him in trouble when the *Lexington* and a submarine competed for the same anchorage. (Ernest J. King Collection at Naval War College; courtesy of Thomas B. Buell and Anthony S. Nicolosi.)

was apoplectic with rage and made some very uncomplimentary remarks about the submarine, her captain, and so forth. In the meantime, the *Lexington* had had to back down hard to keep from ramming the submarine.

Lieutenant Commander Forrest P. Sherman, the staff navigator, had quietly watched this situation developing. As it approached the critical stage, he checked the ship's navigation and discovered that it was the *Lexington* which was out of position and so informed Admiral Yarnell. The admiral interrupted Captain King's tirade by quietly suggesting that he might be the one who was wrong. There was almost a dead silence while Sherman made his point with the ship's navigator, and it was clear that the aircraft carrier was fouling the submarine's berth, not vice versa.

Captain King almost exploded with rage. I am quite certain that, if looks could have killed, his navigator would have been a casualty that morning. As it was, Ernie King took a grip on himself, things quieted down, and the *Lexington* was soon anchored in her berth. Before we all secured from the sea detail, Captain King appeared on the flag bridge. Those of the staff still there did not know whether the admiral had sent for him or whether he had decided it was best to present himself quickly. At any rate, the admiral and the captain had a quiet huddle by themselves, and that was the end of the incident, as far as all of us knew. I must say, though, that Ernie King seemed quite subdued and almost pleasant to everyone for the rest of the cruise.

Arthur William Radford (1896–1973) was graduated from the Naval Academy in 1916 and served in surface ships before being designated a naval aviator in 1920. He then served in the Bureau of Aeronautics, the tender *Aroostook*, Observation Squadron 1, and in command of the 1929 Alaskan Aerial Survey. He commanded Fighting Squadron 1B, then served on the staff of Commander Aircraft Battle Force and in the tender *Wright*. He commanded NAS Seattle, was executive officer of the *Yorktown*, established NAS Bermuda, and directed naval aviation training. As a flag officer during World War II, he commanded carrier divisions and served in the Office of the Chief of Naval Operations. After the war, he was active in the Navy's fight for air power. He was Commander in Chief Pacific and later Chairman of the Joint Chiefs of Staff until he retired from active duty in 1957. Admiral Radford's posthumous memoir *From Pearl Harbor to Vietnam* was published in 1980 by the Hoover Institution. (National Archives: 80-G-461543.)

Even as Arthur Radford and others were helping to develop U.S. carrier doctrine in the 1930s, the Imperial Japanese Navy's air arm was emerging. Among the most innovative Japanese thinkers in the area of naval air warfare was Minoru Genda, the tactical planner of the Pearl Harbor raid. In the selection that follows, he traces the growth of his navy's carrier fleet and acknowledges the unwitting help provided by the maker of an American newsreel.

Evolution of Aircraft Carrier Tactics of the Imperial Japanese Navy

By General Minoru Genda, Japanese Self-Defense Force (Retired)

The tactical concepts for employing aircraft carrier formations in the Imperial Japanese Navy developed primarily in the following phases:

Phase One: From 1923 through 1928. This period began when the light carrier *Hosho* went into service for use in the conducting of fundamental studies and training. In 1928, with the addition of the converted battle cruiser *Akagi*, she and the *Hosho* were formed into the First Naval Air Wing (carrier division) and integrated into the Combined Fleet. The main emphasis by the Japanese Navy during this period was on torpedo attacks.

Phase Two: From 1928 to approximately 1935. The Navy built up to four carriers during this period by adding the *Kaga* and the *Ryujo*. Two of the ships were a permanent part of the Combined Fleet, while the other two were normally regarded as reserve vessels. The latter two were integrated with the fleet in the event of major naval maneuvers.

War games were held matching the Red Fleet (supposed to represent the U.S. Navy) against the friendly Blue Fleet. During the early part of this phase, however, the number of carriers and planes was still too small for the use of wide-scale tactical maneuvers. The chief missions assigned to the carrier fleet were reconnaissance, attack (torpedo and horizontal bombing), and air patrol for the benefit of battleships and carriers. In the case of warfare between two belligerent fleets, the patrol fighters overhead were assigned to repulse the target-observation planes sent by the enemy and to protect our own target-spotting aircraft.

During this period, especially at the beginning, there seemed to be no unified concepts within our Navy regarding the selection of targets to be attacked. Generally, aviation experts considered enemy carriers to be the primary targets, while the gunnery staffs emphasized going after enemy battleships.

In phase two, and indeed throughout the history of Japanese naval aviation, the prevailing philosophy was to emphasize attack, particularly by torpedoes. This tactical philosophy grew out of the Washington naval disarmament conference of 1921–1922 in which Japan came out on the short end of the 5:5:3 allocation ratio for battleship and aircraft carrier tonnage. Since we could build to only 60 per cent of the levels allowed the major powers, we were forced to compensate by developing our capabilities with the torpedo, submarine warfare, and other supplementary areas.

Theoretically, once warfare began, we would try to build our strength to at least 70 per cent of that of the U.S. Fleet before engaging in a decisive battle. We would do so through an attrition campaign against the dominant U.S. warships, and that became one of the essential subjects of our naval training. Of course, some of us hoped to contest the final fleet engagement under a condition of complete air superiority, and I'm sure that was the aim of the U.S. Navy also. However, as a result of the ratios mentioned above, there was scarcely a chance for us to gain such superiority unless the carriers were loaded mainly with fighter planes. And that, of course, would have cut down on our ability to use bombers and torpedo planes.

As aircraft development progressed year after year, operational tactics advanced as well, and so our record in naval maneuvers grew better. Thus it was in 1932–1933 that the philosophy of surprise attack started to be accepted within Japanese naval aviation. Our objective would be to destroy the enemy carriers and thereby gain the air superiority that would give us a range of choices for employing the fleet.

The trend of enlarging aviation units was accelerated after the London conference of 1930, when Japan failed to secure a hoped-for 70 per cent strength against the United States in supplementary units such as heavy cruisers. In 1933, we introduced dive-bombing and found it to be highly destructive and superior as a method of surprise attack. It also enabled us to put more stress than previously on the offensive potential of carrier planes. Until that time, carriers had been used to escort battleships; the carriers were expected to operate on the unengaged side of the formation in the event of a major battle with the enemy. From this time on, frequent maneuvers and training were conducted specifically to practice surprise attacks on enemy aircraft carriers by cooperating with advance units or by operating entirely independently.

Phase Three: From approximately 1935 to 1940. As surprise attacks on enemy carriers became the most important mission of our naval aviation units, we also experienced an increase in the number of our carriers. This enabled us to employ a wider variety of tactics. It was during the period between 1934 and 1936 that naval tactical experts debated how best to deploy our carriers in formation—concentrated or dispersed. Those of a more progressive frame of mind advocated dispersion, because an aircraft carrier is almighty in attack and extremely vulnerable in defense. The basis of the argument for spreading carriers out was that it would lessen the chances of their being discovered. Moreover, those that weren't discovered would then still be available for launching strikes against the enemy's carriers.

The superiority of the dispersed arrangement proved itself both in experimental maneuvers around 1936 and in tactical research conducted at the Naval College. We considered a number of types of arrays and decided that the most effective in the long run was one in which we surrounded the enemy force. That, after all, was our conventional way of using destroyer flotillas in night torpedo attacks against battleships. In the case of aircraft carriers, however, we concluded that we would have difficulty surrounding the enemy, because he would probably also have dispersed his carriers.

The reports of air warfare in the Sino-Japanese Incident, which broke out in 1937, revealed the magnificent capability of fighter aircraft. When the enemy had powerful defensive fighters, we would have to increase the sacrifice of our attacking bombers if we did not provide a substantial fighter cover of our own. Moreover, our bombers would not have been able to secure the desired results if we had not attacked with large concentrated formations. Of course, this was a lesson learned from land operations, but it still suggested the necessity of considerable modification to the conventional way of thinking within the Japanese Navy.

The idea that then emerged was that of simultaneous and intensive attacks by large formations combining various offensive techniques. That is to say, we conceived of attacking with a large group of torpedo planes and dive-bombers operating together. We would also send along defensive fighters to repel the interventions from enemy fighters. This idea, which was later used at Pearl Harbor, was practiced in our Combined Fleet in 1939–1940. The results were satisfactory, and we thus concluded that no other offensive techniques were to be considered.

The most difficult problem we faced was how to concentrate the deployed seaborne aircraft to a certain point in operational waters. The problem was made even more difficult when we operated under radio silence. Moreover, if the planes required much time to get together, the distance from which we would have to launch the attacking force might diminish our ability to surprise the enemy. This was one of the main problems to be solved for the Combined Fleet and Naval Air Wings in 1941.

Phase Four: From the end of 1940 to the end of the Battle of Midway. In the Combined Fleet of 1941, the dominant carrier/aircraft units were the First Naval Air Wing (the *Kaga* and two destroyers) and the Second Naval Air Wing (the *Hiryu*, *Soryu*, and four destroyers). These carrier divisions were subordinate to the Second Fleet, which was supposed to be an advance force. Already by that time, the necessity for simultaneous and intensive attack by a large formation had brought about a command arrangement which placed both carrier divisions under Rear Admiral Michitaro Totsuka.

I was assigned to the operational staff of the First Naval Air Wing soon after I came back from overseas at the beginning of October 1940. I was destined to grapple with the problem on all fours. I realized that in order to solve the problems of carrier allocations and simultaneous, intensive attacks, we would have to introduce new concepts to replace our conventional methods.

While staying in Tokyo during the month of October, I was absorbed in thinking of the matter day after day. Then I happened to see a newsreel in a certain metropolitan theater. It showed four American carriers steaming in a single column. In Japan, two carriers were assigned to each division, so a formation of two was quite normal. But we had never experienced an instance of four of them together. I didn't know why that many American carriers had been together; I simply thought about what a strange formation it was and left the theater.

Several days later, when I was stepping out of a streetcar, a new concept suddenly hit me. If several carriers were concentrated in one group, the time necessary for all of the planes to join up in a giant formation would be relatively short. The weak point of the method would be that if the concentrated carrier group were discovered by the enemy, they could all come under attack simultaneously. On the other hand, we would be able to mount a much larger combat air patrol of fighters over the whole carrier group than would be the case with carriers operating independently. What's more, the carriers and their escorts would also be able to supply more effective antiaircraft firepower. I saw this concentrated grouping as a rather good policy in

A newsreel showing four U.S. carriers steaming in column inspired Commander Genda to concentrate Japanese aircraft carriers in larger formations than the pairs used up to then. Shown here are the *Lexington, Ranger, Yorktown,* and *Enterprise.* (U.S. Navy: Naval Institute Collection.)

order to provide a decisive blow against the enemy attacking force by attracting them around our carrier formation.

As I contemplated the various possibilities involved in such a new tactical scheme, I also contemplated whether or not it was right in terms of military doctrine. Sun-tzu, the ancient Chinese philosopher of war, wrote: "Wherefore in conduct of war, do not depend on the enemy's not coming, but rely on your own preparations. Do not count on the enemy not attacking your fortress, but leave nothing undefended." This philosophy was first accepted by Rear Admiral Totsuka and later by Vice Admiral Chuichi Nagumo. Collective employment of carriers was from then on exercised frequently, but all-out drill was not practiced until the final rehearsal for the Pearl Harbor attack, just one month before the real assault.

By early 1941, we had four powerful carriers in

commission—the *Akagi, Kaga, Hiryu,* and *Soryu.* Doubt had arisen about the conventional idea of attaching them to the First Fleet (mainly battleships) and to the Second Fleet (mainly heavy cruisers). From 1939 onward, there had been discussion of joining the carriers with appropriate patrol vessels in order to form a special fleet whose mission would be to destroy enemy carriers. This objective was realized on 10 April 1941 when Vice Admiral Nagumo took command of the newly constituted First Air Fleet. It was comprised of the First Naval Air Wing (*Akagi* and *Kaga*), the Second Naval Air Wing (*Soryu* and *Hiryu*), and the Fourth Naval Air Wing (*Ryujo, Zuiho,* and *Hosho*). The new fleet launched exclusively into research and training in naval air warfare. The Eleventh Air Fleet, a land-based naval air force, was organized in January 1941. It was composed of land attack aircraft and fighter units and participated in maritime air operations together with the First Air Fleet. In the autumn of 1941, two new carriers, the *Shokaku* and *Zuikaku*, joined the Combined Fleet and formed the Fifth Naval Air Wing.

The subsequent combat operations at Pearl Harbor, in the Indian Ocean, and at Midway were all attacks on powerful enemy ground bases. So we used a box-type formation of carriers steaming alongside each other in pairs. This arrangement worked satisfactorily for attacking land targets, but the box-type formation was not so fit for defense against carrier attacks. This was particularly demonstrated in the Battle of Midway, and the formation was never used again after that.

Phase Five: From the end of the Battle of Midway to the end of the Battle of the Marianas. The tactics of carrier operation during this period are universally known already, so nothing is to be added here. Throughout this period, the standard number of vessels in a carrier division was three, growing out of our experience at Midway.

The *Hiryu* and *Soryu* steam in formation en route to the attack on Pearl Harbor. Genda's disposition of aircraft carriers in a boxlike arrangement worked well in the strike against Hawaii but had disastrous results in the Battle of Midway six months later. (National Archives: 80-G-182259.)

The *Kaga*, which was completed in 1928, was one of Japan's first large aircraft carriers, having been converted from her intended role as a battleship during construction. Initially, she had two decks for launching planes in addition to the main flight deck, and her exhaust was ducted almost to her stern. After being rebuilt in 1935, she had one flight deck, a starboard-side island, and a smokestack amidship, as can be seen in the second picture: this is essentially how she looked at the time of the attack on Pearl Harbor. The *Kaga* and three other carriers that took part in the raid on Pearl Harbor were sunk in the Battle of Midway. (Pacific & Atlantic Photos, Inc., and Imperial War Museum.)

The *Shokaku* (shown here) and her near-sister *Zuikaku* were completed in August and September of 1941, respectively, and thus were available to participate in the Hawaii Operation. (Courtesy of Norman Polmar.)

In examining the five phases outlined above, we found the biggest shortcoming in Japanese Navy carrier tactics to be in the employment of patrol and search aircraft. Although we were fully aware of the fact that reconnaissance was the fundamental prerequisite of all tactics, we esteemed attack forces too highly. Because we expected a great deal (too much as it turned out) from our land-based patrol planes, we decided to sacrifice the patrol power of our carriers. That decision proved to be the vital cause of our defeat in the Pacific theater of war.

Minoru Genda (1904–   ) was graduated from the Imperial Naval Academy in 1924 and completed flight training as a fighter pilot in 1928. He subsequently served in the cruiser *Izumo* and the carriers *Akagi* and *Ryujo*. After a tour as assistant naval attaché in London, Genda became operations officer of the First Naval Air Wing in late 1940. The following year, he became operations officer on the staff of Vice Admiral Chuichi Nagumo, Commander First Air Fleet. In this capacity, he planned all the tactics, including the use of shallow-running aerial torpedoes, used by the six Japanese carriers employed in the Pearl Harbor attack. He was involved in carrier operations through much of World War II, and in 1945 took command of the 343rd Fighter Group for defense of the homeland. In later years, he was chief of staff of the Japanese Air Self-Defense Force. He now lives in Atsugi, Japan. (Naval Institute Collection.)

One of the real ironies connected with the Pearl Harbor disaster is that the officer who sent out the first message informing the world of the air raid was the same man who had virtually "predicted" that type of attack four years earlier. In 1937, Lieutenant Commander Logan C. Ramsey, a naval aviator, discussed at length (more than is reproduced here) the strategic and tactical considerations that would be involved in attacking a fleet either at anchor or in port. His analytical article was an entry in the Naval Institute's annual General Prize Essay Contest, which has been conducted since 1879. Lieutenant Commander Ramsey did not specify any geographic locations, but he was nonetheless remarkably prescient in describing many of the factors involved in the eventual attack. The only important factor that he did not foresee was that aerial torpedoes would be perfected for use in the shallow waters of a protected harbor, a breakthrough that was achieved shortly before the British attack at Taranto, Italy, in 1940. (His analysis was correct at the time he wrote it; in 1937, a fleet in a harbor of restricted size, with the ships moored to docks or other structures, was still immune to aerial torpedoes.) Ramsey's proposed countermeasure against the type of attack he was discussing was what he called a "dynamic defense"—detecting the attacking force early and launching a counterattack before the planes could reach their targets. Both the Italians at Taranto and the Americans at Pearl Harbor were caught by surprise and, consequently, prevented from so defending themselves.

Also reprinted here is a part of Ramsey's testimony before the Navy's Pearl Harbor court of inquiry, which was conducted in 1944. In it, he tells of his own reaction on the morning of 7 December 1941, at which time he was a commander, serving on the staff of Rear Admiral Patrick N. L. Bellinger, Commander Patrol Wing 2.

Following his retirement from active duty and promotion to rear admiral, Ramsey explored the results of the attack in an article titled "The 'Ifs' of Pearl Harbor," which was published in the *Proceedings* in April 1950. In considerable detail, he speculated on how different things might have been if the United States had reacted differently in 1941—if it had concluded from the diplomatic situation in late November that Japan might attack Pearl Harbor in the near future; if the nation had reached such a conclusion around 3 December on the basis of radio intelligence; if 700-mile aircraft patrols had been in effect in early December; or if a last-minute warning transmitted by any means had afforded Admiral Husband E. Kimmel and Lieutenant General Walter C. Short about an hour in which to react. Admiral Ramsey hypothesized seven possible outcomes different from the one that actually occurred. Five of the seven, he wrote, "probably would have been more disastrous than the real Pearl Harbor; the seventh would have had no really material effect on history." He concluded that, given the political and strategic circumstances in late 1941, a Japanese attack on Pearl Harbor was almost universally considered to be unlikely. To Ramsey, the fact that it happened the way it did was a reflection of the Japanese mind and a blessing for the United States.

Aerial Attacks on Fleets at Anchor

By Lieutenant Commander Logan C. Ramsey, U.S. Navy

In the first place, a fleet is designed for one main purpose—to control the sea. To accomplish that mission it must, of necessity, be able to move freely across the sea despite hostile opposition. That in turn demands of the fleet the ability to repel all forms of enemy attacks while under way. In other words, if the ability of the fleet to defend itself while cruising is not at the maximum possible degree of efficiency, then something is radically wrong with that fleet. It follows then, that the vulnerability of a fleet to aërial attack must necessarily be greater in port than at sea, from the standpoint of design alone.

It is therefore necessary to weigh the defensive liabilities assumed by a fleet which enters port—whether it be a regular naval base or merely a fleet anchorage—against the assets it acquires in the form of base defenses. On the strategical side two distinct disadvantages accrue immediately. Naturally, with the fleet in port, no major operations may be undertaken against the enemy, which in turn permits him to assume a certain strategical freedom of movement. In addition, any operations he may contemplate against the opposing fleet will not require as extensive strategical scouting as would be the case if his objective should be at sea. In all probability, the enemy would hardly undertake any aërial operations in the vicinity of the naval base or anchorage until after obtaining information, and hence his entire aërial strength should be available for the actual attack. Further, the attack itself would occur at his chosen moment rather than at a more indeterminate instant such as might be expected as a result of unanticipated contacts at sea.

On the tactical side, the disadvantages of the fleet in port are many and varied. First of all, the fleet and its individual units are deprived of their tactical mobility. This diasability operates doubly to the defensive detriment of the fleet. The hostile aërial attack has to contend with two fewer variables—the course and speed of the target—which should very materially improve the accuracy with which its projectiles may be launched. In addition, the individual targets have lost all opportunity to evade the bombs or torpedoes by maneuver. Next, the disposition of the fleet units within the harbor

is often the result of hydrographic and logistical, rather than tactical, considerations. Hence the fleet in port lacks the defensive cohesiveness of the fleet formation at sea. Hostile aircraft may be able to reach the most important units of the fleet without first being subjected to the anti-aircraft fire from the smaller fleet units, as must often be the case at sea. In addition, it is quite possible that the greater portion of those anti-aircraft batteries of the fleet which happen to be within range of the hostile aircraft may be masked by docks, buildings, or other ships.

There is also the logistical angle to be considered. The basic reason for the fleet to put into port in time of war is to make it possible for that fleet to go to sea again. This involves refueling, provisioning, rearming, repairs, and adjustments, and other operations which, for the time being, reduce the fighting efficiency of the unit or units concerned. Concomitant to the logistical is the personnel problem. From time immemorial, coming to anchor has had the connotation of a certain surcease from the rigors of the seafaring life. Rest, recreation, and shore leave have always been the watchwords on anchoring. And unless anti-aircraft gun crews are provided in duplicate or triplicate such duty is quite apt to be highly unpopular—in port at least. Hence as far as the fleet itself is concerned, its defensive ability against hostile aërial attacks is almost certain to leave much to be desired while at anchor.

The security of the fleet at anchor [against aërial attack] calls for a defense the outstanding characteristic of which may well be termed dynamic. This necessity arises from the extremely short time interval between the appearance of the attacking planes within visual range of the fixed defenses of the port and the delivery of the actual attack upon the fleet. Even the static defense of anti-aircraft batteries requires dynamic assistance, at least to the extent of needing some warning of the approach of an aërial enemy. Under the most ideal conditions, an aërial attack develops with such speed and may come from so many directions simultaneously that it may break through all static defense and seriously damage vital units of the fleet. The only sure defense is to tackle the ball carrier before he crosses

These are the two photographs that accompanied Lieutenant Commander Ramsey's article in the August 1937 issue of the *U.S. Naval Institute Proceedings*. In the first, the U.S. Fleet is at anchor in Lahaina Roads, Hawaii, and in the second in Guantánamo Bay, Cuba. Although Ramsey's analytical article did not deal with a particular place, in a number of respects, it proved to be remarkably prophetic of the Japanese attack at Pearl Harbor. (U.S. Navy: Naval Institute Collection.)

the line of scrimmage—in other words, to stop the aërial attack before the planes are launched.

Naturally, before we can discuss intelligently the dynamic methods of defense against aërial attacks on our fleet in port, we must examine the nature of such raids and determine their probable composition and tactical conduct. As a starting point we may rule out all of the hostile shore-based aircraft, as a naval base or fleet anchorage located within range of such aircraft is absolutely untenable. It [thus] follows that only aircraft operating from mobile bases need be considered in aërial attacks of the kind in which we are here interested. The battleship- and cruiser-based planes have only limited offensive potentialities as, while they might damage the flight deck of a carrier, sink a destroyer or two, or set fire to oil tanks on shore, they lack the weight-carrying ability to constitute a real menace to a fleet in port. This, then, limits a serious attack to aircraft based on carriers making a raid and to patrol planes operating from tenders occupying a geographically advanced position. This restriction, in addition to imposing a numerical limitation on attacking aircraft, defines the areas within which the appearance of a hostile carrier or aircraft tender indicates the possibility of an aërial raid upon the fleet at its base. The safety of that fleet demands that such mobile aircraft bases be detected and destroyed before they are able to penetrate these danger areas and launch their aircraft for the attack.

The defenses of the naval base, then, must extend considerably beyond the immediate vicinity of the fleet anchorage; and that range must be further expanded with each new aëronautical development which permits of any material increase in the operating radius of ship-based aircraft. Therefore, the base defense force, in order to maintain the security of the fleet under its protection against hostile aircraft, must extend its influence to or beyond the outer limit from which hostile carrier planes are able to attack and cover the entire area to seaward of the base. In the case of enemy task groups, consisting of tenders and patrol planes, its protection need extend only to the general vicinity of locations known or suspected to provide sheltered bodies of water suitable for seaplane operations. This necessity involves practically continuous operation of powerful forces over extensive areas as long as the fleet remains in port; except in those happy instances where previous operations have accounted for all of the hostile carriers and aircraft tenders.

Before further discussion of the strategical aspect, let us examine briefly some of the tactical features of the problem. The traditional concept of a suitable naval base or fleet anchorage includes such features as a relatively large body of sheltered water with anchorage depths and entrances large enough for ready access, yet small enough to be readily defended. The terrain has been considered of secondary importance. Roughly speaking, the primary requisite has been room for the fleet to anchor. Like animals entering the Ark, each type has been accustomed to anchor, "after his kind," in a fashion reminiscent of an oriental caste system. However, such an anchorage system for the units of the fleet in a harbor of generous size would certainly simplify the tactical problem confronting the commander of an attacking aërial group. For example, most of the readers have seen battleships at anchor swing to the tide so that, from certain directions, the ends of one ship have apparently overlapped the silhouette of a ship in the second line, giving the entire group the appearance of one enormous and continuous structure. A magnificent sight; but also a perfectly marvelous target for a squadron of hostile torpedo planes! In fact, the entire conception of a fleet anchorage as a commodious body of water appears to be made to order for this form of aërial attack. With the usual anchorage plan, the broadside batteries of the ships could not be used very effectively, not only because of masked fire, but also because any fire might cause damage to adjacent units. The anti-aircraft batteries of the fleet would be subject to much the same disabilities, as the fire control problem against such a menace is one bearing a very close analogy to that of broadside fire, due to the very low altitude of the attacking planes. It may be necessary to hark back somewhat to the past and to provide the more important units of the fleet with detachable torpedo nets for port use, or to lay down lines of such nets to protect the rows of anchored heavy units. Such a·solution may, or may not, prove practicable; and, in the absence of proof, it may be stated that the only sort of fleet anchorage immune to torpedo plane attacks would be one of restricted size, with the fleet units moored to docks or other structures, and with no clear approaches to such positions from which aërially launched torpedoes might strike home.

While such a base would provide freedom from the threat of torpedo planes, there is another form of aërial attack to be considered. Because of the greater altitudes at which such bombing planes must operate, the anti-aircraft batteries of the fleet should be more effective than against torpedo planes. Fewer guns will be masked and there will be less chance of the fire damaging other units of the fleet. On the other hand, nets and a restricted

This aerial view of Pearl Harbor, made in the mid-1930s, shows what a compact place it is. Ramsey's comment that "the only sort of fleet anchorage immune to torpedo plane attacks would be one of restricted size, with the fleet units moored to docks or other structures, and with no clear approaches to such positions from which aerial torpedoes might strike home" was true in 1937. By 1941, however —to the great surprise of the U.S. Navy—the Japanese had developed an aerial torpedo that was capable of operating in shallow, restricted waters. (Naval Historical Center: NH 54301.)

anchorage would not bar a bombing attack. Hence, while the conformation of the anchorage or the use of nets may virtually eliminate the danger of a torpedo plane raid, no naval base can be considered as affording immunity to bombing attacks.

Thus far in this discussion we have not elaborated upon the aids that may be provided the fleet in port to augment the defense against air attacks. These will consist of anti-aircraft batteries on shore and shore-based defensive aircraft. If the guns are to have the maximum effectiveness they must surround the anchorage in order to provide opposition regardless of the direction from which the final stage of the air attack develops. This feature likewise indicates the desirability of a harbor more moderate in size than has heretofore been considered ideal, not only because outlining the entire periphery of a large harbor with anti-aircraft batteries would be prohibitively expensive, but also

because certain of such emplacements would necessarily be too distant from the fleet they were designed to defend for effectiveness. Parenthetically it may be stated that, in general, the fixed anti-aircraft defenses of a base will provide greater protection for the fleet from bombers than from torpedo planes, in the final stages of any aërial attack, for much the same reasons that control the relative effectiveness of such fire from the fleet itself. Broadly, the efficiency of anti-aircraft batteries on shore is dependent upon the geographical features of the anchorage and, in many cases, cannot provide protection against attack from all directions. Inevitably, in the case of such bases, hostile aircraft will use just those sectors for their final approach. For this reason, floating anti-aircraft batteries—perhaps in the form of a new and special type of surface craft—may be required. Several such vessels might be organized as part of the fleet base force and proceed from base to base in conformity with the movements of the fleet. It must not be construed from the foregoing that the proposed type should be designed to provide anti-aircraft protection for the fleet at sea. Its primary mission would be to provide such defense to the fleet in ports where anti-aircraft batteries on shore are lacking, or where the conformation of the harbor precludes the effective use of such defenses. This type holds out a prospect of considerable over-all economy by permitting a reduction in the otherwise excessive number of anti-aircraft installations that would be required to afford complete protection for all of the naval bases and fleet anchorages a nation possesses. From this standpoint alone, the possibilities of such a type merit the most careful investigation.

Even with the most adequate system of anti-aircraft batteries, whether afloat, ashore, or in combination, it would be extremely difficult, if not impossible, to keep all of the guns manned continuously and ready to open fire immediately. Therefore observation units, located at some distance, are required to give the necessary warning of the approach of hostile aircraft. These must cover the land approaches to the anchorage as well as those to seaward. Under certain weather conditions these units would have only aural indications to guide them which, in view of the world-wide attention being given to the problem of noise elimination in aircraft, are apt to prove insufficient. Hence, anti-aircraft gunfire as a defense for the fleet at anchor, while necessary, cannot be considered a complete solution.

Likewise, defending shore-based aircraft may be evaded by hostile planes and thus afford only incomplete protection. To go even further, there is a school of thought in Europe which holds that aërial combat is a thing of the past and that greater military efficiency will be obtained by the elimination of fighting planes in favor of types designed for other missions. Adherents of this theory would, in these premises, discard the idea of purely defensive planes designed to intercept and combat hostile attacks in the air and concentrate on aircraft of longer range and greater striking power: the types that could intercept and destroy enemy carriers and tenders before their aërial complements could be launched for the attack. Without discussing such a controversial theory, it must be conceded, solely on the basis that they can be evaded, that purely defensive shore-based aircraft do not provide a sufficiently positive defense for a fleet base.

This brings us back to the prior assertion that such defense must be dynamic and extend considerable distances beyond the location where the fleet is anchored. Extensive aërial and surface patrols are therefore indicated. For illustrative purposes, let us assume that we have the problem of defending an isolated island naval base during the stay of the fleet there. The location of the base is beyond the range of hostile shore-based aircraft, nor does that range overlap the area around our base from within which hostile carrier planes may reach our fleet. In other words, our base is at least 2,000 miles from the hostile mainland. Considering first the steps that are required to defend against hostile carriers, let us assume solely for the purpose of this discussion the arbitrary figure of 400 miles as the maximum distance at which such planes may be launched for the attack and still have sufficient fuel to regain their parent vessels. With 12 hours of darkness and an assumed speed of 30 knots for the hostile carrier, we must cover a circle with a 760-mile radius from our base each day prior to sunset. This would merely enable us to ascertain whether or not hostile carriers are in a position from which their attack may be launched prior to daylight the next morning. Such a daily effort would require the services of a large number of patrol planes. In addition, an aërial striking force with sufficient power and speed to reach and destroy the hostile mobile aircraft bases before they could reach their launching point would have to be kept at the base in a ready condition. Obviously, the greatest danger of the enemy carriers being able to penetrate this defense area without detection will occur at the end of a period of bad weather or reduced visibility conditions which would impair the efficiency of such an aërial patrol.

We have still to consider the defense against hostile patrol planes. This problem may present grave difficulties as many parts of the world provide areas in which seaplane anchorages abound. If any such region lies within striking distance of our base, then our long range aërial scouts must search such areas daily. Even if this is done there still exists a possibility that an enemy tender may slip in to some obscure anchorage shortly after it has been visited by our patrol planes and there receive its complement of aircraft. If timed correctly, either by good fortune or by skillful planning, sufficient time might elapse before the next daily search of the area by our patrol planes to permit the tender to refuel its planes and allow the planes to take off for the attack.

Let us return, in closing, to the strategical aspect of the question. There is a fairly large section of public opinion in the United States which fears that, in the unhappy event that this nation should become involved in war, our cities and towns might be subjected to indiscriminate and widespread bombing or gas attacks by literally thousands of hostile planes. That portion of the public fails to realize that as yet planes cannot cross an ocean carrying a military load and still return to their origin. It has not yet learned that any plane, in order to attack the continental United States, must be brought within striking distance by the medium of a hostile carrier or tender and that the greatest possible number of aircraft that could be so aided is relatively small, and directly in proportion to the number of such vessels possessed by any potential enemy. This apparent digression has been interpolated in this discussion solely to emphasize the belief of the present writer that any transoceanic aërial raid would be undertaken, not with the purpose of destroying our cities or aircraft factories, but in the hope and expectation of inflicting damage upon our fleet while it is in port. Such a long-distance operation would involve great risk of loss to the enemy of the entire raiding force, either before or after it made its attack. As has been argued previously in this article, the loss of the fleet air arm of any enemy would result in an immediate increase in the strategical freedom of movement of our fleet by making available for our use fleet anchorages previously denied us by the mere existance of this aërial contingent. As the hazards in such an attempt would be enormous, compensating damage upon our fleet could hardly be inflicted unless the maximum force available should be employed. To risk the complete loss of such a vital part of his fleet by using it in such an operation with any objective other than our fleet would constitute a strategical blunder unexcelled by any in naval history.

"Air Raid, Pearl Harbor. This Is No Drill."

Testimony by Captain Logan C. Ramsey, U.S. Navy

Our patrol planes covering the operating areas were carrying live depth charges and had specific orders to sink any submerged submarine sighted outside of the submarine sanctuary and without a close escort. At approximately 7:30 on the morning of December 7th I received a telephone call from the staff duty officer who informed me he had received a message from 14-Prep-1 [a PBY aircraft in Patrol Squadron 14] to the effect that they had sunk a submerged submarine one mile off the entrance to Pearl Harbor. I asked him if the message had been properly authenticated, because there was in the back of my mind the feeling that it was quite possible that it was a mistake, a drill message of some variety that had gotten out by accident. So I ordered the staff duty officer to request an authentication of the message immediately. However, that did not stop me from making an immediate report of the information to the staff duty officer of the Commander-in-Chief of the Pacific Fleet. I believe at the time that I did not consider that as definite information of any enemy attack. I went immediately to the Command Center and for no reason that I know of, drew up a search plan for our aircraft under the conditions prevailing that day. I prepared it in dispatch form. Meanwhile, I was waiting for an authentication of this message. There was a slight delay, and approximately 5 or 10 minutes after I reached the Command Center, I saw, together with the staff duty officer, a single plane making a dive on Ford Island. The single plane appeared at the time to both the staff duty officer and myself in the light of a young aviator "flathatting" [flying low in a reckless manner] and we both tried to get his number to make a report of the violation of flight rules. He completed his dive, pulled up and away. We were commenting together on the fact that it was going to be difficult to find out who the pilot was, when the delayed action bomb which he had dropped, and which we had not seen drop, detonated, and I told the staff duty officer, "Never mind; it's a Jap." I dashed across the hall into the radio room, ordered a broadcast in plain English on all frequencies, "Air raid, Pearl Harbor. This is

no drill." The detonation of the bomb dropped by that first plane was my first positive knowledge of an enemy attack.

Logan Carlisle Ramsey (1898–1972) was graduated a year early in the Naval Academy class of 1919, then served in the battleship *Texas* before taking flight training. During the 1920s, he served with air squadrons in the Atlantic Fleet and was at Naval Operating Base Hampton Roads before reporting to the Navy Department Hydrographic Office. His *The Navigation of Aircraft* (1929) was long the standard textbook on the subject. He was subsequently in the aviation units of a number of ships, studied at the Naval War College, and served in the Bureau of Aeronautics and Patrol Wing 2. He was instrumental in the 1942 defense of Midway and later the first commanding officer of the carriers *Block Island* and *Lake Champlain*. He also had aviation duties at Norfolk and Philadelphia. Upon his retirement in 1949, he was promoted to rear admiral and later became executive vice president of the Spring Garden Institute in Philadelphia. (Courtesy of the *Philadelphia Evening Bulletin*.)

In the matter of its policies toward Japan during the years leading up to World War II, the United States certainly had stability in its top leadership. Joseph C. Grew, a career Foreign Service officer, became U.S. Ambassador to Japan in 1932. Franklin D. Roosevelt became President and Cordell Hull became Secretary of State in 1933. In Japan, it was completely different. Changes of government came frequently, and during those many changes, the momentum toward war built steadily. The Japanese Ambassador in Washington during much of 1941 was a naval officer and longtime friend of Americans, Admiral Kichisaburo Nomura. In the following article, he maintains that, despite the preparations for war being made in Japan, he did not find out that his government had decided on war until after the bombs started falling at Pearl Harbor. Soon thereafter he was interned, along with the rest of the Japanese Embassy staff, and spent a number of months in a hotel in Hot Springs, Virginia. He returned to Japan in mid-1942.

Stepping-Stones to War

By Admiral Kichisaburo Nomura, former Imperial Japanese Navy

Around the time of the Washington Disarmament Conference of 1921, Lieutenant General Guichi Tanaka was in office as War Minister. I have been told by a certain ex-ambassador that Tanaka then encouraged the Foreign Office to bestir itself, going so far as to say to the Foreign Minister, Viscount Yasuya Uchida, "The military has no intention of conducting diplomacy. If a diplomatic policy to cope with the situation is shaped on your part, I will willingly stamp my approval seal on it without looking."

A few years before the outbreak of the Manchurian Incident of 1931, when General Hisaichi Terauchi came back to Tokyo relieved of the post of Commanding General of the Manchurian Garrison Army, I was told by him that enthusiasm for re-

covery of national prestige by the Chinese people had become prevalent in Manchuria. So much so that unless measures were taken immediately to meet the situation properly, all that had been achieved as a result of the Russo-Japanese War would be lost eventually, and that this Chinese resurgence had all the makings of a crisis.

In 1928, Chang Tso-lin died due to the bomb explosion when his train was bombed on his way back to Mukden from Peking. At that time Tanaka, being Premier and concurrently Foreign Minister of Japan, endeavored to deal with the case lawfully, examining closely the causes of the matter. However, the matter became complicated contrary to his intention. And, due to lack of thoroughness of the measures taken, the Tanaka cabinet resigned, fail-

Admiral Nomura was long a friend of American naval officers, as evidenced by this portrait which he inscribed and autographed for Admiral Pratt in October 1929. Pratt is shown on board ship during his tenure as Chief of Naval Operations, which lasted from 1930 to 1933. (Naval Historical Center: NH 75881 and 55470.)

ing to satisfy His Majesty on the matter. Around that time I, along with General Gen Sugiyama, went round North China and Manchuria, paying visits to the Sixth Division, then located in Tsinan, and to the headquarters of the Kwantung Army, then located in Mukden. On our return to Tokyo we reported to Tanaka on the situations we had found. Tanaka himself seemed to have been shocked by Chang's death, and it was evident that he had had no part in the bombing.

The Manchurian Incident was taken advantage of, however, to consolidate Japan's position in Manchuria. The military command had regarded this area as the very front line of our national defense. This violated the Nine Power Treaty, so that U. S. Secretary of State Henry L. Stimson proposed economic sanctions against Japan. However, instead of going to the length of such a measure, the United States instituted the policy of non-recognition. As a result the cabinet of Baron Reijiro Wakatsuki resigned, and Baron Kijuro Shidehara, the Foreign Minister, also retired from the active diplomatic service. Thus the diplomacy of Japan came to be weighed in the balance from this time on. It may well be said that the dual government, civil and military, brought about by the independence of the military command from the civil government effectuated by virtue of the Meiji Constitution, was the cause of the downfall of the Empire of Japan.

Japan did not adopt the Open-Door policy in Manchuria. In 1932 the Manchurian Incident developed its effect on Shanghai where armed conflict occurred. Being then appointed Commander in Chief Third Fleet, I went there in haste to assume the post. Admiral William V. Pratt of the U. S. Navy, my intimate friend and then Chief of Naval Operations, had said casually to Ambassador Katsuji Debuchi that it would be best to "allow Nomura to deal with the case." Thus it happened that I went there to settle the conflict and succeeded in bringing about a local settlement of it, cooperating with General Kenkichi Ueda, General Yoshinori Shirakawa, and Mamoru Shigemitsu. General Sadao Araki, then War Minister, withdrew the troops from Shanghai after the settlement of the conflict. On 29 April of the same year, several of those who were present at the ceremony in Shanghai for the commemoration of the Emperor's Birthday, were seriously wounded by the bomb thrown by a Korean. I lost my right eye, and more than one hundred splinters still now remain in my body; Shigemitsu lost one leg, and Shirakawa died later.

In 1937 another incident occurred in Peking. It developed into the "China Incident" which became so complicated that it remained unsettled even after eight years. Prince Fumimaro Konoye as Premier and Koki Hirota as Foreign Minister both endeavored in vain to bring about a local settlement of this incident, with the result that the Military Command became more and more dominant over the Civil Administration. In other words the professional diplomats became more and more impotent. As a result the Nine Power Treaty was violated and the Open-Door policy was discarded, so that the relations between Japan and the foreign powers deteriorated precipitately to the point where the

U.S. and Japanese naval officers pose outside the Foreign Office in Tokyo in May 1935. Admiral Nomura is second from right in the front row. All the way to the left in the front row is Admiral Osami Nagano who was Chief of the Naval General Staff at the time of the attack on Pearl Harbor. The senior U.S. officer pictured is Admiral Frank B. Upham, fifth from left in the front row. (National Archives: 80-G-45960.)

end result was eventually the Pacific War. However, even though it may be said that the Military Command acted arbitrarily in the course of the above mentioned developments, still no declaration of war had been made. And there was a definite limit in the scope of the actions taken by the Military Command, so the Konoye cabinet cannot be absolved from the responsibility of bringing the situation to the ultimate crisis regardless of their laying it at the door of the arbitrariness of the Military Command.

In 1939, I was appointed Foreign Minister. As the first step for settlement on the issue of the Open-Door policy I talked with U.S. Ambassador Joseph C. Grew relative to the opening of the Yangtze-kiang and Si-kiang (West River). Although I had the support of the Premier, General Nobuyuki Abe, the War Minister, General Shunroku Hata, and the Navy Minister, Admiral Zengo Yoshida, the diplomats along with the military authorities on the spot looked with disfavor on the matter, so that before it was put in execution the Abe cabinet resigned.

In 1940, the second Konoye cabinet was born in which Yosuke Matsuoka took the portfolio of Foreign Minister. Matsuoka wished me to take the office of Ambassador in Washington. But in my talk with him at that time I became acquainted with his intention of strengthening the relations of Japan with Germany after the arrival of Mr. Max Stahmer, who was coming to Japan shortly. Thinking that this intention and the idea of improving U. S.-Japanese relations would be incompatible, I said as much to Navy Minister Yoshida, and at the same time I declined Matsuoka's offer.

Both Konoye and Matsuoka entertained the fallacy that, by means of the Tripartite Alliance, Japan would be able to extricate herself from her state of isolation and yet at the same time reach an understanding with America. It is quite astonishing that they should show such a lack of understanding of the mentality of the American people. Admiral Koshiro Oikawa, Yoshida's successor as Navy Minister, also desired to avoid a U. S.-Japanese war, yet nevertheless supported the Tripartite Alliance. But Oikawa felt somewhat uneasy, it seems, after the conclusion of the said alliance. Therefore he again urged me to go to America as ambassador so earnestly that I, on my part, had to accept the proposal. Matsuoka also approved it. This may be attributable, I surmise, to the mentality of a drowning person who will catch at a straw, because he knew that I knew President Franklin D. Roosevelt well—an acquaintance going back to the time when Mr. Roosevelt was Assistant Secretary of the Navy.

Matsuoka was more than enthusiastic in regard to the Tripartite Alliance and regarded the conclusion of the said alliance as a success. At the time of the cabinet of Baron Kiichiro Hiranuma, before Konoye's administration, the question of the Tripartite Alliance had been proposed, but no decision on the matter could be made even after scores of debates and arguments. In the meanwhile, the Nonaggression Pact had been concluded between Germany and the Soviet Union. Hence the Hiranuma cabinet resigned, voicing its utter astonishment in the statement of "complicated and baffling." The alliance proposed at that time, after all, aimed at substantially the strengthening of the Anti-Comintern Pact. The Foreign Minister at that time was Hachiro Arita.

After the Hiranuma cabinet, two cabinets of short duration, Abe's and that of Admiral Mitsumasa Yonai, succeeded in turn. At the time of the administration of the Yonai cabinet the question of the said alliance was again raised, and again the cabinet resigned because of it. After that the Konoye cabinet was reinstated. The Tripartite Alliance proposed at the time of the administration of the Konoye cabinet differed in its nature from that at the time of the Hiranuma cabinet. Essentially it took up the United States as its objective and aimed at restraining her from becoming a participant in the war in Europe. There are even some who assert that as there were included some leftist elements in Konoye's brain trust, the Tripartite Alliance concluded by his cabinet had been engineered by the leftist element.

Konoye, being a peer, was a refined gentleman and a man of popularity in every sphere of society. He was clear-headed and a good talker, being very logical in his arguments. Having a liking for new ideas, he undertook various new schemes. However, becoming the premier at such a youthful age, he lacked experience, so that he installed in key posts some persons who were popular yet who were also stubborn and who were sources of worry to him later. He did not have the perception to discern the sheer difficulty of obtaining the two incompatible things, the Tripartite Alliance and the U. S.-Japanese understanding, just as the maxim puts it, "No man can wear two pairs of shoes at the same time." This was a shortsighted blunder on the part of Japan, although man becomes clever only after failure and even the great mind sometimes commits a fault.

In 1941, the second Konoye cabinet resigned in a body and the third Konoye cabinet was born. This change was all brought about in order to oust Matsuoka and install Admiral Teijiro Toyoda in his place. Nevertheless, the new cabinet carried out immediately the dispatch of troops to southern French Indochina as had been planned, thereby inviting the U. S. severance of economic relations with Japan. The cabinet, although deeply desirous of amicable relations between Japan and the United States, actually caused the relations to deteriorate more and more, eventually bringing about the economic severance between the two nations, a step just short of war. And my talk with Secretary of State Hull came to a halt with this and the subsequent pronouncements on his part.

I think now that what proved to be the insurmountable obstacles to friendly relations between the United States and Japan were: (1) the China Incident, (2) the Tripartite Alliance, and (3) the advance of Japanese troops into southern French Indochina. But it was only after the end of the war that I learned the whole truth, especially in connection with the following matters:

At the Imperial conference held on 2 July 1941, it was decided that in order to establish the Greater East Asia Co-Prosperity Sphere preparations should be made for a war with Great Britain and the United States; and that the structure for the southern advance would be strengthened even at the risk of an armed conflict with Great Britain and the United States. Hence, the advance of troops into southern French Indochina was planned by the second Konoye cabinet and was put into execution by the third Konoye cabinet, so that Konoye's purpose in reorganizing his cabinet was discarded immediately, and by himself.

Therefore, after profound mental anguish, he made desperate efforts to ease this crisis even to the extent of trying to arrange a conference with President Roosevelt, who had always exhibited friendliness toward him, but this objective he could not attain. Konoye was opposed to a war against the United States, and moreover he had fully understood after deliberation with Admiral Isoroku Yamamoto that in the case of war, even though our armed forces would be able to display activity with vigor at the earlier phase, the war would eventually be protracted and no probability of ultimate victory could be expected.

The resignation of the third Konoye cabinet was due to the difference of opinions between Konoye and General Hideki Tojo. And the Navy at that time, in spite of its inherent opposition to a war against the United States, was still mindful of its public popularity. So instead of taking a resolute antiwar attitude, it evaded the responsibility of deciding between war or peace by putting it solely on the shoulders of Konoye. This also, it seems, strengthened Konoye's intention of resigning. If at this critical moment Yamamoto had been in office as Navy Minister, he might have taken a determined attitude and the history of Japan might have taken a far different course. Or he might have been assassinated by the opposition party in that case.

The below-mentioned matter, which also came to my knowledge only after the termination of hostilities, is also of great importance.

In the decision made by the Imperial conference held on 6 September 1941, are included the following:

1. The Empire of Japan should perfect the preparation for war by the latter part of October, with the determination not to shrink from a war with the United States (as well as the United Kingdom and the Netherlands) in order to ensure the self-existence and self-defense of the Empire.

2. Parallel with the above, the Empire of Japan should try to obtain the demands of the Empire through negotiations with the United States and Great Britain, exhausting all diplomatic means for this purpose.

3. The Empire of Japan should determine to commence war at once on the United States (as well as on the United Kingdom and the Netherlands) in

General Hideki Tojo, Japanese Prime Minister at the time Japan decided to go to war against the United States. (National Archives: 208-AA-248N-5.)

case by the beginning of October the negotiations should not have produced any prospect of obtaining the demands of the Empire.

At that time, Emperor Hirohito looking with great disfavor on this plan, closely questioned Konoye on the matter one day before the Imperial conference. In accordance with Konoye's advice, the Emperor then summoned General Sugiyama and Admiral Osami Nagano in audience, with Konoye also present, and vehemently questioned them on the plan. All things considered, it was decided at the Imperial conference that primary importance should be attached to diplomacy; at the same time preparations for war were being made.

Nagano, my close friend, was a good-natured man who was well aware of the national potential of the United States. After my return home from the United States he told me that although he could not say definitely that Japan would be able to win the war, the situation had come to such a point as left no alternative but to resort to war. Even then there was criticism of his irresponsibility in consenting to begin the war without any prospect of victory.

At the Imperial conference held on 1 December, commencement of the war against the United States, the United Kingdom, and the Netherlands was decided upon, and on that occasion Tojo made a general report to the Throne, and Shigenori Togo made a report on the progress of the U. S.-Japanese negotiations.

It was not until the end of August 1942 that I returned to Japan. As the war had broken out contrary to my intention, I thought that an *ex post facto* report need not be made immediately. But I submitted a written report to the Foreign Minister in lieu of an oral one. One day thereafter, Togo held a customary garden party at his official residence. On that occasion he reminiscently told me in particular that before he was installed as Foreign Minister the foundation stones for the conflict had been laid, so that there was left no alternative but to take the course thus set.

The official document of the Japanese Government proposing severance of the negotiation was to be delivered to the U. S. Government at 1:00 p.m., 7 December, Washington time, but it was delayed in preparation at the Japanese Embassy in Washington. Therefore it was already 2:00 p.m. when I reached the State Department and I interviewed Mr. Hull at 2:20 p.m. This delay was a matter of great regret to me. The Japanese Govern-

Emperor Hirohito, shown here with a Japanese officer bowing to him, acquiesced reluctantly in his government's decision to make war on the United States. (National Archives: 208-PU-935-1.)

ment's note, of course, had been drafted by the Foreign Office, and consultation had been made thereon with the military authorities. Although the Foreign Minister, I think, might not have been acquainted with the operational orders, he should, of course, have been fully aware of the general tendency of the situations to be brought about thereafter. However, in Washington nothing was known, and I myself became acquainted for the first time with the attack upon Pearl Harbor by the radio news.

Kichisaburo Nomura (1877-1964) was graduated from the Japanese Naval Academy in 1898 and served in the Russo-Japanese War in a number of ships, one of which was sunk by a mine. In 1908, he went to Russia as a naval attaché and later served similar duty in both Vienna and Berlin. Back in Japan, he was secretary to the Navy Minister before becoming naval attaché in Washington during World War I. He was a delegate to the Washington Disarmament Conference of 1921-1922 and in 1926 attained flag rank. He commanded the Japanese Third Fleet during the "Shanghai Incident" in 1932 and held a number of other posts before leaving the active Navy in 1937. He continued to serve Japan, including as ambassador to the United States from February 1941 until interned in December. He was repatriated in 1942 but was not given any military or naval duty during the war. (Naval Historical Center: NH 75857.)

Shortly after the end of World War II, Nomura appeared in "Report From Tokyo, 1946," a film designed to show American audiences how humble the Japanese were in defeat. Nomura was the Japanese ambassador to the United States in December 1941 but claimed he had no advance knowledge of the attack on Pearl Harbor. (National Archives: 80-G-606887.)

"My God, They Can't Do That to Me"

By Vice Admiral George C. Dyer, U.S. Navy (Retired)

On 6 January 1940, Admiral James O. Richardson took command of the United States Fleet. At that time, the U.S. Fleet included units that were in both the Atlantic and the Pacific. I had served with Admiral Richardson before, and now I was his flag secretary. He was a long, rangy Texan—a very good-looking man. He was a man of tremendous energy. He had an extremely keen mind, great determination, and great character. Admiral Richardson called things the way they were. On the other hand, he had a very human touch; he was full of funny stories. He loved golf and played any time he could. He had had a very broad experience in the Navy, primarily in the fields of engineering and gunnery. Prior to taking over as CinCUS, he had been Chief of the Bureau of Navigation and Commander Battle Force, two of the most responsible flag officer assignments in the prewar Navy. He had a tremendous galaxy of friends. I've yet to find a person who spoke ill of Admiral Richardson.

I think his downfall as CinCUS came because he misjudged Franklin D. Roosevelt and how much criticism of himself the President would take. The factor that has gotten the most attention was that Admiral Richardson believed the principal ships of the fleet could do a far better job of preparing for war by returning to their West Coast bases than by being kept out in Hawaiian waters. I do not know, but I think one of the reasons for the admiral's objection to keeping the fleet at Pearl Harbor was that he felt daily patrol plane searches were necessary there, and we didn't have nearly enough planes to do a 360-degree search. The admiral had known FDR for many years and probably thought that he could bring him around to his viewpoint and get the fleet back to California. Even though that's my opinion, I don't think Admiral Richardson would have done things differently in any case, because he was a person who believed in being frank with his seniors.

On 10 October 1940, the Commander in Chief U.S. Fleet, Admiral James O. Richardson (right), was in Washington to meet with the Chief of Naval Operations, Admiral Harold R. Stark (left) and Secretary of the Navy Frank Knox (center). Richardson protested the continuing deployment of the fleet to Hawaii because, in his view, it could better prepare for war at its West Coast bases. President Franklin D. Roosevelt did not agree and fired Richardson. (Naval Historical Center: NH 81942.)

In October 1940, Admiral Richardson made his case to FDR during a visit to Washington. When he came back to Hawaii, he said he had been told by Admiral Harold R. Stark, then Chief of Naval Operations, that he would remain as commander in chief for one more year. It was only a little more than two months later, in early January, that a dispatch came in ordering Richardson to be relieved by Admiral Husband E. Kimmel. I was the staff duty officer when the message arrived. It was on a Sunday, so I went out to the course where the admiral was playing golf. I delivered the dispatch to him, and Richardson's remark was, "My God, they can't do that to me." But, of course, they could and did.

Since Kimmel would be bringing in his own staff when he took over as fleet commander in chief, that left the old staff to look out for itself. I received orders to report to the Bureau of Navigation, but I didn't want to go ashore. So I sought and received permission to request another assignment and asked for sea duty—"any ship, any ocean." I was really putting my neck on the line, because I could have been sent anywhere and would have had no complaint. As it turned out, I couldn't have gotten a better job if I had asked for it specifically. I was detailed as executive officer of the heavy cruiser *Indianapolis*, a ship I had enjoyed serving in previously. That's where I went in early February.

As the year dragged on, things were becoming more and more tense between the United States and Japan. About August, I finally got the ship's department heads together and told them I didn't think we had the ship in a sufficient state of readiness. I wanted to step up our watches while in port, but I couldn't get much support. So I went in to see my skipper, Captain Edward W. Hanson. Much to my pleasure, he said, "I've just been hoping that you'd come in and say something like this to me. I think it's most inadequate what we're doing." He backed me all the way as we doubled our readiness condition. We shifted the watches to what we called a "modified Condition II." In other words, everybody was on duty two days out of four instead of one day out of four. In port that meant we could man 100 per cent of our antiaircraft battery, all of its fire-control equipment, and have our ammunition supply largely manned. Either the skipper or I was on board ship all the time.

This new setup hadn't been going on for forty-eight hours when I got word from Mrs. Dyer, "All the wives have been calling me, asking, 'What's the *Indianapolis* trying to do, fight the war all by itself? Fight some war that doesn't exist?' Their husbands aren't coming home, and they're upset." I told her I was sorry, but that's the way things had to be. Things got tauter and tauter, and people grew more and more disgruntled. When I handed the captain the dispatch saying, "Air raid, Pearl Harbor. This is no drill," we were at Johnston Island. He said to me, "You and I are lucky this dispatch came. In another week, the crew would have thrown us overboard."

As it happened, it wasn't much more than a week

Admiral James O. Richardson (center), CinCUS, and his two principal subordinates in 1940. At left is Admiral Charles P. Snyder, Commander Battle Force, and, at right, Vice Admiral William S. Pye, Commander Battleships Battle Force. When Husband E. Kimmel relieved Richardson in February 1941, Snyder declined to serve under him and thus paved the way for Pye to take command of the Battle Force. (Naval Historical Center: NH 54893.)

after that when we got a setback that was an entirely unanticipated side effect of Admiral Richardson's summary relief earlier in the year. At that time, Admiral Charles P. "Peck" Snyder had been Richardson's number one subordinate as Commander Battle Force, even though he was two classes senior (Snyder was 1900, and Richardson was 1902) at the Naval Academy. Admiral Kimmel was from the class of 1904, and Admiral Snyder said that while he was perfectly willing to serve under Admiral Richardson, he would not do so under Kimmel. So, Snyder was relieved, and Vice

Admiral William S. Pye became Commander Battle Force. The side effect came when Kimmel himself was summarily relieved in December and Pye became acting Commander in Chief Pacific Fleet. Admiral Pye was a great theoretical tactician, but what we needed was a great fighting sailor like Snyder.

Our war plan—Rainbow Five—called for a raid on the Marshall Islands as one of the early acts in a war against the Japanese. Having been set on our rear ends by the attack on Pearl Harbor, there was a great deal of feeling among the officers of the fleet that the least we could do would be to go down and take a smack at them. A week after the attack, 14 December, we shoved off a goodly portion of the combatant fleet. Task Force 11, built around the carrier *Lexington*, was under Vice Admiral Wilson Brown, Jr., Commander Scouting Force. The *Indianapolis* was his flagship. We also had along the heavy cruisers *Chicago* and *Portland*, Destroyer Squadron 1, and the fleet oiler *Neosho*. Our attack on the Marshalls would be a diversionary effort designed to draw attention away from a relief expedition to Wake Island.

After a run of nearly a week, we were due to make the raid on the Marshalls at next daylight. About four o'clock in the afternoon, Admiral Brown ordered everything buttoned up. We went to battle stations, worked up to 28 knots, and started in. We had been running in for four or five hours, and as it was getting dark, Commander Turner Joy, who was Brown's operations officer, came down from the flag bridge to the ship's bridge and showed me a dispatch. It was from Admiral Pye, the temporary Commander in Chief Pacific Fleet, telling us the Marshalls operation was canceled and that we should swing north toward Wake instead. It felt like

In the weeks immediately following the attack on Pearl Harbor, Vice Admiral Wilson Brown, Jr., commanded a task force sent to attack the Japanese-held Marshall Islands. At the time, Commander Dyer was executive officer of Brown's flagship, the heavy cruiser *Indianapolis*, and was bitterly frustrated when the planned raid was called off by Vice Admiral William S. Pye, acting Commander in Chief Pacific Fleet. (National Archives: 80-G-302401, and U.S. Navy: Naval Institute Collection.)

a kick in the groin. Here we were all enthusiastic that we were finally going to do something—to satisfy the American people who were asking, "Where's the fleet?"—and now the operation was off.

Joy said to me, "The admiral hasn't seen this; what do you think we ought to do with it?" I told him he ought to tear it up and throw it over the side. Captain Hanson of the *Indianapolis* gave the same advice. But Joy showed it to Brown's chief of staff, who was "an old woman," and he told Joy to pass it on to the admiral. Brown consulted with the captain of the *Lexington* and the commander of the destroyer squadron, and they both recommended going ahead with the operation. But Admiral Brown didn't take the advice. Instead, he followed Pye's orders. A little while later, we changed course to the north and slowed down.

Admiral Pye had had a scare, apparently visualizing the Japanese fleet all over the Pacific Ocean, and insisted that the operation ordered by Admiral Kimmel be canceled. I later talked with any number of people who served on the Pacific Fleet staff at the time, and I was told that only one other senior officer recommended that the raid be called off. All the rest wanted to go ahead. That cancellation, and the parallel cancellation of the Wake relief expedition itself, were both tremendous disappointments to the fighting men of the Pacific Fleet.

As it turned out, that missed opportunity was the last chance for action that I had for some time. Soon afterward, I was relieved as exec of the *Indianapolis* and ordered in as flag secretary on the new U.S. Fleet (CominCh) staff that Admiral Ernest J. King was putting together in Washington. At that time, the flag secretary's job was really an involved one— legal officer, intelligence officer, public relations officer, and secretary. So I would be the first one the admiral would turn to when something of an administrative nature came up. About twenty-four to forty-eight hours after I had reported in, Admiral King called me in and said, "This Pearl Harbor disaster has a terrible smell. Something went completely wrong with our intelligence activities. I want you to make a study, interrogate people within the department here, and come up with a report to me. I would like to have a report in about four or five days, certainly no longer than a week."

At that point, I was getting down to the office at seven o'clock in the morning and leaving at nine or ten o'clock at night, so this was really quite an additional chore. I talked to a lot of people and tried to learn as much as I could. Eventually, I got it down to a written report. Among the recommendations I came up with for Admiral King was that the functions of naval intelligence be placed under

the Plans Division of the CominCh staff. Intelligence information was obviously one of the bases on which plans would be made, so it seemed logical to have the functions combined. That put the noses of some of the people in the Office of Naval Intelligence out of joint, but at least it was better than continuing the internal squabbling over who was supposed to do what. In addition, I concluded that a larger number of capable naval officers should be encouraged to go into the intelligence field. There were a few individuals such as Commander Arthur H. McCollum in ONI who had had the language training and a series of intelligence billets, but there weren't nearly enough of them. In the months that followed, the intelligence and planning functions were strengthened as Admiral King put them under the CominCh organization and exercised a great deal of personal control.

Shortly thereafter, I was shifted from being flag secretary to concentrating on intelligence for the

Patrol Squadron 8 flies in left-echelon formation shortly before World War II. During much of his tenure as CinCUS, Admiral James O. Richardson turned down requests that he halt long-range reconnaissance patrols by PBYs based in Hawaii. Later, at the instigation of Admiral Stark, he did call them off, and that, maintains Dyer, was a major factor in the surprise achieved by the Japanese in December 1941. (U.S. Navy: Naval Institute Collection.)

 CominCh staff. I believe, but do not know, that the reason for the shift had its origins in that report. I was also made an assistant plans officer under Rear Admiral Kelly Turner, who headed the Plans Division. I was told by both Admiral King and Admiral Turner that I was there to ensure that Plans got all essential intelligence.

Since my retirement from active duty a number of years later, I have supplemented the knowledge I picked up in the near aftermath of the attack. In the course of collaborating on Admiral Richardson's autobiography and writing a two-volume biography of Admiral Turner, I sat down and read the thirty-nine volumes of the congressional report on Pearl Harbor. It's a major operation, because the report has only a limited index. So in order to obtain the basic story and necessary background, one has to read the whole thing. I doubt if more than twenty people in the United States have read all thirty-nine volumes. As a result of all my research into the subject, I have come up with three principal conclusions.

First, in my opinion, one of Admiral Kimmel's great derelictions was the failure to maintain the proper state of readiness in his ships. If one reads the Pearl Harbor report with any degree of care, he'll find that it was minutes and minutes after the initial attack came and the Japanese had dropped their bombs before there was a gun that could shoot. The reason was that the proper condition of readiness was not being maintained. The ships didn't have the proper fire-control gear manned. Sure, they had a bunch of ammunition sitting up alongside the guns and a few people standing there. But they didn't have fully manned gun crews or fully manned ammunition crews. And things just didn't happen.

The second thing that contributed to the success of the attack was the lack of U.S. air reconnaissance. When he was CinCUS, Admiral Richardson maintained 300-mile air patrols from Hawaii from May 1940 to 5 December of that year. Patrol Wing 2, with about sixty PBYs, was the principal naval air patrol and reconnaissance force in Pearl Harbor. When Admiral Richardson started requiring 300-mile patrols seven days a week, the flyboys were bitterly opposed—for what they thought were perfectly logical reasons. There were a lot of new aviators coming into the Navy then, and the more senior ones wanted the new men to be well rounded, able to do a lot of things instead of just one thing, long-range patrol.

About every six weeks or two months, Commander Patrol Wing 2 would come through the

Admiral Husband E. Kimmel (center), Commander in Chief Pacific Fleet during most of 1941, is flanked by his two principal staff officers, Captain Walter S. DeLany (operations officer, left) and Captain William Ward Smith (chief of staff, right). (National Archives: 80-G-456842.)

chain of command with a long-winded letter saying he couldn't train his people properly and that he was wearing out his airplanes. The Patrol Wing letter would come up through Vice Admiral Brown, Commander Scouting Force, and he was sympathetic was canceling the flights. So we'd have a staff conference. The aviators that we had on the staff—first, Commander Osborne Hardison and, later, Commander Art Davis—would tell of the horrendous effects that these patrols were having on training young aviators. Each time, it came right down to a dogfight on the staff. Each time, Admiral Richardson had to make the decision, and each time he decided that we would continue the patrols from Pearl Harbor. He finally called off the flights in early December 1940 when Admiral Stark wrote that he didn't believe they were necessary "at this time." In my opinion, had we continued air reconnaissance until Admiral Richardson was relieved, and had Admiral Kimmel continued it after that, there never would have been a disaster at Pearl Harbor. When the international events heated up in the summer of 1941, Admiral Kimmel just completely missed the boat when he didn't stand up under the pressure from the aviators. He should have issued an order to start up the patrols again when the situation with Japan tightened up. It was surely within the prerogative of Kimmel to start air reconnaissance whenever he felt a compelling need for it.

The third point in which I found fault with Admiral Kimmel is that he did everything he could to discourage officers and men from bringing their families out to Pearl Harbor. He did not even bring his own wife out. When the question of a greater degree of readiness of the ships and so forth was raised, I have heard from other people that he turned it aside. His reasoning was that he would be criticized by those with families in Hawaii because they would say that the only reason he didn't mind stepping up readiness was that his own family wasn't out there anyway.

Mrs. Dyer was out in Honolulu. Thousands of officers and men had their wives out there. Kimmel's wife's absence provided him with an excuse, in my opinion, for not doing his job properly. Had his wife been there, he could have explained the situation to her and got her to work along with him. In fact, my own wife helped me a great deal in that regard when we went to the modified Condition II in the *Indianapolis*. It is my very humble opinion that women play a tremendous part in such things. You can many times sell something through your wife that you can't sell yourself. So Kimmel should have brought his wife out to Hawaii and put her to work on the other wives. Having her back in the States was just no good at all.

By naming these three points, I in no way wish to imply that Admiral Kimmel was the only person who had responsibilities. What I do say is that his defenders—instead of taking a realistic point of view and saying, "Yes, there are things that he didn't do"—have tried to paint him as lily white. And he was far from lily white. I've been asked several times how I apportion the blame for the disaster at Pearl Harbor. I think 40 per cent of it belonged to Admiral Kimmel, 40 per cent belonged to Admiral Stark, and 20 per cent to President Roosevelt. The ultimate responsibility has to rest with the President, because he is the one who decided to get rid of Admiral Richardson.

George Carroll Dyer (1898-   ) was graduated from the Naval Academy in the class of 1919. He served in nine submarines, three of which he commanded: *D-3*, *L-10*, and *S-15*. Subsequent commands included the submarine rescue ship *Widgeon*, the minelayer *Gamble*, Submarine Division 8, and, during World War II, the light cruiser *Astoria*. Before the war, he served in the *Arizona* and *Indianapolis* and was on three of Admiral Richardson's staffs: Destroyers Scouting Force, Battle Force, and U.S. Fleet. After leaving the CominCh staff, Captain Dyer was wounded in the Italian campaign while serving as Rear Admiral Richard Conolly's chief of staff. During the Korean War, Rear Admiral Dyer commanded Task Force 95. He retired from active duty in 1955 and now lives in Annapolis, Maryland. He is the author of *Naval Logistics* and *The Amphibians Came to Conquer* and coauthor of Richardson's *On the Treadmill to Pearl Harbor*. (Naval Historical Center: NH 77048.)

The Navy Was Not Ready for War

By Admiral Robert B. Carney, U.S. Navy (Retired)

In the summer of 1940, I was executive officer of the battleship *California*, then located in Hawaiian waters. One day, my skipper, Captain Harold M. Bemis, received a message from the Commander in Chief U.S. Fleet, Admiral J. O. Richardson, stating in effect that he wished to talk to Commander Carney, the exec. Wondering what I had been caught at, I hastened to comply with the commander in chief's wish.

Without preamble, Admiral Richardson stated that in his opinion war with Japan was inevitable, that it would be long-dragged-out, that people in my age bracket would be wartime leaders, and that he wanted to talk to some of that group about the realities as he saw them. Flattering as it was, it seemed farfetched to consider me as a potential wartime leader. Mind you, I was then a commander. The admiral then proceeded to paint the readiness—or lack of it—picture. To me it was shattering.

Pointing out the lack of advanced bases, the slow pace of updating the fleet's offensive and defensive characteristics, the fact that there were fatal shortages in ammunition replacements and backup stocks of fuel, spare parts, and essential supplies, and the tenders and logistic ships needed to support an advanced-positioned fleet—he was saying in plain and understandable language that the Navy was not ready for war. Step by step, he dismantled my confident belief that the U.S. Navy could win a quick decision. Instead, proceeding from our deficiencies, he foresaw the United States hanging on for a couple of years while the country and the service built the strength necessary for an offensive campaign, and then a hard fight of a year or two before victory could be won.

Probably a *four-year* war!

I considered myself a competent professional, versed in all the experiences and skills required for advancement. At least, I *had* so considered myself. When Admiral Richardson finished with me, I was sure of nothing. Mentally and spiritually, I staggered back to the *California*. I was so profoundly disturbed that I had stomach butterflies, I was almost nauseated, and sleep would not come. My tight little professional world had collapsed.

Finally, I pulled myself together. Accepting Admiral Richardson's views as irrefutable, I would throw out every previous professional belief and make a new thinking—start from scratch. No matter what the conventional wisdom held on any given subject, I would challenge it, disregard it, and make my own evaluation.

It was a turning point in my life, and later I expressed my gratitude to Admiral J. O. Richardson.

Admiral James O. Richardson, shown on board his flagship, foresaw the nature of the naval war in the Pacific and provided an appropriate warning to up-and-coming Commander Carney. (Naval Historical Center: NH 77344.)

Robert Bostwick Carney (1895-   ) was graduated from the Naval Academy in 1916. In World War I, he was gunnery officer of the destroyer *Fanning* when she sank the *U–58*. He commanded the *Reno, Laub, Buchanan, Reid, Sirius*, and briefly the *California* (during his tour as executive officer). In 1941, he reported to the staff of Commander Support Force Atlantic Fleet and was later chief of staff. He commanded the light cruiser *Denver* in the Pacific, then was chief of staff to Admiral William F. Halsey, Jr., Commander Third Fleet. Admiral Carney took the surrender of the naval base at Yokosuka, Japan. After World War II, he was Deputy CNO, Commander Second Fleet, Commander in Chief U.S. Naval Forces Eastern Atlantic and Mediterranean, Commander in Chief Allied Forces Southern Europe, and Commander in Chief Allied Naval Forces Southern Europe. From 1953 until he retired in 1955, Admiral Carney was Chief of Naval Operations. He lives in Washington, D.C. (Naval Historical Center: NH 51587.)

The Last Months of Peace at Pearl Harbor

By Commander Lawrence R. Schmieder,
Chaplain Corps, U.S. Navy (Retired)

Even before Hawaii was annexed to the United States, the desirability of Pearl Harbor as a naval base was recognized. Consequently, as quickly as these things could be pushed, the different lochs, or channels, which collectively form the mouth of the dreamy Pearl River, were dredged, and facilities for the use of naval vessels were constructed. East Loch was developed first.

Pearl Harbor had a submarine base and a shipyard. For many years, only a few ships operated out of there, but in October 1939, a Hawaiian detachment of heavy cruisers and supporting ships was based there. This invasion began to change the leisurely tropical routine of the submarine base; hence, the cruisers were not too popular. It also meant the arrival of an additional group of sailors with all the various problems they can bring. Then, in April 1940, the U.S. Fleet held its spring war games off Hawaii, and subsequently twelve battleships and two or three carriers were based at Pearl. This new influx of ships brought in many more white uniforms. Long Beach, California, however, continued to be designated as the fleet's official home port, and no government funds for dependents' transportation to Hawaii were available.

The carrier *Saratoga* did her airplane training off the West Coast of the United States, but the *Lexington, Yorktown,* and *Enterprise* operated mostly with the fleet. Usually, one or two battleships were undergoing overhaul in West Coast shipyards, so that ordinarily about ten battleships would be in Hawaii at one time.

On 1 February 1941, Admiral Husband E. Kimmel relieved Admiral James O. Richardson as Commander in Chief U.S. Fleet on board the flagship *Pennsylvania* in Pearl Harbor. Kimmel also took on the newly created title of Commander in Chief Pacific Fleet. Under him were Vice Admiral William S. Pye, Commander Battle Force, in the USS *California;* Vice Admiral Wilson Brown, Jr., Commander Scouting Force, in the heavy cruiser *Indianapolis;* and Vice Admiral William F. Halsey, Jr., Commander Aircraft Battle Force, in the *Yorktown.* The carrier force consisted of the *Enterprise, York-*town, and *Lexington.* The battleship force was made up of four divisions of three ships each: Battleship Division 1—the *Arizona, Nevada,* and *Oklahoma;* Battleship Division 2—the *Pennsylvania, California,* and *Tennessee;* Battleship Division 3—the *New Mexico, Idaho,* and *Mississippi;* Battleship Division 4—the *Maryland, Colorado,* and *West Virginia.* There were two divisions of four light cruisers each, with 6-inch guns, and three divisions of four heavy cruisers each, with 8-inch guns.

In the old concept of a full fleet engagement, the battleships would form the battle line, with an inner screen of light cruisers and an outer screen of destroyers. Carriers launching planes would stay to the rear, and scouting forces would make the initial advance to see what they could do.

Early in 1941, the Battle Force and the Scouting Force usually operated on separate schedules. Every Wednesday, five battleships would leave the harbor, and later in the morning, five others would return, so that there were never more than five battleships in the harbor at one time. Operating schedules for light and heavy cruisers and carriers were about the same; thus, not more than half the fleet was in the harbor at one time.

As ideas shifted away from the conventional fleet engagement with the "Orange" (Japanese) enemy, different types of task-force deployments were initiated. This, of course, radically revised operating schedules, but usually it was a week in and a week out for each ship.

After February, other changes occurred. Submarines disappeared more and more in the direction of Manila and Tawi-Tawi in the Philippines. So did a tender or two. Early in May, without warning, the *Yorktown,* Battleship Division 3, a division of *Brooklyn*-class light cruisers, and about twelve destroyers were detached and ordered to the Atlantic Fleet. At this time, various cruisers were also escorting many convoys to Manila. Usually the route would be via Suva, Torres Strait (between Australia and New Guinea), Balikpapan (Borneo), and then to Manila. The cruisers would come back through the Central Pacific by themselves.

Two aerial views of Pearl Harbor, taken in October 1941, provide different perspectives of the area in the last months before the Japanese attack. The triangular pattern at the top center of the upper photo and near the center of the lower photo is formed by the runways at the Army Air Forces's bomber base, Hickam Field. (National Archives: 80-G-182874, and Naval Historical Center: NH 89041.)

Sailors on liberty found Waikiki Beach a popular spot as peacetime neared its end. (U.S. Navy: Naval Institute Collection.)

Around July or August, the fleet commander in chief moved his headquarters ashore to the top deck of a building at the submarine base. Prior to that time, his flagship *Pennsylvania* was often moored at the old Ten Ten Dock (so named because it was 1,010 feet long) in the navy yard. The *California* had the forward Fox mooring quays at Ford Island, and astern of her was the *Enterprise*, which had Commander Aircraft Battle Force embarked after the *Yorktown*'s departure. The rest of the battleships were moored at a string of quays farther along in Battleship Row. The *Lexington* was usually on the Pearl City side of Ford Island, and when in port the target ship *Utah* or a tender was also there. Also in the vicinity were the hospital ship *Relief* and, never to be forgotten, the old cruiser *Baltimore*, part of Commodore George Dewey's force in the Spanish-American War. The *Indianapolis*, as flagship of the Scouting Force, had a berth at what is now the supply center. The other cruisers, unless they were being overhauled in the shipyard, were at the "X" and "C" mooring floats between Aiea Landing and the Pearl City Peninsula. Docking facilities in 1941 consisted of one large graving dock, one floating dry dock, and one marine railway.

The hospital was still located in the shipyard. As one entered Pearl Harbor Channel, Fort Kamehameha was on the right. The Central and West Lochs

A Pan American Clipper moored at its float on the Pearl City side of Pearl Harbor. (Pan American World Airways.)

had not been much developed by that time. The present deep-water channel toward the area of the naval receiving station was still undredged and unimproved. At the end toward Honolulu and the main gate, and opposite the supply depot side, were the officers' boat landing, parking lot, and officers' club. This channel was broadside to Battleship Row on Ford Island, and it was near the officers' boat landing that the Japanese planes started their over-water torpedo runs on the battleships.

The enlisted men's landing was Pier 19 (B–19). After the arrival of the battleships, liberty for single men expired at either midnight or 1:00 a.m. There was always a huge mob of sailors, all trying to catch the last liberty boats back to their ships. Since the slip was not too wide, the coxswains had a glorious time clanging their bells and maneuvering their motor launches in tight circles. Every night, a few drunks would fall into the water. Usually, the bow boathook man would fish them out of the drink, and about thirty pairs of uncertain hands would try to haul the tipsy one back aboard. Sometimes, a few more fell over the side while trying to haul in the first swimmer. This only multiplied the number of rescue missions.

In 1941, Pan American Clippers landed in the Pearl Harbor Channel. Many seaplanes from Ford Island did so also, making quite a scene of confusion when ships, boats, and planes were all trying to fight for the right of way. As a result, elaborate rules governed all of this heavy traffic.

There was a YMCA building at the site of the present swimming pool at the receiving station. Rear Admiral Claude C. Bloch, Commandant Fourteenth Naval District, had this organization moved out of the yard. Right inside the shipyard was a nine-hole golf course.

Only one road ran from the main gate of the Pearl Harbor Navy Yard to Honolulu, and it was only two lanes wide. Now and then, taxicab drivers and others tried to make it three lanes—with discarded wreckage as evidence of their lack of success. Each taxicab carried seven passengers at twenty-five cents apiece from Pearl Harbor to the Army and Navy YMCA in Honolulu. The Oahu railroad was still in fine running shape, and many of the boys liked to ride it, especially after a rest camp was opened by Commander Cruisers Scouting Force.

In late 1941, apprentice seamen made twenty-one dollars a month, seamen second class made thirty-six dollars, and seamen first class made fifty-four dollars a month. Family allowances for the higher ratings were coming in. The Naval Academy class of 1941 hit the fleet. Ensigns still made $1,500 a year and could not marry until two years after grad-

uation. Selections of the class of 1922 to the rank of commander were made that fall. Everyone was busy reading confidential reports of British naval experiences against the German Navy, such as the sinking of the *Hood* and the *Bismarck* the previous spring. U.S. Navy bluejackets in trouble were anxious for a second chance in life—by volunteering for Asiatic Fleet duty and getting out to the Far East in the faithful old transport *Henderson*.

There was much arguing about the depth of water required for the launching of aerial torpedoes. The degaussing range at Maui was busy, because everyone was magnetic-mine-conscious. There was trouble with some sailors writing directly to their Congressmen to protest one thing or another. Ship's service (now the Navy exchange) was still run mostly by seamen first class, who got extra pay as soda jerkers, barbers, cobblers, and the like. At that time, no rated man could work in ship's service, and it was controlled by an officer as a collateral duty. Servicemen in Pearl Harbor sensed the ultimate arrival of hostilities, and blackout drills were conducted, but there was quite a bit of anxiety lest the civilian population be alarmed, perhaps resulting in the loss of key men who might leave for

The Army and Navy YMCA in Honolulu. (Courtesy of YMCA.)

the mainland. The navy yard continued to expand rapidly; some sections worked around the clock.

Housing was very tight, and people were sleeping on cots along the lanais, or porches, of the Army and Navy YMCA in Honolulu. Still, dependents kept coming over. It was not all one way, however, because persons of the more reflective type were starting to send their wives and children home in the summer of 1941.

There were lots of fights in town. In those days, enlisted men had to go on liberty in uniform. Officers, if in civvies, had to wear a shirt, tie, coat, and hat. Schofield Barracks was still one of the largest U.S. Army posts. In the evening, Army officers stationed there either had to wear a good uniform or black trousers, white coat, and tie.

In September 1941, the *Lexington* and the heavy cruiser *Pensacola*, in which I was serving as chaplain, had an odd fleet problem. We had to stay within 15 miles of Barbers Point lighthouse until dark. We attacked Pearl Harbor by plane at dawn; then the planes returned to the carrier. Captain Frederick C. Sherman, the skipper of the *Lexington*, was not too impressed with land-based aerial reconnaissance, so he stayed within 15 miles or less of the plane-launching point until the big Army planes finally discovered us about 2:00 p.m. There was much muttering about this, since the ships were not allowed to return to port until they were discovered.

This was the era of the fancy painted-on bow waves, and the *Lexington* had a beautiful one. People who were asked to estimate her speed from a distance guessed about 30 knots when she was going only about 8 knots. There was also one operation in which the *Lexington* or *Saratoga* operated inside a protecting screen of four battleships. The battleships could make only 20 knots—if they secured their galleys. The *Lexington* was much faster.

It was also the day when torpedo planes would lay down two long smoke screens before an attack. They were at right angles to each other, like two adjoining sides of a square. Then the planes would attack after a low-altitude run, so they would be protected from surface-ship fire. Such tactics didn't get much use after the war started, mainly because opposing fighters intervened. Somewhat prevalent at this time was the theory that no carrier-based planes could attack land-based planes. The wise youngsters had a time-sustained comeback on that one—after the plane was in the air, no one bothered much about its ancestry.

In 1941, a good many ships were armed with only their main batteries and small surface-ship-repelling secondary batteries. They also had .50-caliber machine guns. A ship that had 20-mm. or 40-mm. weapons was considered new. Radar was just beginning to appear, and that was mostly the foremast or mainmast search type rather than fire-control radar.

Various runs by different ships were made to Midway, Wake, and the like. Ships would operate outside the harbor with no flags flying. The dark color of the ships made them very hot for those on board. Enlisted men wore white shorts and skivvy shirts as the daytime uniform on board ship. Late in 1941, officers were authorized to wear white shorts and white shirts with open collar and rolled-up sleeves. The khaki uniform for officers was worn only at work on board most ships. Only the aviators wore khaki at lunch, never at dinner, in the larger ships. The aviators took the rank sleeve stripes off their khaki uniforms in favor of shoulder boards. Their green uniforms were still the old style—black sleeve stripes for rank.

There were many inspections, although everybody decried their frequency and peacetime aspect. They were held, nevertheless, including open double-bottom material inspections. Inspecting officers still concerned themselves in looking for a speck of dirt behind a shoulder-high bulkhead.

Operations began to be more realistic. Oftentimes in squalls they would get a bit mixed up. The *Enterprise* and the *Oklahoma* sustained a small swiping collision. Then the *Oklahoma* and the *Arizona* had a bigger and better collision; several destroyers ran into one another. Otherwise, all went off pretty well.

Family separations were quite a problem. Ships seldom returned to the West Coast. The *Pensacola*, for instance, was away from the West Coast from October 1939 to late August 1941, and this caused plenty of trouble, even as long deployments do now. Some groups of ships returned to the West Coast for about two weeks' "morale" leave, and then the crewmen were subject to telegraphic recall.

In late 1941, a task force of carriers could stay 500 miles from a target until darkness, then come in at 30 knots for twelve hours, attack at dawn only 140 miles away, have its planes return, and then quickly steam away. This 500-mile radius would have required a geometrical scouting area of nearly 800,000 square miles before dusk—an almost impossible task. Shore-based radar was in its infancy and often erratic; it had apparently caused some earlier false alerts.

And so it was at 7:45 on the morning of 7 December 1941. A few minutes later, the era of (more or less) national peace which had begun on 11 November 1918 would rudely come to an end—along with a way of life now remembered but dimly.

Lawrence Richard Schmieder (1911-   ) was graduated from St. Gregory's Seminary, Cincinnati, in 1932 and Mount St. Mary's Seminary, Norwood, Ohio, in 1936. He was ordained as a priest in 1936 and received a direct commission in the regular Navy in October 1940. He served in the *Pensacola* until March 1943, including participation in the Battle of Midway and the Battle of Tassafaronga (Guadalcanal). He was with the 1st Marine Division during the invasion of Okinawa. After World War II, he served as chaplain at Farragut, Idaho; on board the battleship *Missouri;* at Camp Pendleton, California; receiving station, Pearl Harbor; Military Sea Transportation Service Atlantic Area; 1st Marine Air Wing in Korea; Marine Corps Air Station, Miami, Florida; and the 2nd Marine Division at Camp Lejeune, North Carolina. He retired from active duty in 1960, has served a number of parishes since then, and now lives in Minster, Ohio. Art Center Studio, Honolulu. (Courtesy of Commander Lawrence R. Schmieder, CHC, U.S. Navy [Retired].)

In the following account, written in the mid-1950s by Vice Admiral Shigeru Fukudome, the reader gets a look into the planning and internal struggles that went into the Japanese decision to raid Pearl Harbor. Even more compelling, though, is the insight into the Japanese viewpoint, especially as it contrasts with the one Americans are accustomed to. For example, Admiral Fukudome cites the analysis of the attack offered by Rear Admiral Samuel Eliot Morison in Volume III of his celebrated naval history of World War II. In the opinion of this editor, Morison's is among the most penetrating and concise analyses to be found. He does very well in assessing the reasons for the great surprise of the venture and the effects the attack brought about. In a passage not quoted in the following article, Morison writes: "Never in modern history was a war begun with so smashing a victory by one side, and never in recorded history did the initial victor pay so dearly for his calculated treachery."

In the account that follows, Admiral Fukudome takes Morison heavily to task. To American eyes, Fukudome's protests appear to be excuses and rationalizations for an event that was the first step on a road to catastrophic defeat. To him, they represented reality. He, after all, took part in the thinking and planning that produced the attack. Having held certain opinions before it took place, it is not surprising that he viewed the reasoning for it in fairly similar fashion afterward.

Hawaii Operation

By Vice Admiral Shigeru Fukudome, former Imperial Japanese Navy

Numerous criticisms have been voiced since the end of the war, both at home and abroad, regarding the Hawaii Operation.* As far as the writer's knowledge goes, however, domestic criticism appears to be restricted to that of a political nature aimed solely at laying the blame on the Hawaii Operation for having ignited a rash war. In other words, there seem to be no instances yet of any attempt to analyze and criticize the operation from a purely strategical or tactical standpoint.

Naturally enough, this subject has been given the most serious attention by the United States. In his work, *The Rising Sun in the Pacific*, Volume III of *History of United States Naval Operations in World War II*, Dr. Samuel Eliot Morison bitterly criticizes the Hawaii Operation in the following manner: "One can search military history in vain for an operation more fatal to the aggressor. On the tactical level, the Pearl Harbor attack was wrongly concentrated on ships rather than permanent installations and oil tanks. On the strategic level it was idiotic. On the high political level it was disastrous."

Dr. Morison goes on to remark: "They [the Japanese aviators] knocked out the Battle Force and decimated the striking air power present; but they neglected permanent installations at Pearl Harbor, including the repair shops which were able to do an amazingly quick job on the less severely damaged ships. And they did not even attempt to hit the power plant or the large fuel oil 'tank farm,' filled to capacity, whose loss (in the opinion of Admiral [Thomas C.] Hart [Commander in Chief Asiatic Fleet]) would have set back our advance across the Pacific much longer than did the damage to the Fleet."

Dr. Morison explains his contention that, strategically, it was a ridiculous and stupid operation, as follows: "The Rainbow 5 War Plan, which would have gone into effect upon declaration of war if the Pearl Harbor attack had not taken place, called for the [U.S. Pacific] Fleet to capture Japanese positions in the Marshalls and Carolines, including Truk, before proceeding to the relief of the Philippines or elsewhere."

This meant that, had the Hawaii Operation not been conducted by the Japanese, the U.S. Fleet would instead have launched an offensive, and the Japanese Navy, accordingly, could have launched its long-cherished countering operations by calmly remaining in waiting. The Japanese Navy had, for thirty years, been arduously engaged in studying and training in the so-called "counter-attack decisive battle against the U. S. Fleet," in which an American onslaught was to be countered and destroyed in the seas adjacent to Japan, as the only sure way of gaining a victory. No offensive operation against Hawaii had ever been contemplated in the past.

Dr. Morison's contention, therefore, may mean that, by carrying out the Hawaii Operation, the Japanese Navy committed the folly of forever losing an opportunity to realize its fundamental operational plan. In contending that it was an unredeemable political blunder, moreover, Dr. Morison points out that the Pearl Harbor attack served to arouse the united determination of the American people, fighting under the slogan *"Remember Pearl Harbor!"* to crush the Japanese Empire.

At complete variance to this view of Dr. Morison, however, is that held by Admiral William V. Pratt,

Rear Admiral Samuel Eliot Morison's fine analysis of the attack on Pearl Harbor is challenged in this article by Admiral Fukudome. In preparing his multivolume history of U.S. naval operations in World War II, Morison (left) interviewed many Japanese naval officers, such as Jisaburo Ozawa (center). At right, wearing glasses, is Roger Pineau, Morison's interpreter and the editor of the article by Captain Fuchida on page 1. (Little, Brown and Co.)

*"Hawaii Operation" was the Japanese Imperial Headquarters' official name for the Pearl Harbor surprise attack.

one of the most illustrious figures of the modern U. S. Navy. In commenting upon the Hawaii Operation in a letter addressed to former Admiral Kichisaburo Nomura, who is his intimate Japanese friend, the American admiral described the Japanese attack upon Pearl Harbor as a most thoroughly planned and daring project—a strategical success of rare precedence in history. The question as to which of the two, the historian or the strategist, holds the more correct view will be left to the good judgment of the reader.

Since the Pacific war ended so tragically for the Japanese people there seem to be some among them who do not wish even to be reminded of the Hawaii Operation, feeling that the entire prosecution of the war was an act of folly. On the other hand, there are a considerable number who feel that those actually concerned in the operation should compile a true and unbiased historical account of it. This essay is a contribution towards that end.

The Roles of Admirals Shimada and Yamamoto: Admiral Shigetaro Shimada, the Navy Minister at the time Japan went to war, wanted by all means to prevent the United States from becoming an enemy and taxed himself to find some means of enabling Japan to declare war only after the United States had opened hostilities. His idea was for Japan to declare war on Britain and the Netherlands, but to resort to arms against the United States only after she was challenged by the latter.

Admiral Shimada had long been with the Naval General Staff when he was appointed Navy Minister, and he had a profound knowledge of naval operations. He advocated passive operations against the United States, but at the same time requested the Naval General Staff, which was the responsible office for operations, to make a study of the problem. He preferred, if worse came to worse, to let the United States strike first, thus enabling Japan to declare war with honor. Had things turned out as Shimada wished, not only would there have been no cry of *"Remember Pearl Harbor!"* but the political developments pointed out by Dr. Morison would have taken a different course.

Shimada believed there would be little chance to exploit a conquest of Southeast Asia if our long Southern Operation line, stretching far below the equator, was flanked by a dominant U. S. fleet, prepared to strike at the best time and in a manner of its own choosing. A political guarantee of non-intervention by the United States was a desired prerequisite for launching the Southern Operation, but that was out of the question in the situation prevailing both at home and abroad. Since there was no sure political guarantee, it was obvious that the

Admiral Shigetaro Shimada, Japanese Navy Minister at the time of the attack on Pearl Harbor. (Naval Historical Center: NH 63427.)

United States would sooner or later join on the side of Britain and the Netherlands in a war against Japan, even if she could be prevented from entry in its early stage.

In reply to the Japanese Government's inquiry with respect to its attitude toward Germany, the U. S. Government stated in a note dated 16 July 1941, "the use of our right of self-defense against Germany is our own proper responsibility"; and moreover, "any state attempting, at this juncture, to compel the United States to remain neutral shall be regarded as belonging to the same camp of aggressors." From its extremely scathing tone, it could readily be surmised that the note not only indicated the stern stand of the United States toward Germany, but also clarified her attitude toward Japan.

Even though the United States could be kept out of the war at its outset, it was absolutely certain that she would not remain as an idle spectator forever. Therefore, the final judgment reached in 1941 was that there was no other way of Japan's gaining victory except by forestalling America's armed intervention, since a war with the United States had already been deemed inevitable.

Since the Japanese realized that there was no means of isolating the United States from operations in Southeast Asia, the main target of the Japanese Navy from the outset was to be the U. S. fleet, and all other objectives were to be treated as secondary. How to accomplish the destruction of the U. S. fleet was the grave responsibility entrusted to Admiral Isoroku Yamamoto, Commander in Chief Combined Fleet.

During basic maneuvers of the Combined Fleet, held sometime between April and May 1940, I was Admiral Yamamoto's chief of staff. One feature of the exercises was a mock air attack. The fleet skillfully eluded the first and second assault waves of the imaginary torpedo bombers but sustained theoretical heavy damage, reducing its strength to one-half, when the "enemy" successfully launched aerial torpedoes from both flanks in spite of the skillful elusive action of the fleet.

"There is no means for a surface fleet to elude aerial torpedoes simultaneously launched from both sides," I said to Admiral Yamamoto. "It seems to me that the time is now ripe for a decisive fleet engagement with aerial torpedo attacks as the main striking power."

"Well," replied Yamamoto, "it appears that a crushing blow could be struck on an enemy surface force by mass aerial torpedo attacks executed jointly with shore-based air forces." The admiral was undoubtedly thinking at that moment of the powerful U. S. fleet concentrated in Pearl Harbor.

Ever since 1909, the Japanese Navy had made the U. S. Navy its sole imaginary enemy. It was but natural that, in the fleet training of 1940, due consideration was given to the strategic situation under which the U. S. fleet was concentrated in Hawaii and steadily making preparations for war, thus showing its determination to resort to armed intervention in opposition to Japan's policy toward China. The Japanese Fleet had for thirty years studied and trained for a decisive fleet counteroffensive as its basic evolution, but such an operation, whose nature was in the final analysis passive, involved the great disadvantage of leaving the initiative in the enemy's hands. Moreover, the situation was such that, as time passed, the balance of naval strength between the two would gradually favor the United States, with the chance of Japan's gaining a victory steadily diminishing. The Japanese Navy was accordingly compelled to find some means for assuring an early decisive engagement. Now, with the U. S. fleet already advanced to its Hawaiian base, it could readily advance to the Western Pacific, thus creating a definite threat to Japan. As long as it remained at its Hawaiian base, it created

As Commander in Chief Combined Fleet, Admiral Isoroku Yamamoto argued for the strike against Pearl Harbor in order to eliminate the threat of the U.S. Pacific Fleet on the flank of the Japanese Navy during its planned offensive against targets in Southeast Asia. (Naval Historical Center: NH 79462-KN.)

a strategical situation incomparably more tense and threatening to the Japanese than had existed when it was based on the Pacific coast. Every Japanese naval officer realized that a crushing blow could be inflicted if a successful attack could be launched on distant Hawaii, thereby depriving the enemy of the initiative and assuring us an impregnable position. However, it was not believed that the Japanese Navy could undertake a Hawaiian attack because of the operational limitations of its warships. But Fleet Admiral Yamamoto, the "father of naval aviation," had long believed that future wars would be decided by air power, and he had improved and developed the Japanese Navy's air arm to that end. As a consequence, he alone originated the idea of an aerial surprise attack—and thus made the impossible possible.

The battleship *Nagato* was the flagship of the Combined Fleet during the attack on Pearl Harbor. As a captain, Fukudome commanded her. Thereafter, he served as chief of staff to Admiral Yamamoto. (Naval Historical Center: NH 2716.)

Rear Admiral Takijiro Ohnishi, an experienced air officer, was responsible for the planning of the Hawaii Operation. Near the end of World War II, he founded the kamikaze special attack force. (Naval Historical Center: NH 73093.)

My Connection with the Hawaii Operation: Upon promotion to rear admiral on 1 November 1939, I was transferred from command of the fleet flagship, the battleship *Nagato*, to duty as Chief of Staff, Combined Fleet, under Admiral Yamamoto, until I was transferred in April 1941 to duty as Chief, First Bureau, Naval General Staff. Since the position of the Chief of the First Bureau placed me in charge of operations, my duties in both capacities associated me with the Hawaii Operation from beginning to end. It may be said that except for the late Admiral Yamamoto, I was the only person acquainted with detailed plans of the operation from the moment of its conception.

"I want a flier, whose past career has not influenced him in conventional operations, to study this problem," Commander in Chief Yamamoto said, and then asked me what I thought about it. This occurred toward the close of 1940, after the annual fleet training exercises had been completed.

"It is a fine idea, sir," I replied.

"For the time being, I will keep the matter secret from other fleet staff officers, except for the aviator assigned to the problem, and would like to ask you to keep it for your personal study," he said. Thereupon, the admiral secretly summoned his selected naval aviator, Rear Admiral Takijiro Ohnishi, and entrusted him with planning the Hawaii Operation.

Ohnishi had long been an airman to the core and ranked foremost in the practical field, in contrast to Admiral Yamamoto, whose main experience had been in the field of naval air organization and administration. They were congenial friends of long standing. Since Ohnishi had not been long with the Naval General Staff, there was little fear that he might be hampered by conventional operational doctrine. Moreover, he was noted for his cautious and logical thinking as well as for his vast experience. Admiral Yamamoto could not have made a better choice in his selection of an officer to whom to entrust this important study.

Toward the end of April 1941, Admiral Ohnishi completed the general plan. He called on me at my office in the Naval General Staff and explained his plan as follows:

"This operation involves two difficult problems. One of them is the technical difficulty of launching aerial torpedo attacks in Pearl Harbor, which is so shallow that aerial torpedoes launched by ordinary methods would strike the bottom. The other concerns the tactical problem—whether a surprise can be made successfully. This operation apparently cannot be carried out without a surprise element."

Even though he pointed out numerous difficulties involved in the operation, Ohnishi estimated, in the early stage of planning, that it had a 60 per cent chance of success. I thought its chance to be 40 per cent, since I took operational difficulties more seriously than did Ohnishi. Opposition to the operation which was later raised by the Naval General Staff arose mainly from my opinion. Had I from the very beginning been entrusted with the study of the idea instead of Ohnishi, I would certainly have recommended to Commander in Chief Yamamoto that the Hawaii Operation be abandoned.

In the early part of September 1941, I remember that Ohnishi called on me again in the Naval General Staff and said that the Hawaii Operation now seemed too risky and he wanted to recommend to Admiral Yamamoto that it be given up. Later, Ohnishi, accompanied by Rear Admiral Ryunosuke Kusaka, then chief of staff to Vice Admiral Chuichi Nagumo who later commanded the Hawaii Operation Force, called on Admiral Yamamoto on board the flagship *Nagato*, and earnestly advised the admiral to give up the operation. But Admiral Yamamoto firmly stuck to his guns.

The General Staff's Opposition: With Japan's resolution to go to war with the United States when necessary—a decision made at the Imperial Conference held on 6 September 1941—war preparations were put in full swing.

Previously, Admiral Yamamoto had received Ohnishi's plan for the Pearl Harbor attack, and he had made it one of his fleet's operational studies, and his staff continued to work on it. As a result, the admiral succeeded in drafting an operation plan upon which he could place full confidence of success. From about the middle of September earnest discussions were exchanged between the Naval General Staff and the Combined Fleet headquarters with regard to the general operational plan which was to be carried out in the event of war. With it, the problem of the Hawaii Operation inevitably came to the fore.

In early October, staff officers of the Combined Fleet went up to Tokyo under orders of Admiral Yamamoto and reported to the General Staff that they desired to launch an attack on Hawaii at the outset of war, if and when it should be started. But the General Staff did not approve the proposal, on the ground that the Hawaii Operation was inadvisable from the standpoint of the overall operational concept. The Naval General Staff doubted that the Hawaii Operation would succeed. Much would be lost if the operation failed. Moreover, the operation gave rise to the fear that it might cause an unfavorable effect on the negotiations then being conducted between the United States and Japan, because preparatory initiation of the operation was necessary prior to the termination of the negotiations.

The objections of the Naval General Staff were essentially five in number:

1) *Success of Hawaii Operation was dependent upon the achievement of surprise.*

The powerful American fleet concentrated in Hawaii was too strong for conventional attack by our task force. Without surprise, our fleet could never achieve success. The prerequisite for a successful surprise attack was the secrecy of the movements of its task force. Since the operation was on a large-scale, employing as many as sixty ships which had to be dispatched one month before the outbreak of war in the Eastern Pacific, it was likely to attract attention, especially since the southerly advance was generally believed to be Japan's chief strategy in the event of war. In view of the tense international situation, it was believed that the close intelligence network of the United States and Great Britain had been widely extended, and that of their ally, Soviet Russia, was also thought to be dangerous. Therefore, much apprehension was entertained on whether the secrecy of the operation could be kept.

Besides, there was the fear that the task force might meet hostile or neutral ships en route to the point of attack. All would be lost if our task force were to meet a ship that might be expected to send a radio dispatch stating, "Japanese fleet proceeding eastward in great strength."

2) *The Hawaii Operation was not so indispensable as to be executed regardless of risk.*

Unless a blow was dealt at the outset of war by carrying out the daring Hawaii attack, the American fleet would certainly come out to attack us. It seemed unlikely that the enemy would come straight to our homeland seeking a decisive battle; rather it would first establish advance bases in the Marshall Islands and then attempt an island-hopping strategy by gradually advancing its bases.

In that case, we would be given ample time to concentrate all our available strength in a decisive contact engagement for which our Navy had long studied and trained. It would be wiser to seek a decisive battle in familiar waters than to attempt the Hawaii Operation with its risk of failure.

3) *Almost all naval vessels participating in the Hawaii Operation would have to be refueled at sea en route; destroyers at least twice.*

Since the establishment of the "Empire's National Defense Policy" in 1909, the Japanese Navy had accepted defensive operations against the United States as its fundamental policy, so that the radius of action of our ships and planes was generally short. Meteorological statistics showed that on only seven days during the month were conditions favorable for refueling destroyers at sea on the North Pacific route which the fleet would have to take to avoid commercial traffic lanes. If refueling could not be carried out, not only would the Hawaii Operation fail, but all the units involved would have been uselessly diverted from other planned operations.

Lastly, one hitch was apt to lead to another. If refueling at sea met with difficulties, it would necessitate the transmission of radio dispatches. Radio transmission would immediately break the secrecy of the operational force's movement, thus tragically spoiling the elaborately planned operation at the last moment. A good example of this was seen later in the Battle of Midway. Should the secrecy of the Hawaii Operation be broken en route to the attack, not only would the Hawaii attack force itself be endangered, but the indispensable southern operation, as a whole, would be adversely affected.

4) *High probability that the task force would be spotted by enemy patrol planes at the point from which the attacking planes were to be launched, with consequent enemy interdiction.*

Alertness around the Hawaiian Islands had gradually been intensified. The Radio Intelligence Section of the Japanese Naval General Staff knew that the daily air patrol had been extended to 600 miles from Oahu. Since our carrier force had to close to within 200 miles of the target, there was a considerable risk that it might be counterattacked by the enemy before launching its attacks.

5) *Knowledge that it would break down the negotiations between the United States and Japan.*

The Navy did not give up hope of success in the negotiations until the last moment. Admiral Osami Nagano, Chief of the Naval General Staff, had placed much hope in Admiral Kichisaburo Nomura, the Ambassador in Washington, who was one of his close friends. Nagano, who had believed that "nothing can be done here in Japan with the negotiations between the United States and Japan, and only Admiral Nomura can break the deadlock," rejoiced greatly at the news received from Ambassador Nomura about 20 October to the effect that there was some hope of solving the stalemate. The chief of staff repeatedly told me, "Nomura is a great fellow, and no one but he could succeed." The firm confidence Nagano placed upon Nomura may well be seen from the fact that, even when Admiral Yamamoto came up to Tokyo on 1 December on his last visit, the policy of withdrawing all forces in the

Admiral Osami Nagano, Chief of the Japanese Naval General Staff at the beginning of World War II. (Naval Historical Center: NH 63422.)

event of a favorable turn to the negotiations was confirmed between Nagano and Yamamoto.

Verdict Given by Admiral Nagano: In the meantime, Admiral Yamamoto, as Commander in Chief Combined Fleet, had trained his fleet in the Inland Sea and had drawn up emergency operational plans. After receiving his staff's report that they had failed to secure the approval of the Naval General Staff on the Hawaii Operation upon which he placed the utmost importance, the admiral elaborated on his plan. Rear Admiral Matome Ugaki, Yamamoto's chief of staff, and other staff officers went up to Tokyo again to submit his recommendation to the General Staff. Salient points stressed on that occasion as Yamamoto's opinion were as follows:

> The present situation, i.e., that of the U. S. fleet in the Hawaiian Islands, strategically speaking, is tantamount to a dagger being pointed at our throat. Should war be declared under these circumstances, the length and breadth of our Southern Operations would immediately be exposed to a serious threat on its flank. In short, the Hawaii Operation is absolutely indispensable for successful accomplishment of the Southern Operations.

> Moreover, when we consider the naval strength ratio between the United States and Japan, we would have no chance of victory unless a decisive attack was launched at the earliest possible opportunity. Therefore, the Hawaii Operation is truly indispensable to the accomplishment of the mission

assigned the Japanese Navy. Unless it is carried out, the Commander in Chief Combined Fleet has no confidence that he can fulfill his assigned responsibility.

This operation is beset with numerous difficulties, none of which, however, makes it impossible. What concerns us most is the weather condition; but, if there are seven days in a month when refueling at sea is possible, the chance of success is by no means small. If good fortune is bestowed upon us, we will be assured of success. Should the Hawaii Operation by chance end in failure, that would merely imply that fortune is not on our side. That should also be the time for definitely halting all operations.

An extremely grim resolution could be clearly read between those lines.

After carefully listening to Ugaki's detailed explanation of Yamamoto's real intention and his practical plan, Nagano, as chief of staff, finally gave the following verdict on the issue: "If he has that much confidence, it's better to let Yamamoto go ahead."

As far as the Navy was concerned, with these words the Hawaii Operation was formally approved as a plan. Needless to say, the Naval General Staff thereafter did its best to make this operation successful. At the same time, it also drew up a plan whereby the Hawaii Operation force would turn back immediately in the event that a setback or hitch occurred en route.

The Time for Going to War: In the Imperial Conference held on 6 September 1941, it was decided that, "in view of the potentiality of the Empire's national strength, Japan is determined without delay to go to war with the United States (Great Britain and the Netherlands) in the event that there is little prospect of achieving our aims by as late as early October." This decision meant that, considering the possible severance of the flow of essential import materials because of the embargo against this country by the so-called ABCD ring (American-British-Chinese-Dutch), no time should be wasted if and when war was finally deemed unavoidable. Among those essential materials, particular importance was placed on oil.

"One of the major causes for this war, I think," said Admiral Nagano in the U. S. Strategic Bombing Survey's interrogation which was conducted after the war, "was the oil problem. Not only the Army and Navy, but the government also, showed a great concern in this problem, because this country faced a serious oil shortage, since the United States, Britain, and the Netherlands refused to sell oil to our country."

"We believed that we would be able to get oil from the southern region," stated Ambassador Nomura during the same interrogation. "Our oil resources were so limited that we had to secure oil from those islands at all costs."

The Japanese Navy's operational plan called for a stockpile of oil for two years' consumption as the minimum prerequisite for going to war. Thanks to its oil policy, which had been followed for a long time, the Japanese Navy had stored up enough oil to meet that demand, but the Army barely had done so. Therefore, a further continuation of the oil import embargo was considered intolerable from the point of view of maintaining the fighting strength of Japan. War should be avoided, if possible; but, if and when war was finally deemed unavoidable, the sooner it was started, the better.

Of course, the oil problem was not the only factor determining the time for going to war. There were many others, political and military. Another consideration was the possibility that the operation might well be hampered by foul weather because it was the northeast monsoon season. Still another consideration was preservation of secrecy of the operation prior to the outbreak of the war. From the operational standpoint, it was apparent that "one day's delay would mean one day's disadvantage." Reflecting the tense international situation, war preparations in the ABCD ring were rapidly being pushed. The U. S. fleet standing by at Hawaii was improving its war preparations, and the U. S. Army Air Forces in the Philippines and the British air strength in Singapore were rapidly being augmented.

When the so-called Ogikubo conference was held on 12 October 1941, in which the final attitude of the third Konoye cabinet toward "peace or war" was decided, Admiral Koshiro Oikawa, the Navy Minister, made the following statement of the Navy's view:

"Now we have reached a cross-road where a choice for 'peace or war' should be made. Speaking for the Navy, we will find ourselves at a complete loss, if asked to go to war, until such time as the current negotiations between the United States and Japan reach a deadlock."

Based on the belief that an early commencement of operations would be advantageous for the aforementioned reasons, the Imperial General Headquarters originally intended to go to war on 1 December. But when top-ranking Army and Navy officers, including the War Minister, General Hisaichi Terauchi, and Admiral Yamamoto, assembled in Tokyo at the beginning of November 1941, for a briefing on the Southern Operations, the date was postponed to 8 December (Tokyo time) by request of Yamamoto, who considered a successful execution of the Hawaii Operation a prerequisite. Yamamoto indicated complete accord with the idea of attacking the U. S. fleet on Sunday, when the ships were likely be in Pearl Harbor for the weekend, but he preferred the second Sunday of December over the first because his fleet would not have sufficient time to prepare for the original date. The Imperial General Headquarters approved his request.

Thus, it was decided to raise the curtain on the Pacific War, with the first attack on Hawaii to be launched at 8:00 a.m. of 7 December (Hawaii time).

The Hawaii Operation and its Promulgation: Since Nagano's approval, as Chief of the General Staff, of Yamamoto's Hawaii attack plan meant no more than an informal decision within the naval command, various procedures had to be worked out before a formal decision could be made. Under the old Japanese Constitution, the opening of hostilities was the prerogative of the Emperor's supreme command. The Chief of the Naval General Staff was responsible to the Throne for naval operations. After the China Incident broke out in 1937, the Imperial General Headquarters had been established with membership made up of the Chiefs of the Army and Navy General Staffs and the ministers of both War and Navy. It was, therefore, necessary for the Chief of the Naval General Staff to propose the plan of the Hawaii Operation to the Chief of the Army General Staff and to the ministers of War and Navy.

The operation plan had also to be discussed at the liaison conference between the government and the high command. The liaison conference had been established about a year before, when the need of a supreme body for maintaining a close and smooth relation between military strategy and politics was keenly felt as a result of the China Incident. The first meeting of the conference was held on 27 July 1940. This body, which later became the Supreme War Directing Conference, was composed of the Premier, Foreign Minister, War Minister, Navy Minister, and Chiefs of the Army and Naval General Staff as regular members. As necessity arose, the Finance Minister and the Minister of the Interior also attended the conference. But, since the Hawaii Operation was an important operation which required top secret security, it was disclosed only to the Premier and the Foreign Minister in addition to the Army and Navy members of the conference.

After the above procedures were followed, the Chief of the Navy General Staff asked for Imperial sanction, thus formally acknowledging it as the Japanese Navy's operational plan. This occurred on 5 November 1941.

On the same day, Imperial Naval General Staff Order No. 1 was issued ordering the Combined Fleet to make operational preparations as follows:

Admiral Yamamoto (fifth from right, front row) and his Combined Fleet staff in early 1942, shortly after they shifted from the *Nagato* to the new flagship *Yamato*. (Courtesy of Captain Roger Pineau, USNR, Ret.)

Imperial Naval General Staff Order No. 1

5 November 1941

To: Commander in Chief Combined Fleet, Isoroku Yamamoto

Via: Chief of Naval General Staff, Osami Nagano
By Imperial Order

1. The Empire has decided to schedule various operational preparations for completion in the early part of December in view of great fears that she will be obliged to go to war with the United States, Britain, and the Netherlands for her self-existence and self-defense.

2. The Commander in Chief Combined Fleet will make necessary operational preparations.

3. Detailed instructions will be given by the Chief of the Naval General Staff.

Japan's Declaration of War Accidentally Delayed: How to integrate diplomatic policies and military operations is a problem of the utmost importance. The case of the last Pacific war was no exception. Since the war was to be started by the attack upon Hawaii, the manner in which Japan arranged the time of commencing that attack and the sending of the ultimatum to the United States still leaves much room for discussion as an important subject related both to the government administration and to the high command.

The Hawaii Operation obviously could not be conducted without surprise. This is the very reason why it was decided that the war was to be started with that operation. Under no circumstance, should diplomatic steps be taken which would give the United States time to prepare countermeasures to our surprise attack.

Since international law experts maintained that it is legal to declare war if the declaration precedes the commencement of hostilities—even though only one or one-half second in advance (the interval of time is of no concern), it was believed that the operation could be carried out in accordance with diplomatic usage if the declaration could be sent to the United States at such time as to prevent it from making preparations. In this way, it was expected that no hitch in the execution of the operations would occur. Thus the government and the high command mutually decided to send the declaration in accordance with the procedure of international law.

The issue of Japan's sending the declaration subsequent to the attack involved various factors. After the war, this was filed as one of the important charges made by the Far East International Military Tribunal. To this day, even after this country has regained her sovereignty, some people still seem to entertain doubts about it.

The indictment filed in the Far East International Military Tribunal included three categories of charges: first, offenses against peace (charges 1 to 36); second, offenses of murder (charges 37 to 52); and third, ordinary war crimes and offenses against humanity (charges 53 to 55).

To these charges, Mr. Ichiro Kiyose, a defense lawyer, delivered a refutation in his introductory argument. He pointed out that the Potsdam Proclamation stated in Article 10, "We do not intend that the Japanese shall be enslaved as a race or destroyed as a nation, but stern justice shall be meted out to all war criminals, including those who have visited cruelties upon our prisoners." Accordingly, the terms laid down at Potsdam, as Kiyose asserted, "constituted the only grounds for the war crime tribunal. Since Japan accepted that [proclamation] because she was defeated in the Pacific war, the military tribunal should be limited to crimes committed in the course of that war, and not include cases in 1928, as was done in the indictment." With the addition of six other points, Kiyose concluded that those seven points should be beyond the jurisdiction of the military tribunal. As one of those seven points, Dr. Kiyose strongly insisted that the offense of murder should not exist in war itself—not only from the legal aspect of international law, but also from that of custom.

The offense of murder was from the beginning charged in the indictment, with the Pearl Harbor attack as its case in point. Since that attack was made without a declaration of war, it was unlawful in that it disregarded international law. The prosecution charged therefore that the attack constituted the offense of murder.

At 2:20 p.m. on 7 December (Washington time), Japan's declaration addressed to the U. S. Government was formally delivered by Ambassador Nomura and Special Envoy Saburo Kurusu to Secretary of State Cordell Hull at the State Department. The original schedule called for its delivery at 1:00 p.m. (Washington time), which was 7:30 a.m. Hawaii time, thirty minutes before the scheduled commencement of the attack upon Hawaii.

As it turned out, due to a mishap, the declaration was not delivered until 2:20 p.m. This caused the declaration, which should have been delivered thirty minutes *before* the commencement of the attack, to be given to the U. S. Government about one hour *after* the actual attack. The prosecution charged that the attack launched before the delivery of the declaration was an unlawful one which constituted the crime of murder. The prosecution furthermore contended that the sending of the declaration was nothing but a trick conceived by the Japanese Government and the military, who had from the outset no intention of sending it before the commencement of the attack but used it as an excuse for their disregard of international law. The prosecution even branded it as the same kind of trick as the dispatching of Kurusu to the United States just before the outbreak of war in an attempt to camouflage the intention of going to war.

If the Pearl Harbor attack was judged to constitute a crime of murder, many top military leaders at the time of the outbreak of war, including Admiral Nagano, would have to be indicted for the offense of murder. The development of the controversy accordingly was watched with keen attention by all Japanese officials.

From November to December 1945, I was questioned about the Hawaii attack by Mr. Joseph B. Keenan and four other prosecutors. A surprise attack of itself cannot be censured, as it is a tactic which has been most ardently advocated both in Japan and abroad. The issue under dispute was whether the attack on Pearl Harbor violated international law by being launched without a previous declaration of war. Although I explained the situation in as much detail as I could, the prosecutors seemed to be prejudiced by their first suspicion, i.e., that the attack was a trick planned by the Japanese, who had no real intention of declaring war before the commencement of hostilities. Examinations on this point were also made of other persons concerned with the Pearl Harbor attack, but the indictment presented to the tribunal showed that the prosecutors refused to change their previous view. Prosecutor John P. Higgins severely attacked the Hawaii Operation as treacherous.*

All charges of murder (charges 37 to 52), however, were dismissed by the ruling that only offenses against peace would be subject to the judgment of the tribunal. In effect, the court made the decision that it had no jurisdiction in connection with the murder charge.

Units Employed in the Hawaii Operation: The operational units employed in the Hawaii Operation were divided into two groups, one being the task force with aerial attacks as its main objective, and the other being the submarine force for submarine attacks. Vice Admiral Chuichi Nagumo, Commander in Chief First Air Fleet, was appointed as its overall commander.

The units of the task force were organized as shown in the upper table on page 67.

* Admiral Fukudome refers to Higgins as a prosecutor; officially, he was the U.S. judge on the international tribunal. Editor.

After completing their war preparation at the Kure Naval Station, those thirty-three warships, consisting of six carriers, two battleships, two heavy cruisers, one light cruiser, eleven destroyers, three submarines, and eight tankers, left their bases in several groups during the period from 10 to 18 November 1941. By 22 November, they had assembled at Hitokappu Bay, on the southern coast of Etorofu Island in the Kurile Islands. The crews for the first time were informed of their grave mission of launching attacks upon Hawaii, and they exhibited excellent morale. Presumably there had been no discovery of the plan by foreign agents.

On 25 November, Yamamoto issued an order to the effect that "the task force will proceed to Hawaiian waters and, under a separate order to be issued later, operate in such manner as to destroy the U. S. fleet at the outset of war." The order was supplemented by instructions calling for an immediate withdrawal of all Hawaii Operation forces in case diplomatic negotiations were successfully concluded between Japan and the United States.

At 6:00 p.m. on 26 November, in a dense fog, the task force sortied from Hitokappu Bay into the Northern Pacific en route to its historic attack.

In conjunction with the movements of the task force, submarines of the submarine force were stealthily converging on Hawaii from other directions.

The submarine force was organized as shown in the lower table on page 67.

These twenty-seven submarines, the cream of the Combined Fleet, had undergone the most rigid training over a long period. Because the Naval General Staff estimated the chance of a successful aerial attack by the task force to be 50 per cent, they considered it necessary to have the submarine force participate in the Hawaii Operation and launch underwater attacks coordinated with the aerial attacks. A plan was accordingly made to encircle Oahu Island with all available crack submarines simultaneously with the aerial attack upon the U. S. fleet in Pearl Harbor. These submarines were not only to sink enemy vessels confused by the aerial attack, but also to intercept enemy reinforcements and supplies from the West Coast. The submarines had to be sent to their assigned positions in advance of the task force in order to reconnoiter Hawaiian waters. That is why the submarine force was named in Japanese the Advance Force.

Among those responsible for the operation, I counted heavily on the activities of the submarine force. It was my belief that, even if the task force's aerial attack ended in failure, the submarine force's

Units	Mission	Commander
1st Carrier Division (*Akagi* and *Kaga*) 2nd Carrier Division (*Soryu* and *Hiryu*) 5th Carrier Division (*Zuikaku* and *Shokaku*)	Aerial attack	Vice Admiral Chuichi Nagumo, Commander in Chief 1st Air Fleet
1st Destroyer Squadron (*Abukuma*) 17th Destroyer Division (*Tanikaze, Urakaze, Isokaze,* and *Hamakaze*) 18th Destroyer Division (*Kasumi, Arare, Kagero, Shiranuhi,* and *Akigumo*)	Guard and Escort	Rear Admiral Sentaro Omori
3rd Battleship Division (*Hiei* and *Kirishima*) 8th Cruiser Division (*Tone* and *Chikuma*)	Guard and Support	Vice Admiral Gunichi Mikawa
2nd Submarine Division (*I-19, I-21, I-23*)	Patrol	Captain Kijiro Imaizumi
7th Destroyer Division (*Akebono* and *Ushio*)	Bombardment of Midway Island	Captain Kaname Ohishi
1st Supply Train (*Kyokuto Maru, Kenyo Maru, Kokuyo Maru, Shinkoku Maru,* and *Akebono Maru*) 2nd Supply Train (*Toho Maru, Toei Maru,* and *Nihon Maru*)	Supply	

Units	Mission	Commander
Katori (cruiser)	Flagship of 6th Submarine Fleet	Vice Admiral Mitsumi Shimizu, Commander 6th Submarine Fleet
1st Submarine Squadron (*I-9, I-15, I-17, I-25*)	Blockade of Oahu and raiding operations	Rear Admiral Tsutomu Sato
2nd Submarine Squadron (*I-7, I-1, I-2, I-3, I-4, I-5, I-6*)	Same as above	Rear Admiral Shigeaki Yazazaki
3rd Submarine Squadron (*I-8, I-68, I-69, I-70, I-71, I-72, I-73, I-74, I-75*)	Same as above	Rear Admiral Shigeyoski Miwa
(*I-16, I-18, I-20, I-22, I-24*)	Special Attack Unit*	Captain Hanku Sasaki
(*I-10, I-26*)	Reconnaissance of key points	Commander Yasuchika Kashihara

*(Note: Each submarine of the Special Attack Unit took a midget submarine on board.)

operation would not fail. My belief was based on the expectation that no hitch would arise in the submarines' operations. They had a cruising radius of 10,000 miles, with no need for refueling at sea. Besides, submarines were best suited for stealthy movements, and a blockading operation of Hawaii would be very easy for the highly trained Japanese submariners. Furthermore, I expected that more damage would be inflicted by submarine attacks, which would be continued over a longer period, than by the air attacks, which would be of comparatively short duration.

The submarine force left Kure and Yokosuka between 18 and 20 November, and proceeded to Kwajalein in the Marshall Islands, where the final refueling was carried out. Then they headed straight for their operational positions.

Thus, the Hawaii attack force proceeded eastward, the task force taking the northern course and the submarine force the southern. The strictest radio silence was maintained all the way.

On 2 December, the famous code word telegram, "Climb Mt. Niitaka," was received from Admiral Yamamoto. It meant that the date for opening hostilities had been set for 8 December as scheduled and that the attacks would be made as planned.

No obstacles were encountered in the movements of any of the operational forces. The weather, which the Naval General Staff and the operational forces feared most, eventually turned out favorably and the secrecy of the operation was safely maintained by the grace of Heaven. Although fear no longer existed that a change of plan would be necessary, there was one factor that we could not determine until the last moment. It was whether the U. S. fleet would be in Pearl Harbor at the time the attack was launched. If it was neither there nor within the limits of our attack radius after departing for maneuvers and training, the operational objective would be lost. By means of secret intelligence, designated as "A" information, we could learn of the daily activities of the U. S. fleet in Pearl Harbor until the day before the attack. The last information on the enemy which the attack force received was as follows:

Received 2050, 7 December
"A" Information (issued 1800, 7 December)
Utah and a seaplane tender entered harbor the evening of 5 December.
Ships in harbor as of 6 December:
9 BB, 3 CL, 3 seaplane tenders, 17 DD
In docks: 4 CL, 3 DD
All carriers and heavy cruisers at sea. No special reports on the fleet. Oahu is quiet and Imperial General Staff is fully convinced of success.

This last information enabled us to expect with confidence the presence of the enemy fleet in the harbor, and therefore everyone concerned with the Hawaii Operation felt relieved. But, at the same time, it worried me that there were no enemy carriers in the harbor, upon which the utmost importance was placed. Not only would our force be unable to destroy them, but we might in turn be attacked by them. Judging from the activities of carriers and cruisers for several days, going in and out of the harbor, it was thought that they were at sea for training; but at the same time there was the possibility that they might be in Lahaina, a customary training anchorage. If so, it was estimated that those enemy carriers and cruisers would be discovered by submarine reconnaissance prior to the aerial attack, and that they could be attacked and destroyed by submarines even if the aerial attack failed to get them.

But actual events were entirely contrary to this estimate. Except for the USS *Enterprise*, which was then steaming 200 miles off Oahu Island, the carriers and heavy cruisers were far away in waters near Wake Island for training exercises against the Japanese. It was only learned after the war that the Nagumo force, on its return to Japan after the attack, passed those ships at a distance of about 500 miles to the north. Had these forces met, the first engagement in history between carriers would have occurred.

Damages Inflicted: Although the "A" information of the day before the attack reported, as already mentioned, the presence of nine battleships, seven light cruisers, three seaplane tenders, and twenty destroyers in the harbor, there were actually eight battleships, two heavy cruisers, six light cruisers, twenty-nine destroyers, five submarines, one gunboat, nine minelayers, ten minesweepers, ten seaplane tenders, three repair ships, two oilers, two ocean tugs, one hospital ship, one surveying ship, one supply vessel, one ammunition vessel, one submarine rescue ship, one antique cruiser, and one submarine tender—totaling ninety-four vessels in harbor when the air attack hit. As a result of the attack, six battleships were sunk, two others seriously damaged, one heavy cruiser and two oilers sunk. Heavy damages were also inflicted upon one heavy cruiser, six light cruisers, three destroyers, and three auxiliary vessels.*

*Admiral Fukudome's lists of ships are not in accord with standard figures in histories of the Pearl Harbor attack. Far fewer ships were sunk and damaged than he reports. He comes closest on battleships. Five were sunk, and the other three sustained varying degrees of damage. Eventually, only the battleships *Arizona* and *Oklahoma* and the target ship *Utah* were not repaired and restored to service. Editor.

Damages inflicted upon the enemy air force were no less heavy. The United States admitted that in the Pearl Harbor attack heavier damages were inflicted on the air force than on the surface force. Even though attacked by surprise, warships can retaliate, as they actually did, but planes lined up wing to wing are absolutely defenseless when attacked by surprise from the air. Maintenance crews and fliers at several bases on Oahu did all they could, and bravely fought even by mounting displaced airplane machine guns on work benches and trash boxes. But most of the United States air force on the islands was destroyed before such makeshift defense measures became effective—ninety-nine Navy and sixty-five Army planes being thus destroyed and many others damaged.

As a result of the attack, a total of 2,403 Navy, Army, and civilian personnel were killed, and 1,178 wounded.

It was most noteworthy that all this damage was inflicted by the air attack, not by the submarine attack upon which much hope was originally placed.

In comparison with the damages inflicted, our attack force lost eight fighters, fifteen dive-bombers, and five bombers. In addition, one flier was killed in a plane and several wounded. Seventy-four planes were holed. One fleet submarine and all five midget submarines of the submarine force failed to return.

Few could doubt the tactical success of the Hawaii Operation after comparing damages inflicted on both sides. Dr. Morison's criticism of the Hawaii Operation was focused on the point that the Japanese overlooked in the attack a greater victory which they could easily have gained.

When it is recalled that the success of this air attack upon Pearl Harbor nullified the U. S. Navy's Rainbow No. 5 operational plan, and that it took two full years to recover its strength; further, that our forces, in the meantime, were able to complete without interruption the occupation of the southern resources area, we, who are students of strategy, cannot agree with Dr. Morison's criticism which assailed the tactics employed by the Japanese. In the event that the Japanese Navy had not launched the Hawaii attack and had consequently encountered the U. S. fleet advancing on the Marshall and West Caroline islands in pursuance of their Rainbow No. 5 operational plan, it would have been impossible for the Japanese Navy to have inflicted greater damage on them than they did in the Pearl Harbor attack, however favorable an estimate may be applied to the case.

Dr. Morison's view maintains that, from the political viewpoint as well, the operation was a foolish one, for the attack incited the Americans to their slogan of "Remember Pearl Harbor." Their firm determination to defeat Japan made the idea of a negotiated peace absolutely untenable to them. But does this really hit the nail on the head? While admitting that the Pearl Harbor attack really angered the Americans, it is yet inconceivable that their fighting spirit depended upon the point on which the first attack was made, since Japan in any case would have declared war, attacked U. S. forces, and occupied enemy territory. I cannot agree with Dr. Morison's view.

The Submarine Special Attack Unit: Everyone knows that the Japanese submarines were a total failure in the Pearl Harbor attack. There are many descriptions and discussions of the air operations at Pearl Harbor as well as of the special attack "kamikaze" at the last stage of World War II, but there is almost no mention made of the Special Attack Unit's midget submarines. For this reason, I should like to describe their operations in particular.

Toward the evening of 18 November 1941, five large type submarines, *I-16*, *I-18*, *I-20*, *I-22*, and *I-24* of the "Special Attack Unit" under the command of Captain Hanku Sasaki left the Kure Naval Station under the cloak of secrecy and headed eastward. Each of them carried on board a secret weapon called "Target A" which was stored in a large tube on deck. These secret weapons were the midget submarines which tried to penetrate deep into Pearl Harbor on 7 December in conjunction with the air attack.

Incidentally, the midget submarine was not a weapon which was produced overnight for use at the Pearl Harbor attack, but a product of the tireless work of technicians over a period of many years. Back in 1933, a group of torpedo technicians got a hint from "A Sure Hit with Human Piloted Torpedo" advocated by Captain Noriyoshi Yokoo, who distinguished himself as one of the heroes of the Port Arthur Blockade Unit in the Russo-Japanese War, and started to study a method of "assuring a hit by releasing a torpedo piloted by one man from a mother torpedo." For security reasons, this mother torpedo was named "Target A," and it was this midget submarine which participated in the Pearl Harbor attack.

Why, then, was such a weapon produced? The mission assigned the Japanese Navy since the establishment of the national policy in 1909 was to safeguard the national security with inferior strength against the superior strength of our potential enemy, the U. S. Navy. All aspects of strategy, tactics, preparations, education, and training had since then been concerned with gaining a victory over the U. S. Navy as their principal objective. Particular emphasis was placed on the use of submarines and on long-range torpedoes in a decisive fleet engagement as a method to be employed by our inferior naval strength. A weakness inherent in the submarine was her slow submerged speed, a disadvantage which often made her miss an opportunity to attack. The limited range of torpedoes also often made them unsuccessful in attacks. The answer to the problem of how to use the advantages of both submarines and torpedoes and overcome their defects in a decisive battle materialized in this "Target A."

Its characteristics, which showed a considerable enlargement over the early types, were in general as follows:

Total length	25 meters
Diameter	2 meters
Underwater displacement	50 tons
Torpedo tubes	2
Torpedoes	2
Underwater speed	19 knots
Radius of action	Capable of making 8-hour run at low speed after 50-minute underwater run at 19 knots
Crew	2

Its shape was a perfect enlarged replica of a torpedo, to which a small conning tower was attached. Midget submarines were successfully constructed about one year after work on them was started. Then the building of their three tenders, *Chitose, Mizuho,* and *Nisshin,* was begun with the object of using them in a decisive battle against the main body of the enemy's forces. In the spring of 1941, the first test launching of a midget submarine from the *Chitose* was successfully conducted.

Although those midget submarines were originally built for use in a decisive engagement, a study was conducted of various methods of employing them in other operations, and we became convinced that they could be effectively used against vessels at anchor in a harbor. Since studies and preparation for the Hawaii aerial attack were being made at that time, all "Target A" personnel ardently wished to volunteer for a special attack. Their requests were granted, and some eventually penetrated into Pearl Harbor on 7 December. At the start of hostilities, twenty midget submarines had been completed, of which five participated in the Hawaii Operation as the Special Attack Unit.

Since it was of primary importance for the Hawaii Operation that the aerial attack be successful,

it was directed that those midget submarines would first lie in waiting outside of the harbor and then stealthily enter to make an attack after the initiation of the air strike. It was extremely difficult to determine the results of those midget-submarine attacks because of the confusion which followed the aerial attack, and also because none of those five boats returned to report. But the Japanese military, and the people as well, believed in their success before the true facts were uncovered following the end of the war. These erroneous opinions were principally based on the fact that one of our submarines on watch outside the harbor entrance the night of 7 December observed a huge explosion inside the harbor at 9:01 p.m. Hawaii time, and also on the fact that a secret message which stated "succeeded to make attack" was received from one of the midget submarines at 10:41 that night. According to records made public by the United States after the war, however, only two of them finally succeeded in entering the harbor and no torpedo hits were scored.

Similar attacks by midget submarines were later made in Sydney Harbor, Australia, and Diego Suarez, Madagascar Island. Recognition was given to each as a valiant and glorious act of warfare conducted in the name of special attacks and excelling all the former deeds of the so-called suicide bands.

In a strict sense, however, there was some distinction between the midget submarine special attack and those special attacks which were widely conducted toward the end of the war. The difference lay in the fact that a means for rescuing crews was provided in the midget submarine special attack, while in the later attacks there were actual body crashes in which there was no hope of returning alive. This may clearly be understood by the fact that, when the plan of "Target A" was advanced in the early part of 1933, Fleet Admiral Prince Fushimi, then Chief of the Naval General Staff, gave his approval only after he was assured that "this weapon is not to be used for body-crashing." When midget submarine attacks were planned in the Pearl Harbor attack, Admiral Yamamoto, Commander in Chief Combined Fleet, in like manner gave his consent to it only after he had his staffs exhaustively study the feasibility of rescuing the crews of midget submarines and their chances of survival. As a matter of fact, those midget submarines possessed sufficient cruising radius to return to a safe point outside the harbor, after completing their attacks in the harbor. Upon reaching this point, they were to be picked up by the waiting mother submarines.

Nine of the ten men who operated the midget submarines of the Special Attack Unit died during the attack on Pearl Harbor. The nine who did not come back were memorialized in this Japanese painting. (Courtesy of Captain Roger Pineau, USNR, Ret.)

But none of the ten men who participated in the attack expected to return alive. They were determined to hit by ramming themselves, their spirit being identical with that of later special attack units. Ensign Kazuo Sakamaki, whose boat went aground outside the bay due to engine trouble, had the misfortune of becoming prisoner of war No. 1. Mr. Matsura Hashimoto, who was the torpedo officer of the *I-16* which released Sakamaki's midget submarine outside Pearl Harbor, wrote in his book titled *I-58 Safely Returns to Base* as follows:

When Ensign Sakamaki's personal effects which were left behind were checked, his hair and nails were found carefully wrapped up together with a letter of farewell addressed to his parents. Even the required postage was attached to the list of addresses to whom these keepsakes were to be forwarded. The balance of his money had been given to his boy. The special precaution he took to prevent matches (to be used for destroying his boat) from getting wet by wrapping them in oil paper was proof of the grim determination of this young officer who did not expect to return alive.

The first Japanese prisoner of war was Ensign Kazuo Sakamaki. He was captured when his two-man submarine was beached near Bellows Field, on the southeastern shore of Oahu. His shipmate was killed in the attack. (National Archives: 80-G-32680.)

Strategy Pros and Cons: As previously stated, Dr. Morison severely criticized the Japanese aerial attack in that it committed a strategical blunder in selecting its targets. He even said that it was the height of folly for Japan not to have attacked land military installations, especially oil tanks, since much more damage would have been inflicted by setting on fire those oil tanks than by directing attacks on battleships in the harbor.

I think that if Vice Admiral Nagumo had executed two or more air attacks, no doubt he would have ordered those oil tanks and other military installations on land attacked. But Vice Admiral Nagumo had planned from the beginning only one wave of air attacks on Pearl Harbor, and he selected for his targets the direct battle forces rather than the indirect military elements, and decided to concentrate all air attacks on ships and planes. In my opinion, Nagumo made the best choice of targets for the simple attack which he launched.

Another argument among military students both at home and abroad about this aerial attack is concerning the number of attacks. Why did the Japanese Air Force, blessed by such a rare opportunity, discontinue its attacks after launching only a single attack? Why didn't it exploit the gains made by repeating attacks upon the enemy two or three times? These criticisms, in other words, meant that had the Japanese repeated their attacks several times for two days, as the U. S. task forces used to do later in the course of the war, almost all of the naval craft in Pearl Harbor, numbering 100, would have been completely destroyed, and land military installations also wiped out.

But I do not agree with this view. It was not until 1944, three years after the war started, that the U. S. task forces could gain control of the sea; by this time the Japanese Navy had lost its integral fighting strength tactically as well as strategically. The U. S. forces had become so powerful that they no longer encountered a rival enemy anywhere. There was no need for them to risk a surprise attack, as the Japanese Navy did in the Hawaii Operation. They could launch an attack in strength any time and anywhere they wished. To compare those attacks of the U. S. task forces with our Hawaii Operation can only be called irrational.

No greater surprise attack could have been planned

The large tank farm for the storage of fuel oil, situated near the submarine base at Pearl Harbor, was left untouched by the attackers. Had Vice Admiral Chuichi Nagumo, the officer in tactical command of the attack force, not passed up the chance to make a second attack, these tanks, which proved extremely valuable as the U.S. Navy mounted its counteroffensive in early 1942, might have been destroyed. Admiral Fukudome, however, defends Nagumo's decision, on the basis that he had already accomplished what he set out to do. (National Archives: 80-G-182880.)

than the Hawaii Operation. Our estimate of the available strength and state of preparation of the American forces precluded any advance plan for launching repeated attacks lasting two or three days.

But a war situation is liable to undergo kaleidoscopic changes. To alter original plans to meet the actual situation of an engagement, therefore, is entirely left to the discretion of the commander in the area.

This criticism does not hit the mark. The fact that there were no enemy carriers in the harbor meant that enemy carrier-borne air forces might suddenly come out to attack our force while our planes engaged in attacking Pearl Harbor. Since our force achieved much greater results in its initial attack than had been expected, credit might even preferably be given to Nagumo's wise decision to terminate the attacks instead of going too far with them.

One thing which I regret is that Nagumo's aerial reconnaissances over the entire area within the radius of his attacks were not sufficient. Since he had already been informed by the "A" information on the night before that there were no enemy carriers in the harbor, he should have conducted a thorough and close air reconnaissance over the whole area to locate targets of attack as well as to safeguard his own force from their attacks. Had such air reconnaissance been carried out, the *Enterprise*, which was then sailing within 200 miles from Hawaii, should have been discovered. I think that there would have been no occasion for criticism of Nagumo's conduct in the Hawaii Operation if he had repeated the attack on Pearl Harbor just once more, while carrying out air reconnaissance over the entire area more closely. At the same time, it should be considered as going too far under the circumstances to repeat attacks more than three times.

Admiral Nagumo's insufficient air reconnaissance around his force was not limited to this case only. In the Midway operation in June 1942, he committed the same blunder, as a result of which the Japanese Navy sustained fatal damage and a crippling blow to subsequent naval operations. Although those facts were kept secret at the time in the interests of the war's direction, they are now well known to the public.

Shigeru Fukudome (1891–1971) was graduated from the Imperial Naval Academy in 1913 and subsequently served in a variety of ship, aviation, and staff assignments. He had temporary duty in the United States in 1932 and 1933 and afterward was a senior staff officer of the Combined Fleet, commanding officer of the battleship *Nagato*, and chief of staff to Admiral Yamamoto during Yamamoto's tenure as Commander in Chief Combined Fleet. In April 1941, he became Chief of the First Bureau (operations) of the Naval General Staff, and in 1942 again became Combined Fleet chief of staff. Later in the war, he was simultaneously Commander Second Air Fleet and Commander Sixth Base Air Force, commanding land-based air forces in the defense of Formosa and the Philippines. At the end of the conflict, he was serving concurrently as Commander in Chief Tenth Area Fleet, Thirteenth Air Fleet, and First South Sea Fleet. (Naval Historical Center: NH 63419.)

The story of the Japanese attack on Pearl Harbor is, of course, much broader than just the events in Hawaii itself. Washington, D.C., was another focus, as Admiral Nomura and Admiral Fukudome have suggested by referring to Japanese diplomatic efforts. The next several articles, most of them by officers who were on the staff of Admiral Harold R. Stark, the Chief of Naval Operations, illuminate events in the nation's capital during the period leading up to and immediately following the attack.

The Taranto Lesson

By Rear Admiral Walter C. Ansel, U.S. Navy (Retired)

I reported about the end of November 1940 to the Office of the Chief of Naval Operations for duty in the War Plans Division. I was junior among ten or twelve officers. Some of the others in our outfit were Captain Harry Hill, Captain Carl Moore, and Captain "Savvy" Cooke. The division of duties was rather vague, and in fact the work was done mostly off the top of the head whenever something came up in the office of the Secretary of the Navy or of the Chief of Naval Operations. There was no continuing systematic planning. We met things as they came and did what we could by conferring with the Army or with other agencies.

Captain Moore really tried to do something about organization, but we were not fitted either to plan a war or to conduct a war. We couldn't even keep track of the corrections that were supposed to be made in the Rainbow war plans, which were locked up. It was too difficult to get them out to make corrections. This sounds facetious, but the situation was almost that nonchalant. I was a greatly disillusioned young commander. Problems over which we had broken our hearts and broken our backs at sea in the Asiatic Fleet counted for little in the Navy Department. At sea, answers had been demanded of us. I now found out that not much was done with those answers when they arrived in Washington. Certainly the tone of doing something was quite different. I finally had to give up and treat this as the way things ran in Washington; they ran on expediency.

When Captain Richmond Kelly Turner, soon to be promoted to rear admiral, came to head the War Plans Division, the picture changed somewhat. He saw the troubles and was sharp enough and irascible enough to do something. For example, he suggested a CNO war room, an idea we'd heard about from the British. Captain Frank Leighton of the Ships' Movement Division was the logical one to get it together. We would then have committee meetings in there each morning to read the daily dispatches and keep track of where the ships were on big wall charts. Unfortunately, the war room was used mostly as a place we could march Congressmen and other VIPs through. (It wasn't any good for practical work, because the charts were not precise enough.) And there was still no systematic division of staff duty for taking or ordering action.

The prize thing that fell to me during the period before the war was Admiral Harold R. Stark's anxiety about the fleet at Pearl Harbor. This started with him after the successful British air attack on the Italian fleet in Taranto Harbor on 11 November 1940. Three Italian battleships were sunk, the *Conte di Cavour*, *Littorio*, and *Caio Duilio*. It was a disaster of Pearl Harbor proportions. It hadn't shocked us very widely, but it did get to the Japanese, and it got to Admiral Stark. The Japanese were crazy to photograph the area and study the situation and all its factors. Some years later, though, when General Minoru Genda visited the Naval Institute, he said unequivocally that Taranto had no influence on the Japanese preparations for Pearl Harbor.

Admiral Turner thought he knew the Japanese. In 1939, when he was commanding the heavy cruiser *Astoria*, he had taken the Japanese ambassador's ashes home, and he formed great friendships in Japan. On the way home, he came through Manila, where I was a destroyer division commander, and we had some opportunities for talks. Later, he was sure the Japanese couldn't possibly get to Pearl Harbor. No one else believed they could either, so here poor old Admiral Stark was alone in insisting that a study be made. I was told to do it, and the fact that the junior man should get the assignment is an indication of how unimportant the rest of them thought it was. In order to find out about the Army planes and antiaircraft guns in Hawaii, I had to spy around. We had no authentic, up-to-date information, and yet the Army was protecting our fleet. We in the War Plans Division really had no idea what the defenses were. And it turned out that they were very sketchy. It was not hard to see. I wrote the following letter for Secretary of the Navy Frank Knox's signature, saying what Admiral Stark wanted. The letter was addressed to Secretary of War Henry L. Stimson and dated 24 January 1941. It was in preparation for more than a month.

My dear Mr. Secretary:

The security of the U.S. Pacific Fleet while in Pearl Harbor, and of the Pearl Harbor Naval Base

The surprise carrier attack launched by the Royal Navy against Taranto, Italy, in November 1940 raised Admiral Harold R. Stark's concern about a possible attack on Pearl Harbor. Nevertheless, Pearl Harbor was surprised. Shown here are Italian warships leaking oil at Taranto, and the Italian battleship *Caio Duilio* sinking as a result of the attack. (British Official Photo, and Imperial War Museum: HU 2058.)

itself, has been under renewed study by the Navy Department and forces afloat for the past several weeks. This reexamination has been, in part, prompted by the increased gravity of the situation with respect to Japan, and by reports from abroad of successful bombing and torpedo plane attacks on ships while in bases. If war eventuates with Japan, it is believed easily possible that hostilities would be initiated by a surprise attack upon the Fleet or the Naval Base at Pearl Harbor.

In my opinion, the inherent possibilities of a major disaster to the fleet or naval base warrant taking every step, as rapidly as can be done, that will increase the joint readiness of the Army and Navy to withstand a raid of the character mentioned above.

The dangers envisaged in their order of importance and probability are considered to be:

(1) Air bombing attack.
(2) Air torpedo plane attack.
(3) Sabotage.
(4) Submarine attack.
(5) Mining.
(6) Bombardment by gun fire.

Defense against all but the first two of these dangers appears to have been provided for satisfactorily. The following paragraphs are devoted principally to a discussion of the problems encompassed in (1) and (2) above, the solution of which I consider to be of primary importance.

Both types of air attack are possible. They may be carried out successively, simultaneously, or in combination with any of the other operations enumerated. The maximum probable enemy effort may be put at twelve aircraft squadrons, and the minimum at two. Attacks would be launched from a striking force of carriers and their supporting vessels.

The counter measures to be considered are:

(a) Location and engagement of enemy carriers and supporting vessels before air attack can be launched;

(b) Location and engagement of enemy aircraft before they reach their objectives;

(c) Repulse of enemy aircraft by anti-aircraft fire;

(d) Concealment of vital installations by artificial smoke;

(e) Protection of vital installations by balloon barrages.

The operations set forth in (a) are largely functions of the Fleet but, quite possibly, might not be carried out in case of an air attack initiated without warning prior to a declaration of war.

Pursuit aircraft in large numbers and an effective warning net are required for the operations in (b). It is understood that only thirty-six Army pursuit aircraft are at present in Oahu, and that, while the organization and equipping of an Anti-Air Information Service supported by modern fire control equipment is in progress, the present system relies

When he was head of the War Plans Division in late 1941, Rear Admiral Richmond Kelly Turner thought that, because he made a trip to Japan in 1939 as commanding officer of the heavy cruiser *Astoria*, he knew the Japanese. He is shown here in April 1939 meeting with Japanese Foreign Minister Hachiro Arita and U.S. Ambassador Joseph C. Grew. (Naval Historical Center: NH 69109.)

wholly on visual observation and sound locators which are only effective up to four miles.

Available Army anti-aircraft batteries appear inadequate if judged by the standards of the war in Europe. There are now in Oahu 26—3" fixed anti-aircraft guns (of which something over half are grouped about Pearl Harbor), 56 mobile 3" guns, and 109 .50 caliber machine guns. The anti-aircraft batteries are manned in part by personnel which is also required to man parts of the sea coast artillery. Should an attack on Oahu combine air attack with a gun bombardment, one or the other countering fires would suffer from lack of men. If the prevailing high ceiling is taken into account the caliber of the anti-aircraft guns might be inadequate against high altitude bombing attack.

By late summer the defenses will be considerably strengthened by additions in guns, planes, and radio locators. It is understood, sixteen additional 3" Mobile, twenty-four 90 mm., and one hundred twenty 37 mm. guns will be on hand; the pursuit aircraft strength is to be expanded to a total of 149; the new radio locators [radar] will have an effective range of 100 miles. Although the caliber of the guns will still be small for effective action against high altitude bombers, this augmentation will markedly improve the security of the Fleet. It does not, of course, affect the critical period immediately before us.

The supplementary measures noted in (d) and (e) might be of the greatest value in the defense of Pearl Harbor. Balloon barrages have demonstrated some usefulness in Europe. Smoke from fixed installations on the ground might prove most advantageous.

To meet the needs of the situation, I offer the following proposals:

(1) That the Army assign the highest priority to the increase of pursuit aircraft and anti-aircraft artillery, and the establishment of an air warning net in Hawaii.

(2) That the Army give consideration to the questions of balloon barrages, the employment of smoke, and other special devices for improving the defenses of Pearl Harbor.

(3) That local joint plans be drawn for the effective coordination of naval and military aircraft operations, and ship and shore anti-aircraft gun fire, against surprise aircraft raids.

(4) That the Army and Navy forces in Oahu agree on appropriate degrees of joint readiness for immediate action in defense against surprise aircraft raids against Pearl Harbor.

(5) That joint exercises, designed to prepare Army and Navy forces in Oahu for defense against surprise aircraft raids be held at least once weekly so long as the present uncertainty continues to exist.

Your concurrence in these proposals and the rapid implementing of the measures to be taken by the Army, which are of the highest importance to the security of the Fleet, will be met with the closest cooperation on the part of the Navy Department.

Sincerely yours,
/s/ Frank Knox

The Honorable
The Secretary of War.

Copies to: CINC, U.S. Pacific Fleet
Com14
Op–22
Op–30

Walter Charles Ansel (1897-1977) was graduated a year early in the Naval Academy class of 1919 and was soon involved in wartime convoy escort on board the *Rambler*. He later served in the *Howard, McCawley, Macdonough, Bulmer, Mervine, Converse, New York*, at the Naval War College, Marine Corps Schools, Battleship Division 3 staff, *Milwaukee*, and as a Naval Academy instructor. He commanded the destroyer *Bulmer* and Destroyer Division 14 in the Asiatic Fleet before assignment to the War Plans Division. During World War II, he commanded the oiler *Winooski*, took part in amphibious operations in the Mediterranean, commanded the light cruiser *Philadelphia*, and served in OpNav. Afterward, he served in Japan and with the U.S. Naval Mission to Brazil prior to retiring from active duty in 1949. He was named a Forrestal Fellow in 1951 and later wrote two books: *Hitler Confronts England* and *Hitler and the Middle Sea*. (Courtesy of Mrs. Walter C. Ansel.)

One of the most remarkable aspects of the attack on Pearl Harbor is that the Japanese were able to achieve such complete surprise at a time when the U.S. Government was intercepting and decoding Japanese diplomatic messages. It is so remarkable, in fact, that one school of thought cites it as proof of a conspiracy—that information indicating Japan was about to break diplomatic relations with the United States was deliberately withheld from Hawaii. The object of withholding the information, according to the conspiracy theory, was to allow the attack to do enough damage to arouse American public opinion and thus get the United States into the world war already raging. A key figure in the matter of the intercepted diplomatic messages was Commander Arthur H. McCollum, an American who was born in Japan and educated in the Japanese language. In late 1941, he was an experienced naval officer, and was serving in the Office of Naval Intelligence in Washington. His vantage point enabled him to see the war coming, but his desire to get timely warnings to the fleet ran into obstacles. In his view, there was no deliberate effort to withhold warnings from Admiral Kimmel in Hawaii. Rather, the events surrounding Pearl Harbor seemed to him to be a case of well-meaning men being stymied by the bureaucratic structure they had helped create.

Unheeded Warnings

By Rear Admiral Arthur H. McCollum, U.S. Navy (Retired)

I reported for duty in the Office of the Chief of Naval Operations and was detailed as head of the Far East Section of ONI in November 1939. My predecessor who had been head of that section, Commander John M. Creighton, had already gone and in temporary charge during his absence was Lieutenant Commander Alwin D. Kramer.

Basically, there were three sections within the Far East Section—the Japan desk, the China desk, and the Philippine desk. We didn't do much about this latter, because the Philippines at that time were still possessions of the United States, although independence was coming on. The head of the Japan desk was Lieutenant Commander Kramer. We had a Chinese linguist, a Marine, who was heading the China desk. That was traditional. That covered pretty much everything other than Japan, and they did collate the best way they could the information that came in. Then we started issuing about every week or two a sort of an appreciation of the situation in the Far East. It was supposed to go to important commands afloat as well as the Navy Department.

I had a very close personal relationship with Rear Admiral Walter S. Anderson [the Director of Naval Intelligence].* He had been captain of the *West Virginia* and I had served on that ship during the period of his command. He got to have, apparently, a very high regard for me. When I came in he welcomed me, and I was Admiral Anderson's fair-haired boy. Captain Howard D. Bode at that time was head of foreign intelligence. I rated with him because I rated with Anderson. He was really very good, but "Ping" Bode was very much of a martinet who stood on ceremony quite a lot. As far as I was concerned, we got along fine and he was helpful. I've seen him treat other people somewhat less well, but I got on all right. Later on, we got another fellow in ONI, Lieutenant Commander Ethelbert Watts, a Japanese-language man. He took over the Japanese desk, and that enabled Kramer to devote full time to the code-breaking business.

ONI, with the exception of the Far East desk, [was] primarily a library-type operation which col-

lected papers of various sorts and filed them away in their archives, and very little of this could be disseminated because the machinery for writing it up and getting it out was lacking. There were just not enough bodies or enough money to run it. Now there was a monthly bulletin, but that was largely filled with technical information—ship design, for instance, and that sort of thing. But starting under the direction of Captain William D. Puleston, who was director of intelligence, in 1934, I think, the Far Eastern desk had been cranked up to be a comprehensive intelligence-gathering and evaluation organization. We were charged with the job of issuing estimates of enemy intent—we didn't use the word "enemy" but obviously in the Far East we had to keep track of what the Japanese and Chinese might do.

When Rear Admiral Walter Stratton Anderson left the Office of Naval Intelligence, he sought to take Commander McCollum to the fleet with him, but the Assistant Chief of Naval Operations intervened. As a result, McCollum was in Washington, not Pearl Harbor, when the Japanese struck. (Naval Historical Center: NH 001827.)

---

* Words in brackets have been inserted in Admiral McCollum's oral history transcript in the process of editing. Sections have been rearranged to achieve continuity.

The problem that was constantly facing ONI was the lack of knowledge on the part of our own people on the Japanese and the terrific propaganda against the Japanese, fomented to a great extent by the Chinese and the missionaries to China who could see nothing good in Japan. The propaganda was exceedingly strong. Our own press took a jaundiced view of anything Japanese—"They're funny little people, they can't march, and they can't work, and so on." Actually, at this time that we're talking about now, in 1940, Japanese armies had overrun any part of China they wanted to. They could go anywhere they wanted to go, and most of the big Chinese victories, with one exception that I recollect, were more or less propaganda.

You had the same idea—these Japanese guys can't fly, because the pilots are no good. Why aren't they any good? Because as children they're carried on the backs of their mothers or their older sisters, and their older sisters play hopscotch. The child's head bounces around and it destroys the balance in the inner ear. It didn't do any good to point out that you've got a thing called Japan Airlines operating on dirt strips, which wasn't unusual in the 1930s, of course, anywhere, and over terrific terrain and using single-engined biplanes mostly. They were running a regular route between Tokyo and Osaka and down to Nagasaki and back on quite a good schedule for the time, and with remarkably few passenger casualties. The Japanese aviators were good, and any time that we would send out something that said how good they were, we would get a storm of, I wouldn't say abuse, but "You can't say this; the papers don't say it."

In late 1940 we had a shift of people in our naval attaché forces in Japan. A young fellow named Steve Jurika had been the assistant naval attaché for air in Tokyo; he was at that time a lieutenant (j.g.). He came back. He had made a very comprehensive study of Japanese naval aviation, and he impressed me terrifically, so I started him on a round of what you might call propaganda talks. I had him appear before the General Board in the Navy Department to tell these people that the Japanese aviators were darned good. They would only half believe. I sent him around not only in the Navy Department but sent him out in the country to carry the message, but it just didn't percolate. It's awfully difficult for a thing like naval intelligence to counter the constant daily drumfire from our press. I'm not derogating the press at all, but you see, speaking now of our press corps in Japan, none of those fellows could talk Japanese.

The War Plans Division [of the Naval Operations staff] in the early autumn of 1940 got a new chief in the person of Captain Richmond K. Turner, a very capable man. The Director of Naval Intelligence at that time was [still] Rear Admiral Anderson. Shortly after Turner became head of War Plans, Naval Intelligence—I think partly at the suggestion of Captain Turner—set up a new periodical called the *Fortnightly Summary*. It had a longer title than that, but it was a short, biweekly magazine having to do mostly with operational type intelligence, what was going to happen or what we thought was going to happen. The first of those was issued on the first of December 1940. The content, I thought, was pretty good.

To get a periodical of this sort out and get it back out into the Pacific area where it would be at all timely was almost impossible. There was very little air mail, or at least not in bulk to handle this sort of stuff, so it took four or five days by train across the country. Then to get out, for instance, to Pearl Harbor, it was another five to seven days by ship. So that by the time this thing got out there, any news value it had was pretty well gone. At least it was widely read around the Navy Department. About the middle of December 1940, or shortly thereafter, Admiral Anderson was detached as Director of ONI and ordered to the Pacific Fleet to take command of the battleships. That job had, up until that time, carried three stars with it, but there was a reorganization of the forces afloat in the works at that time. Anderson got the command all right, but he never got the third star.* Admiral Anderson had done me the honor to invite me to be his operations officer, the number two spot on the staff. The chief of staff was number one. I was quite junior for that job, and naturally I was very much flattered.

The admiral said he was going to leave right away and that I would have to stay for three weeks or so in ONI until the new man [Captain Alan G. Kirk] got things running. About that time, Captain Kirk was back from London [where he had been U.S. naval attaché], and he was very much impressed with what the British called the COIC, combined operations and intelligence center system. He suggested that some such arrangement as that be put up within the precincts of the Navy Department. That was enthusiastically received, and in early January of 1941 there was a conference presided over by Rear Admiral Royal E. Ingersoll, the Assistant Chief of Naval Operations. Captain Frank T. Leighton, who had been selected for flag rank, was selected to get this thing in operation. I don't think he wanted the job particularly, and he was very much in a fog as to what was required.

Anyhow, at this conference, each section within

---

* *See* article by Vice Admiral Anderson on page 126. Editor.

ONI had a person designated to make sure that Leighton and his outfit got the necessary intelligence to make the situation work. War Plans also came into it very much. Turner was getting more and more into everything, which was very fine. When they designated me to be the Far East liaison with this outfit, I made the mistake of saying, "Well, now, you'd better designate someone else because I'm under orders to go." And Admiral Ingersoll looked up quickly and said, "You are? Well, we'll stop that right now." He picked up the telephone in my presence and called the Bureau of Navigation and said, "Cancel McCollum's orders." I had to write Admiral Anderson that I had pleaded with Admiral Ingersoll to let me go. I would much have preferred to go to sea, particularly with Anderson whom I knew I could get along with very well indeed, but I couldn't get shaken loose.

I think it well at this time to review certain things that happened. Admiral James O. Richardson was relieved of command of the fleet. Admiral Husband E. Kimmel was chosen as his successor. Richardson had been Commander in Chief U. S. Fleet. Kimmel was never that. Kimmel was Commander in Chief Pacific Fleet. Theoretically, the United States Fleet under the new setup was considered to comprise the Atlantic Fleet, the Pacific Fleet, and the Asiatic Fleet. If all three of them ever got together, the Commander in Chief Pacific Fleet would be designated as commander in chief of the whole works, but the chances of anything like that ever happening were most remote. So the title and the function of the Commander in Chief U. S. Fleet virtually disappeared. The new organization went into effect the first of February 1941. That's the time that Kimmel assumed command.

Both Kimmel and Kirk were, I understand, personal selections for their respective jobs of the Secretary of the Navy, Mr. Frank Knox. Mr. Knox was very much impressed with Admiral Kimmel on one of his trips out to the Hawaiian Islands—now this is what I've been told, it's hearsay. And he was very much impressed and taken with Captain Kirk who, [had] a very engaging personality. I don't think he had very much regard for Admiral Anderson, because Admiral Anderson was rather outspoken and rather blunt. Mr. Knox didn't like too much outspokenness or too much bluntness.

Shortly after Admiral Kimmel relieved Admiral Richardson, he was constantly concerned about the fact that he was losing the reconnaissance type of aircraft and ships on which possibly a warning of attack would come. At that time he was completely bemused that the attack was probably building up or could be building up in the mandated islands—Truk and those kind of places. In February 1941, I

drafted a letter to him which was signed by Admiral Harold R. Stark [Chief of Naval Operations] in which I told [Kimmel] that the Japanese did not plan an attack in the foreseeable future. Right at that time, there was a very sensible easing of the diplomatic tension between the United States and Japan. Admiral Kichisaburo Nomura had recently arrived in Washington as Japanese ambassador. From reading the Japanese diplomatic codes, [we knew] his plan was to try to tread water and ease the situation, which he was doing. It just didn't seem possible at that time that the Japanese contemplated an attack anywhere. And, of course, how far does one foresee the future? Maybe two weeks or a month or what-have-you. The situation can change, and it did change. It changed radically. Yet Kimmel in his defense [brought] up this, that he was told in February 1941 that they weren't going to attack, and that's what he [based] it on. Since that time, of course, he had been told repeatedly that an attack might come most any time and would come presumably on a Sunday or a holiday. We didn't know where it was coming from. There was no intelligence that certainly I had, and as far as I've been able to read and judge, that Lieutenant Commander Edwin T. Layton had out there—he was Kimmel's intelligence officer—as to the possibility of an attack on Pearl Harbor.

Captain Charles H. McMorris, who was the war plans officer on Admiral Kimmel's staff, is quoted in the reports as telling Admiral Kimmel flatly that the Japanese simply weren't going to attack. You had the same feeling in Washington. In spite of the fact that the Japanese were moving steadily southward into French Indochina, which they went into in a big way in March, I think it was, of 1941. Here in May of 1941 they came to the grand conclusion that the war was going to be fought in the Atlantic. So all the emphasis was on the Atlantic and at the very time that the Japanese were building up their [strength] in the south, apparently that was completely disregarded. Now, I'm speaking of the people on the General Board. Rear Admiral John W. Greenslade is one that I have in mind. I don't know whether they got their orders from the White House or what-have-you. Anyhow, the decision was made somewhere around May 1941 that if there was going to be a war, as far as the United States was concerned, it would be in the Atlantic and we could forget about the Pacific, or that was a corollary. Of course, that was not my view at all. Naturally, forgetting about the Pacific or making it of lesser importance deflated my ego a little bit. I talked to people like Captain Dudley Knox and some others and said, "Look here, we're underestimating these people."

In early February 1941, following [ONI's] usual custom, I sent out a dispatch forecasting a move of the Japanese into French Indochina. Their forces seemed to me to be so disposed, and they had the capability certainly of doing it. About the third or fourth of February, I was sent for and was told that hereafter War Plans would do all of the evaluating of probable enemy intent. We had to be particularly careful that the Director of War Plans [Turner] in person got all of the pertinent information. Now, he was a very busy man and here he was going to do that, not only for the Far East, but, my goodness, for the British, the Germans, and everybody else.

I commenced to wonder why this had taken place, so I did a little snooping on my own and found that about the same time that my dispatch had gone out predicting an invasion of French Indochina to take place within a month or so, Turner had issued, without any knowledge of ONI at all, a prognostication that the Japanese were going to invade Siberia! And he continued in that view, on what basis I don't know. At one time, I think I made him rather angry when I suggested that maybe he was privy to some intelligence that I certainly didn't have. Anyhow, he was convinced that the Japanese were going to invade Siberia. So I finally went to Commander Charlie Wellborn, who was the administrative aide to the CNO, a friend of mine, and I said, "Charlie, what is all this business about?"

He said, "Well, I'll tell you, maybe you'd better go and see the admiral," meaning Admiral Stark. Admiral Stark said he realized that it was a function of ONI to talk about intentions, it was in the [ONI] manual, and all that, but he thought that it ought to be coordinated and that Turner was the man to do the coordinating. Well, of course, that didn't make any sense because once you start a coordinating job you've got your hand on the gullet, you've got a stranglehold, and that's exactly what happened.

Another thing, they had a complex on secrecy around there, which was all very well, but it tended to make people so secretive that they didn't tell anybody what was going on, so ONI was put in the unenviable position of having stuff going out about enemy intentions and what-have-you that they didn't know about at all. Anyhow, these things were going on, and the only way you found out about it was to have a private pipeline to some of these places, which is not a good way to do. But that was the situation, and I brought this up to Admiral Ingersoll, and Ingersoll said, well, he knew that in the Army the Military Intelligence Division did the evaluating, but the Navy didn't do it that way. In the Navy, War Plans always did it. I said, "Admiral, if that's the case, how about issuing an order in writing amending that part of the ONI manual?" He said, "Get the hell out of here. A verbal order is enough." By his decision, ONI was put on the spot, saying in effect, "All right, if there's anything

The top officers of the Army and Navy gather in late 1941 for a meeting of the Joint Board. Clockwise from left, they are Brigadier General H.F. Loomis, Major General Henry H. Arnold, Major General William Bryden, General George C. Marshall, Admiral Harold R. Stark, Rear Admiral Royal E. Ingersoll, Rear Admiral John H. Towers, and Rear Admiral Richmond K. Turner. (U.S. Army: Naval Institute Collection.)

wrong with the evaluation, you guys did it, and you guys and not War Plans must take the onus." That's what it amounted to. It was a very unenviable spot.

The War Plans Division would prepare a dispatch and send it out without reference to or even consideration by ONI at all. These dispatches would frequently be released either by Admiral Ingersoll or by Admiral Stark, presumably assuming that ONI had been consulted, but neglecting to look to see if there was the initial of the [Director of Naval Intelligence] on it. The result is that you had a situation which left intelligence without any information as to what our own government was doing, and we frequently picked it up only as a result of decoding Japanese diplomatic ciphers, which is a ridiculous situation. On the twenty-fifth of July, for instance, War Plans prepared a dispatch, perfectly properly so, but again ONI was not told. Everybody else was told about it apparently. The following is a joint dispatch from the U. S. Army Chief of Staff and the Chief of Naval Operations:

> Addressed to the Commander in Chief Pacific, Commander in Chief Asiatic, Commander in Chief Atlantic, Com 15, SPENAVO [Special Naval Observer in London, Vice Admiral Robert L. Ghormley].
>
> Appropriate addressee, please deliver copies to the commanding generals of Philippines, Hawaii, and Caribbean Defense Command, and also to General [James E.] Chaney in London. You are herewith advised that on July the 26th at 1400 GCT [Greenwich Civil Time] the United States will impose economic sanctions against Japan. It is expected that these sanctions will embargo all trade between Japan and the United States subject to modification through the medium of a license system for certain materials. Import licenses may be granted for raw silk. It is anticipated that export licenses will be granted for certain grades of petroleum products, cotton, and possibly some other material. Japanese funds and assets in the United States will be frozen except that they may be moved if licenses are granted for such movement. It is not expected that the Japanese merchant ships in ports of the United States will be seized at this time. U.S.-flag merchant vessels will at present be ordered to depart from or not to enter ports controlled by the Japanese. CNO and Chief of Staff [Army] do not anticipate immediate hostile reaction by Japan through the use of military means, but you are furnished this information in order that you may take appropriate precautionary measures against any possible eventuality. Action is being initiated by the United States Army to call the Philippine Army into active service at an early date. Except for immediate Army and Navy subordinates, the contents of this dispatch are to be kept secret. SPENAVO London inform [British] Chief of Naval Staff but warn him against disclosure.

The Ships' Movement Division, which was traditionally an admiral-maker, at that time was headed by Rear Admiral Roland M. Brainard who in that position was made a vice admiral. [His division] was left more in the dark as to what in heck was going on than ONI was. I remember one morning Brainard came in so damned mad he could hardly talk. He found that all this that he was supposed to be looking at, monitoring the movements of our own ships, was being ordered from some sources without his knowledge at all. Yet he was the guy responsible for knowing where these ships were. Movements of ships actually were ordered from War Plans. His hair was standing on end—what little he had. So that ONI by no means was alone. There had grown up in the office of the Chief of Naval Operations a coterie of officers—Stark, of course, the head of it, and Ingersoll and Turner. They were sort of a triumvirate. Turner would bring in the ideas, and these guys would execute them, frequently without any staffing of the matter.

In hearings [held after World War II] before the Congress, it has become very apparent that there was no lack of effort, because these were all very able men. They just felt that these things were so secret that they didn't dare discuss them. You'd hear, for instance, [that] Admiral Stark [testified] at the hearings: "Why, yes, we had a conference on the subject." Well, who were the conferees? They were Stark, Ingersoll, and Turner. That was the conference.

About the eleventh of October, I went to Captain Theodore S. Wilkinson [who had recently replaced Alan Kirk as Director of Naval Intelligence] and I said: "Look, this thing in my view is getting more and more serious and I would like your permission to put my section on a twenty-four-hour watch basis. I want to have either myself, Lieutenant Commander Watts, or Major [Ronald A.] Boone, in that office day and night." We went on a heel-and-toe watch. When the day's work was over, usually around four o'clock, whoever had the watch stayed there, always with an assistant or two along to help, until six o'clock the next morning, when we came back to work. If it was a holiday, you stayed right on. It was not an ONI watch; it was the Far East Section watch so that we would be immediately available to Lieutenant Commander Kramer and his staff of translators and to the decoders and so on, in case they needed help. In the process of decoding or trying to decode an encrypted message, it's frequently very helpful to have collateral information, background, where did this take place, and things of that sort. The whole business of the conditions under which things occurred is sometimes

In the view of Admiral McCollum, one of the problems in the handling of naval intelligence in the weeks before the attack on Pearl Harbor was that a triumvirate had walled itself off from much normal staff work, conferring only with one another. The three men were Admiral Harold R. Stark, Chief of Naval Operations; Rear Admiral Royal E. Ingersoll, Assistant Chief of Naval Operations; and Rear Admiral Richmond K. Turner, Chief of the War Plans Division. (Naval Historical Center: NR&L (MOD) 23853; Naval Photographic Center: K-9272; and U.S. Navy: Naval Institute Collection.)

very, very helpful to the people who are making an effort to unlock the secrets of the code.

Right up to the outbreak of war, ONI [was] constantly sending out information, but I saw no action. I got considerably worried, because I hadn't seen any warning dispatches going out to anybody. So in the latter part of November I sat down and drafted a memorandum about what had been going on in the Far East. I took it up to Captain Wilkinson, and he took it to Admiral Stark. Admiral Stark called a conference of his principal flag officers, and I went over what the Japanese had done in preparation for war, step by step, outlined it and so on. [I] deliberately asked whether the Pacific Fleet and the Asiatic Fleet had been warned and was answered in the affirmative. They had been warned and they had been ordered to take every step necessary to be ready for war.

Turner, Ingersoll, and Stark repeatedly assured both Wilkinson and me that adequate and ample warnings had gone out. We hadn't seen any. Now, for instance, there [was supposedly] a war warning dispatch, but I hadn't seen it. I had drafted another dispatch, and they said it was unnecessary to send it because of the others. Finally, I raised so much sand in Turner's office that he showed me the dispatch—the "war warning." That was the first I'd seen of it [on] the first of December. This "war warning" dispatch went out on the twenty-seventh of November. So here we're talking about four or five days later.

On the third of December, ONI issued instructions to the naval attachés at Tokyo, Peking, [and] Bangkok, [and to] the assistant naval attaché at Shanghai to destroy all of their codes and ciphers and all secret and confidential material whatsoever, and be prepared to be taken over, and that when this had been accomplished to send us a code word. The word, as I remember it, was "Gobbledygook." I got the [approval] of the Director of Naval Intelligence on it and went down and personally saw that this message was sent. All messages, under instructions from ONI, relating to the Far East were relayed through or [addressed] to both the Commanders in Chief of the Asiatic Fleet and of the Pacific Fleet, both going and coming. I had the confirmation in my hands that this had been accomplished by the fifth of December, which was Friday. In other words, the top American naval commanders in the area affected knew, or should have known, that our own people had been more or less directed to batten down and get ready for hostilities. That's what it amounted to.

A multiple-address dispatch [had been] sent on 3 December to the Commandant of the Sixteenth Naval District, Commander in Chief Asiatic Fleet,

Commander in Chief Pacific Fleet, and the Commandant of the Fourteenth Naval District. The Fourteenth District, of course, is the Hawaiian Islands, and the Sixteenth is the Philippines. It [said]: "Highly reliable information has been received that categoric and urgent instructions were sent yesterday to Japanese diplomatic and consular posts at Hong Kong, Singapore, Batavia, Manila, Washington, and London to destroy most of their codes at once and to burn all other important, confidential, and secret documents." That dispatch was released by Captain Wilkinson.

As soon as we got [the intercepted Japanese instructions about code-burning], I got hold of domestic intelligence and I said, "I think you people ought to put a special watch on the Japanese Embassy to see if this is actually taking place." They did, and, sure enough, found them toting papers out and putting them in an incinerator and then burning them. So we not only had the code order, but we saw it being carried out.

It was generally agreed that war was imminent—any time within the next two weeks. What we didn't know and did not find out [was] that the commencement of war would entail an attack on Pearl Harbor. It might. It might entail an attack on Manila, as it did. And it might entail an attack in other places. In other words, there was no—what we have come to term now—hard intelligence that Pearl Harbor, as such, would be subject to an attack at the outbreak of the war. It should have been understood. It seems to me that anybody sitting out in a place where he's outside of support of something can expect an attack on the outbreak of war. Admiral Kimmel and Admiral Thomas C. Hart [Commander in Chief Asiatic Fleet] had been warned at least on three occasions throughout the summer of 1941 that it was the Japanese and the German custom to attack without warning, frequently on a holiday, and so on and so on. It's very difficult to know what else could have been done.

When I left the office on Saturday [6 December], I knew that the thirteen parts [of an intercepted Japanese diplomatic message] were coming in. Kramer was staying on on duty, [but] the translators weren't necessary because this particular note came in in English. Sometime on the night of the sixth, Kramer called me at my home in Alexandria and said rather cryptically that [the thirteenth part] had come in and he was going to make his rounds. He briefly discussed over the telephone what he meant by "his rounds," who he was going to see, and to whom he was delivering the booklet with the thirteenth part in it. Sometime around midnight, he called me again at my home to tell me that he had made delivery, but he had not been

able to reach Admiral Stark. He had made the other deliveries pretty much and he was all through and was going home to catch a good sleep for a little while, which he did.

I was taking over the watch to be on duty all day on Sunday. I don't mean to say that I was alone. I had an assistant with me, John Clark, as I remember it, who was one of our very fine civilian analysts. He knew Japanese and so on, he was a very, very fine man. So I came down to the Navy Department and got there about 7:30 a.m. After chatting with Watts for a little while, Kramer came on in and brought up the thirteenth part and we read it together. Then Watts went home to get breakfast.

The thirteenth part was building up to a climax which, was coming in the fourteenth part, which they said was coming. At the end of the thirteenth part, it was very significant, we thought, there came a sort of thank-you message from the Foreign Office. This was in Japanese, not English, and it was thanking the [diplomats] for their work and so on and so forth and telling them, "Well, it's too bad, but we didn't make it this time but it wasn't due to any lack of effort on your part," or words to that effect. That seemed rather odd. The thirteenth part came on through with the fourteenth to follow.

Admiral Nomura was the ambassador, and Mr. Saburo Kurusu had been sent over to assist Ambassador Nomura. Kurusu was a career diplomat. I knew him when he was in a much lower grade in the foreign service. He had for a long time been consul or consul general in Chicago, and his wife was a native of Chicago. He had had a very wide diplomatic experience, both in South America and

Special Envoy Saburo Kurusu was sent to this country in November 1941 to assist Ambassador Kichisaburo Nomura in negotiating with the U.S. Government. Mrs. Kurusu, an American whom he married in 1914, did not accompany her husband on the trip to Washington in 1941. Their son Ryo, an aeronautical engineer, was killed during World War II. (Asahi Shimbun.)

Europe. His last job in Europe was as ambassador to Belgium, and he handled the signing of certain treaties or had attended as the chief Japanese plenipotentiary to handle treaties between Germany and Japan. Nomura, of course, was a man of tremendous prestige in Navy circles, but he was not a professional diplomat, which Kurusu was. That's why Kurusu was sent over here. For one thing, the [Japanese] felt that maybe Nomura in his dotage was a little bit too pro-American to be real tough, and they sent this man over to toughen it up.

Shortly after I got in the office [on Sunday morning], Captain Wilkinson came in. The minute I heard that he was there, I took the whole set of dispatches and went down and discussed the situation with him. We thought it was very important to make sure that Admiral Stark knew about this, so Captain Wilkinson called Admiral Stark's quarters at the Naval Observatory and found that the admiral was on his way down to the Navy Department. So I went up and asked the admiral's orderly, a Marine corporal I believe, the minute Admiral Stark came in the office to give me a ring so that we'd be up there. Around nine o'clock, we got word from the orderly that the admiral was in his office. Captain Wilkinson and I went up to see him and showed him the thirteen-part message and discussed the whole situation with him.

Around ten o'clock or maybe a little bit before, Kramer came in with the fourteenth part. That was the end. In other words, diplomatic relations were being broken. The fourteenth part was the final: "In spite of everything, you people have wronged us and so on," summing up the case and breaking off diplomatic relations.

[The fourteen-part note was] from the Tokyo Foreign Office, and the [diplomats in Washington] were directed to present it in exactly the words it came in. In other words, the Foreign Office did not wish the ambassador here to add anything or change one line or dot. That's why it came in English. They didn't want to take a chance on these people here trying to calm it down or polish it up. So the note itself came on in English precisely as it was to be presented. In the fourteenth part they said instructions on the timing of the presentation would follow. Well, the fourteenth part was coming in and Kramer hot-footed it over to the White House along with Captain John R. Beardall, who was the President's naval aide, and tried to get it to the President, which they did or someone did, and also to [Secretary of State Cordell] Hull, the Secretary of the Navy, and so on.

I continued to haunt Admiral Stark's outer office. Kramer came in about 10:30 and said, "We have

the final—we've got the instructions for delivery," and it repeated over and over that it must be delivered to Mr. Hull at precisely one o'clock Washington time. Kramer and I thought about it for a minute and said, "Let's see what the times are." In the Far East Section of ONI, whenever we got anything that had to be worked on a time basis, we always thought in terms of the three or four time zones: Washington time, Hawaiian time, Manila time, and so on. Of course, we had sighted and had under observation the Japanese task force in the Indian Ocean, heading for the [Isthmus of] Kra, and we were concerned with that. On the wall of the outer office of Admiral Stark, there was a time-zone chart—blue, light blue, and pink, with the zones. We quickly looked it over and said, "All right, here it is one o'clock would be 7:30 a.m. Hawaiian time roughly." It would be sometime later in Manila— I forget offhand what the time was, but we figured it out, and it would be just about dawn at Kota Bharu which is on the [Isthmus of] Kra. And, of course, that would be the ideal time, as we then thought, to create a surprise amphibious landing. We figured out this time, and it was taken in to Admiral Stark.

I sent an orderly down to get Captain Wilkinson, who came in promptly to Admiral Stark's office. We both went in there and talked about the message and pointed out the time elements in it. Admiral

Captain Theodore S. "Ping" Wilkinson, as Director of Naval Intelligence, urged Admiral Stark to telephone Admiral Husband E. Kimmel in Pearl Harbor on the morning of 7 December 1941, but Stark declined to do so. (Naval Historical Center: NH 83931.)

Stark understood right away, and he didn't seem to be very much perturbed. Captain Wilkinson asked again, it was almost monotonous, whether the Pacific Fleet had been alerted. Admiral Stark said, yes, they had. Captain Roscoe E. Schuirmann, who was the head of the [Naval Operations] Central Division, came in and out, and we were in and out of Admiral Stark's office and the outer office most of the time. I mean not any formal conference, but everyone of those who were there were coming in. Admiral Turner had not arrived and, as far as I knew, didn't plan to come, but I understand that Admiral Stark called him at his home and asked him to come down, apparently on another matter.

Admiral Turner showed about eleven o'clock in the morning. At this time, we asked again whether the Pacific Fleet had been warned, and I believe Captain Wilkinson suggested to Admiral Stark that he pick up the telephone and call Admiral Kimmel. I thought he was going to do it, but apparently he changed his mind and tried to get through to the White House and was told the President wasn't available. About eleven o'clock, apparently the office of General George C. Marshall [Army Chief of Staff] called up and talked to Admiral Stark. Admiral Stark said he didn't think any further warning was necessary, that they'd had ample warning and he couldn't see it would do any good. Then he talked a little while and called back on the phone and apparently got the Chief of Staff of the Army and said, add on to your message [to Lieutenant General Walter C. Short, Army Commander in Hawaii] "tell Navy."

Rear Admiral Leigh Noyes [Director of Naval Communications] had come in by that time, and he said to Admiral Stark, "Why don't they let us send it? I know I can send it and we'll have a definite confirmation in less than twenty minutes." Well, of course, Admiral Stark said, no, we would let it be handled by the Army. I got the impression—and this is purely an opinion—that they had had a regrouping of responsibilities for the joint action Army and Navy group, and that had been approved and gone into effect a little bit before. This time, the defense of the Hawaiian Islands was placed as an Army responsibility, and I got the impression then that Admiral Stark was bending over backwards to let the Army exercise their prerogative. The Army wanted it for a long time and it had never been definitely settled. The Navy was just as glad it was settled. It was an Army responsibility, the defense of the islands and the defense of the naval base, and that was fine. In other words, the fleet based there went in and out and operated offensively. The fleet itself was not a part of the Hawaiian

defenses, although as long as they were there and had a certain amount of artillery mounted they would participate in any defense that came up and so on.

So that was Sunday morning about eleven o'clock. The general feeling in the office was that everything had been done and all preparations had been made to minimize any damage that would be resulting. It was realized that with a surprise attack coming, if it did come, anywhere—Manila or anywhere else—that we were going to have to take it on the chin. The problem actually was one for people such as Admiral Kimmel and Admiral Hart to hope that they could minimize the extent of the damages. I don't know that Admiral Kimmel ever seemed to clearly understand that feature of it. He must have. Certainly Admiral Hart did, judging by his actions and writing subsequently.

Arthur Howard McCollum (1898–1976) was born in Nagasaki, Japan, the son of Baptist missionaries. He was graduated from the Naval Academy in 1921 and underwent three years' study of Japanese. After submarine training, he commanded the O-7 and was executive officer of the S-11. He later had several tours involving intelligence, including attaché in Tokyo, the Office of Naval Intelligence in Washington, and the staffs of U.S. Fleet and Southwest Pacific Force. McCollum served in the battleship *West Virginia*, commanded the destroyer *Jacob Jones*, and was the first commanding officer of the heavy cruiser *Helena*. Following World War II, he was involved in the formation of the Central Intelligence Group (later, the Central Intelligence Agency) and was Commander Military Sea Transportation Service Atlantic. He retired from the Navy in 1951 but remained with the CIA until 1953 as a consultant, then was in the insurance and real estate business in northern Virginia until his final retirement in 1964. (Naval Historical Center: NH 68797.)

Aide to Admiral Stark

By Vice Admiral William R. Smedberg III, U.S. Navy (Retired)

My association with Harold R. Stark began in 1937 when he took command of Cruiser Division 3, with the four-stack light cruiser *Concord* as flagship. After that, he moved up to become Commander Cruisers Battle Force. As such, he rated a seven-man staff, and because he was white-haired, we got our nickname from a movie which came out about then: *Snow White and the Seven Dwarfs*. I have a hard time now remembering which officer was which dwarf. The funny part of it was that the characteristics of the dwarfs were very aptly applied to each member of the staff. You couldn't necessarily see your own, but you certainly could see everybody else's.

In 1939, while still a rear admiral, Stark was chosen to become Chief of Naval Operations. It was a big surprise to everybody in the Navy. I don't think he was selected because of what he had done in command, although he had been a very good Chief of the Bureau of Ordnance and was well thought of. He was jumped over the heads of a number of more senior admirals, and I think he must have been a compromise choice.

When he was a young officer, Stark had known

Because Rear Admiral Harold R. Stark had white hair, he and the seven members of his Cruisers Battle Force staff were known as "Snow White and the Seven Dwarfs." Front row, left to right: Lieutenant Commander Charles Wellborn, Captain Willis A. Lee, Rear Admiral Stark, and Lieutenant Commander Ellsworth Roth. Back row: Lieutenant Commander Horace Butterfield, Lieutenant Commander William F. Jennings, Lieutenant Commander Harold D. Krick, and Lieutenant William R. Smedberg III. (Courtesy of Vice Admiral William R. Smedberg III, USN, Ret.)

Admiral Stark takes the oath as Chief of Naval Operations before Rear Admiral Walter B. Woodson (right), the Navy's Judge Advocate General. The outgoing CNO, whom Stark relieved on 1 August 1939, was Admiral William D. Leahy (left). Second from left is Acting Secretary of the Navy Charles Edison. The fact that all four men are attired in white suits testifies to the heat of a Washington summer in the years before air-conditioning. (Wide World.)

Franklin D. Roosevelt, so the two had formed a pretty good rapport and friendship. Of those who were in the approximate rank and age bracket to be considered for the job of CNO, Stark was the least controversial and the fellow Roosevelt probably thought he could get along with best. And he fit in with Roosevelt's practice of serving as his own Secretary of the Navy. The man then in the job, Claude Swanson, was sick most of the time and in fact died that year. Even when he came to the Navy Department, Swanson would often be on a cot in his office. Many times, documents were signed by the chief clerk—a man who could sign Swanson's signature better than Swanson could.

When Admiral Stark got the news he had been chosen to relieve Admiral William D. Leahy as Chief of Naval Operations, he was flabbergasted. He could hardly believe it. But he had quite a bit of ego, and it didn't take him very long to feel that the President had made a good choice. He was a dear old man, and I loved him very much, but he's not the man that I would have chosen as Chief of Naval Operations.

The admiral asked several members of his cruiser staff to go along with him to Washington. One of them was his chief of staff, Captain "Ching" Lee, and he also took Lieutenant Commander Charlie Wellborn to be his flag secretary, and me, a lieutenant then, as his aide and flag lieutenant. I told him I didn't want to go, because I was due to be

executive officer of a destroyer, and I figured it would ruin my career if I went ashore then. But Lee and Wellborn persuaded me that it was a good opportunity, and I finally consented to go.

Wellborn and I were detached early so we could report to Washington and have a sort of break-in period during the summer while Admiral Leahy was still CNO. Up to then, I had known only ships and nothing whatsoever about how the Navy Department operated. The whole three months were spent in being briefed in every office in the CNO's staff and in all the bureaus. We found out about what everybody was doing, what all the secret projects (such as radar) were, so that we would be able to keep Admiral Stark advised of what was being done in the Navy. The man at the very top is often shielded from the specifics of things going on in different places. I also found out who the men were who made the Navy tick in Washington. Charlie and I soon got to know to whom we should go if the admiral wanted something done in a hurry. At the end of the summer, Rear Admiral Husband E. Kimmel relieved Stark as Commander Cruisers Battle Force, and then Admiral Stark proceeded to Washington to become Chief of Naval Operations.

The three years I spent there were probably the most interesting from the point of view of learning about the Navy that I ever had. I learned of its shortcomings, how you got things accomplished, and who the really up-and-coming officers were. I mean you'd spot a commander down the line some-place who was really the spark plug in his whole organization, and you'd know that he was the fellow who could always get something going. There were other individuals to be avoided, because you knew nothing would happen when you got them with a project.

Another interesting part of the job was the contact it afforded with the man at the top, President Roosevelt. I kept a wax cylinder record of everything the President said to the admiral, because often Roosevelt would bypass the Secretary of the Navy. Instead he would call up and say, "Betty, I want this done right away," and he'd give five or six things in rapid-fire order.

The admiral would say, "Yes, Mr. President. Yes, Mr. President. Yes, Mr. President."

"Have you got that, Betty?"

"Yes, Mr. President." And he'd hang up.

The buzzer would ring, and I'd go in to hear Admiral Stark say, "Did you get all that, Smeddy?"

"Yes, Sir."

"Well, get going on it."

I monitored nearly every conversation he had, and I made a record of almost all of them. Every now and then, when it was a personal thing, Stark would tell me to destroy the record. But I kept most of them until I left that job after the war started. At that point, I said, "I made them, and I'm going to destroy them." That disgruntled some people, but just think, if President Nixon had destroyed all his tapes, he'd be in a lot better position today than he is. I guess those wax cylinders would be worth a million dollars now if I still had them.

Although I was very close to Admiral Stark in those years, there were some things that even I didn't learn about, particularly our war plans and the fact that we were able to read the Japanese codes. Because Wellborn was the flag secretary, he was cut in to some degree, but I wasn't. Rear Admiral Walter S. Anderson was Director of Naval Intelligence, and there were times he would think he was fooling us by going into Stark's office with a folder hidden under his coat. Stark wouldn't tell us about the meeting afterward. That's how secretive the intelligence people were, and really it was for a good reason. If word had ever leaked out about our codebreaking, we never would have had the success we did in World War II.

One of the biggest jobs that the CNO had in 1940 and 1941 was to try to build up the size of the fleet and the number of naval personnel. It's hard to pinpoint the things Stark did, but I know he was constantly on the telephone to the President, asking

One of Admiral Stark's finest achievements as CNO was that he persuaded Congress to provide the Navy with the ships and men it needed to fight a two-ocean war. He is shown here in June 1940 with Representative Colgate W. Darden of Virginia. Stark was preparing to testify before the House Naval Affairs Committee on behalf of a $4 billion fleet-expansion bill. (Wide World.)

for insignificant little bits and pieces here and there. For instance, he would ask for more men to fill a shortage in a new ship or class of ships being built. He was asking for permission to go to the House and Senate Naval Affairs Committees to ask for additional men. In those days, you couldn't do that unless you had the President's okay. The President would often begrudgingly say, "Okay, Betty, okay." The hardest thing to get from Roosevelt was men. The admiral finally got so he'd get them in jumps of 1,000 or 5,000, but we were always short of personnel.

Admiral Stark also led the fight to build what we then called a two-ocean navy. On occasion, headlines would come out and accuse him of being a warmonger. Or the press would go after other people, like Rear Admiral Joe Taussig, who were thinking along the lines that Admiral Stark was espousing. Because of his knowledge of Far Eastern affairs, Taussig was called to testify before the Senate Naval Affairs Committee in April 1940, when it was considering a naval expansion bill. Taussig identified Japan as a potential enemy of the United States, and he really stirred things up when he said, "I cannot see how we can escape being forced into

Rear Admiral Joseph K. Taussig's testimony before a Senate Committee almost got him fired by President Franklin D. Roosevelt. (National Archives: 80-G-454560.)

eventual war by the present trend of events." He turned out to be right, of course, but that wasn't the sort of thing Americans wanted to hear then.

Before the day was over, Admiral Stark issued a statement saying that Taussig was expressing his own personal views and not speaking on behalf of the Navy or the government. The next morning, there was one of the biggest headlines I ever saw in *The Washington Post*, calling Taussig a warmonger. The President was furious. He called Admiral Stark and said he wanted Taussig sent home "awaiting orders"—removing him from his post as Commandant of the Fifth Naval District. Admiral Stark argued and begged the President to reconsider, to sleep on it. Gradually, he got Roosevelt to agree that Taussig didn't have to be fired. The upshot of it was that Stark gave Taussig an oral admonition by telephone, and the thing blew over. Taussig stayed on the job until the following year, when he reached the mandatory retirement age.

Congressman Carl Vinson, chairman of the House Naval Affairs Committee, pitched in with some of the others in Congress, and we got a lot of money for a two-ocean navy, which was starting to take shape at the time of Pearl Harbor. This was a buildup which I think Admiral Stark had more to do with than anybody else. He was very much concerned over the fact that we didn't have enough oilers, we didn't have enough transports, we didn't have enough supply ships, we didn't have enough ammunition ships. Because if we had a war in the Pacific, we would have to have a lot of these auxiliary ships to service the fleet that would be operating a long, long way from any base.

The President was a very perceptive man, and he knew about the need for these ships, but, of course, politics came first with him. There was probably no shrewder politician than Franklin D. Roosevelt. Admiral Stark, by contrast, was a very simple sort of man. He was not devious in any way. I think because of his honesty he got as much from these congressional committees as any man could have done in those days. Charlie Wellborn went with Admiral Stark to the committee sessions more often than I did, but I went enough times to see that Congressmen listened to him.

Stark was constantly trying to improve our state of readiness, and when our fleet was kept in Hawaiian waters, it was really for political reasons, not Navy reasons. Stark did his best to get more long-range PBY patrol planes so we could protect our fleet base. We had nothing like the number of planes that we had to have in order to fly proper reconnaissance. Admiral James O. Richardson was removed from command of the fleet because he insisted to the President that it was foolhardy to keep the fleet in Pearl Harbor under the inadequate protection that was then in existence. I think the President just removed him because he got irritated with him, the same way he wanted to do with Admiral Taussig.

One day in November 1941, a young naval officer from the Japanese Embassy came to my office. He was wearing civilian clothes and told me he had a very personal message for Admiral Stark. Ambassador Kichisaburo Nomura felt it was most important that he have a private meeting with Admiral Stark and that nobody else know about it. I went to the embassy and met with Admiral Nomura, and we arranged a little scheme whereby the next afternoon I would be driving up Massachusetts Avenue. Dressed in civilian clothes, I would stop and offer a lift to Nomura, and then I would drive him to Stark's house at the Naval Observatory, also on Massachusetts Avenue.

We arranged this, and the next day, I did exactly that. I took him to the admiral's house, and the two of them were closeted there for quite a long time

The CNO's house on the grounds of the Naval Observatory in Washington was the site of a clandestine rendezvous between Admiral Stark and Ambassador Kichisaburo Nomura in late 1941, as they sought to stave off war between their two nations. (Naval Historical Center: NH 75726.)

while I sat outside. When they came out, Ambassador Nomura had tears in his eyes. I then dropped him off on Massachusetts Avenue. What Admiral Stark told me afterward was that Nomura was extremely worried about the possibility of the war party in Japan making some drastic decisions. He said the Japanese Army, which headed the war party, didn't understand the power and potential of the United States. He said he had tried in vain to tell them that Japan could never win in a war against the United States. "But," he had said to Admiral Stark, "Admiral, if the United States doesn't ease up on these sanctions against Japan, the military men in my country are going to be driven to do something desperate, in my opinion. I know that my country can only come out second best in any war with the United States."

That's the best recollection I have, and Admiral Stark was deeply impressed. I think it was as a

result of that that he and General George C. Marshall, Army Chief of Staff, got together and went to see the President. Both of them told Roosevelt that under no circumstances could the United States accept a war in the near future, because we were so unprepared. We still needed many, many months. Secretary of State Cordell Hull was also there, and the President had him read a proposed answer to the Japanese request for an easing of sanctions. Hull's proposal was a very strong resistance to any easing of sanctions. Stark and Marshall both said that sending such a message could be disastrous, so the President told Hull to modify it. But, after that, our Navy people were doing practice decryption on State Department messages and discovered that Hull's strong reply to the Japanese went out with no modification whatsoever.

When this came to Admiral Stark's attention, he and General Marshall got together. I'm not sure whether they both went to see the President or whether Stark called the President on the phone. But they got the President to admit that after Hull had gotten back to the State Department, all his advisers had impressed on him the fact that the Japanese respected firmness, and if he gave in, he would lose face and so forth. So Hull called the President and apparently told him that his people were absolutely against weakening the position paper. The President agreed and never notified the Army or Navy that he had changed his position. That to me had the greatest potential for disaster of many things in our history. Later, we heard that message described as an ultimatum to Japan, although it wasn't discussed as such at the time.

After the President admitted that he had changed his mind, he apparently called Hull and must have said to him: "Didn't you tell the Army and the Navy about this?" Right after that, which was somewhere around the second or third of December, I would guess, Hull called Stark and said, "Admiral, I'm afraid the fat's in the fire. It's up to you military fellows now." I heard that conversation. It was on one of those wax cylinders I broke up. Now, I wish I hadn't destroyed them. If we could just document what happened with all the material we did have, it would be very significant. The real significance is that we should never get into that kind of position again. In those days, State rarely talked to Army or Navy. Nowadays, I hope that through the National Security Council we have complete knowledge by everyone about everything.

The Japanese had sent Special Envoy Saburo Kurusu to Washington shortly before that. Nomura told me in Japan after the war that he didn't know Kurusu's mission when he arrived. Nomura didn't know anything about the plan that Kurusu divulged at the time of the attack on Pearl Harbor. He was sent over and instructed, apparently, to keep Nomura in the dark, because the Japanese Government didn't trust its ambassador. The Japanese felt that Nomura was so close to the Americans that he might leak the plan.

On the night of 6 December, we worked long in our office, but there was no great excitement. Through our intelligence, we had been watching the Japanese warships and transports that were headed for the Isthmus of Kra. I remember leaving the office that Saturday night between seven and eight o'clock, with Wellborn and Captain John McCrea. The latter was then a special assistant to Stark. As we left the office, one of us said, "Well, the British are sure going to catch it tomorrow at Singapore." We didn't have the slightest suspicion that there was any threat to Pearl Harbor. Kemp

Tolley, who's a good friend of mine, is absolutely convinced that Roosevelt planned this whole thing and that he had information he didn't share with us.* But I'm certain that the President was caught just as unaware as the rest of us.

On Sunday morning, Admiral Stark went to his office, but he let Wellborn and me have the day off. I was flooring the attic in my house in Arlington when my daughter called from downstairs and said, "Daddy, the radio says the Japanese have bombed Pearl Harbor."

"Oh," I said, "don't be ridiculous."

"No, really, Daddy, come on down here." So I went and listened to this thing, put on my uniform, and rushed to the Navy Department. I got there just as Charlie Wellborn did, and then all the natives began to gather.

Like most of the people in Washington, Admiral Stark was stunned by the attack. I think the man who was least stunned was Rear Admiral Ben Moreell, Chief of the Bureau of Yards and Docks. The admirals were all sitting around in Stark's office when Moreell walked in. "Bouncy" is the only word I can use to describe him. He was always on his toes and full of pep and energy. He said, "Well, gentlemen, I've lined up every heavy contractor in the United States ready to go to Pearl Harbor to start raising those ships." This was within twenty-four hours of our getting the word about the damage that had been done out there. Moreell was right on the ball. Practically everybody else was sitting around in a state of shock.

Secretary of the Navy Frank Knox went out to Pearl Harbor and then came back to give us the first real details of what had happened. Of course, it was some days before we had more than fragmentary accounts. People weren't sure for a while what had happened. Knox really got involved after Pearl Harbor. I thought he was tremendously interested in public relations, but in those days the Secretary of the Navy did pretty much what he was told to do. Frankly, the secretary did pretty much what the admirals advised him to do. The first real secretary who took charge was James V. Forrestal; he started telling the admirals what to do.

Admiral Ernest J. King came to Washington shortly after that, and he had a lot of consultation with Roosevelt and Knox. It was also about that time that Admiral Kimmel began to develop a lot of bitterness toward Admiral Stark, because he felt that Stark had let him down. Stark actually had been giving Kimmel as much information as he had himself, which really wasn't very much. Stark, I

*See article by Rear Admiral Tolley on page 122. Editor.

think, was fearful of crying "wolf" too much. It was easy to sit in Washington and say "Look out for this" and "Look out for that." He felt that if he did that too much, it would dull the edge of a real warning.

It was apparent to Stark that some of the blame for the Pearl Harbor disaster would rub off on him. After all, he was the head of the Navy, and the head of the Navy has to be responsible, just as Kimmel was solely responsible at Pearl Harbor. Yet I'd been in Kimmel's squadron when he was a destroyer squadron commander in the late 1920s, and there was never a man in the Navy who worked harder to prepare a Navy for war than Kimmel. He put us through things that no other squadron commander had ever done, and it kept us on our toes. Kimmel was a man who really, I think, would have been a great wartime commander and had already done a great deal to get his fleet ready with what he had. He was just caught in a vise. He was the fall guy on the scene. It was just criminal, and, of course, he was bitter the rest of his life. I don't blame him, because all his life he had done more than his contemporaries to get the fleet ready—every unit he'd ever had.

It wasn't long after the new year when I left the CNO's office. Admiral Stark was told he was going to London as Commander U.S. Naval Forces in Europe. He asked me to go with him, and I said, "Admiral, I'm sorry, but if you don't mind, I've got to go to sea. I want to go to sea, and I'm told I can get command of a new destroyer."

"Well," he said, "I don't blame you. I understand how you feel, but I just feel that you're deserting me, and I need you."

I said, "Admiral, I've been with you five straight years—five consecutive years. I've got to get out in this war."

And so we left on that note, a tearful farewell. I know he felt I was running out on him after he'd been disgraced by Pearl Harbor, but I had to think about my career too. As it turned out, he did a fine job in London and I had some times in the South Pacific when I wished I had gone to London with him.

William Renwick Smedberg III (1902–   ) was graduated from the Naval Academy in 1926 and had postgraduate education in communications. He served in the *New Mexico, Mullany, Northampton,* and on the staffs of Commander Cruiser Division 3 and Cruisers Battle Force. From 1939 to 1942, he was aide to the CNO. During World War II, he commanded the destroyers *Lansdowne* and *Hudson* in the Pacific, was chief of staff of Task Force 39 (cruisers and destroyers), and combat intelligence officer for CominCh. After the war, he was naval aide to Secretary of the Navy James V. Forrestal, Commander Destroyer Squadron 3, a Naval Academy department head, and commanding officer of the *Iowa.* Later, he was DesLant chief of staff, directed the CNO's Politico-Military Policy Division, and was Superintendent of the Naval Academy, Commander Cruiser-Destroyer Force Pacific Fleet, Commander Second Fleet, and Chief of Naval Personnel. He retired in 1964 and now lives in Crystal River, Florida. (Courtesy of Vice Admiral William R. Smedberg III, U.S. Navy [Retired].)

The Fog of War

By Vice Admiral Charles Wellborn, Jr., U.S. Navy (Retired)

Right after the attack, there was something called the Roberts Commission appointed by President Roosevelt to investigate. I think it was pretty accurate in its assessment of the situation that existed at the time. There was a general belief on the part of practically everybody that the Japanese were on the point of doing something, and everybody thought the target might be the Philippines or the Malay Peninsula, with the latter more likely. There may have been a few voices in the wilderness who were saying "Pearl Harbor," but they weren't very loud voices, and nobody really thought it could happen there. I mean, nobody of real consequence. When it did happen, I think most of the military people were just as surprised as the general citizenry. I think that came out quite well in both the Roberts Commission report and in Roberta Wohlstetter's book *Pearl Harbor: Warning and Decision.*

The commission was composed of Supreme Court Justice Owen J. Roberts, Admiral William H. Standley and Admiral Joseph M. Reeves, Major General Frank McCoy, and Brigadier General Joseph T. McNarney. In my book, all five were very able people. I think they came up with a good report. Admiral Standley and a number of other people have held the view that the commission's report was a whitewash. I don't agree with them. I saw all the messages that went out from both the War Department and the Navy Department. They were sent to Admiral Thomas C. Hart of the Asiatic Fleet and Admiral Husband E. Kimmel in Pearl Harbor. I think it's worthy of note that Admiral Hart very accurately interpreted the intent of all those messages, and I think he did exactly what was expected of him. On the other hand, at Pearl Harbor the intent seemed to have been missed. This was essentially what the Roberts Commission said—that Washington did give adequate information and warning to the commanders in the field and that the responsibility lay with those commanders. This is my view also. Of course, I'm a little biased, because I was sitting there in Washington.

To have sent Admiral Kimmel information copies of all we had would have cluttered his communication system and added to what Roberta Wohlstetter calls "the background of noise." It really wouldn't have materially improved the Pacific Fleet intelligence position. Instead, I think the problem lay in the attitude of the people in Pearl Harbor who assumed that when the war started, it surely wouldn't be in Hawaii or on the Pacific Coast of the United States. As a result, they failed to recognize the warnings that were sent. One in late November started off, "This dispatch is to be considered a war warning." How that could be interpreted as just kind of a mild, innocuous thing, I don't know. To me that says, "This is it; be ready any time." I do think Admiral Kimmel and his staff were given adequate information, although this, of course, was the heart of that great controversy—did Washington keep the commander in chief adequately informed?

As for issuing a warning at the last minute, there was telephone communication, but it was wholly insecure. With voice communication, there was no scrambling or coding in any way. Although I very definitely recall Admiral Harold R. Stark, the Chief of Naval Operations, talking in the clear to Rear Admiral Claude C. Bloch, Commandant of the Fourteenth Naval District, after the attack occurred, the telephone was not used when security was involved. There was rapid secure radio telegraphic communication. Both the Army and the Navy had their circuits, and they were pretty fast, although not like voice communication.

I was not actually in the office the morning of 7 December. I arrived about two o'clock in the afternoon after hearing about the attack while at my home in Chevy Chase. As soon as I heard, I jumped in the car and went on down. It took perhaps half an hour. During that afternoon, Admiral Stark was the only one who talked directly to people in Hawaii. There was a continuing flow of radio messages coming in, and getting things all sorted out and presented in a way that gave us a real picture of what was happening was pretty much of an undertaking. In my memory, that afternoon stands out as the best example I've ever experienced of the fog of war. There were various rumors, some of which made the dispatches that came in to Washington, as to what was happening. There was one, for instance, of a landing on the west coast of Oahu by hostile forces. I recall having to run that one down and find out that it wasn't the case. Then sorting out all of the welter of messages and information that the admiral had been able to get by telephone and putting together an accurate picture of what really had happened was very difficult. I think this is the way it usually is in war, particularly in a surprise situation. You never have adequate information either on the enemy forces or your own forces and what's happened to them.

I think Admiral Stark was as much surprised that it happened at Pearl Harbor as were all the rest of us. I think it required his collecting his thoughts and adjusting them to this new situation. His thinking up to that point had been that the most important thing to do was to proceed with getting ourselves in a better state of readiness and that any actual assault very probably was going to be in the Southeast Asia area. He had assumed that even after hostilities commenced, we still would be proceeding in a way not too different from the one that we had been using up to that time. Here, all at once, the situation was radically changed, and it called for a lot of very quick reassessment. I think he recognized the magnitude of this problem right away.

My recollection of Secretary of the Navy Frank Knox that day was that he was superbly calm and collected; a lot of the rest of us seemed to be running around in circles yelling and shouting—although, of course, this is an exaggeration. Secretary Knox seemed to be able to view things with considerable detachment and to take quite a philosophical and practical approach to it all. I had great admiration for him in the days following the attack. He seemed not to be panicked at all and proceeding along good

sound lines. During this period, I think he was probably the instrumental force in pushing for the replacement of Admiral Kimmel by Vice Admiral William S. Pye. With his rather calm overall view of the situation, Knox seemed to feel that, for a number of reasons, the commander in chief out in Hawaii should be replaced. There had been a disaster, and whether a change was required from a strictly professional military point of view, it was necessary from the point of view of public confidence, if nothing else.

I think in due course, after a chance to reflect on things a little bit, Mr. Knox probably felt that the people in Pearl Harbor were the ones who should bear the greatest responsibility for this disaster. But at the time, I think the prime consideration was the need for a new boss in a situation of that sort. There may have also been some feeling that Admiral Kimmel and his staff were overwhelmed by this catastrophe. Before it happened, they might have been highly competent and thoroughly capable of doing the job, but after it happened, there was sufficient psychological effect to render them something less than completely effective in the job at that time.

There was also some thought about the need for a change in Washington. Let me backtrack a little to explain the change. Shortly before Admiral Stark became Chief of Naval Operations in 1939, Ernest

In the early months of the war, Secretary of the Navy Frank Knox (left) saw the need for a more aggressive Chief of Naval Operations than Admiral Stark was. Thus, he tapped Admiral Ernest J. King (center), shown here being sworn in as CNO in March 1942 by Rear Admiral Walter B. Woodson, the Judge Advocate General. (U.S. Navy: Naval Institute Collection.)

J. King, who was a vice admiral while serving as Commander Aircraft Battle Force, had reverted to his permanent rank of rear admiral. He was then assigned to the General Board, which at that time was regarded pretty generally as a graveyard for senior admirals. It was a planning and advisory board which would allow a senior rear admiral to serve out his declining years with a reasonable degree of dignity, then gracefully retire when he reached the statutory retirement age of sixty-four. Admiral Stark felt that Admiral King's capabilities were such that he should not be relegated to the shelf, and he was alert to openings in various commands in which King's great capabilities might be successfully used.

An ideal opening came with the upgrading of our forces in the Atlantic. Admiral King was first ordered as Commander Patrol Force and soon afterward as Commander in Chief Atlantic Fleet. This got Admiral King back into the flow of those who were exercising important high commands. He, of course, did an outstanding job of making the Atlantic Fleet a real fighting force rather than a group of ships just visiting and showing the flag. And I think his talents were seen pretty clearly during this period by both the Secretary of the Navy and the President. Because of the armed neutrality aimed at the Germans, it was quite an active period in the Atlantic, and Admiral King's aggressive, activist characteristics were quite apparent. Following the Pearl Harbor disaster, it seemed to me that the Secretary of the Navy, who was something of an activist himself, felt that what was required to direct the operation of the Navy was an activist, and the characteristics that Admiral Stark had may not have completely fitted into this picture.

Admiral Stark, I think, was a much more considerate individual than Admiral King. He had shown a great deal of patience and a great deal of—maybe empathy is the word—in trying to understand what congressional views might be and to convince the members of Congress that they should go along with his thoughts on building up the Navy and readiness for a possible war. I think, after the Pearl Harbor attack, the Secretary of the Navy felt that all military people now had to do was to name what they wanted and Congress would give it to them, so that what we needed was the Admiral King type. There was a complete change in the whole atmosphere as a result of Pearl Harbor.

At first, Admiral King came in as just CominCh, an abbreviation which he personally selected. Previously, the Commander in Chief of the U.S. Fleet had been known as CinCUS, and Admiral King thought that this was an utterly inappropriate name. It could have been used propaganda-wise, because it was pronounced "Sink us."

Originally, Admiral King's responsibilities were to be simply the direction of the operations of the Navy, and the logistic side was left with the Chief of Naval Operations. Admiral Stark did, in fact, remain for some months as CNO after Admiral King's arrival and was purely a logistician. Ironically, during the last few months of his tenure as Chief of Naval Operations, Admiral Stark had nothing to do with operations.

Charles Wellborn, Jr. (1901–   ) was graduated in the Naval Academy class of 1921 and subsequently received postgraduate education in ordnance engineering. He served in the *New Mexico*, *Gilmer*, *Nevada*, and in the Bureau of Ordnance. After commanding the destroyer *Perry*, he served in the *Concord* and on the staff of Commander Cruisers Battle Force. He was aide to the CNO, then commanded Destroyer Division 19 and Destroyer Squadron 8. He served in the Fifth Amphibious Force and the Bureau of Personnel before commanding the battleship *Iowa*. As a flag officer, he was chief of staff to Commander Fifth Fleet, on the staff of CinCPacFlt, Deputy Chief of Naval Operations for Administration, Commander Cruiser Division 4, Commander Destroyer Force Atlantic Fleet, Commander Second Fleet, Commandant of the Armed Forces Staff College, and Commander Eastern Sea Frontier. He retired from active duty in 1963 and now lives in Washington, D.C. (National Archives: 80–G–386426.)

War Plans Under My Mattress

By Vice Admiral John L. McCrea, U.S. Navy (Retired)

One of the best jobs a commander could hold in the prewar Navy was executive officer of the fleet flagship *Pennsylvania*, and I was fortunate enough to have that job. In late 1939, when I had been there about a year, I received a letter from Captain Trood Bidwell, the senior detail officer in the Bureau of Navigation in Washington. We had been shipmates in the old armored cruiser *Rochester* and remained good friends. In his letter, Bidwell wrote, "I know you'd like to have a command. I think you have a good chance of being selected as captain, and I'm going to have to find six or seven young captains and send them to the cruisers. Would you like a command like that? The only catch is that I'd like you to stay at sea for the time being and await the selections."

The following year, about midsummer, I got another letter. It said that the plans had changed; I would be going to the office of Chief of Naval Operations Harold R. Stark instead. I did want that cruiser, but this looked all right too. Bidwell asked me to stop by and see him before I reported to the CNO—this in September 1940. He started off the conversation by saying, "I think I should tell you, John, that Stark doesn't want you. He has nothing against you, but he doesn't know you. You've never served with him, and he just would prefer to have somebody he knows." While I was digesting that, Bidwell added, "I told him that I'd go on the line that you two would get along well, and that's what you're going to do." As it turned out, Bidwell was right.

I got set up with a big office—about four times as large as I needed—in the old Main Navy building and started to work on a paper originated by the General Board. Its title was "Are We Ready?" and the reference, of course, was to the war that many of us expected to be involved in. The General Board had done the paper for the Secretary of the Navy, who in turn sent it to the CNO for implementation. Admiral Stark put me in charge of the project, and in the course of it, I went around to the various divisions within the Navy—the Bureau of Ordnance, the Bureau of Engineering, and so forth. I asked questions concerning items in "Are We Ready?" and incorporated what I learned into my report. I had been at it for a few weeks when Captain

Richmond Kelly Turner reported to the Office of the Chief of Naval Operations as director of the War Plans Division and took an office right around the corner from me.

One day, shortly after Turner's arrival, he came charging through the door that led from his office to mine and said, "The Orange [Japan] war plan is in a hell of a shape, and I've got to get out a new one right away. Now I'm locking the door to my office. The only way anybody can get at me is through your office. If anybody comes in looking for me, you ask, 'Did he send for you? If not, you can see him after five o'clock tonight.'" Even though he was busy, I guess he needed someone to talk to. So he came into my office quite often to chat, and that's how I came to know Kelly Turner. I'd never laid eyes on him before this. I had heard that he was a tough guy to shave—and he was too. But we got along splendidly, and I liked his brain. He drank too much, but I didn't contribute to that. I did like the way he did things; he was a "no-fooling" guy.

Finally, Turner completed the new war plan, and one day he said to me, "You are to take these war plans out to the Pacific and the Orient." That caught me by surprise, so I said, "Captain Turner, I'm working for Admiral Stark. I just left the Pacific about three months ago. Sending me back out there for this thing, I don't know what you'd have in mind. I know nothing about war plans, and you've got a stable full of smart guys around here who are supposed to know all about them. Why don't you send one of these fellows?"

"I want you to go," he said. "You won't have to know an awful lot, because in two weeks I can fix you right up so that you can answer any questions." He meant questions from the fleet commanders who would be called upon to implement the plans if war came. I didn't rush right out to accept the assignment, because I still hadn't finished my report on the General Board paper. I just sat there and kept on working. In about an hour, Admiral Stark sent for me and said, "Turner wants you to be officer messenger and go to the Pacific and to the Orient and take out the changes in the war plans."

"What about 'Are We Ready?'?" I asked.

"Well, from the papers that have been flying by

In the years before World War II, Pan American Airways received a good deal more in payment for carrying mail than for carrying passengers. Consequently, in late 1940, when Captain McCrea was ordered to take new war plans to U.S. commanders in the Pacific, he needed special pull to get aboard a Clipper to carry him from Alameda, California, to Pearl Harbor. The recounting of his long trip illustrates the vagaries of transoceanic air travel forty years ago. (Clyde H. Sunderland, Photo, Oakland, California.)

here, you've probably taken the biggest chunk out of that. So right now, I'm inclined to go along with Turner. He has some particular reason. He just wants you to go, that's all." I wound up going.

I still have my notes from the trip, and the more time passes, the more amazing my itinerary looks to me. It illustrates particularly how far we have come since then in air travel; flight was filled with a good many vagaries and uncertainties in the winter of 1940–1941. I set out from Washington on 13 December and was grounded that night in Kansas City. The following morning—together with other "air" passengers—I took a train to Albuquerque, New Mexico. There I picked up a plane bound for Los Angeles, where I chartered a single-engine plane to San Pedro. And from there I took a shore boat to get me to the Pan American float in San Pedro Harbor. Thus, I managed to catch the Clipper flight leaving for Hawaii on 15 December, and even at that, the Clipper had to be delayed about fifteen minutes until I got there. I needn't have bothered. The plane completed about one-half the distance to Pearl Harbor before being forced to turn back by adverse weather. San Diego and San Pedro were fogbound, so we landed at San Francisco after about twenty-two and one-half hours in the air. Not surprisingly, we didn't have much fuel left by the time we touched down.

Bad weather kept me grounded in San Francisco for another four days. I stayed at the St. Francis Hotel and lived with those war plans twenty-four

hours a day. I couldn't put them in the Twelfth Naval District's safe, because it had a time lock, and Pan American told me I had to be ready to go on four hours' notice as soon as the weather cleared. At night, I put the war plans under my mattress. I took them in the bathroom with me when I went to shave in the morning. I took them to the movies one night and sat with them in my lap.

The morning of the fifth day in San Francisco, I was called by Pan American with the news that the Clipper was leaving early that afternoon for Pearl Harbor via San Pedro. The airline regretted that it could not take me, because the U.S. mail contract with Pan Am gave priority to mail. All the tables, bunks, and excess gear were being removed from the plane, but it still wouldn't be able to accommodate all the mail on hand. "So sorry," the caller told me, "but don't worry. Pan Am is picking up the tab at the St. Francis Hotel."

"Well, my friend," I answered, "don't count me out just yet. I have important documents which must be delivered earliest. You will hear from me later."

I put in a long-distance call to Admiral Stark in Washington and told him the story. Quick as a flash came his reply, "I shall call the Postmaster General immediately and ask that he order removal of enough mail so you can get to Pearl."

"While you are at it, Admiral, may I suggest that enough mail be removed to make room for Commander Vincent Murphy [war plans officer on the staff of Admiral James O. Richardson, Commander in Chief U.S. Fleet], who is in Long Beach and urgently wants to get to Pearl?"

Within minutes after that, Pan American called back to say that the Postmaster General had ordered the removal of mail in sufficient quantity to accommodate two adult males. About 1:00 p.m., the Clipper left San Francisco and went to San Pedro to pick up Vince Murphy and some more westbound mail.

Every vestige of furniture had been removed, but after we were airborne Pan Am came up with a good stout drink to help us weather the discomfort. We were given a satisfying supper, and with the help of the plane's steward, Vince and I moved mail bags about in order to get the proper mattress effect. Sleeping fully dressed on mailbags is not bad if the drink is stout enough—and it was. We made Pearl about eight o'clock the following morning.

In Hawaii there was another six-day delay because no plane could get through from the West Coast to carry me onward. I was able to put the time to good use, though, because it gave Admiral Richardson and his staff a chance to pick my brains about the war plan changes. And I profited from the discussion also by getting myself in better shape to talk about the plans in the Orient. Once I got going again, there was a one-day holdup in Midway because of an aircraft engine failure. I finally reached Manila on 6 January. The whole journey could be made in a day or two now; it took me more than three weeks.

While in the Philippines, I had thorough and most profitable discussions with the Commander in Chief Asiatic Fleet, Admiral Thomas C. Hart, in his flagship, the heavy cruiser *Houston*. And, because General Douglas MacArthur had been graduated from the Military Academy the same year, 1903, that Admiral Stark was graduated from the Naval Academy, a call on the general was a must. He gave me his views on the war to date, and I see in my notes that Admiral Hart described General MacArthur as being positive in his views and knowing a lot. At the same time, the admiral cautioned, MacArthur "knows many things that are not so." Admiral Hart stated that he had a "shrewd guess" that if it weren't for the salary, General MacArthur would "duck out, because he doesn't appear to be too happy in the job."

Another individual with whom I talked was Lieutenant Commander Redfield "Rosie" Mason, Hart's intelligence officer, who was fluent in the Japanese language. He gave me a rundown on a number of Japanese flag officers, and there was one capsule portrait I found myself turning back to several

months later, after the Pearl Harbor attack. This is how Mason described Admiral Isoroku Yamamoto, Commander in Chief of the Combined Fleet:

> Energetic. Highly able. Bold in contrast to most who are inclined to be cautious. Decisive. He has American viewpoint. Formerly Naval Attaché in Washington. London Arms Conference delegate. Well versed in international affairs. A wounded veteran, having lost two fingers at Tsushima. Highly thought of by rank and file in ORANGE Navy. Personally *likes* Americans. Plays excellent bridge and poker. Alert in every way. Very air minded.

I was still with Admiral Hart on board the *Houston* when a dispatch came in from Washington, saying that Rear Admiral Husband E. Kimmel was under orders to relieve Admiral Richardson. And then, of all things, I got a dispatch from Admiral

Admiral Thomas C. Hart, as Commander in Chief Asiatic Fleet, warned the CNO's emissary, Captain McCrea, that General Douglas MacArthur "knows many things that are not so." (Naval Historical Center: NH 83511.)

Stark, telling me to contact Admiral Kimmel on my way back to the United States. I'll never forget Admiral Hart's reaction—he was a great one! He pulled his neck down inside his high white collar and said, "God, if Stark didn't think you had enough sense to do something like that, he never should have let you come out here in the first place." I just laughed, because he was right; certainly, I would have gone anyway.

I arrived at Pearl Harbor on 22 January 1941, two days after leaving Manila on a 3:00 a.m. flight. When I met with Admiral Richardson, I didn't get any impression from him that he was bitter over his sudden relief. And I think I was in a good position to gauge his mood, because it hadn't been all that long before when I was executive officer of his flagship. I had gotten to know and like him greatly during my service in the *Pennsylvania*.

While I was there, I talked to both Admiral Richardson and Admiral Kimmel about the war plan I had delivered. Rainbow 3, as it was called, prescribed essentially defensive operations in the Pacific. This was in contrast to the standard "Orange" plan during the interwar years. That strategic concept had dictated a U.S. Pacific Fleet offensive toward the Japanese mandated islands. Now Germany was to be considered the primary threat. It was in light of this new role that Admiral Richardson remarked that the antiaircraft defenses of Pearl Harbor left much to be desired; Kimmel quickly agreed when Richardson said of the defenses, "They are, in my judgment, wholly and completely inadequate." Then Richardson continued, "The Army must realize that the protection of this base is their paramount consideration of the Pacific. The principal thing that is needed here now is: (1) increased

The *Pennsylvania*, flagship of the U.S. fleet, was the site of Captain McCrea's meetings with the outgoing CinCUS, Admiral James O. Richardson, and his successor, Admiral Husband E. Kimmel. McCrea was executive officer of the *Pennsylvania* before his tour of duty in Washington. (U.S. Navy: Naval Institute Collection.)

Army land plane strength; (2) increased antiaircraft guns up to 5-inch and 37-mm.; (3) a most liberal supply of ammunition for target practice and action."

Admiral Kimmel added his view that consideration should be given to establishing a balloon barrage in and near Pearl Harbor but that he didn't think effort in that direction should detract from the supplying of badly needed additional planes. Richardson didn't completely concur, saying that he didn't think a balloon barrage would be all that much assistance and might even be an annoyance to U.S. forces. But Kimmel persisted, and he also suggested that the Navy should consider providing torpedo nets for ships in Pearl Harbor. He remarked that the technical difficulties might be "almost insurmountable." When the Japanese torpedoes struck our battleships eleven months later, I'm sure he wished that protective nets had been in place.

Admiral Kimmel was due to take command of the fleet on 1 February, so we were within a week of the change of command during my stay in Hawaii. He and his staff had been holding discussions with Richardson's people, and I was there at a good time to assess Kimmel's concerns and the problems he expected to face. We talked over these things while walking up and down the deck of Admiral Kimmel's flagship. It's customary, of course, for a junior to walk on the left side of a senior, so that's the way I fell in with Admiral Kimmel for our first walk. But he pushed me over to his right, saying, "Come on and get on the other side here, because the left is my bad ear."

The new fleet commander in chief knew that I was to report back to the CNO and could thus serve as a pipeline for expressing his thoughts to Admiral Stark. In looking back at my notes, I see that I quoted a list which Admiral Kimmel asked me to head "Things I am thinking about." They included such items as the need for instantaneous communications between Army and Navy airfields; concern that personnel and material not be worn out by alert watches; provision for prompt detection of enemy planes; command arrangements for local air defenses; satisfactory aircraft recognition signals and training; Army practice at using Navy airfields and vice versa.

Admiral Kimmel told me to tell Admiral Stark: "I am either going to be good friends with the Army and get things done, or I am going to have a hell of a fight with them. My preliminary conversations with [Lieutenant] General [Charles D.] Herron [top Army Commander in Hawaii] and his air man indicate that we are going to be good friends but we haven't yet got down to cases. I am perfectly willing

Rear Admiral Husband E. Kimmel was Commander Cruisers Battle Force when President Franklin D. Roosevelt appointed him in January 1941 to command of the U.S. Pacific Fleet. In briefing Captain McCrea, he voiced his concern over the deficiency in fleet defenses at Pearl Harbor. The Japanese attack proved that his concerns were well founded. (National Archives: 208-PU-108 FF-1.)

to make concessions to get the answer and I'm not going to get too much obsessed with any one thing. However, the defenses against aircraft for Pearl Harbor *must be improved*."

I had encountered Admiral Kimmel off and on since World War I, and I had a high regard for him. In 1924, for example, I fell in with him out in the Philippines. We played golf together often, and he was a delightful companion. Following a round of golf one day, we walked across the road from the Intro Muros course to the Army-Navy Club and had a beer. While we were chatting, he told me that he had gone out there, where he was commanding a destroyer division, without his family. Even though it meant being separated from his wife and children, he thought his boys needed their mother because they were still in school. He also said he wanted to get firsthand impressions of the Far East, because he expected that the United States would eventually be involved in a war in that area. His experiences wound up being for nought, because circumstances forced him to spend World War II on the sidelines. Admiral Kimmel was a fine officer. He deserved a better fate than being an unsuccessful commander. No one worked harder at being a *good* officer.

On 28 January 1941, four days before Admiral Kimmel took over, I flew back to San Francisco and then on to Washington. That flight worked out better than the westbound leg, although it was grounded for part of a day and a night in Cheyenne, Wyoming. I was back at work on 31 January and prepared to write a formal report from the notes I had scratched out from time to time during my long journey. But before I could do that, Admiral Stark came by my desk, saw my notebook, and took it home with him. He liked what he saw and told me the next morning to get the notes typed up in just

Up to the time of Captain McCrea's trip to the Pacific, Admiral Stark's two principal aides were Charles Wellborn (left) and William Smedberg (right), shown here in the CNO's office. Stark asked McCrea to make the group a trio, which McCrea was reluctant to do, explaining, "I didn't want to muscle in on them. I was senior to both of them, but that wasn't my fault." (Courtesy of Vice Admiral Charles Wellborn, Jr., USN, Ret.)

the form they were in. Certainly they make for interesting reading with the advantage of hindsight.

The results of my trip must have made an impression on the CNO, because a couple of weeks after that, he arranged for me to move into his front office. I was reluctant to do so, because he already had two aides, Commander Charlie Wellborn and Lieutenant Commander William Smedberg. I didn't want them to think I was trying to muscle in on them. I was senior to both of them, but that wasn't my fault. So I asked Admiral Stark to make it clear that the impetus for the move came from him and not me. This he did. He carved out an office for me, and then he said, "I suppose you have a secretary." I told him I did and that I wanted to bring her with me, to which he replied, "I'm pretty particular about the secretaries we have around here."

"Well, Admiral," I said, "I don't know just how particular you are, but I can assure you that the gal I'd like to bring up here is attractive and capable in all respects." I did bring her with me, and the funny part of it was that in almost no time I had to work hard to get anything out of her for myself, because Admiral Stark had appropriated her. Not that it mattered all that much, though, because he had appropriated me too. From then on, I wrote drafts of a good many of the CNO's letters for him. They were his letters, of course, but I collected the information required and gave him a first version before he put in his contributions. Quite a few of them were to Admirals Hart and Kimmel, and I was in good position to answer questions raised by them because I had been in contact with them so recently. The tone of Admiral Stark's correspondence with the two fleet commanders was businesslike and most friendly.

As the year 1941 progressed, it was hard to escape the feeling that war was coming ever closer. There were overt (but undeclared) hostilities in the Atlantic, including the sinking of one U.S. destroyer and the torpedoing of another. The pot was warming up in the Pacific as well, and it really seemed to come to a boil in late November. One day, Kelly Turner came in with a message he wanted to send to the Pacific commanders. It's quite famous by now, particularly because of the first sentence— "This dispatch is to be considered a war warning." Admiral Stark was startled. He sent for Rear Admiral Walton R. Sexton, chairman of the General Board, and for Rear Admiral Royal E. Ingersoll, Assistant Chief of Naval Operations. Charlie Wellborn and I were also present. I think Admiral Stark was taken aback by the suddenness and the directness of that opening sentence. When Admiral Stark hesitated about approving the message, Turner said, "But, Admiral, you think we're going to have a war, don't you?"

"Well, everything seems to point that way," replied Stark.

"That's the way I feel about it," said Turner, "and I think it's time we have a 'war warning' dispatch go out from the Navy Department. Nobody's told these fellows out there anything specific like that." There was general agreement that the dispatch should go as drafted. It did go that way, and when war came and people started investigating everything in the world, a good many people relied upon that dispatch.

Even though we got to the point of expecting the Japanese to attack in the Far East at any time, we still had our lives to lead until they did something. On the last weekend in November, I took my twelve-year-old daughter Meredith to Philadelphia to see the Army-Navy game. We came back, and on the Sunday morning of the following weekend, 7 December, we saw in the newspaper that the Translux theater in Washington was going to show twenty minutes of highlights from the football game we'd seen a week earlier. We went downtown that afternoon, and I stopped across the street from the Army-Navy Club to cash a check. While I was standing there, a fellow officer came down the steps and asked, "You going back to the Navy Department?"

"No, I'm going to the movies," I told him.

"Well, evidently, you haven't heard."

"No, what?"

"Pearl Harbor is under attack."

As soon as I heard that, I told my daughter to find her own way home, and I hurried to the office. Admiral Stark had been there most of the forenoon, and because I was downtown already, I was among the first to get there after the announcement of the attack. One of the things I was involved in that afternoon was the monitoring of Admiral Stark's telephone calls with Rear Admiral Claude C. Bloch out in Hawaii. Bloch was Commandant of the Fourteenth Naval District and was giving the CNO reports on the damage. I particularly remember Admiral Stark asking, "Claude, how about it?"

"Well, Betty, it's pretty bad. I don't know how secure this telephone is."

They were using the conversation scrambler, so Admiral Stark said, "Go ahead and tell me." And Bloch did. He told him all sorts of things, and then as he wound up, he said, "If any unauthorized person has heard the remarks I have just made to the Chief of Naval Operations, I beg of you not to repeat them in any way. I call on your patriotic duty as an American citizen."

Secretary of the Navy Frank Knox (left), who shared a furtive drink with Captain McCrea on 7 December 1941, congratulates McCrea upon taking command of the new battleship *Iowa* at her commissioning ceremony 22 February 1943. (Naval Historical Center: NH 70496.)

There were several of these calls, adding new information each time. One was around six o'clock that night, and I wrote a memorandum about it, as I had with the earlier ones. Admiral Stark looked at it and said to me, "You take this down to the Secretary [of the Navy, Frank Knox]. I think he's seen enough of me today."

So I went down to Knox's outer office and asked for him. Somebody said, "Well, he's in there. Go right on in." So I opened the door and went in— but nobody was in sight. I stood there for a moment or two, and then I finally coughed a few times to see if I could attract any attention. It worked, because the secretary's head then emerged from the little bathroom he had in his office.

"Oh," he said, "Captain, it's you."

"Yes, Mr. Secretary."

"This has been quite an afternoon," he told me.

"Yes, it has."

"You know, I'm just mixing myself a drink. Would you join me?"

"Well, Mr. Secretary, I've never taken a drink in the Navy Department, but being invited by the secretary, it's almost a command."

So, with that, the two of us stood there in the little bathroom and drank Mr. Knox's bourbon.

John Livingstone McCrea (1891–   ) was graduated
from the Naval Academy in 1915 and later received two
law degrees from George Washington University. He
served in the battleship *New York* during World War I
and had several tours as aide to Admiral Hugh Rodman.
He commanded the minesweeper *Bittern* and destroyer
Trever and was navigator of the heavy cruiser *Astoria* and
executive officer of the *Pennsylvania*. Between wars, he
had three tours in the office of the Navy Judge Advocate
General. After his OpNav duty, he was naval aide to President Franklin D. Roosevelt, first commanding officer of
the battleship *Iowa*, and Commander Cruiser Division 1.
After World War II, he served in the office of the CNO,
as Deputy CinCPac, in the office of the Secretary of Defense, and as Commandant First Naval District. He retired from active duty in 1953 and now lives in Chestnut
Hill, Massachusetts. (Naval Historical Center: NH 47941.)

Cutting the Red Tape

By Admiral James L. Holloway, Jr., U.S. Navy (Retired)

The car pools brought on by the energy crisis are nothing new. I can remember being on iron rations in 1941—one parking spot for each group of five officers. We all worked until six o'clock in those days. If anybody had to work past six, we left without him. That usually meant he walked home, which was often to Arlington, from the old Main Navy at Seventeenth and Constitution.

We weren't working Sundays yet, and that's why I was at home on the afternoon of 7 December. One of my Naval Academy classmates called me from his home and said he'd heard on the radio about the Japanese attack.

"Oh, bushwa. I don't believe it," I told him.

"Yea, it's true."

So, pretty soon after that, I got on down to the office where I was serving as head of the gunnery section in the Division of Fleet Training. Fleet Training was still part of the staff of the Chief of Naval Operations at that point, although it soon became the Readiness Division when Admiral Ernest J. King became CominCh. Captain "Ching" Lee was head of Fleet Training, and he wasn't fazed at all by the abrupt change from peace to war. As a matter of fact, it was just the thing he needed, because now it meant we could get on with the business at hand—providing the fleet more to fight with than it had been getting up to then.

Lee and Rear Admiral "Spike" Blandy, Chief of the Bureau of Ordnance, were alike in that regard, which helped enormously. The two were close friends, and they worked harmoniously together. They didn't worry about red tape and whether a particular item of business belonged on one side or the other of the dividing line between their two bailiwicks. Ammunition for .50-caliber machine guns is a good example. There may not have been more than half a million rounds in the whole Navy inventory at that moment! It was discomfiting to be starting a war with so little ammunition, especially when we had been giving part of our production to the British under Lend-Lease and would continue to do so. Lee made me the custodian for the .50-caliber ammo, and I had to dole it out in dribs and drabs because it was so damn scarce. Blandy made Lieutenant Commander Freddie Withington, with whom I served in the *West Virginia* in 1926, the liaison man for the Bureau of Ordnance, and things went smoothly. The bureau had the material, and I made the decisions on where it went.

Up to the time when we got actively involved in the war through the Japanese attack, many people still had a cautious approach about weapons development and production. But the attack really took the lid off things. There had been two major reactions—disbelief and shock. At first, people just couldn't believe that the Japanese would do such a thing. After they found out what a terrible blow we had taken, they were a little stunned. But there

The Navy Department at 17th and Constitution in Washington, D.C., was the Navy's headquarters throughout World War II. (National Archives: 80-G-47092.)

When the Navy needed antiaircraft training centers, Rear Admiral Ben Moreell worried less about the niceties of the law than about getting the job done. (Naval Historical Center: MCN-379-1.)

Captain Willis "Ching" Lee and Rear Admiral William "Spike" Blandy accomplished much by working together because neither was concerned with the dividing line between their responsibilities. (Photo of Lee by Vice Admiral Milton E. Miles, USN, Ret., courtesy of Mrs. M.E. Miles. Photo of Blandy, Naval Historical Center: NH 56198.)

was never any doubt in the minds of Navy people that we could come back and lick the Japanese. That kind of attitude was exemplified by Rear Admiral Ben Moreell, Chief of the Bureau of Yards and Docks. One of the things we needed to do was build antiaircraft training centers, because we knew that the light guns—20-mm. and 40-mm.—were going to be vitally important. Lee and Blandy had worked together on pushing for the guns and the Mark 14 directors to go with them; now, Moreell was in our corner for building the training centers. "Hell, I'll give you all the money you want," he said. "I don't give a goddamn what the law says." That was just the spirit we needed—do it now and worry about the paperwork later. He had G-U-T-S.

We were busy as bird-dogs in those weeks following the attack. It's hard to describe just how much the workload moved up. We stopped all routine computation of training and competitive exercises that Fleet Training had been responsible for, and we went into expediting production and perfecting the performance of weapons. Ching was a real genius on that, and he didn't hestitate to rely on the people who worked for him. And with good reason, because the commanders (which is what I was then) were really the hard-working reservoir of experience in the Navy. Usually a commander was at least eighteen years out of the Naval Academy, had been a department head in a battleship or cruiser, and had had a destroyer command. That's probably why two commanders and a fresh-caught captain were picked as the Navy Department duty officers. (You'd probably have vice admirals today.)

We stood a watch in three from six in the evening to six in the morning—four hours each. The other two besides myself were Captain "Chick" Glover and Commander Forrest Sherman, later Chief of Naval Operations. Those two were from the War Plans Division of OpNav. We were all well-seasoned officers who had authority to call up Admiral Harold Stark or the President if we needed to—and we did. One night, we got a report that there was a dirigible off New York. I put out an emergency on the whole East Coast and called Rear Admiral Royal E. Ingersoll, Assistant Chief of Naval Operations. As it turned out, it was one of our own blimps from Lakehurst, New Jersey. It had sort of lost altitude and was drifting around in the breeze, but it was better to be safe. Ingersoll backed me up on it. After what had happened at Pearl Harbor, we went to general quarters in case of doubt.

James Lemuel Holloway, Jr., (1898–   ), was graduated from the Naval Academy in 1918 (class of 1919) and served in the destroyer *Monaghan* in European waters. As a junior officer, he served in destroyers, battleships, at the Naval Academy, and as aide to Vice Admiral Harris Laning. He had two tours in Fleet Training and, during World War II, he commanded Destroyer Squadron 10, trained destroyer escort crews, served in the Bureau of Naval Personnel, and commanded the battleship *Iowa*. As a flag officer he devised the Holloway Plan for NROTC; was Superintendent of the Naval Academy; Commander Battleship-Cruiser Force Atlantic Fleet; Chief of Naval Personnel; and Commander in Chief Naval Forces Eastern Atlantic and Mediterranean. He retired from active duty in 1959 and now lives at Vinson Hall, McLean, Virginia. His son, Admiral James L. Holloway III, was Chief of Naval Operations from 1974 to 1978. (U.S. Navy: Naval Institute Collection.)

This Is a War We Could Lose

By Hanson W. Baldwin

About three weeks before the Pearl Harbor attack, General George C. Marshall gave an interview to about eight or ten Washington-based correspondents, and one or two other people, with the purpose of preparing them for the shock of war. He thought that war was coming, and in an oblique way he wanted to get the press ready for it. The interview was completely off the record and wasn't even reflected in background stories of the time. It wasn't for publication at all. Though I wasn't there, I heard about it from some of my friends, including Bob Sherrod of *Time*, who attended.

Much later—I think it was during the war or just afterward—I got transcripts of the notes from two of my friends who had attended, and the notes were nearly identical. I remember that they showed Marshall had made some egregious errors of judgment. He was talking about the defensibility of the Philippines. He was telling about the plans for getting large reinforcements to the Philippines, but he said they were already defended by the biggest concentration of B-24s anywhere in the world. And he said that if the Japanese attacked the Philippines, they'd lose a lot of ships. And, of course, we would hit the paper cities of Japan with B-24s and set them on fire.

It was pointed out to him by one of the correspondents there who knew more about the B-24s than he did that they didn't have the range to reach Japan from the Philippines and return to base. Marshall said they could fly above the altitude of any Japanese antiaircraft guns, and he added, rather naively, "Oh, well, they will continue on to Vladivostok in shuttle bombing." In fact, we had no such agreement with the Russians whatever and were scarcely even speaking to them at that time.

I remember this very vividly, because after the war was over I was writing a book called *Great Mistakes of the War*. In doing my research into the early phases, I wrote to Marshall to ask if these transcripts were accurate. In addition to the point about B-24s, he had also made other statements which were way off base when he talked about the merchant marine and various other things. It's a measure of the size of the man that he said that, to the best of his knowledge and belief, those transcripts were correct. It takes a rather large man to

admit his errors in the light of history four or five years later. It was a revealing admission, because it indicated that the prewar Marshall was not the up-to-date great strategic brain or technological thinker that people imagined he was. Neither were a good many Navy people, of course, but this press conference revealed a great over-appreciation of the effects of air power and had, I'm convinced, been sold to him by the Army Air Corps when he gave them their head.

When the attack itself came, it turned out to be the Japanese who had the better use of air power. On that Sunday, I was at my home in Chappaqua, in Westchester County, New York. I think I heard the news on the radio and was absolutely appalled. Then I headed to my office and tried to make heads and tails out of the thing for the next day's paper. Within three or four weeks, I wrote an article called "This Is a War We Could Lose," and it shook up a lot of Americans, because we had always regarded the Japanese as these curious little people who didn't know how to fly. There were a lot of other myths, as it turned out.

In the first week after the attack, the *Times* sent Foster Hailey to Hawaii as a correspondent. He sent

Soldiers guard the Munitions Building, home of the War Department, on the night of 7 December 1941. (United Press International [International News].)

When in the elevated arcade connecting the Navy Department and the Munitions Building (which are shown here from the rear), Correspondent Baldwin found himself in a quandary. He had no pass and, for a while, guards would not let him into either building. He was trapped in between. (National Archives: 80-G-187406.)

a message to the paper, roughly describing the damage that had occurred. The Navy objected greatly, because it said his story evaded censorship, as indeed it did. I don't think we printed the story; it was for the benefit of the office. After that, heavy censorship was put into effect, and nothing else got through.

That same week, I traveled to Washington and went to the Navy Department building to talk to Under Secretary James V. Forrestal and to everyone else I could. At the time, the Army's Munitions Building was right next to the Navy headquarters on Constitution Avenue. I remember going through a little arcade that ran from the Navy building into the Munitions Building. When I started into the War Department, a couple of Army policemen stopped me and asked for my pass. I said, "I haven't got any pass yet. I've just come in here."

So they said, "Well, you can't come in." So I shrugged and went back toward the Navy Department, where I found the doors guarded by a couple of Marines. They wouldn't let me in the Navy building. I was marooned in there until I could finally convince one or the other. It was one of those early war panic situations in which no one knew what was going on or what passes were required. It was funny in retrospect.

Things were in too much of a tailspin for me to find people to talk with in Washington. They were all frantic; nobody knew what was going on. They were all trying to pick up the pieces, and there was virtually no organization. Although I did get in to see Forrestal and some of the other civilians, they were so busy that I just didn't want to take too much of their time. There was a real sense of frantic worry, and this was reflected in the early January piece I did in which I said we could lose the war.

The thing I remember next most vividly is the

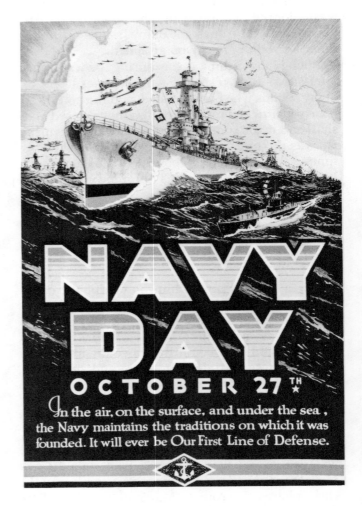

The overwhelming confidence that America exuded before the war is reflected in this poster created for Navy Day 1941, six weeks before the attack on Pearl Harbor. There are airplanes and battleships galore, including far more of the *North Carolina* class than were built. Curiously, though, there are no aircraft carriers, the ships that were preeminent in leading the Navy to victory in World War II. (Naval Historical Center: NH 77239.)

fall of the Philippines and the shocking fact that the Japanese took them without a single major Japanese ship being sunk. I think no Navy man before the war would have said that was possible. We had the greatest concentration of submarines in the world there, but they didn't do a thing. Despite General Marshall's optimistic estimates, our bombers didn't do a thing. The Philippines fell just about as had originally been thought long before the war and as some Navy people felt even after the war started. But it was not the official estimate; it was not the belief into which a lot of people had talked themselves.

Of course, the loss of Manila hurt even more because of the way it was done. General Douglas MacArthur didn't tell the Navy about his "open city" ploy until the last few minutes. As a result, a lot of Navy stores were left there which would have been useful. Instead, they went up in smoke. But even greater damage than that was done by the Japanese raid on Cavite, where the torpedo warhead storage was ignited. As it developed, that wasn't as much of a handicap as people thought, because the torpedoes didn't work anyway.

I think this was a shock. I reflected this shock, and it irritated some in the Navy. On the other hand, I had written just after Pearl Harbor that the job of defending Hawaii was primarily the Army's. A naval base, to be secure, had to be defensible, and attacks against it were supposed to be primarily the Army's job, which was the doctrine at the time. The Navy was not supposed to be defending its own bases, particularly overseas. Many Navy people were looking for a crutch at the time, especially those who were emotionally involved, and many of them were. I think most of them liked that particular article.

Some time after that, around late December or early January, I had the painful experience of interviewing the youngest son of Admiral Kimmel. This boy called me up, told me who he was, and said he'd like to see me. So he came up from Princeton, where he was a student. He started by asking, "Do you think my father is really as guilty as everybody says he is?"

I tried to be as kind and gentle as possible. I felt so sorry for this youngster. I explained again what I had said in my article, that the job of defending the bases was primarily the Army's, that I knew very little about the details of the attack or what went on before the attack. But I also said, "I think there's been a national state of mind that it can't happen here, and we reflected this." I couldn't offer him very much solace, but I did the best I could. The main thing I remember about it was that it was

a painful interview. But the boy's opening remark really stuck with me, "Do you think my father is really as guilty as everybody says he is?" That's an awful thing for a youngster to have to face.

Hanson Weightman Baldwin (1903-   ) was graduated from the Naval Academy in 1924 and served in the battleship *Texas* and destroyer *Breck* —on the East Coast, Caribbean, and in the European Squadron. He resigned his commission as a lieutenant (junior grade) in 1927, then worked for *The Sun* (Baltimore) as police reporter and general assignment reporter for a year. From 1929 until 1968, he was with *The New York Times*, first as a reporter, then as military and naval correspondent until 1942, finally as the newspaper's military editor. He wrote numerous reports and analyses from World War II battlefronts. He has been a frequent contributor to the *Proceedings* and other magazines and has written more than a dozen books, including *Men and Ships of Steel* (1935), *What the Citizen Should Know About the Navy* (1941), and *Sea Fights and Shipwrecks* (1955). Mr. Baldwin now lives in Roxbury, Connecticut. (Courtesy of Hanson W. Baldwin.)

The role of Franklin D. Roosevelt in connection with the surprise attack on Pearl Harbor is one of history's enduring controversies. Throughout the years 1940 and 1941, President Roosevelt was trying desperately to aid Great Britain in its fight against Nazi Germany. He traded fifty old destroyers, which were badly needed by the British for antisubmarine warfare, for bases in the Western Hemisphere. He managed to get the Lend-Lease bill through Congress so the United States could supply Britain with war materials even after Britain had exhausted its ability to pay for them. He instituted an increasingly aggressive Neutrality Patrol in the Atlantic to aid in getting convoys through to Britain. During these maneuvers, he had to be cautious—he had to avoid getting too far out in front of an isolationist American public. And he had to avoid or bypass the restrictions imposed by U.S. neutrality laws.

At the same time, he was faced in the Pacific by a bellicose Japan which had been carving out larger and larger chunks of territory in the Far East in establishing its "Greater East Asia Co-Prosperity Sphere." Manchuria had become a Japanese puppet state. Japan had been at war with China since 1937, and in 1941 sent its troops into Indochina. The policy of the United States was to restrain Japan's aggressive tendencies through the use of economic sanctions—embargoes on the shipment of scrap metal and petroleum and the freezing of Japanese assets in the United States. By denying Japan the raw materials it needed to continue waging war in Asia, President Roosevelt left Japan with two alternatives; it could either cease its imperialistic campaign or widen the war and seize the things it needed. Japan chose the latter course.

The President was an extremely astute politician and covered his tracks well. In the wake of the attack, he fired his top Army and Navy commanders in Hawaii, Lieutenant General Walter C. Short and Admiral Husband E. Kimmel, ending their military careers in disgrace. They became scapegoats, victims of a political move designed to tell the American people that the blame for the surprise attack belonged in Hawaii rather than Washington. In a very real sense, the economic sanctions did push Japan into war, but was the push really as deliberate and sinister as Roosevelt's critics suggest? Did he deliberately withhold information from Pearl Harbor in order to lessen the fleet's ability to defend itself?

The following two articles focus particularly on the President at the beginning of the war. The first, by Roosevelt's Secretary of Labor, suggests that FDR was as surprised as anyone else by the debacle in Hawaii. The second, by a naval officer who was half a world away at the time, argues that Roosevelt was willing to sacrifice him in order to bring about an overt act of war.

The President Faces War

By Frances Perkins

In November, it was obvious that things were getting tighter and tighter. Both Secretary of War Henry Stimson and Secretary of the Navy Frank Knox were exceedingly secretive. They said less in cabinet meetings and appeared to be needing longer conferences with the President, either together or separately, afterward. The President obviously worried about it a great deal.

On Friday, 5 December, we had a regular cabinet meeting. Secretary of State Cordell Hull said practically nothing except to talk about his complete gloom over the conversations he was having with the Japanese envoys then in Washington. He said:

> They don't mean business, Mr. President. I'm sure they don't mean to do anything. With every hour that passes, I become more convinced that they are not playing in the open, that what they say is equivocal and has two meanings to it. As soon as you proceed on what is the desirable meaning, they then switch to another meaning. I'm convinced that they don't intend to make any honorable agreement with us about anything, or to come to any understandings. I think this is useless and futile. They are the worst people I ever saw.

Secretary of State Cordell Hull. (National Archives: 111-SC-99912.)

In December 1941, President Franklin D. Roosevelt's cabinet expected the Japanese to strike but did not know where they would do it or whether the United States would become involved. (United Press International [Acme].)

Secretary of the Navy Frank Knox. (National Archives: 80-G-399009.)

Secretary of War Henry L. Stimson. (National Archives: 18-HP-79-2.)

He was more disgusted with Ambassador Kichisaburo Nomura than with Special Envoy Saburo Kurusu, I think because he had known Nomura before and Nomura was Western-educated. Hull thought Nomura was in a better position psychologically to really say what he meant and to trust Hull to speak the truth. He was very disgusted with the Japanese and used the strongest language I ever heard him use. That, of course, started the cabinet conversation at once into the area of the war that was then going on in the Pacific, with questions as to what the Japanese were going to do next.

Stimson, of course, contributed a good deal to the conversation. The rest of us didn't have much to say, except to express general consternation at the direction that things seemed to be taking. There was never a flicker of an idea expressed by anybody that the Japanese might at that time engage in war with the United States. Instead, the discussion involved how we thought the Japanese would go about attacking the British, who had done nothing to the Japanese, but did hold Singapore, which was presumed to be the key to Asiatic control.

Knox then piped up and said, "Well, you know, Mr. President, we know where the Japanese fleet is." The President looked up and looked around and then asked Knox to tell us. "Well," said Knox in his sputtering way, "we have very secret information that mustn't go outside this room that the Japanese fleet is out. They're out of harbor. They're out at sea."

The President interrupted Knox and kept him from going much further. Then he said, which Knox agreed to, "We haven't got anything like perfect information as to their apparent destination. The question is in the minds of the Navy and in my mind whether the fleet is going south. . . ."

Several people asked, "Singapore?"

He nodded, "Probably. That's the presumed objective if they go south."

Then Knox interrupted to say, "Every indication is that they are going south, Mr. President. That's the obvious direction."

Then Roosevelt said, "But it's not absolutely certain that they're not going north. You haven't got information with regard to direction."

"That's right, we haven't, but we must conclude that they are going south. It is so unlikely that they would go north."

Knox indicated that he thought the Japanese were up to something. The President then went around the table, asking us one by one what we thought the United States should do. Almost everybody said he thought we should go to the relief of the British if Singapore were attacked. It looked to me as though we were drifting to war anyhow, and we had to do that. I know it was the majority view of the cabinet. Although most of us knew that it was an area of action in which we could not give competent advice, we knew that the President was seeking our moral advice—based not on our knowledge of strategy or foreign affairs, but what we knew about life. He was testing through us what most decent people would be likely to feel and think in this situation. It was partly to get a political estimate of what the public reaction would be if we did go to the support of the British at Singapore or if we let the British perish there and didn't do anything. I could find no trace of opinion on the President's part. We all knew that he felt it would be a horrible thing for the British to be knocked to smithereens. The loss and damage of British prestige in Asia certainly evoked concepts not so much of the weakening of the British Empire as of the weakening of British civilization in the East.

That afternoon, nobody mentioned the Philippines as possible targets, but they had been discussed previously. We had talked about their exposed position if the Japanese should undertake to do anything. Stimson had said, "The plan for the Philippines is absolutely letter perfect. The Philippines are indefensible. We have always known it. Every Army officer in the United States above the rank of lieutenant is familiar with the plan for the handling of the Philippines in case of war." As Stimson had explained, the plan was to abandon them. I had thus learned with horror from the mouth of the Secretary of War that the U.S. Army had never expected to defend the islands. It had never crossed my mind that there had been a realistic acceptance for years of the idea that the Philippines would be left to the Japanese.

One thing I recall from that period is that there was a complete sense of confidence in the American Navy. Nobody asked where it was or how it was dispersed. It would have been extraordinarily bad form to have asked. We would have been promptly told that the admirals had charge of that, which we knew, anyhow. It was strictly the business of the Navy to take care of itself, and there was complete confidence that it could do so. One thing that kept coming through was that we must be extraordinarily careful that nothing we did was provocative. There must be no action on our part. The President turned to Mr. Hull and said: "We must strain every nerve to satisfy and keep on good relations with this group of Japanese negotiators. Don't let it deteriorate and break up if you can possibly help it. Let us make no move of ill will. Let us do nothing to precipitate a crisis."

Someone said hopefully, "Maybe the fleet is out for maneuvers."

I remember that Knox laughed with a sort of hollow, "how ridiculous" sort of a laugh.

As we went out of the room that Friday afternoon, I suppose everybody felt the same way, that we had a dreadful, dreadful situation. I remember going back to my office and just sitting down kind of limp, trying to face the music. It was a very shattering day, but there was still no sense of anything immediate. One would have supposed that within the next two weeks, they would find out where the Japanese fleet was. As a matter of fact, Knox more or less ended on that note, "We've got our sources of communication in pretty good shape, Mr. President, and we expect within the next week to get some indication of which way they are going." So we went off to our various activities planned for the weekend.

I went to New York. Saturday, I had an engagement, and Sunday afternoon, I was locked in my room at the Cosmopolitan Club, dictating a report to a stenographer. I had a bite of lunch sent up to the room where I was working, so it wasn't necessary to go downstairs all afternoon, except for a brief visit with a girl who came to see me. It got to be about six o'clock, and I had a dinner engagement. As I was getting ready to leave, my chauffeur, Bill Delaney, telephoned me from Washington, "Miss Perkins, this is Delaney. I wanted to know what time you want me to meet you."

I answered, "You don't need to meet me. I'll be down on the morning train. I'll take a cab."

"You'll be down tonight, won't you?"

"No, I'm coming on the midnight train."

"Miss Perkins, they say on the radio that the cabinet's been called in for tonight." He didn't say anything about war. He just said, "The radio says the cabinet's all been called back on account of the trouble." I didn't understand what he meant, and I never believed anything anybody heard on the radio. People like Delaney were always listening to the radio anyhow. I started to get dressed and wondered what in the world he meant. Then the telephone rang again; it was a White House operator, Louise Hachmeister, saying, "This is Hackie. The President wanted me to find you and tell you that there will be a cabinet meeting at eight o'clock tonight. He wants everybody there."

I asked, "Hackie, what's the trouble? Surely, I'll be there, but what's the matter? Why are we being called in tonight?"

She said, "The war, you know," then hung up. My stenographer and I hopped a taxicab and started to the airport. There was nothing on the

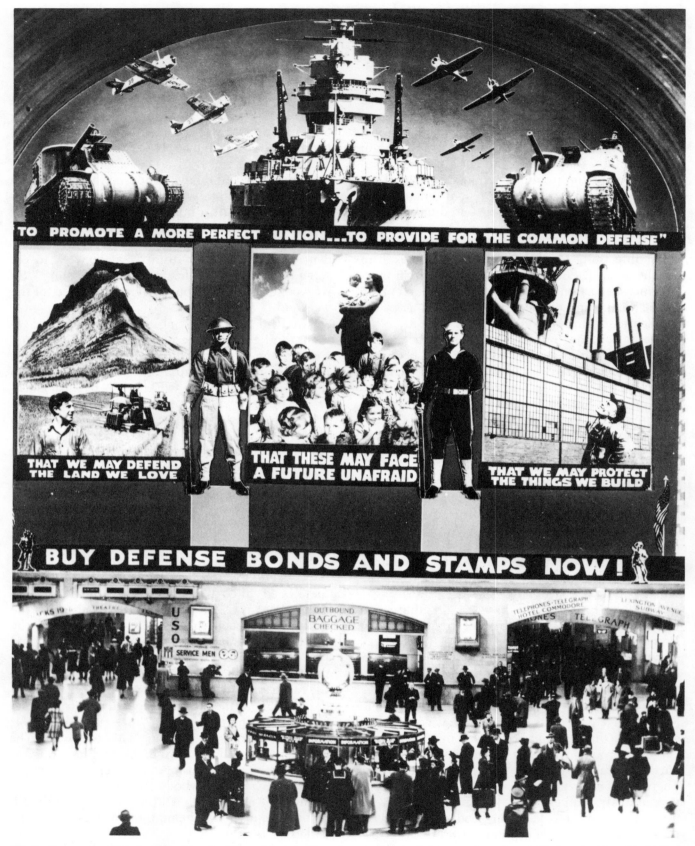

While Secretary of Labor Frances Perkins was spending the weekend of the attack on Pearl Harbor in New York City, a huge photo mural in Grand Central Station reflected the pride the United States felt in its armed forces. (United Press International.)

streets that would make you think anything had happened. There were no boys crying "EXTRA!" It was just an early Sunday evening in New York. By the time we got to the airport, I was slightly embarrassed. I didn't know what was going on, and I was afraid to ask anyone. There were lots of things in government that were not to be gossiped about. Asking might have started speculation and rumor.

In a few minutes, I was told to go to the plane. I saw a young man from Washington whom I knew. He said, "I suppose everybody will be rushing back."

I answered, "Oh yes," sounding as though I knew. I wasn't going to let on that I didn't know, nor was I going to spread false rumors.

The young man had apparently gotten a report from a radio broadcast and said, "I don't know exactly where, but I gather that there's been some shooting in the Pacific. That's all I know. When I heard that, I thought that I had better get back to Washington."

We talked about other things—the way you do when you're in a moment of intense dread. People do that in situations like that. They all know that something terrible has happened, or they think they know, but they talk deliberately about the state of the garden or whether the trees are a little bit more advanced than usual for this time of year—perfectly reasonable nothings in order to keep control of themselves.

It was a quick flight to Washington, and Delaney was there waiting. I got into the car along with Vice President Henry Wallace and Postmaster General Frank Walker, two of the people who had come down on the plane from New York. Delaney knew more than we did, so we all said, "What happened?"

He said, "It was on the radio that the Japs were shooting at us."

We said, "The Japs?"

"That the Japs were shooting at American ships. They've been dropping bombs on them."

"Where?"

He responded, "I couldn't quite make it out, but it sounded to me like it was Honolulu."

We said, "That's impossible."

So he said, "I don't know where it was, but that's the way it sounded to me."

We got a little from that. Honolulu was a new idea. We were still blinking going into the White House. We gathered in the President's study, that big oval room on the second floor over the south portico. The room was quite full with a lot of extra chairs. There were a number of maps up, but I had often seen maps hanging there, because the President was a map-minded person. When we came in,

he was sitting at his desk with his back to the wall. He was preoccupied and didn't notice us right away with so many people coming and going. He was looking at papers and had a cigarette in his mouth. Frank Knox was among those who were right close to him and showing him something or other.

Cordell Hull was there already and seated quietly in a Chippendale type armchair right up in front of the desk. He was the opposite type from Frank Knox. However angry he might be, Hull had a calm, almost cold, exterior. Knox was the physically active type. When he was angry or disturbed, he would buzz around and move his hands and head. His face would grow red, and the flushes would go up and down. He would talk a lot. His voice would tend to rise in tone. He was the exact opposite of this cold, pale, white-haired person sitting in the chair. Hull had his fingers together, as he so often did, and he looked as gloomy as he could possibly be.

I can't say who it was, but I think it was one of the Assistant Secretaries of the Navy, or one of the naval aides with Knox, who gave us the first coherent report we received. When I say "coherent," I mean that he began at the beginning and told us something. All he said was, "This morning a Japanese fleet launched airplanes and bombarded Pearl Harbor, which is a great naval installation in Hawaii, with a very serious loss of ships and Army and Navy personnel. We don't know how much has been lost. We don't know the circumstances. We just know that it happened."

That was very shocking. I hadn't heard the whole story before—not that that was the whole story. We sat down near the President's desk, because the principal focus of conversation was there. Knox was coming in and out. Press Secretary Steve Early was rushing back and forth saying, "They've had another telephone conversation with Admiral 'So-and-So'. Things are worse than were reported earlier."

It must have been nearly nine o'clock before any kind of order developed. Knox began to cool off as he told the President various things. Stimson sat down, looking very disturbed. The President then looked up for the first time. He was very serious. His face and lips were pulled down, looking quite gray. He said, "I'm thankful you all got here. Of course, you all know what's happened." Then he plunged into the present, not into the story. He said, "We've been able to get the Navy twice on the telephone. They're making efforts to get another connection. We were very alarmed because for several hours we weren't able to get a telephonic connection, but we've gotten through. We only had four

At the cabinet meeting on the night of 7 December, Secretary Perkins observed that President Roosevelt's "pride in the Navy was so terrific that he was having actual physical difficulty in getting out the words that bombs dropped on ships that were not in fighting shape." (Naval Historical Center: NH 77347.)

minutes of conversation, and then it died away. What caused it to die away we don't know. All we got was the information that the destruction is much worse than it was reported at first." After mentioning some of the actions being taken, Roosevelt said, "And Frank Knox declares he's going himself tomorrow morning to Hawaii, that he's flying."

"Yes, indeed I am. I've got to go myself."

The President said, "I don't know that it's necessary, Frank. There's nothing you can do when you get there. We've got to know what's going on, and you can't tie the wires together. That's a technician's job."

"I know, but I've got to go. I've got to be there. I know it's my duty to go."

The President nodded and said, "I guess you're right, Frank. I guess you're right. You may not be able to do anything, but you're right. It is your duty to go."

I remember feeling that Knox had the right idea. He was the boss of this show, and he should go where the trouble was.

The term "sitting duck" wasn't used in connection with all this until the next morning, but what

we heard was a pretty sad story. I remember that the President could hardly bring himself to tell us this. His pride in the Navy was so terrific that he was having actual physical difficulty in getting out the words that bombs dropped on ships that were not in fighting shape and prepared to move, just tied up. I remember that he said twice to Knox, "Find out, for God's sake, why the ships were tied up in rows."

Knox said, "That's the way they berth them."

It was obvious to me that Roosevelt was having a dreadful time just accepting the idea that the Navy could be caught off guard. However, at that time, there were no recriminations. There was no thought of anybody being blamed for this. Naturally, people asked what Admiral Kimmel was doing. They couldn't get Kimmel, because he wasn't available. He was out there where he belonged, at his battle station. Before we left that room, we knew that most of the high naval personnel were not on board ship. I got a feeling that it was humiliating for the President to have to acknowledge the fact that it was Sunday morning and the naval officers were otherwise occupied. Quite subordinate officers had been in charge, had had to give what orders were given and to do what should be done.

We just got scraps of information, an episode here and there. We got a picture of total confusion. Still, nobody knew exactly what had happened. Nobody knew where the planes had come from. This young naval aide had said they were from a carrier, but he was only assuming. There was no other place to fly from. The question that popped into my head, and I think I asked it—if I didn't, somebody right next to me did—"How could it be? Why didn't our patrols find it out?"

The answer was, "We do not know how it could have happened. The guess here is, and we haven't had this confirmed from Hawaii, that a Japanese fishing fleet, which had seemed innocent enough, had been not only the conveyor of messages, but may even have been a disguise for actual weapons of bombardment. But we do not know. We haven't yet got sufficient information."

I suppose there arose in everybody's mind, as they did in mine, the questions, "Where was that Japanese fleet that we knew to be out of the harbor? Where was it on this particular Sunday? Does anybody know?"

Before the story was more than half over, Frank Knox came back from the other room, where he was obviously telephoning. He was very red in the face, flustered, with every mark of excitement on his face. He was excited and tense, barely holding himself in. He said, "Well, I've made all the arrangements. I'm going in the morning."

The White House is ablaze with light on the night of 7 December. People gather outside the fence while the President and his cabinet meet inside. (United Press International [Acme].)

Although the President tried to project an air of calm, one that had a sort of studied quality, there were others who seemed to share Knox's mood. I remember that one or two Congressmen present were very red and flushed, muttering profanities to express their distaste and revulsion at this whole episode. It was an incident that civilized men found impossible to describe. There's no word to say, "How shall we endure this humiliation? How could this enemy do this to us? We've never shown ourselves anything but decently disposed to them." There's nothing to say except, "The dirty bastards! I hope they roast in hell!" The words that mean something are not to be said, so people revert into some kind of language which may be profane or exaggerated.

Along with the other things the President told us that night, he said: "The Secretary of State has already dismissed the Japanese envoys, and they are in our care and custody. We will take care of them until they can be sent back to Japan. Nothing will happen to them, but they will not be in a position to communicate with the press or the public."

Hull added a little bit: "You know, Mr. President, to the last minute they were protesting. When I told them this was the end and everything was over, they protested that they didn't know anything about it. They had the nerve to tell me that there

was some mistake, that we must be misinformed, that there had been some accident. But you know what we know." To this day, I don't know what they knew, but I assume that some intelligence had at some time intercepted communications to Nomura and Kurusu which indicated the Japanese Government was in communication with them, telling them that something of this sort was going to happen. At the time, I don't think I gathered that, although I knew that Hull was very angry and believed that they were just plain lying. He described how patient he had been that day and how utterly stubborn they had been. He said that there had never been any real meeting of the minds. One could see that this deceitfulness struck him as being the most dreadful aspect of all.

Through all of the discussion, the President remained intent on communication with Hawaii. He was obviously absorbed in that. I noticed that most of the evening his face remained tense and screwed up around the mouth. His upper lip pulled down, and his lower lip sort of pursed in—an expression that I've seen him have many, many times. Sometimes I've seen it when he was not particularly pleased or proud of a situation in which he found himself. I've seen it on his face when I thought he was not making everything quite clear and open personally, when he was not exposing the total sit-

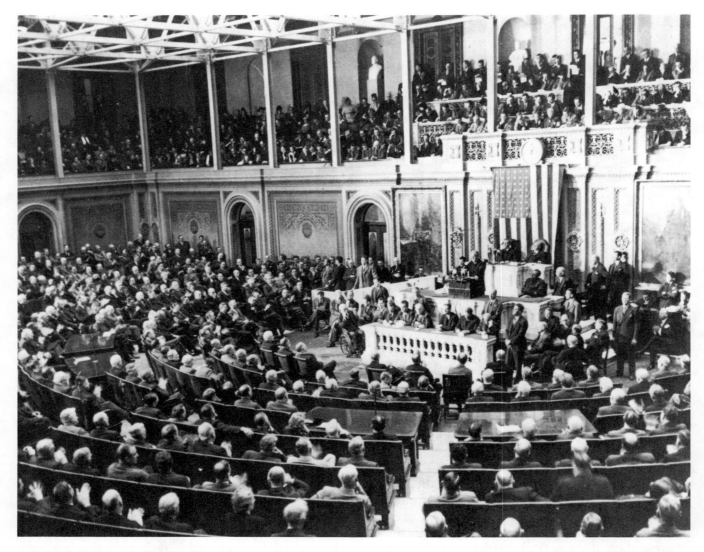

On Monday, 8 December, President Roosevelt tells Congress of the "date which will live in infamy" and asks for a declaration of war against Japan. (National Archives: 208-CN-3992.)

uation. It was the sort of expression that he sometimes used when people were making recommendations to him that he didn't have the slightest intention of doing anything about. In other words, there have been times when I associated that expression with a kind of evasiveness. I had a deep emotional feeling that something was wrong, that this situation was not all it appeared to be.

Now I see that it would have been impossible for a man in the position of Roosevelt to have acted in a natural, easy, relaxed fashion. None of us were easy or relaxed. Therefore, he was playing a role as the leader of a nation that had been attacked by surprise by an enemy we had always thought of as inferior. It was an awful role to play. What do you show the world? I don't know.

I've been asked if it might be possible that the President, recognizing that this thing had hap-pened, felt a certain element of relief that the long tension of wondering what the Japanese would do and when they would do it was over. We didn't have to think any longer about what we would do in defense of Singapore if there was no apparent attack on ourselves. That very wave of relief might have produced in him that psychological atmosphere—reflected partially in his facial expression of calmness and tenseness. And yet it seemed to me also that there was a slight evasion there. It could have been expressed in what Frank Walker said to me. The Postmaster General was very close to the President. He said, quietly under his breath, "You know, I think the boss must have a great sense of relief that this happened. This is a great load off his mind. I thought the load on his mind was just going to kill him, going to break him down. . . . At least we know what to do now."

I remember saying, "Yes, I think so."

I think I should say something else about that evening. There was never any question put to the cabinet or members of Congress present, "Shall we declare war on Japan? Shall we declare war on Germany?" Roosevelt already had a rough draft of the message he was going to give Congress the next day. He read his declaration of war to us, and in my own mind, there wasn't any question about what we should do.

The next day, we all went to Congress to hear the President. I don't recall anything except the terrible tenseness and the absolute lack of the usual loose-mouthed jollity that goes on whenever Congress meets in full session. We assembled in the speaker's room, as we always did, and then marched in, solemn as owls, and took the places reserved for us in the chamber. Everybody knew we were in for something terrible. It was a spiritual strain as well as a physical one. We had all been trained to think of the United States as invincible, and now we were faced with the fact that our Navy had cracked—how badly we were not sure, but that invincible defense was not there.

After we took our places, it seemed to me that the chaplain prayed a little longer than usual, although he was a long-winded man, anyhow. The President's message, on the other hand, was very brief. He was greeted with resounding cheers and applause, which was an expression of men trying to say, "We stand with you."

Frances Perkins Wilson (1880–1965) was graduated from Mount Holyoke College in Massachusetts in 1902 and later earned a master's degree from Columbia University. In the early years of the century, she was a school teacher and social worker, concerned with improving working conditions for women and children. From 1913 until his death in 1952, she was married to statistician Paul C. Wilson but retained her maiden name in professional life. For a number of years, she headed the New York State Industrial Commission, then was Secretary of Labor from 1933 to 1945, the nation's first woman cabinet member. Much of the New Deal legislation, including the Social Security Act and the Fair Labor Standards Act, resulted from her influence. She remained in government as a civil service commissioner until 1953, then taught at Cornell University until her death. Her book *The Roosevelt I Knew* was published in 1946. (Department of Labor.)

The Strange Assignment of the USS *Lanikai*

By Rear Admiral Kemp Tolley, U.S. Navy (Retired)

The summer of 1941 was clearly a prelude to war in the Far East for which the United States was by no means prepared. In the Philippines, desperate efforts were being made to close the gap between near defenselessness and a fair posture of readiness which might give pause to the advancing Japanese.

Secretary of War Henry L. Stimson, who as Secretary of State had crossed swords with the Japanese over the Manchurian incident, was eager to square accounts and vindicate his earlier judgment of the inevitability of continued Japanese expansion. He had taken the line that our only hope for a quick power buildup in the Far East lay in a great augmentation of our heavy bomber force in the Philippines. General George C. Marshall urged the President to buy time, to draw out negotiations, to stall off hostilities until at least April 1942. By late November, it had become clearly apparent that Japan was then tactically disposed to commence a major operation. Her naval forces were massed in Indochina. A large convoy was being shadowed by our submarines as it passed south through the Formosa Strait.

The big question in everyone's mind was where the Japanese would strike next. There was no real clue as to their next target. There was, however, the distinct possibility that Japan would bypass the Philippines, attack Singapore and the East Indies, and thus destroy our potential allies while we sat on the sidelines. American public opinion at this point almost certainly would not have supported a war against Japan.

No one was more acutely aware of this danger than President Roosevelt. A memo by Harry Hopkins described his days in England in early 1941:

> [British Foreign Minister Anthony] Eden asked me repeatedly what our country would do if Japan attacked Singapore or the Dutch East Indies, saying it was essential to their policy to know. Of course it was perfectly clear that neither the President nor Hull could give an adequate answer to the British on that point because the declaration of war is up to Congress, and the isolationists and, indeed, a great part of the American people, would not be interested in a war in the Far East merely because Japan attacked the Dutch.[1]

Undersecretary of State Summer Welles added:

> He [Roosevelt] did, however, make it very plain to me that he thought the immediate danger was an attack by Japan upon some British possession in the Far East, or even more probably upon the Netherlands East Indies. What worried him deeply was that, though this would immediately threaten our vital interests, it might be impossible to persuade either the Congress or the American people that it was tantamount to an attack upon our own frontiers and justified military measures of self-defense. He felt, however, that Japan would not attack the United States directly until and unless we found ourselves involved in the European War.[2]

The President was by no means alone in this belief. In a letter to me, dated January 1961, Admiral T. Fukuda stated:

> I didn't think that war with the United States was near because it was a top secret in our Navy Department. Besides, the opinion of most Japanese naval officers was that we should not have war with the United States but keep the Japanese Navy as it was as a stability force in Asia. It was a common idea of naval officers. Admiral [Kichisaburo] Nomura, ex-ambassador to the United States, told me when he came to my office in Hokkaido before the war that we should keep out of war with the United States and maintain the Japanese Navy as a stabilising force in the Far East. Then no country could venture to have war with us.

Toward the end of November, the Japanese envoys in Washington offered a plan to the President and Cordell Hull wherein they promised to stop sending troops to Indochina. They did not, however, agree to withdraw any from the large number already there poised to strike south or east. This proposition was rejected by Roosevelt, who must have realized by this time that the game had about run its course.

---

[1] Robert E. Sherwood, *Roosevelt and Hopkins* (New York: Harper & Brothers, 1950), p. 259.

[2] Sumner Welles, *Seven Decisions That Shaped History* (New York: Harper & Brothers, 1951), p. 89.

The *Lanikai* lies at anchor south of Java during the course of her long journey from the Philippines to Australia. She had been intended as sacrificial bait to lure the Japanese into committing an overt act of war. The old schooner was spared that fate when the Japanese struck far more lucrative targets at Pearl Harbor, thousands of miles away. (Courtesy of Rear Admiral Kemp Tolley, USN, Ret.)

Secretary Stimson, after attending a cabinet meeting late in November, confided in his diary his surprise at hearing the President say that "we" might be attacked soon, perhaps over the weekend. In further describing the President's remarks, he said: "The problem was how we should maneuver them into the position of firing the first shot without allowing too much danger to ourselves."[3]

On 12 December 1937, antedating Pearl Harbor almost four years to the day, the USS *Panay*, a Yangtze River gunboat, had been bombed and sunk near Hankow by Japanese military hotheads anxious to precipitate war. This action had served to incite American public opinion to a high point. Tempers were cooled only by a swift Japanese apology and more than $2 million in reparations. It was a good object lesson in *casus belli*.

Thus, on 2 December 1941, Admiral Harold R. Stark, Chief of Naval Operations, personally received a directive from the President—a somewhat unorthodox order directing in detail the carrying out of "reconnaissance" by the Commander in Chief Asiatic Fleet, Admiral Thomas C. Hart. The preamble to this message to Admiral Hart left no room for doubt as to the source: "President directs that

the following be done as soon as possible and within two days if possible after receipt this despatch." The message continued: "Charter three small vessels to form a defensive information patrol. Minimum requirements to establish identity as U.S. men of war are command by a naval officer and to mount a small gun and one machine gun would suffice."[4] The Philippines were our major base of operations in the Far East; it was essential that the Filipino people be rallied enthusiastically to the U.S. cause. To this end, the following would contribute, provided, of course, that the Japanese could be provoked into a repeat performance of *Panay*: "Filipino crews may be employed with minimum number naval ratings to accomplish purpose which is to observe and report by radio Japanese movements." The specific geographic locations to which the three ships were to be sent were carefully laid down; they were the entrances to the concentration points of the Japanese fleet in Indochina.

Representative Frank B. Keefe said of this project:

> The President's directions were that . . . the ships were to observe and report by radio Japanese movement in the West China Sea and Gulf of Siam. The President prescribed the point at which each vessel was to be stationed. One vessel was to be stationed between Hainan and Hue; one between Camranh Bay and Cap St. Jacques; one off Pointe de Camau. All these points were clearly in the path of the Japanese advance down the coast of Indo China, and towards the Gulf of Siam. The Navy Department did not originate this plan. The Navy Department would not have directed it to be done unless the President had specifically ordered it. Admiral Hart was already conducting reconnaissance off that coast by planes from Manila. So far as the Navy Department was concerned, sufficient information was being received from this air reconnaissance. Had the Japanese fired upon any one of these three small vessels, it would have constituted an overt act on the part of Japan.[5]

Indeed, the CNO, according to his testimony before the committee, not being party to anything more ulterior in the President's directive than its wording stated, was sufficiently mystified as to this unusual intervention on the President's part to add a postscript on the directive to Admiral Hart: "Inform me as to what reconnaissance measures are being regularly performed at sea by both army and

[3] Relman Morin, *East Wind Rising* (New York: Alfred A. Knopf, Inc., 1960), p. 353.

[4] OPNAV 12356 CRO313 of 1 December 1941 to CinCAsiatic.

[5] *Report of the Joint Committee on the Investigation of the Pearl Harbor Attack* (Washington: U. S. Government Printing Office, 1946), p. 266-P.

If the *Lanikai* had encountered Japanese warships, her defense would have been limited to this puny three-pounder gun of Spanish-American War vintage. (Courtesy of Rear Admiral Kemp Tolley, USN, Ret.)

navy whether by air surface vessels or submarine and your opinion as to the effectiveness of these latter measures."

Admiral Hart's reply covered in some detail the extensive reconnaissance already in effect and concluded with a touch of the brusqueness for which he was well known: "When it is considered called for will increase air patrols and send out more subs." In another message, Admiral Hart reported on progress with the "three small vessels." He told the CNO, "have obtained two vessels. One now en route Indochina coast. Second one sailing soon as ready."

The "one now en route" was the *Lanikai*. I was her prospective skipper. Arriving in Manila from Shanghai on board the flat-bottomed Yangtze River gunboat *Oahu*, I had been ordered immediately to the commander in chief's headquarters ashore. "At Cavite," I was told, "you will find a schooner. Commission her. Man her with a naval crew including Filipinos. Have a gun mounted, load ammunition, food and water, and report back here in 24 hours ready to put to sea on a voyage of not less than two weeks." To my feeble protests about requisitions, work requests, and certain delays inherent therein,

it was made quite clear that the navy yard commandant at Cavite had been thoroughly impressed with the fact that the President himself had given the order. No paperwork would be involved.

Probably never before in recent peacetime has a fitting-out been less encumbered by conferences and signatures in triplicate. The four simple Filipino fishermen who came in a package with the lease for the ship found themselves in white hats and sworn into the Insular Force of the U.S. Navy with only the dimmest understanding as to what was happening; none of them spoke more than a dozen words in English. Six U.S. Navy chiefs and petty officers drifted down to the dockside at intervals through the morning of 4 December, each surveying the *Lanikai* in obvious doubt, scarcely believing she could indeed be the *Lanikai* to which they had been shanghaied on half an hour's notice. Filipino workmen streamed aboard to strengthen the deckhouse for the three-pounder and its bright brass pedestal. The moss-encrusted radio resisted all efforts to make it produce a beep and so it remained a silent witness to the fable that the *Lanikai* would be on a "reconnaissance" mission. The two-masted, 75-ton auxiliary schooner was commissioned as a U.S. naval vessel on 5 December. Then came provisioning.

Thousands of inch-long cockroaches scuttled for concealment as bags of rice and cases of salmon came slamming down the hatches. Sails were shaken out and running rigging checked. The auxiliary engine groaned and coughed and chugged into action to test its all-out speed of 6 knots. I found space for a portable typewriter, camera, and three sets of tropical whites. Class ring, sword, uniforms, and all the small treasures of a young bachelor were consigned to storage ashore and never seen again.

The schooner and crew then lay at the entrance to Manila Bay awaiting the dawn of 7 December to transit the minefields there. I gratefully recalled the training in sail which the Naval Academy had given me, as I cogitated over my unusual instructions, the seal of which I broke on leaving Manila for what now appeared to be the last time. The instructions were short and to the point, "Patrol off the entrance of Camranh Bay and report the direction taken by the Japanese Fleet when it emerges."

There were also oral instructions. "If the Japanese want to know what you are doing, tell them you are looking for the crew of a downed plane," said the fleet operations officer at a final briefing. The *Lanikai* was built for the island trade in the South Pacific; her fresh-water capacity was calculated to supply a crew of four or five whose thirst traditionally ran more to beer than to water. "If you run short of water," added the operations officer, "use your international signal book. Ask the first passing Japanese man of war for some."

But even as the *Lanikai* awaited the dawn, Japanese forces already had struck a blow at Pearl Harbor that was to provide an incident infinitely more spectacular and satisfactory than anything the *Lanikai* could have furnished. My journal notes: "0615 underway on orders to return to Manila, feeling very glad to be alive. Notified the crew a state of war existed with Japan. Hoisted foresail, jib staysail and jib." The radio could receive, even if it could not transmit.

With our original purpose having become unnecessary, we stayed in the area until the situation became untenable. It was shortly before the end of the year that the schooner sought to escape. At dusk on 26 December 1941, we threaded our way out through the minefields, "destination unknown," according to the journal entry I laboriously pecked out on the *Lanikai*'s only typewriter. Ahead, before we reached safety in southwest Australia, lay 4,000 miles of hazardous waters controlled by the powerful Imperial Navy of Japan.

Sailing in the soft tropical nights, holing up in jungle-fringed island hideouts by day, crossing open water under cover of blessed typhoons, the *Lanikai* worked her way south to Makassar, Soerabaja, Tjilatjap, and Fremantle. Twice given up for lost, arriving unheralded in Australia twenty days out of Java as one of the few surface survivors of the East Indies debacle, I was greeted incredulously by the U.S. Navy in Perth. "My God! What are you doing here?" cried Rear Admiral William R. Purnell, chief of staff to Commander Southwest Pacific. "You're supposed to be dead!"

Kemp Tolley (1908–   ) was born in Manila, the son of an Army officer. He was graduated from the Naval Academy in 1929 and served in the *Florida, Texas, Canopus,* Asiatic Fleet staff, *Wyoming, Mindanao,* and *Tutuila.* After instructing at the Naval Academy and serving in the *Wake,* he commanded the *Lanikai,* the story of which he told in more detail in a Naval Institute Press book, *Cruise of the Lanikai: Incitement to War,* published in 1973. Later, he was assistant U.S. naval attaché in Moscow and navigator of the *North Carolina.* He subsequently commanded the attack cargo ship *Vermilion* and LST Squadron 2. He served at the Armed Forces Staff College, on the staff of Amphibious Group 2, and then commanded Amphibious Squadron 5, and Fleet Activities Yokosuka, Japan. He retired from active duty in 1959 and lives in Monkton, Maryland. He is the author of *Yangtze Patrol: The U.S. Navy in China.* (Courtesy of Rear Admiral Kemp Tolley, U.S. Navy [Retired].)

The articles that follow are about ships that were at Pearl Harbor during the attack. The battleship *Nevada* receives the lion's share of attention; there are several reasons for that. The primary one is the availability of articles. All those here presented appeared in the *Proceedings* in one form or another, although one has been rewritten for this volume, one has been rearranged, and a third has been shortened drastically. Another reason for the focus on the *Nevada* is that the *Proceedings* format allows substantial followup comment on published articles. Thus, one of the articles here spawned two of the others. In addition, there is value in telling the entire story of one battleship—the attack itself, the immediate aftermath, the refloating and salvaging, the repair and rebuilding, and finally her career during the remainder of the war—and letting her act as representative of the others.

The USS *Nevada* was an old ship at the time of the attack, but she was still full of spirit. Ever since her commissioning in 1916 under Captain William S. Sims, her crews had known her as the "Cheer-Up Ship." That tradition served her well through the trauma of Pearl Harbor and the events beyond.

Worse Than Dante's Inferno

By Vice Admiral Walter Stratton Anderson, U.S. Navy (Retired)

There used to be a morning conference in the office of the Secretary of the Navy, attended by the Chief of Naval Operations, the Commandant of the Marine Corps, the naval aide to the President, the Director of Naval Intelligence, and sometimes others. On one of these occasions, in 1940, when it came my turn to say what we were proposing to do in Naval Intelligence, I mentioned that I wanted to send confidential agents into North Africa. My reason was that when I was in London as naval attaché in the mid-1930s, I had been told that the Admiralty realized that in a war the situation might arise in which their communications would be interrupted. Therefore, obviously, North Africa's importance would be enhanced.

When I said that we were thinking of sending these agents, the Secretary of the Navy, Mr. Frank Knox, owner and publisher of the *Chicago Daily News*, said, "We will send *Daily News* men."

This knocked me a little off my balance, and I said, "Oh, Mr. Secretary, we couldn't do that!" My response angered him, and he never forgave me. To do him justice, I doubt if he would have gone through with any such thing. I think it would have been better if he had laughed and said, "Oh, of course not." But that incident had an adverse bearing on my naval career from then until he died.

About the end of 1940, Rear Admiral Chester W. Nimitz, then Chief of the Bureau of Navigation, came to my office and told me I was going to be sent as Commander Battleships Battle Force with the rank of vice admiral. I was a rear admiral at the time, and he told me to proceed to have my uniforms changed for vice admiral rank, because I would go in a few days. "Furthermore," he told me, "in about four months, Admiral [Charles P.] Snyder [Commander Battle Force] will be relieved, and you will fleet up and take his job with four stars."

I started to have my uniforms changed, and a few days after that, I met Admiral Nimitz and Admiral Harold R. Stark, the CNO, in the hall. They were deeply concerned about something, which I soon learned. One of them said, "You're not going to get those three stars. They're going to be given to Admiral [Ernest J.] King in the Atlantic."

So I said, "Well, I can see that he's entitled to three stars more than I am if there's only one set of three stars available, but do I get the job in command of the battleships?"

"Yes," was the reply.

And I responded, "Well, will I be given three stars, like all my predecessors, as soon as there are three stars available for me?"

Again, the reply was "Yes." But, for some reason, it didn't work out that way.

I was detached as Director of Naval Intelligence and reported as Commander Battleships Battle Force, with my flag in the *West Virginia*. I had additional duty as Commander Battleship Division 4, comprised of the *West Virginia*, *Colorado*, and *Maryland*. I was very happy to be given this command, my only regret being that I didn't have the same rank as all my predecessors had had.

Having had command of the *West Virginia* in 1932 and 1933, I realized that there must be some men on board who had been there when I was captain. Therefore, I ordered that the men should be brought to the quarterdeck in a group, along with the visiting officers who were to witness the ceremony at which I took command. After my two-star flag had been broken, I was able to go down the line and shake hands with my old shipmates, most of whom were by then chief petty officers or at least first class petty officers. There were forty or fifty of them.

When I took command, there were twelve battleships in the Battle Force, four divisions of three ships each. I should say here that I was very fortunate in the staff I had. In fact, I was always fortunate in my staffs. These men served me well during our operations, which were centered around Pearl Harbor up to the coming of the war. We were always at least in readiness Condition III when we operated at sea, which means that we were always at least partially prepared to commence action without delay. As one of our preparedness measures, I issued an order, on my own initiative, a few weeks before the Japanese attack. I directed that on board each ship, two of the 5-inch antiaircraft guns and two .50-caliber machine guns would be manned at all times, night and day. That was carried out. I also realized that in case of air attack, it might be impossible in the few seconds available

In 1933, Captain Anderson was relieved of command of the battleship *West Virginia* by Captain Harold R. Stark. Both were members of the class of 1903 at the Naval Academy, but thirty years later, Anderson appeared to be ahead of Stark because he got his major ship command first. Indeed, Anderson appeared headed for the top in the Navy, but somewhere along the way, he got sidetracked. In December 1941, Stark was the four-star Chief of Naval Operations and Anderson was the two-star Commander Battleships Battle Force. Anderson did not get his third star until late in World War II, by which time he was out of the running for major combat command. In the overview, Anderson is at the microphone and Stark is standing behind him. In the close-up, Stark is in the center, wearing glasses, and Anderson is the four-striper standing beside him. (U.S. Navy: Naval Institute Collection.)

for a control officer to get the word through to the guns. Therefore, the men were to be instructed that if they were absolutely sure that they were being attacked by enemy planes, they were to open fire without waiting for an order from anybody. These orders were to prove useful when the Japanese staged their surprise attack on 7 December 1941.

Actually, my thought in issuing the orders concerned what should be done to make us as ready as possible, in case we ever got into war or were attacked. I can't say that I particularly visualized an attack on Pearl Harbor, because the message which Admiral Husband E. Kimmel received on the twenty-seventh of November, from the Navy Department, indicated that from the location and organization of the Japanese fleet, the Navy Department believed that the attack might come on the coast of French Indochina or perhaps in the Philippines. This rather relieved the minds, I think, of those in the Hawaiian Islands. And, as a matter of fact, this message was found by the commission the President sent to investigate the attack to be a contributory cause to the surprise.

In any event, it was a surprise when the Japanese did strike Hawaii. By that time, my flag had been shifted to the *Maryland*, and on board were my chief of staff, Captain Worrall R. Carter, my operations officer, Commander William F. Fitzgerald, and two or three other officers of my staff. There was also another battleship division commander, Rear Admiral Isaac C. Kidd, in the *Arizona*. Subsequent investigations proved that more than half the officers were in the ships at the time of the attack, and so were about 97 per cent of the men.

During the weekend when the Japanese struck, I had gone out to an apartment my wife and I occupied. I was dressing when she answered the telephone Sunday morning. It was a message from one of my aides that an attack was taking place. I hastily repaired to the navy yard and got aboard my ship, about nine o'clock in the morning, while the attack was still in progress. I went to the officers' landing to get a boat and was greatly impressed by two things. One was the terrible aspect of the harbor. There was the bottom of the overturned *Oklahoma* facing me and the sunken, blasted *Arizona*. Great clouds of black smoke were billowing up from the oil afire on the water. There was the most comprehensive antiaircraft fire that I had ever seen, and yellow Japanese planes were flying back and forth, almost literally hedge-hopping. I thought to myself, "Dante's inferno never looked like this."

The other thing that impressed me was the fact that there were two or three boats at the landing, and the men on board were as calm and collected and devil-may-care as you could wish. One of them said, "Where do you want to go, Admiral?" And I told them. To get to the *Maryland*, we had to go around her bow, because there was flaming oil on the water that prevented us from going around the stern as usual. As soon as I got aboard, I went to the bridge and joined the members of my staff already there. From then on, we did what we could to mitigate the situation. It was obvious that something should be done to relieve any men that might be trapped in the overturned hull of the *Oklahoma*, and my material officers, Commander Edgar P. Kranzfelder and Lieutenant Richard S. Mandelkorn, discussed it with me. I told them I thought they'd better cut their holes in the shaft alley, because, I said, "You don't want to cut a hole into an oil tank and have a lot more oil catching fire." They did cut a hole in the shaft alley, and they relieved thirty-two men.

Captain Howard Bode was in command of the *Oklahoma*. He was not on board at the time she was torpedoed and capsized. He reported to me on board the *Maryland*, not long after I got there, and I told him to get some men and some boats and get in touch with the ammunition depot so they could immediately begin to bring on an added supply of antiaircraft ammunition. I told him to see that it got out to each of the ships, so that we wouldn't run out. Because, at that time, we didn't know how long the attack was going to continue. This he did.

We also made some attempt to put out the fires burning in the oil on the water, using hoses from the ships. There was one short period when the smoke was so bad that I was afraid that we were going to have to abandon the bridge of the *Maryland*, but it didn't prove to be quite that bad. The *Maryland* had been struck by two heavy shells—that is, projectiles converted to bombs—but they did not really explode with any effect. They hit on the bow and went on through quite a little plating and messed things up in that part of the ship. But they didn't do great damage, except that several men were killed as a result of the flying pieces of the shells. One of the men was an ensign whom I had seen on the ship's bridge when I was going to the flag bridge. The poor fellow had a hole right in his forehead where he'd been hit.

It should be mentioned that, contrary to what the papers have frequently said, the fleet was not a sitting duck in Pearl Harbor. And it should be said that prior to the attack, naval officers, in our country and elsewhere, generally considered that torpedoes could not be launched from planes into water as shallow as that in Pearl Harbor or most

The smoke and fire pouring up from the battleships under his command struck Admiral Anderson as being even worse than the inferno depicted by Dante. In the top photo at left, Anderson's flagship, the *Maryland*, can be seen beyond the hull of the capsized *Oklahoma*. At right in the same photo are the *West Virginia* and *Tennessee*. (National Archives: 80-G-19951 and 80-G-33035.)

One of the projects in which members of Anderson's staff were involved was directing the rescue of thirty-two sailors trapped in the overturned *Oklahoma*. The feat was accomplished by cutting a hole in the bottom of the battleship. The ship in the background is the *Maryland*. (National Archives: 80-G-32748.)

other ports in which we anchored. And it must be said, to the credit of the Japanese, that they had evidently worked this problem out, because their torpedoes functioned even in water that shallow. The big shells that they converted into bombs didn't do a great deal of damage. The real damage was done by the torpedoes. In my opinion, the Japanese failed to do one thing that would have been greatly to their advantage—and that would have been to set on fire the oil tanks that were on shore. Then that burning oil would have gone down into the harbor and would have made a complete mess.

I might add also what, of course, is a matter of history—that Rear Admiral Kidd lost his life in the attack, as did Captain Mervyn Bennion of the *West Virginia* and Captain Franklin Van Valkenburgh of the *Arizona*. Captain Bennion was particularly gallant. He was terribly wounded, practically disemboweled, but he maintained command, although lying on the deck of his bridge. He was a bona fide hero. I did not personally know enough to recommend him for the Medal of Honor, but I am glad he got it, because that captain of the *West Virginia* merited it if anybody ever did.

At the time, bad as things were, I felt great confidence that we would eventually be victorious, because the conduct of the personnel was impeccable. I didn't see a single case of any man or officer showing the white feather in the slightest degree. And another thing which impressed me, and which is very important—that they were masters of expedience. If something was put out of commission by the attack, they would find another way to do whatever was necessary. In other words, my already high opinion of the personnel of our Navy was enhanced by that tragic experience.

A few weeks after the attack, after a little patchwork had been done on the bow of the *Maryland*, I was ordered to proceed to the West Coast along with the *Pennsylvania* and the *Tennessee*. The *Maryland* and the *Tennessee* were ordered to the Puget Sound Navy Yard, and the *Pennsylvania* went to San Francisco. When I entered Puget Sound, I had an escort of about three destroyers, and I ordered them to drop depth charges as we entered the Strait of Juan de Fuca. My theory was that if there were any submarines around—and there might have

Twisted metal and shattered OS2U floatplanes mark the remains of the *West Virginia*, a ship commanded by Anderson in the early 1930s. Beyond is the *Tennessee*. Captain Mervyn Bennion of the *West Virginia*, who lost his life in the attack, was awarded the Medal of Honor for his heroism that day. (National Archives: 80-G-19945.)

Rear Admiral Isaac C. Kidd, Commander Battleship Division 1, was killed when his flagship, the *Arizona*, exploded. He was later awarded the Medal of Honor. (Naval Historical Center: NH 85226.)

been—they would think they had been discovered and would be somewhat embarrassed. Looking back on it, I don't believe there were any Japanese submarines there, but we had no assurance at the time that there wouldn't be.

After we were repaired at the navy yard, I took the *Maryland* down to San Francisco Bay. On one occasion, Vice Admiral William S. Pye, who had resumed his prewar role as a task force commander, sent me with three or four battleships off quite a few hundred miles to the southwest on a reconnaissance in force. He evidently had some reason to think that there might be some Japanese naval force in that area, although I don't think there was. Thereafter, we spent a good deal of time anchored in port with torpedo nets around us.

In the latter part of 1942, I was detached from command of Battleships Pacific Fleet. Both Admiral Nimitz and his chief of staff were kind enough to tell me that an effort had been made to retain me in my command but that they had been unsuccessful. The fitness report that Admiral Nimitz gave me on my detachment was such that I greatly prize the copy of it that I have.

Walter Stratton Anderson (1881–   ) was graduated from the Naval Academy in 1903 and subsequently received postgraduate instruction in ordnance. He served in a number of ships, including the *Brooklyn, Galveston, Nebraska, Utah, Des Moines,* and *Arizona.* He was commanding officer of the dispatch boat *Yankton,* the destroyers *Sinclair* and *Kidder,* and the battleship *West Virginia.* During the mid-1930s, he was U.S. naval attaché in London, then commanded (heavy) Cruiser Division 4 until reporting as Director of Naval Intelligence. After serving as Commander Battleships Pacific, he was president of the Board of Inspection and Survey from September 1942 to July 1944. His final active duty assignment was as Commandant of the Seventh Naval District and Commander Gulf Sea Frontier. He retired from active duty in 1946, then worked several years in the business world. Admiral Anderson, who now resides in Washington, D.C., is the oldest living graduate of the Naval Academy (Naval Historical Center: NH 56038.)

Whatever the reason, Anderson remained a rear admiral until after Secretary Knox died in 1944, even though Congress passed a law authorizing additional vice admirals soon after the war started. In his oral history, Admiral Anderson says:

When I came ashore after [the battleship command], I knew that Admiral King [by then Chief of Naval Operations] was trying to give me a good billet, but was having difficulties in gaining approval of the Secretary. One time, when I was in his office—I knew him very well—I said, "Ernie, it's not right, in a war in which you're carrying all the burden you are, that one rear admiral should be in here taking up your time about his own personal fortunes." And King said to me, "I've always got time to correct a manifest injustice."

Admiral Anderson did get his third star then and became Commandant of the Seventh Naval District and Commander of the Gulf Sea Frontier, with headquarters in Miami. He stayed in those billets for the remainder of the war. The position had been a busy one earlier in the war, when German U-boats were active in the area, but by 1944, the combat commands were elsewhere. In his shore billets, Admiral Anderson had not gained the combat seasoning that the war had provided other admirals by then.

A Tactical View of Pearl Harbor

By Captain Joseph K. Taussig, Jr., U.S. Navy (Retired)

On the morning of 7 December 1941, I was awakened by the assistant quartermaster of the watch of the USS *Nevada*. "Mr. Taussig, it's 0700. You have the forenoon watch, Sir." Promptly at 7:45, I reported on the quarterdeck to relieve the officer of the deck who had stood the morning watch. I am not really sure of the exact details of the next ten to twelve minutes. I do know that the relieved officer of the deck was still on the quarterdeck at about 7:55; possibly he was completing his log. There was a liberty party of about a dozen men waiting for the 8:00 a.m. motor launch. In my twenty-one-year-old mind was the gnawing question of whether the correct-sized national ensign had been ordered for the raising of colors on this Sunday morning. I remember sending a messenger forward to call from our bow to the stern of the *Arizona* moored only 20 or 30 feet ahead of the *Nevada*, and I was watching the sailor pass up the port side of the *Nevada* when I caught a glimpse of a torpedo plane flying from the east and very low over the water.

The bomb-bay doors were open, and out dropped a "fish." My reaction was merely to think of the welcome break in the Sunday morning tedium that we would have watching the salvage operation of digging the torpedo out of the mud under 40 feet of water, the controlling depth of Pearl Harbor. Absently, I tabbed the aircraft as a Douglas TBD type.

Moments later, a plume of water spouted from the side of a ship ahead of the *Nevada* in Battleship Row. The noise of the explosion as the torpedo hit and the incredible realization that the TBD was a Japanese plane, the rising suns on its wings plainly visible, galvanized me into action. Immediately, I left the quarterdeck and climbed the six ladders to my battle station in the starboard antiaircraft director.

Personal involvement in historical happenings creates vivid, lifelong memories for the participant, but rare is the man who, at the moment, can visualize the entire forest being destroyed—he is far too busy ducking the trees that are falling all around him. As an individual, then, my view was restricted to what was going on in my immediate

vicinity. I was conscious of the fact that, before I reached my battle station, the starboard antiaircraft battery was firing and that someone had pulled the safety firing cut-outs which normally restricted the firing elevations of the guns to 65 degrees. As I climbed throught the door of the director, I was conscious that the cross hairs on my check sight were on an airplane, and I saw that it was hit almost immediately and went down trailing smoke.

The director was slewing around for another target when I was hit by a missile which passed completely through my thigh and through the case of the ballistic computer of the director which was directly in front of me. There was no pain, and because I was clutching the sides of the hatch as the director slewed around, I did not fall down. My left foot was grotesquely under my left armpit, but in the detachment of shock, I was not aware that this was particularly bad.

My shipmates carried me into the sky control structure between the two antiaircraft directors and laid me out on the deck. Eventually, a pharmacist's mate arrived with a basket stretcher, administered a shot of morphine, and got me into the stretcher. The rest of the morning was spent "observing" the battle of Pearl Harbor through the eyes of the enlisted personnel who remained with me.

Regardless of how much or how little I saw that morning, there is one thing I have become sure of in the ensuing years: the defeat at Pearl Harbor was basically attributable to the lack of effective antiaircraft guns.

The *Nevada* of late 1941 was as typical a battleship as one might find. Some of the battleships had more antiaircraft protection than the *Nevada*, some had less. One or two cruisers had far better antiaircraft protection than any battleship—although this was not generally known, and certainly not generally appreciated in retrospect. Even then, what was "better" than the *Nevada* was better only in degree. In sum and substance, the fleet actually lacked an antiaircraft protection worthy of the name. It is, in fact, remarkable, that *any* Japanese aircraft were actually shot down by these batteries!

The lesson Taussig learned from the attack on Pearl Harbor was that Japanese torpedoes were effective weapons. In this photo, torpedo tracks can be seen streaking toward the *Oklahoma* (arrow) and the *West Virginia*, just astern of her. This picture was taken only minutes after the attack began, but both ships are already beginning to list to port. The *Oklahoma* soon capsized, while the *West Virginia* settled to the bottom on an even keel, thanks to prompt counterflooding. Taussig's ship, the *Nevada*, is in the lower left corner. (National Archives: 80-G-30550.)

My director was designated a Ford Mark 19. It was considered to be among the very best antiaircraft directors in the Navy. It served seven 5-inch/ 25 antiaircraft guns on the starboard battery. Let us look at these guns and how they were served. The pointer elevated the gun either by matching the signals sent from the director, or by eye. The trainer trained the gun in azimuth by the same method. The fuze setter set a timing mechanism on his "fuze pots," in accordance with the director order, or the order of the gun captain or battery officer if the guns were being fired by local control.

The ammunition was "semi-fixed," the projectile being lodged in a brass casing which held the primer and powder, and which was ejected from the gun after firing. This ammunition was either in cans, stowed in "ready boxes," or arrived at the lip of the ammunition hoists from below-decks magazines. A third loader would strip the protecting wires from the rim of the can and tilt the can so the ammunition could be handled by a second loader. This man then placed the ammunition nose-down in one of the three fuze pots, which set the mechanical/powder fuze. The first loader would

reach over, pick up a shell from the fuze pot, and place it on a tray under the chamber of the gun. The gun captain would shove a lever, and the shell would be rammed home by compressed air. Automatically, the breech would close, and if the firing circuits were also closed, the gun would fire, recoil, and eject the empty cartridge. The first loader would start the action all over again by placing another shell on the tray. This was an amazingly fast and efficient method. We could often load and fire twenty or more shells a minute over a sustained period. The enlisted men were drilled for interminable hours into teams of near-inhuman perfection. Fortunately, too, we had drilled almost every sailor in the ship.

The fire control crews were equally expert. We often spent as many as ten hours a day manning the directors. The range finder operators were superior. The director pointers and trainers, in conjunction with the director officers, were expert in obtaining the "set-up." This amounted to "solving" the course, speed, and altitude of the target; compensating for the drift caused by the winds aloft; calculating the lead angles to properly lead the target during the flight of the projectile; and determining the length of time to set on the fuze to cause the projectile to explode at the predetermined point where it met the aircraft. These signals were sent to the gun crews. This was an electro-mechanical marvel, to be sure—but it was not "electronic." It was certainly better than anything else, but even so, the best was not good enough.

In the first place, despite all our "training," the constraints placed upon us by a combination of the safety regulations and the requirements of fleet "competitions" had restricted our actual firing practices to artificial bounds which were tactically unacceptable. We had never fired the guns at an aircraft towing a sleeve more than 110 knots (in fact, my director was being modified to allow us to track a plane making 180 knots as opposed to its then-capacity of 150 knots). We had never fired at a sleeve target (much less a drone) that was not in level flight, at a height greater than 9,000 feet, or approaching more than 45 degrees forward of or abaft the beam.

Sometimes, even within these constraints, we were able to put a few holes in a sleeve. Many times, we couldn't even get close. This was not the fault of the crews. They were drilled incessantly, and performed perfectly. It was purely a matter of equipment. In essence, the equipment could not possibly perform to meet an actual tactical situation. Once my director was rendered inoperable, all fire was conducted by "local control" which was literally "seaman's eye." Further, by the perversities of design by the Bureau of Ships and the Bureau of Ordnance, the air compressors serving the guns were far below decks, and once the air lines were damaged, the guns had to be rammed by hand. (I was particularly bitter about this, for as a midshipman I had written the Bureau of Ordnance suggesting that they could alleviate the recoil problem as well as the remote air compressor problem if they placed a piston on the barrel of each gun and a cylinder on the slide. Thus, the recoil would jam the piston into the cylinder, compressing the air and taking up some of the recoil. This suggestion was met by a snide letter from the bureau reminding me that I was unsatisfactory in Spanish and on the borderline in math, so perhaps I should spend more time pounding the books than pounding their ears.)

The "secondary antiaircraft battery" on board the *Nevada* was pathetic. Eight old .50-caliber machine guns, on the top of the masts in what we called the "bird baths," were our total battery. Other ships had locally controlled 3-inch/50s, while a couple of cruisers had 1.1-inch secondary antiaircraft batteries.

Six months later, at the Battle of Midway, the ships sprouted all manner of automatic guns of smaller caliber, and *these* held off the devastating effects of torpedoes which played such havoc with the ships at Pearl Harbor. The 1.1-inchers, the 20-mm. and the 40-mm. guns spelled the difference for the remainder of World War II. The United States did not lose a single battleship once these guns were installed.

But, at Pearl Harbor, there was the *Nevada*. We

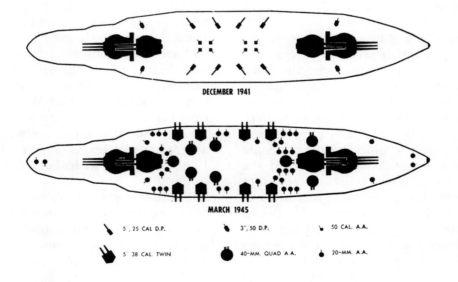

One of the reasons the old battleships fared so poorly at Pearl Harbor was their paucity of antiaircraft guns. These diagrams show the extent to which the *Nevada*'s AA battery was beefed up between the beginning of the war and its end. (Reprinted from *U.S. Navy Bureau of Ordnance in World War II*.)

The *Nevada* was the only battleship to get under way in Pearl Harbor on 7 December 1941. In the foreground is Ford Island. At right, just beyond the ship, is a part of the navy yard, and in the background are the submarine base and the tank farm. (National Archives: 80-G-32559.)

Myth has it that the *Arizona* was devastated by a bomb that went down the uptakes of her smokestack. Many more of her men would have survived if the bomb that did so much damage had gone into her stack. (U.S. Navy: Naval Institute Collection.)

had been outfitted with gun tubs during an overhaul in late 1940, into which the 1.1-inch guns would be installed. But these tubs were still empty in late 1941.

Let us now cross over into the enemy camp for a moment. During my stewardship of the U.S. Naval Institute, I was secretary-treasurer when Captain Mitsuo Fuchida of the Japanese Navy wrote his article, "I Led the Air Attack on Pearl Harbor," which was published in the September 1952 issue of the *Proceedings* and appears on page 1 of this volume.

Captain Fuchida gave the lie to the canard that the "fleet was asleep," by stating unequivocally that he was amazed, as he flew in from the west in the high-altitude bombers, that so much antiaircraft fire was already in the air. Indeed, my experience was exactly the same. Assuming that we should not have been manning the guns twenty-four hours a day, the reaction time to the threat was amazing. I ran up six ladders and along a few feet of deck—and the guns were not only manned and ready, but had been on the "kill."

Previous warning would not have helped much, in my opinion. The real *material* damage at Pearl Harbor was done by the torpedo planes. They caused the *Oklahoma* to roll over; the shock of explosion rolled over the *Oglala* next to the *Helena*.

Torpedoes caused the *California* to settle. Torpedoes undoubtedly broke the back of the *Arizona*, probably allowing a bomb to penetrate the top of number two turret or possibly pass close by the barbette and explode the main battery ammunition. I only wish that bomb had "gone down the stack," as is popularly believed. Hundreds of men would be alive today had this Hollywood scenario been followed, since the stack of the *Arizona* was shaped like an inverted Y, with the uptakes angled radically from the top of the stack to the boiler rooms. A bomb dropping down the stack would have exploded in the "uptakes" and in the spaces below. Even a boiler explosion (and the *Arizona* probably had but one boiler in operation) would not have caused the horrible explosion that did occur in that ship.

Bomb damage to ships was substantial only where the destroyers were struck in dry docks. These relatively fragile ships were penetrated to their magazines, and exploded. But on the battleships, which were the main Japanese targets, the bombs damaged only the superstructure areas. To be sure, they killed a lot of people, started a lot of fires, and broke up a lot of gear. But, structurally, they did no damage of consequence to the battleships, save for the bomb which caused the explosion of the *Arizona*—if indeed it was a bomb. Still, of all the battleships, only the *Arizona* and the *Oklahoma*

During the time his ship was under way, Ensign Taussig was lying in his battle station in the starboard antiaircraft director (indicated by arrow) because a Japanese projectile had damaged his left leg, which he later lost. (National Archives: 80-G-32638.)

The *Nevada* lies beached after her gallant but unsuccessful attempt to leave the harbor was frustrated by the furious pounding she received from Japanese bombers. She is wreathed in smoke from the destroyer *Shaw*, whose magazine exploded while she was on keel blocks in the floating dry dock at left. (National Archives: 80-G-32457.)

did not live to fight another day. Later, the *Oklahoma* was raised, and possibly could have been refitted, but by that time, our war economy was turning out ships newer than the *Oklahoma*, which had been built prior to World War I.

The torpedo lesson was not lost on the Japanese. Had a second Pearl Harbor attack been made under the same circumstances, I am sure that their mix of aircraft would have been entirely different. There probably would have been no high-level bombers at all. Instead, their places would have been taken by torpedo planes. The number of dive-bombers would also have been smaller; again, their places would have been taken by torpedo planes.

How effective were the torpedoes? About 350 pounds of high explosives underwater created a gaping hole in the *Nevada*'s bow almost 20 by 40 feet, whereas a 500-pound bomb (or thereabouts) made a small hole in the boat deck and the gun deck below and exploded in a compartment without even damaging the bulkheads. The *Nevada* sustained about fourteen bomb hits and near-misses. But one torpedo really hurt us badly.

Having often second-guessed the Japanese "mix" of aircraft, I wondered about several other things concerning their tactics during the battle. It was not until 1969, for example, that my curiosity finally impelled me to ascertain why the Japanese

had failed to do certain obvious things, and even now, I am able only to guess why I think they failed.

Their strategy, insofar as the local attack was concerned, was to destroy and paralyze the fleet, particularly the battleships and the carriers. Since the carriers were at sea, the targets were then the battleships. But, in addition, their targets should have included the fuel and ammunition supplies. There, in plain view of every aviator, was the tank farm at the Naval Supply Depot, less than a half a mile from Battleship Row. Yet, not one Japanese aviator took the trouble to drop a bomb on this tempting target. One lucky hit would have sorely curtailed the fuel supplies in the Pacific and created a logistics nightmare, since there were only three oilers in the Navy's entire West Coast inventory on 7 December 1941. This Japanese error or omission freed the U.S. Navy of the replenishment effort for its forward base, and allowed that much more time to put in the effort to win the Battle of Midway in June 1942. Why was it not bombed?

I asked the question point-blank of the senior surviving Japanese officer, General Minoru Genda, and he replied ingenuously that nobody had thought of this target. I do not doubt him. Yet, while the Eskimo may start out his hunt thinking of nothing but succulent seal, he will very quickly start thinking polar bear if one rears up in front of him as vividly as the tank farm must have appeared to some of the Japanese pilots. Perhaps the real answer is that the young Japanese pilots suffered the "medal fever" common to all young people. They got medals for sinking battleships, not for blowing up fuel farms.

Why, also, had not the Japanese dropped a bomb in the ammunition depot at West Loch? Here was a truly tasty target: thousands of 14-inch and 16-inch projectiles, each with two bags of between seventy-five pounds and ninety pounds of smokeless powder, were out there in plain sight. The *Nevada*, alone, had 1,440 14-inch shells at West Loch (we were being furnished new projectiles), and 2,880 seventy-pound bags of smokeless powder. The explosion would have rattled the windows in Topeka, Kansas, but, more importantly for the Japanese, it would have been the kind of solar plexus punch that would have guaranteed that the stunned U.S. Navy would not quickly be back on its feet. Almost unbelievably, the Japanese did not know of the ammunition facility at West Loch—a lack of military intelligence which is astounding. It was no secret in the fleet—in fact, family picnics were often held there.

Finally, I have always been at a loss to understand why the Japanese did not know accurately what ships were in the harbor and their exact placement. They had sent a small submarine around the harbor early in the morning of 7 December and her cramped crew did a truly miserable job of identification. But why this ploy was necessary in the first place is difficult to understand. All the girls in Pearl Harbor knew. And the Japanese spies at Pearl could have found out the same way the ladies did. I must digress in order to explain.

We ensigns—and even some of the older officers—were forbidden to tell our lady friends when we would be in the harbor and when we would be at sea. Thus, like the traditional shipboard announcement, "There will be liberty—but no boats!" a young lady could always get a date, but her male partner might not always be able to keep it. This infuriating policy had produced the most expert group of ship-recognition experts ever trained. The girls would anxiously drive up the public highways to Aiea, slow their cars down, and identify the various ships in the harbor. "The *Aylwin* is out," one girl might say, "I hope that cute ensign from the *Rowan* calls me tonight; it's in."

No matter how hard the U.S. Navy tried to keep secret which ships were in and where, every young lady worth her salt in the Hawaiian area could tell you exactly what ships were in or out, and where the in-port ships were berthed. (This was important intelligence because of the necessity to catch the motor boats to those ships not berthed alongside the docks.)

Today, with almost the same detachment that I studied the Battle of Jutland when at the Naval War College, I try to follow the unending Battle of the Bookcases, as the new "historians" ally themselves—or clash—with the old in refighting Pearl Harbor. Yet, I do not consider myself a Pearl Harbor buff, for I have never made a formal study of the causes and effects of that battle.

Even when I returned to Pearl Harbor in 1949 as administrative aide to the naval base commander, I experienced the same sense of personal detachment insofar as the strategic and policy reasons for the debacle were concerned.

During my tour at the Naval Institute, I was constantly reminded of my very real ignorance of the battle. I was neither a revisionist, an apologist, nor anything else, I told myself. What had happened had happened, insofar as politico-strategic aspects were concerned. Neither as ensign nor as commander were there very many contributions I could make to the guesswork behind the scenes leading to the defeat of our fleet. Yet, I was not without my opinions.

Personally, I felt, and still do, that Admiral Husband Kimmel and General Walter Short were treated in a totally unfair and unethical manner. Even today, I can clearly visualize Admiral Kimmel running out to his lanai when the noise of battle alerted him to what was going on. What should he have done? Dashed to his den and picked up a pistol or a shotgun? Run out to his car and raced to his headquarters? And when he got there, what was he to do? Call Washington?

If, as may be inferred, he and General Short failed to display sufficient foresight, their inquisitors, in uniform and out, later made up for it by their dazzling exhibitions of hindsight. But, of course, someone had to shoulder the blame for a catastrophic tactical situation—which, in the opinion of many, was merely the inevitable result of the actions of the strategic and political planners in Washington.

To be more specific: in my opinion, the only possible result of any "prior alert" that might have given the fleet an opportunity to sortie would have exacted a far greater death toll—though probably fewer wounded, since we would have drowned—than actually occurred. The only hope, had we been at sea, was that the Japanese might not have found us. As for myself, given a second turn, I would choose to be in a vessel that was tied up alongside the quays, exactly as we were.

Joseph Knefler Taussig, Jr., (1920–   ) is the son and namesake of an admiral. Upon graduation from the Naval Academy in 1941, he reported to the *Nevada* and served in her until he was wounded in the Japanese attack. He spent much of World War II in hospitals recovering from the damage to his leg. In 1949, he was graduated from George Washington University Law School, and from 1952 to 1954, while senior instructor in military law at the Naval Academy, he assumed collateral duty as secretary-treasurer of the Naval Institute. After retirement from active duty in 1954, he remained at the Institute as executive secretary for two years and has been a frequent contributor since then. Subsequently, Captain Taussig held positions in industry with Westinghouse, Raytheon, and Joy Manufacturing Company, and in 1962 he established Taussig-Tomb & Associates, a consulting and representative firm in Washington, D.C. In July 1981, he was appointed Deputy Assistant Secretary of the Navy for Civilian Personnel Policy/Equal Employment Opportunity. Captain Taussig lives in Annapolis, Maryland. (Courtesy of Naval Academy Alumni Association.)

The Value of Gold Braid

By Captain Charles J. Merdinger, Civil Engineer Corps, U.S. Navy (Retired)

The *Nevada* was scheduled to stay at sea over the weekend of 7 December. At least that was the rumor we heard in the junior officers' mess. However, there were some reported submarine contacts, so it was decided—again, according to rumor—that because of these contacts we would return early to Pearl Harbor. It's intriguing to think that perhaps we were unnecessarily driven into Pearl when we might have stayed out and avoided what came that Sunday morning.

I went ashore the night of 6 December and bought an artificial Christmas tree. Some of my friends decided to stay ashore all night, and after we got into the war the next morning, I was beginning to wish I'd stayed with them.

Because I slept late on Sunday morning, the first thing I became aware of was the alarm clanging, a little before 8:00 a.m. This wasn't unusual, because we were always being subjected to man-over-board drills or "fire on the *Arizona*," or something else at odd times. So I thought it was a drill. As soon as I heard the alarm, I started to get into my clothes. I always had everything hanging up nearby. I'd put on one sock and was putting on the second when, all of a sudden, I heard a boom and a rat-a-tat. The whole place seemed to erupt, and a fellow ran by my room saying, "It's the real thing. It's the Japs."

My roommate, Ensign Joe Taussig, had left our room some time before to stand watch on the quarterdeck. We never did see each other that day, but I had the unhappy task of requesting medical assistance for him shortly after the action began. In my hurry, I stepped right through my sock, put on my slippers, dungarees, and officer's hat and went to my battle station. It was five decks below the main deck in the main battery plotting room.

Normally, I was the most junior officer in the plotting room. Two other officers were senior to me, but neither of them was on board ship that morning. This left me the only officer at that battle station. Eventually, we stayed in the plotting room until about three o'clock that afternoon. In the meantime, the ship sustained one torpedo and five bomb hits. She not only listed but ultimately was beached and sank. We went right down with her,

and we were actually lower than the surface of the water in our position inside the ship.

Partway through the engagement, I received a call to send about half my men topside to man the guns. We'd had a lot of people killed up there on the 5-inch antiaircraft guns. I picked out those who were manning the least useful phone circuits. We weren't really directing the big guns, because there was no need for them, but we were serving as a communication center. We were connected with the tops, the turrets, and a number of other sections of the ship.

This was a real Hobson's choice, because I felt that those men who were singled out to go topside thought they were going to their deaths. And the ones who were staying thought they were staying to their deaths, because it looked as though we might get trapped down there. So this was a moment when I was faced with what seemed to me at the time a life-and-death decision that had to be made immediately. Most of the men in the plotting room were older than I, a junior ensign at the time. They'd been in the Navy many more years than I, but there wasn't a murmur. People just said, "Aye, aye, Sir," and went. Right then, I was struck by the value of military protocol—including the importance of relatively small items such as saluting and gold braid on the hat—in training for this type of response. All these things, I think, pay off at a moment of crisis.

In the course of all this, with the ship sinking and listing, I was getting reports from topside that the *Oklahoma* had turned over. At this point, we were canting maybe 12 or 15 degrees and it seemed a lot more than that down where we were. To hear that another ship had turned turtle certainly didn't contribute to our peace of mind. Then came a report that the *Arizona* had blown up. I was getting reports that there was a fire in one of the magazines very close to us. We heard that it was just about to blow, and our firefighters couldn't get any water to it. So it seemed that everything that was happening to these other ships in some way was happening to us at the same time. Of course, one's imagination takes one a long way in a situation such as that.

We were without fresh air for a good long time,

Channel buoy number 24 snuggles against her starboard side and a harbor tug plays a stream of water on her port side, as the battleship *Nevada* lies beached and smoking off Hospital Point. Having taken on considerable water through a torpedo hole forward, she is well down by the bow. When Ensign Merdinger found his battle station in main battery plot leaking water, he decided the time had come to escape. His roommate, Ensign Joe Taussig, had already been evacuated from the starboard antiaircraft director (arrow). (National Archives: 80-G-19940.)

and ultimately the main power failed. We shifted to auxiliary power, and it produced an eerie green light. People took off their shirts, and the scene resembled one in a submarine movie with men lying around, sweat on their bodies, and bathed in green light. But we were manning the phones, and I think we were performing a useful function.

Along about three o'clock, water started coming in through the door by which we had entered the plotting room. We knew the ship had sunk, and we knew we were under water pressure. The plates above us were starting to go, and water was beginning to drop from the overhead. In essence, we were in a big air bubble.

I called up the executive officer, told him that it was impossible for us to hold on more than a few seconds longer, and requested permission to secure. He told us to go ahead, so I passed the word. Every-

body took off his phones, wrapped them up, and put them in place on the bulkhead just as he had always done. By then, water was rushing past everyone's feet, but the men were so trained that they did things exactly as they'd done them a hundred times before.

Then we opened the door to the adjacent central station, which was filled with smoke. We didn't really know where we were going from there. Everybody filed in, and finally I closed the door behind us. Going up from the space was a communication tube that ran all the way up to the conning tower. It was just full of wires, and normally nobody ever climbed up inside, but all ten of us managed it that day.

As we got toward the top of the tube, I smelled fresh air for the first time in all those hours, and that was the greatest blessing. I just never felt anything so wonderful as that breath of fresh air.

Charles John Merdinger (1918–   ) was graduated from the Naval Academy in 1941. After the *Nevada*, he served as 16-inch turret officer in the *Alabama* in both Atlantic and Pacific. He then did postgraduate work at Rensselaer Polytechnic Institute, transferred to the Navy's Civil Engineer Corps, won a Rhodes Scholarship, and received his doctorate from Oxford University. Captain Merdinger was director of the Naval Civil Engineering Laboratory, head of the English, History and Government department at the Naval Academy, and assistant chief of the Bureau of Yards and Docks. He held public works, construction, and Seabee billets in Panama, Bremerton, Alaska, Miramar, Japan, and Vietnam. After commanding Western Division, Naval Facilities Engineering Command, he retired from the Navy in 1970. He has since been president of Washington College, vice president of the Aspen Institute for Humanistic Studies, deputy director of Scripps Institution of Oceanography, and is currently a director of AVCO Corporation. He lives at Lake Tahoe, Nevada, and La Jolla, California. (Courtesy of Naval Academy Alumni Association.)

The Cheer-Up Ship

By Vice Admiral Lorenzo S. Sabin, U.S. Navy (Retired)

For several days prior to the attack, the battleships at Pearl Harbor had been replacing their standard-weight main battery projectiles with heavier-than-standard projectiles. This had been ordered by the Bureau of Ordnance, which accepted the loss of a mile or so in maximum range in exchange for a higher penetration factor and a larger and more powerful explosive charge.

In order for the new projectiles to be fired with approximately the same muzzle energy as the old ones, new powder charges were needed also. At the time, I was type gunnery officer on the staff of Com-

mander Battleships Battle Force, Rear Admiral Walter S. Anderson. On Saturday afternoon, 6 December 1941, Lieutenant Commander Armand J. Robertson, gunnery officer of the *Nevada*, reported to me that all old main-battery projectiles and all old powder had been removed from the ship and all new projectiles loaded on board, leaving only the new powder charges to be loaded.

Since his crew had been working around the clock and needed a rest, Robertson said that unless I directed otherwise, he would arrange for the new powder to be barged from the ammunition depot

When Commander Sabin visited the smoking, shattered *Nevada* on the afternoon of 7 December, she bore grim reminders of the devastation wrought upon her during the morning's attack. By the next day, however, her men had done much to put the "Cheer-Up Ship" back in shape. (National Archives: 80-G-32745.)

at Lualualei to the *Nevada* early the following morning. On Sunday morning, that barge was en route to the *Nevada* when the attack started; it was loaded with enough powder to blow up half of Pearl Harbor. Captain Francis W. Scanland, commanding officer of the *Nevada*, was not on board when the attack began, but the command duty officer made the decision to get the ship under way. When the Japanese caught her in the channel, they gave her a terrible beating, hoping to sink her and thus block the channel. They almost—but not quite—succeeded. The *Nevada* didn't blow up and sink, because there was no main-battery powder in her magazines! By superb shiphandling and a valuable assist from the minesweeper *Seagull*, commanded by Lieutenant Commander Daniel B. Candler, the *Nevada* was kept from capsizing and was later secured upright with anchors in the channel and wire hawsers to the shore.

Sunday afternoon, following the attack, Admiral Anderson directed the type material officer, Commander Edgar P. Kranzfelder; the type damage control officer, Commander William V. Hamilton; and me to accompany him on an inspection of the ships that had not been sunk. When we arrived aboard the *Nevada*, we saw a scene of complete shambles, particularly on the main deck, topside, and the upper structure. The grim effects of her punishment were everywhere. Twisted masses of metal and spidery steel were spattered with blood, while bodies and parts of bodies were being pulled from the debris. But the crew had already started to clear the debris on the main deck and to bring some semblance of order out of the chaos. Topside it was worse. All 5-inch antiaircraft guns were out of commission, the ship had no power, wreckage and destruction were everywhere, and the decks and bulkheads were red with blood. Lieutenant Commander Robertson, his face drawn and gaunt from the strain, nevertheless managed a smile. "Come back tomorrow," he said.

I did just that, and what I saw was a complete metamorphosis. Gone were the twisted metal, wreckage, and debris. Decks and bulkheads had been washed down, and already repainting had started. All about were signs such as "This is the 'Cheer-Up' ship," "We'll fight again," "Cheer up the Cheer-Up ship." Topside was almost the same. In addition, all 5-inch guns had been repaired. Auxiliary generators from the beach supplied enough power to train and elevate the guns. "What," I asked Robbie, "are you going to do for air at the guns?"

He took me over to a space and pointed to a torpedo airflask. "We scrounged that from the submariners," he said. "We charged it up to its 1,500 pounds, put a reducer in the line to bring it down

In the wake of the Japanese attack, Rear Admiral William R. Furlong, at right, commandant of the Pearl Harbor Navy Yard, and Commander Harry L. Thompson, acting commanding officer of the *Nevada*, inspect damage to the ship. Furlong is standing on a plank because the deck plating forward of turret 1's barbette has gone. (National Archives: 80-G-323800.)

to the 450 pounds we need at the guns, and connected them up." Then he added; "Sabe, we have a commanding view of the channel entrance. Except for the main battery, all my guns are manned and ready to fire!"

When the three battleships still afloat and able to get under way—the *Maryland, Pennsylvania,* and *Tennessee*—were ordered to Bremerton for battle repairs to ease the load on the yard at Pearl, I guess the *Nevada*'s crew thought we were going out to seek battle with the enemy. They lined the rail and, as each ship passed, they gave her a mighty cheer.

I never served in the *Nevada* myself, but I can understand how proud of her are those who did— including some who, like Ensign Joseph K. Taussig, were critically wounded, plus perhaps those whose spirits hovered over that ship. Certainly, the *Nevada* has earned a place in the glorious history of our Navy as one of our most gallant ships of the line.

Lorenzo Sherwood Sabin (1899–   ) was graduated from the Naval Academy in 1921 and later received postgraduate education in ordnance engineering. Sea duty prior to World War II included the *Tennessee, Northampton, Augusta*, Base Force staff, *O'Bannon, West Virginia*, and Battleships Battle Force staff. During the war, he commanded LCI-L Flotillas 1 and 2 and Landing Craft and Bases Europe before reporting to the OpNav staff. Subsequently, he commanded Destroyer Flotilla 1 and was chief of staff to Commander Destroyers Pacific Fleet before being selected to flag rank in 1948. He held eleven different billets as a flag officer. Among them were command of Amphibious Training Command Pacific, Amphibious Group 1, Task Force 1 during Operation "Passage to Freedom" in Vietnam, Amphibious Task Force Seventh Fleet, Naval Gun Factory Washington, Potomac River Naval Command, and Amphibious Force Atlantic Fleet. Admiral Sabin retired from active duty in 1961 and now lives in La Jolla, California. (National Archives: 80–G–43842.)

The Raising and Salvaging of the *Nevada*

By Vice Admiral Homer N. Wallin, U.S. Navy (Retired)

When the Japanese attack began, the *Nevada* was moored in the berth astern of the *Arizona*. In accordance with the fleet doctrine, she immediately prepared to get under way and was able to do so although suffering from one torpedo hit. As she steamed down the channel toward the sea entrance, she was heavily attacked by dive-bombers and suffered seven or eight bomb hits. Two of these hits in the forward areas induced serious flooding. By the time the *Nevada* reached the entrance, she had taken on a great amount of water, and it was apparent to Lieutenant Commander Francis J. Thomas, the plucky young officer then in command, that the ship should not enter the channel because of the risk of blocking it. Accordingly, he decided to beach her and did a very successful job. The fine spirit of her personnel which permitted the *Nevada* to get under way and fight off her attackers soon was to carry her over the difficulties of refloating and rehabilitation and the eventual return home under the ship's own power.

As the *Nevada* lay beached near the entrance channel to Pearl Harbor, she really was a sorry sight to behold. It was not a pleasant spectacle for new ships arriving to reinforce or support the Pacific Fleet. Her stern was only a few feet from the shore, while her bow was practically submerged in the deep water near the channel. The forecastle was pretty much a tangled mess of twisted steel, and the superstructure up through the bridge had been entirely gutted by fire. The inside of the ship was completely filled with water and fuel oil.

There was considerable doubt in most minds as to whether the ship could ever be floated, and there were very few who even dimly hoped that she could be of any further military value. The "Cook's tour" of damaged ships by newly arrived personnel usually brought forth pessimistic forecasts regarding the *Nevada*—and she was the least damaged of the battleships which had been sunk.

However, the officers and men of the *Nevada* who had not been transferred were full of optimism, optimism that seemed a bit foolhardy perhaps. They insisted, especially Lieutenant Commander George E. Fee, the engineer officer, that the remainder of their crew be kept together in order that the ship when raised might be returned to the mainland under her own power. This fine spirit of the ship's personnel was greatly respected and appreciated. Their request was approved, but with some mental reservations. Yet this time optimism paid off!

Immediately following 7 December, the crew of the ship set to work to remove wreckage and to condition the ship for salvage operations. Salvage personnel, including divers, made a careful check of underwater damage and found that most of the flooding occurred through three large holes—one a torpedo hit on the port side at frame forty and 20 feet below the waterline, and two bomb hits, the first at frame thirteen starboard which passed through the forecastle and out through the shell about 13 feet below the main deck. This bomb exploded alongside the ship and opened up a triangular hole about 25 feet long and 18 feet deep, which was responsible for most of the flooding of the ship. The second bomb passed through the forecastle and eventually out through the bottom of the ship. It exploded in the water and left a hole about 6 feet in diameter. As a matter of special interest, this bomb passed through the large built-in gasoline tanks without igniting the contents.

In order to shut off flooding from the torpedo hole, a large wooden patch was manufactured by the Pearl Harbor Navy Yard. This patch was ship-shape, about 55 feet long and 32 feet deep, and extended around the turn of the bilge. The shape of the patch was obtained from measurements taken from the exposed bilge of the *Oklahoma* which was a sister ship of the *Nevada*. The patch was a massive affair and proved unsatisfactory for the purpose intended. Divers were unable to fit the patch to the hull of the ship satisfactorily for a number of important reasons, one of which was that it just seemed too large to handle satisfactorily in one piece. Eventually it was decided to endeavor to unwater the *Nevada* without this large patch, on the assumption that some of the bulkheads in the area

The *Nevada*'s upper deck was badly ruptured by a bomb that struck forward of turret 1. (Naval Historical Center: NH 64484.)

of the damage would be sufficiently intact to restrict the inflow of water, at least to a degree which would permit internal measures to be taken.

The two holes caused by bombs in the bow area were temporarily covered with wooden patches ordinarily referred to as window frames. The work was done by divers on the outside. The patches were drawn up reasonably tight by hook bolts. The bolts were hooked into holes burned into the small shell plating by underwater cutting torches.

All hull openings were plugged wherever possible by divers. Broken airports under water were made tight by use of wooden plates and draw bolts. Drain scuppers were plugged with mattresses, wooden plugs, and other similar material.

A large number of gasoline-driven suction pumps were used to unwater the *Nevada*, varying in size from 3 inches to 10 inches. Inasmuch as the maximum lift of a suction pump under the operating conditions embodied was about 15 feet, it was necessary to install pumps at various levels throughout the ship. The small 3-inch pumps were used for "clean-up" jobs, such as for the final water in cut-up compartments, corners, etc. An excellent organization was developed to operate the pumps continuously, and this organization became very adept at diagnosing troubles and remedying them.

In the case of ships floated after the *Nevada*, a much improved pump became available. This was the "deep-well" pump which was of the centrifugal type operated by a propeller shaft extending from the topside to the bottom of the vertical piping. Of course, such pumps could be used for straight pipe lines only, and were ideally suited for use in trunks

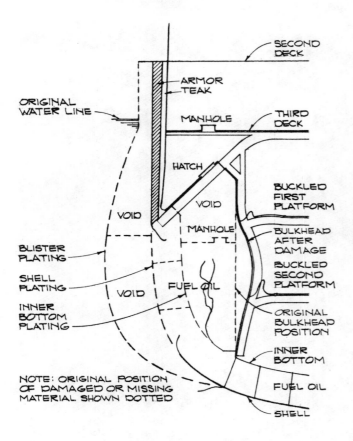

ORIGINAL WATER LINE

SECOND DECK

ARMOR
TEAK

MANHOLE

THIRD DECK

HATCH

VOID

BUCKLED FIRST PLATFORM

VOID

MANHOLE

BULKHEAD AFTER DAMAGE

BLISTER PLATING

BUCKLED SECOND PLATFORM

SHELL PLATING

VOID

FUEL OIL

INNER BOTTOM PLATING

ORIGINAL BULKHEAD POSITION

INNER BOTTOM

NOTE: ORIGINAL POSITION OF DAMAGED OR MISSING MATERIAL SHOWN DOTTED

FUEL OIL

SHELL

such as were common on the battleships under salvage. These pumps came in sizes varying from 8 inches to 12 inches and were capable of handling tremendous quantities of water; the 10-inch pump would handle about 4,000 gallons per minute.

As indicated heretofore, the *Nevada* was completely filled with seawater and oil. The plan for floating the ship contemplated the installation of a sufficient number of pumps to remove the water faster than it could flow into the ruptured shell with patches in place to the extent mentioned. As the unwatering work commenced, it was apparent that there would be no difficulty in floating the vessel. However, the amount of space from which water was removed at any one time had to be governed by a schedule taking into account a large number of considerations. Some of these pertained to stability and list of the ship; others had to do with making temporary repairs inside the vessel as the water was removed, such as stopping off leaks, shoring bulkheads, etc. Others pertained to removal of debris, cleaning, preservation of mechanical and electrical equipment, etc.

As the water level was reduced inside the ship, it was noted that all surfaces were heavily coated with fuel oil. This had some good effects but mostly bad. Steps were taken to organize working parties to remove such coating by hosing down with a hot caustic solution and rinsing with salt water. Sand was placed on the decks to improve footing. As various compartments were uncovered, the ship's force removed the wreckage, stores, provisions, and eventually ammunition. Electric motors and certain items of auxiliary machinery were removed as soon

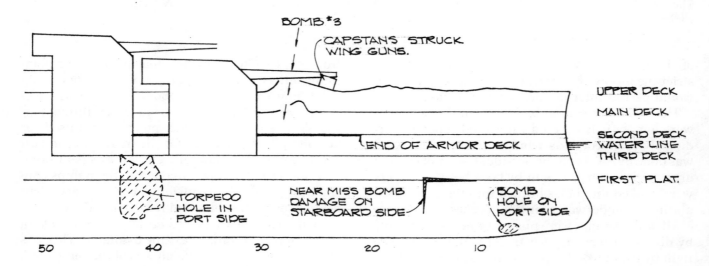

BOMB #3

CAPSTANS STRUCK WING GUNS.

UPPER DECK

MAIN DECK

SECOND DECK
WATER LINE
THIRD DECK

END OF ARMOR DECK

FIRST PLAT.

TORPEDO HOLE IN PORT SIDE

NEAR MISS BOMB DAMAGE ON STARBOARD SIDE

BOMB HOLE ON PORT SIDE

50   40   30   20   10

These diagrams show the effects of bomb and torpedo hits in the forward part of the *Nevada*. The heavy torpedo damage is depicted in both diagrams. It was this torpedo, at frame forty, that caused the ship to take on a great deal of water forward and put her down by the bow as she steamed toward the harbor entrance. (Drawn by Joseph R. Beckenbach, Jr.)

The *Nevada* is afloat again in mid-February 1942. The white streaks on her hull show where her waterline was as she rose steadily higher. (Naval Historical Center: NH 50105.)

as possible after they were unwatered. The motors were sent to the navy yard for reconditioning, as were also many pieces of equipment. As the work went on, it was found that, although the motors had been submerged in saltwater for about two months, some 95 per cent of them could be reconditioned. It was also found that items of mechanical machinery that had been protected by the fuel oil were 100 per cent salvable. It was possible to recondition even such delicate instruments as electric meters.

As the main machinery spaces were pumped out, it began to seem very probable that the machinery could be put in operable condition, and all hands became increasingly optimistic regarding the ability of the *Nevada* to go home under her own power. The crew of the *Nevada* (about one-third original crew) applied themselves most strenuously to the job of cleaning up the ship and especially toward getting the machinery and equipment in running condition.

As successive stages of pumping were undertaken, the bow rose higher and higher in the water, and it soon became clear that no great difficulty would be found in floating the ship. However, it was important to reduce the draft as much as practicable, and for this reason it was decided to remove all the oil still remaining aboard and as much of the storeroom and magazine contents as practicable. The removal of oil was undertaken by operating the vessel's fuel oil transfer pumps on compressed air which was furnished by portable compressors. The operation was wholly successful and marked

the beginning of self-operation on the part of the *Nevada*.

As the unwatering schedule continued, a number of people felt ill effects from the apparent prevalence of gas which seemed to fill the ship. The very dangerous toxic properties of this gas were discovered on 7 February. On that date, Lieutenant James S. Clarkson was in the pumped-out trunk forward of the steering engine room and removed the cap from the air test fitting on the door to determine the water pressure within. The water which entered the trunk from the steering engine room released a large volume of toxic gas and Lieutenant Clarkson was overcome and collapsed. Other persons entered the trunk to rescue him, with the result that eventually six or more persons were overcome. The final result was that Lieutenant Clarkson and Chief Machinist's Mate Peter C. DeVries died as a result of gas poisoning. Thereafter, a very careful investigation was made of the gas situation, and it was determined that the gas was generated by reason of the polluted and stagnated harbor water being under pressure in closed compartments, thus forming hydrogen sulphide which is given off in large volumes in lethal concentrations when the water is released from pressure. Immediately, precautionary steps were taken to provide additional ventilation, mostly suction blowers. Also persons were prohibited from entering compartments without respiratory equipment if the compartments were found to contain dangerous concentrations of gas. There were no more persons overcome by gas on board the *Nevada*, but practically all persons work-

The *Nevada* enters dry dock No. 2 at Pearl Harbor on 18 February 1942, a milestone in the massive effort required to refloat and salvage her. The salvage of the *Nevada* paved the way for raising other, worse-damaged battleships at Pearl Harbor. (Naval Historical Center: NH 83056.)

On 22 April 1942, after preliminary repairs in dry dock, the *Nevada* left Pearl Harbor under her own power to undergo modernization and further repair on the West Coast. (U.S. Navy: Naval Institute Collection.)

ing continuously on the ship were subjected to some gassing.

The vessel was fully afloat on 12 February 1942 and was scheduled for dry-docking two days following. There was some trepidation about towing the *Nevada* across Pearl Harbor Channel because of the possibility of some occurrence which might cause reflooding and possible sinking in the channel, thus blocking it. Careful inspections were made to ensure that all bulkheads and patches were reasonably tight and that there was little if any possibility of reflooding. The dry dock was put in readiness and tugs took the *Nevada* in tow at 6:00 a.m. on 14 February. Within a few hours, the first vessel to be raised was safely tucked away in dry dock No. 2, and there was great jubilation in the hearts of the *Nevada*'s crew and of the salvage personnel. On the coping of the dock stood the Commander in Chief of the Pacific Fleet, Admiral Chester Nimitz, and high ranking officers of his staff, and also the Commandant of the Pearl Harbor Navy Yard, Rear Admiral William Furlong. This show of interest and support was a great boon to the salvage operations still ahead.

With the ship in dry dock, the navy yard turned to with a will to repair the serious hull damage, to recondition the machinery, and otherwise to get the *Nevada* in shape to return to the West Coast. The work proceeded most satisfactorily with the result that the *Nevada* sailed for the Puget Sound Navy Yard under her own power on 22 April 1942. It was a great day for the salvage organization, and indeed was a happy event for all hands of the Navy who were aware of the event.

Within a few months, the *Nevada* was revamped and modernized and took her place in the fleet as a highly valuable antiaircraft and bombardment vessel.

Homer Norman Wallin (1893–   ) was graduated from the Naval Academy in 1917 and reported to the *New Jersey*. In 1918, he transferred to the Construction Corps and underwent postgraduate instruction in naval architecture at MIT. He then had tours of duty in several navy yards and in Washington. At the time of the Pearl Harbor attack, he was material officer on the staff of Commander Battle Force and subsequently became fleet salvage officer. He was involved with shipbuilding and repair during the rest of the war. Afterward, he commanded the naval shipyards at Philadelphia, Norfolk, and Bremerton, interspersed with tours as Chief of the Bureau of Ships and as Department of Defense Coordinator of Shipbuilding, Conversion and Repair. Admiral Wallin retired from active duty in 1955 and now lives in Seattle, Washington. His book *Pearl Harbor: Why, How, Fleet Salvage and Final Appraisal* was published by the Navy in 1968. (Courtesy of Naval Academy Alumni Association.)

The Silver Mine

By Captain Walter J. Buckley, U.S. Navy (Retired)

In August 1942, when I joined the crew of the *Nevada* at the Bremerton Navy Yard, the "Cheer-Up Ship" looked anything but cheerful. She was pretty much a hulk at that point with nothing showing above the main and 01 decks except her turrets. The commission pennant was flying from a "pig stick" because there were no masts.

When I reported to the officer of the deck, he steered me to the ship's office in a building adjacent to the dry dock that held the *Nevada*. In the office I encountered the executive officer; he read my orders, looked up at me, and asked, "Have you ever seen a ship before?"

"Yes, Sir," I replied. "I have a license in my pocket that says I can be chief engineer of any size merchant ship afloat."

He then called the engineer officer, Lieutenant Commander "Gus" Fee, and told him he had a real live engineer for him. I was assigned as senior assistant engineer, and Fee was delighted to have some help, because there was a monumental job in progress to get the ship ready to rejoin the fleet.

After the *Nevada* took a beating from the Japanese planes and was partially submerged in Pearl Har-

bor, her electrical system was completely fouled up. All her wiring had to be replaced, and every motor needed to be rewired or replaced. We also had to rebuild the ship's two direct-current switchboards.

At that point in the war, copper was a critically scarce material. We were able to get around the problem by obtaining silver ingots from the Treasury Department. By rolling them out and fabricating the silver into bus bars, we were able to complete the reconstruction of the DC boards. After we painted them with Glyptal, few people knew what they were made of. They were the most valuable DC boards in the U.S. Navy, so I made frequent inspections to make sure that no electrician's mates were filing off a "poke of dust" in order to have a good liberty. In my seagoing career, I have often heard the engine-room spaces referred to as the "iron mine," but this was the first time I had encountered a "silver mine."

Gradually, we got the ship put back together, and her appearance changed dramatically from what I had seen when I first reported in the summer. The *Nevada* was ready to go back to sea in December 1942, and after we had worked out some bugs, we

In this photo, made on 15 December 1942 at the Puget Sound Navy Yard, the *Nevada* sports a much more compact superstructure than the one with which she began the war. While she was at Bremerton, Washington, her superstructure was completely rebuilt and her antiaircraft gunnery was substantially upgraded. (U.S. Navy: Naval Institute Collection.)

proceeded to Long Beach for training. While we were there, we got a batch of cargo consisting of foul-weather and cold-weather gear. As soon as the loading was complete, we got under way and headed up to the Aleutians where we participated in the invasion of Attu.

One day, we were anchored in Cold Bay, waiting for a provision ship to come alongside. Darkness descended while we were waiting, so the executive officer sent for me and told me that the supply ship had sent a message saying she wouldn't be along until morning. I was trying to figure out where I, as the assistant engineer, came into the act. Then the exec told me that the supply ship had been chartered from the United Fruit Company. He knew I had worked for that company, so he told me to go over and tell the crew that we had an urgent need for provisions. It turned out that she was the USS *Pastores*, in which I had served as junior engineer years before. Well, I rode in a whaleboat for about two miles in heavy weather and saw the Navy supply officer on board. He told me that he refused to work his crew until they'd had some rest. The only bright spot in the whole deal was that I got to see the chief engineer of the *Pastores*, and he gave me a bottle of brandy for the long, wet boat ride back to the *Nevada*.

Weather and supplies weren't our only problems up north. Back in Bremerton we had been able to get only one of six boilers retubed. Our pleas about the rest were to no avail, despite the fact that they had been submerged in saltwater for months at Pearl Harbor. After three months of continuous steaming in the Aleutians, tube ruptures became routine. Fresh water was also a big problem. The *Nevada* had evaporators designed for a peacetime crew of 1,800 men, and we had nearly 3,000 on board. After we left the Aleutians, we stopped at a shipyard in San Francisco and got the other five boilers done. Then we proceeded to the East Coast via the Panama Canal.

After we reached Norfolk, Captain Powell M. Rhea assumed command of the ship. Following the ceremonies, the exec took all the department heads to the captain's cabin to meet the new skipper. By then, I was the chief engineer, so I was included in the group. During the course of the visit, the captain turned to me and asked, "Chief, do you have a shower in your room?" I was the only department head with his own shower, and I was immediately puzzled how Captain Rhea could have gotten around the ship so fast that he had made that discovery. Then he explained: "I had that put in when I was chief engineer in 1930. It is nobody else's business how much fresh water the chief uses."

The bus bar on which the E division officer, Lieutenant (junior grade) Pitsen Berger, is leaning was quite valuable, having been made of silver rather than the customary copper. The latter was in short supply. The author, Lieutenant Commander Buckley, is second from left, wearing a baseball cap. (Courtesy of Captain Walter J. Buckley, USN, Ret.)

In 1944, coveralls were evidently popular among the *Nevada*'s officers, as they show off their World War II campaign ribbons. Captain Powell M. Rhea, the commanding officer, is at the far left in the top row. Lieutenant Commander Buckley is at right in the middle row. The other man in the middle row is Commander Howard A. Yeager, the *Nevada*'s executive officer. (Courtesy of Captain Walter J. Buckley, USN, Ret.)

Upon completion of our Norfolk overhaul (including the installation of additional evaporators), we were assigned convoy duty between New York and Belfast, Ireland. In the spring of 1944, we began training for the invasion of Europe. We got under way one morning from an anchorage in the Clyde River, near Glasgow, Scotland, for shore bombardment practice. Number two turret jammed in train, and the gunnery officer asked me for help. I was in the roller path of the turret as we were returning to anchorage. Then I felt a shudder in the ship, and someone reported that we had just run aground.

I hightailed it for the main control engine room and found that we had lost suction, because the condensers were full of mud. With no help from our engines, a combination of the tide, a British destroyer, and several tugs was able to get us afloat. We worked all night cleaning condensers and got under way the following morning for Belfast. When we arrived, our division commander, Rear Admiral Carleton F. Bryant, convened a board to investigate the grounding. The admiral's first question dealt with my whereabouts at the time of the grounding. I told him I was in number two turret, so the admiral asked if I was familiar with Navy regulations that required the chief engineer to be in main control when entering and leaving port, etc. At that point, the captain told him that I had additional duty as turret-repair officer, so I was excused and my senior assistant testified.

While we were anchored at Belfast, I received a call one morning at two o'clock. I learned that the forward diesel generator room was flooding. When I arrived, the water was about 8 feet deep and rising. No one had seen the man on watch, so a chief and I peeled off and dove in to look for a body. Believe me, the water in Belfast Lough in March was *cold*. We located the source of the flooding, and when we emerged from the space, we found the machinist's mate on watch peering down the scuttle. He said he had gone for a cup of coffee. His next cup of coffee was as a fireman—after an interview with the commanding officer.

During our convoy duty, I had qualified as an officer of the deck, and prior to the invasion of Normandy in June 1944, my battle station was assigned as secondary conn. The first lieutenant and I were the only two senior officers who didn't have battle stations on the bridge or in the foremast structure. Engine control was capably handled by my senior assistant, Lieutenant Donald K. Ross, who had performed heroically on board the *Nevada* during the Pearl Harbor attack and was later awarded the Medal of Honor.

D-Day, 6 June, provided sights I will never forget. Not many engineers ever get a bird's eye view of battle action, and at times I was wishing for the protection of the armored deck. Our 14-inch guns barked time and again, pounding the enemy-held coastline to beat back the Germans and open holes for our tanks to move out from the landing beaches. The *Nevada* came through unscathed, but we didn't get a chance to rest on our laurels. We returned to Plymouth, England, for fuel and ammunition, then went back to Omaha Beach. After another stop at Plymouth, we went to bombard Cherbourg. The *Nevada* was in a task force which had Rear Admiral Morton L. Deyo in the heavy cruiser *Tuscaloosa* as officer in tactical command. Also along were the old battleships *Texas* and *Arkansas* and a couple of British cruisers. The Germans were well prepared and hit the *Texas* and a British cruiser. The *Nevada* was straddled a good many times by enemy shells but not damaged. That afternoon, the skipper called to tell me we were going to retire; he wanted me to give it all we had. I called main control and told the men down there to throw on the coal. The *Tuscaloosa* was operating nearby, and we went past her as though she were stopped. Years later, I met Admiral Deyo and told him I had been in the "armored cruiser squadron" (as we called our batch of World War I-era battleships) at Cherbourg. He asked me how a thirty-year-old battleship had been able to outrun a much newer cruiser, so I paraphrased Caesar to him. We had not stood on the order of our going—only on going like hell to get out of there.

After that, we went through the invasion of Southern France without incident, and then in September returned to the States. A hurricane diverted us to New York for a welcome respite, and from there we proceeded to Norfolk to be regunned and overhauled. In November, we headed for the Panama Canal and Long Beach. Then it was on to Pearl Harbor and Ulithi to prepare for the invasion of Iwo Jima in early 1945. Again, we came out with no damage and returned to the huge fleet anchorage at Ulithi. Okinawa was next on the agenda, and there our luck ran out. Prior to the invasion, we were hit at daybreak by a kamikaze plane. Number three turret was knocked out; there was considerable hull damage; and we had many personnel casualties. After L-Day, we were hit by a shore battery with no serious damage and only a few casualties. We got mail then, and I learned that my wife and I had become parents of a baby boy. (Yes, that had been a pleasant respite between battles in the Atlantic and Pacific.) My son was six months old by the time I first saw him.

What was probably the *Nevada's* finest performance in the years after the attack on Pearl Harbor came in June 1944 when her ten 14-inch guns provided devastating bombardment fire during the landings in Normandy on 6 June and the days that followed. (National Archives: 80-G-231647 and 80-G-252412.)

Painted a bright orange-red to make her identifiable as the "bull's-eye" ship for upcoming atomic bomb tests, the *Nevada* steams past Waikiki Beach in May 1946, en route to Pearl Harbor. After a brief stay there, she steamed to Bikini Atoll in the Marshall Islands, where she was engulfed in a series of bomb blasts; shown here is the Baker Day explosion of 24 July. Her tough structure survived, as it did at Pearl Harbor, but her topside areas were knocked into considerable disarray by the effects of the blasts. Her stack, mast, antennas, and aircraft crane were all knocked askew. (U.S. Navy:Navy Institute Collection; Joint Army Task Force One; United Press International.)

Having survived atomic bomb tests at Bikini, the tenacious *Nevada* finally sank in 1948 when she was used as a target for surface-ship gunfire some sixty-five miles southwest of Oahu. (National Archives: 80-G-498282.)

My relief as chief engineer reported on board at Ulithi, and after the ship got to Guam, I was sent on ahead to Pearl with all our battle damage repair requirements and requisitions. I spent one night on Guam, and in the morning I was on my way to the Pacific Fleet headquarters to arrange transportation to Hawaii. I saw three officers approaching me, and as I saluted, one of them stopped and asked, "Aren't you new here?" It was Fleet Admiral Chester W. Nimitz.

I was new there, because Guam was one of the few places the *Nevada* and I hadn't been to up to then. I went on to Pearl and got detached when the ship arrived there. I was transferred to the new heavy cruiser *Helena*, so I was elsewhere for the last few events in the career of the "Cheer-Up Ship." In 1946, she was in the bull's-eye for atomic bomb tests at Bikini, and then in July 1948, she was finally sunk as a target near Pearl Harbor—a few dozen miles from where the Japanese had used her as a target six and a half years earlier. I have often wondered whether the treasure trove was removed before the *Nevada*'s end or whether, with the passage of time, the silver bars were forgotten and went to the bottom with the fine old ship.

Walter John Buckley (1909–   ) was graduated from Massachusetts Maritime Academy in 1929 and commissioned an ensign in the Naval Reserve the following year. For several years, he served in merchant ships, including holding the position of chief engineer. He reported to active duty with the Navy in 1940 and served with the Inspector of Naval Material and at the Submarine Chaser Training Center at Miami before being ordered to the *Nevada*. Subsequent sea duty included being engineer officer in the *Helena* and *Coral Sea*, executive officer in the *Noble*, and commanding officer of the repair ship *Kermit Roosevelt*. He had several tours with the Office of Naval Material and was twice at the headquarters of the First Naval District. He was retired for disability in 1962 and joined the New Hampshire Insurance Group of Manchester. Captain Buckley, who now lives in Arlington, Massachusetts, is quite active in the Retired Officers Association. (Courtesy of Captain Walter J. Buckley, USN, Ret.)

Why Them and Not Me?

By Commander Paul H. Backus, U.S. Navy (Retired)

After so many years, it is almost impossible to capture in words the attitudes which prevailed and the events which took place on 7 December 1941. Something which today is accepted as a "proven fact" might have been, in reality, a possibility or half-truth in the initial telling. But an event like the attack on Pearl Harbor is a once-in-a-lifetime sort of experience for most of us. Forty years of tarnish in the memory might blur the edges and upset the order, but until death wipes the slate clean, the stark reality of the images never fades.

In remembering the attack on Pearl, it is all too tempting to focus on the events of that morning and to omit mention of the prevailing atmosphere. To me, however, and I think to those who come after us, the story is most meaningful when told within the context of the environment in which we were immersed.

I was the signal officer in the *Oklahoma*. I was lucky to have the job and I enjoyed it immensely. I was blessed with an encouraging department head, Lieutenant Mann Hamm, and a crackerjack signal gang led by Chief Petty Officer Thomas Zvansky, an old-line chief who really knew his job and how to indoctrinate young ensigns. The chief was supported admirably by two superb first class signalmen, Eugene M. Skaggs and Lester J. Williams.

In the *Oklahoma* the signal officer's job was to be the interface between the conning officer and the signal bridge. In those days about 85 per cent of the tactical signals were visual. The signal officer had to interpret these signals for the conning officer and to obtain from him an "understood" before the ship indicated she was ready to "execute" the signal. If asked, the signal officer was expected to advise the officer of the deck how to maneuver the ship in response to the pending signal. While under way, this involved being on the bridge all day and often during the night. Just off the signal bridge was a sea cabin which I was allowed to use. The hours were long but never dull. One certainly learned tactics in a hurry. I found it all fascinating.

There was both a wardroom and a junior officers' mess in the *Oklahoma*. The wardroom was for all the officers except the junior ensigns (those with two years of service or less) and was off limits to the junior ensigns except by invitation. We ensigns

had our own mess on the second deck forward. At the time it was lorded over by those in the Naval Academy's class of 1940.

Approximately two years before the attack on Pearl Harbor, reserve officers from the merchant marine, the organized Naval Reserve, and those who had gone through the NROTC program at such universities as Yale, Harvard, California, and Washington had been ordered to duty. The *Oklahoma* had a number of these officers on board. They were good and were about the same seniority as the Naval Academy class of 1939.

"Ninety-day wonders" also were coming into the fleet. In some wardrooms their presence caused problems. The fact that they had received their commissions after only ninety days of training and, in some cases, outranked those who had been graduated from the Naval Academy was not easy for some to swallow. There wasn't much of this feeling in the *Oklahoma*. We had a good bunch of junior ensigns. On 7 December, there were heroes among the ninety-day wonders.

The *Oklahoma* was a reasonably happy ship, but the atmosphere was in a state of change at the time of the attack. There had been a change in command a few weeks before. Someone who had been liked very much by all hands, Captain Edward J. Foy, had been relieved. The new man, Captain Howard D. Bode, was an entirely different personality. Everyone, including the executive officer, was having great difficulty adjusting to him.

In the weeks just before the attack, the ship had been involved in a collision with another battleship and a very, very near-miss with a carrier. In the first instance, the fact that the *Oklahoma* had an old steam-operated reciprocating main propulsion plant prevented disaster. Steam turbines don't have much backing power. The older reciprocating type had as much power going astern as going forward. This, and the skill of Captain Foy, saved us from plowing into the side of the *Arizona* just outboard of her wardroom when almost everyone was there for the evening meal.

Testimony taken from members of the watch on board the *Oklahoma*, including me, by the board of investigation was thought to be so biased in favor of Captain Foy that I was given to understand much

Junior officers worked hard on board the ships of the prewar Navy. The *Oklahoma* is shown here not long before the beginning of World War II. (Courtesy of Gerald E. Foreman, USS *Oklahoma* Association.)

of it was discounted. (He was not selected for rear admiral as early as he should have been.) In short, Captain Foy was very highly regarded by everyone in the ship. The new man had a tough time coming up against that kind of loyalty and affection.

The only reservation we ensigns had about Captain Foy involved his niece. She lived with the Foys out near Waikiki. Actually, she was a charming and attractive girl, but at least outwardly we objected to being dragooned by the captain for escort duty. Most of the burden fell on a friend and classmate, Ensign Adam De Mers. Adam, like the captain, hailed from Arkansas and was a favorite of the gracious Mrs. Foy.

The other ship-maneuvering incident came when the *Oklahoma* was under the command of the new captain and involved the carrier *Enterprise* turning into us during night maneuvers. She came so close that the overhang of her flight deck bent the flagstaff on the stern as she went by. The safety talker of turret four was on deck manning his telephone and was so stunned he was speechless for several minutes after seeing the overhang of the flight deck pass just over his head. Technically, of course, this too was a collision but it was never treated as such.

There was a great feeling of cockiness among those with whom I worked and played. I don't recall anyone ever expressing any concern about potential combat, naval or otherwise, with the Japanese. That combat was expected, was almost a given fact. After all, my Naval Academy class had had its first-class cruise foreshortened, and its first-class academic year compressed so that we could graduate

in February 1941 instead of June. War was expected. It was just a matter of when. But at no time in my circle was an attack on Pearl considered even a possibility.

We worked hard both at sea and in port. The crews of the battleships were professional. They were competent and well trained but probably to do the wrong things. Competition was keen among the battleships. It included every phase of operations from long-range major-caliber gun accuracy and rate of fire, through the highly structured, but very artificial, short-range battle practice for the 5 inch/51-caliber surface-to-surface secondary battery. Battleship signal gangs vied with each other across the spectrum of visual communications. Even the signal officers became involved in sending and receiving semaphore and flashing-light messages and seeing who could be the most accurate and fastest interpreter of tactical signals.

Competition in athletics also was heated. One of my more embarrassing moments occurred when, as coach of the *Oklahoma*'s softball team, I put myself in as a pinch hitter in the last inning of a championship game against the *Nevada*'s team—and proceeded to strike out.

In port, as long as your work was done, there was ample opportunity to play. Recreation facilities were plentiful. The beaches, of course, were superb. The Army's Fort DeRussy, in the middle of Waikiki, had a marvelous beach. In those days Oahu was not a tourist trap as it is today. It was beautiful, uncrowded, and there were no high-rise apartments anywhere near the beach. The favorite watering

An aerial view of the Royal Hawaiian Hotel on Waikiki Beach. (National Archives: 80-G-411109.)

spots for the "young crowd" were Lau Ye Chai's and the Royal Hawaiian Hotel. The former (a restaurant with a good dance floor) had the better band, and was less formal and more affordable. The dance floor of the Royal Hawaiian, however, was hard to beat. It was right on Waikiki Beach. There, with Diamond Head in the background and the breaking surf luminous in the moonlight, all resistance was said to dissolve.

Some of the more junior ensigns found the state of matrimony irresistible, despite the two-year ban following graduation from the Naval Academy. Almost every big ship had at least one or two ensigns who had married before the end of their initial two years of service. If this fact had become known officially to their superiors, these ensigns would have been discharged from the Navy. A few who married early admitted it and got out; most did not. There were a number in the *Oklahoma* who did not. They avoided taking the first boat ashore and always caught the early mail boat back in the morning. This routine enabled them to avoid the obvious with the senior officers. Those senior officers who might have been suspicious seemed to avoid confronting the ensign unless the latter's actions were so blatant as to demand challenge. Those who had been discharged for marrying too soon were recalled to active duty shortly after the war began.

Like all the major combatants, the *Oklahoma* had a Marine detachment on board. Ours was a good outfit. There seemed to be a fair working relationship between the sailors and Marines. I was one

sailor, however, who thought the Marines were too rigid and unthinking in carrying out their routines. This was caused by the fact that one of the Marines almost holed me with a .45-caliber automatic pistol a couple of months before the Japanese attack. We were under way, and I was on the bridge a few yards from the captain. The corporal of the guard brought up a Marine orderly to relieve the watch. One of the orderlies was going through the damn silly drill of checking his automatic—all show and no substance. He took it out of his holster, raised it to eye level, pulled back the slide to see that the chamber was clear and let it slam forward. The only trouble was he didn't take the clip out and he had his finger on the trigger. As a consequence, a fresh round was levered into the chamber, the .45 fired, the bullet hit the overhead and ricocheted by my ear. No, I didn't have a warm feeling for this routine.

At sea the ships were exercised primarily in type maneuvers. Occasionally, circular task group formations were practiced, but the opportunities were rare. Most of it was of the Turn 9 or 9 Corpen variety. Being able to turn exactly in the wake of the ship ahead and keeping the right distance at night were of critical importance to success as an underway officer of the deck. Far too little attention was paid to damage control, antiaircraft gunnery, and shore bombardment. Radar had just come into the fleet. At least one heavy ship now sported a mattress-spring antenna rotating on her foretop. I remember our astonishment as reports came in to our bridge from the ship with the radar—aircraft contacts at 25 miles or better. Unbelievable!

The *Oklahoma*, and the ships with us, operated darkened and stood condition watches during the two weeks at sea just prior to the attack. The destroyers had orders to attack any submarine contact made outside of the sanctuary areas for our boats. These actions were most unusual. Condition watches and steaming darkened ordinarily were reserved for war games. As soon as we hit port on Friday evening, 5 December, however, everything was relaxed. We went to the regular in-port routine, despite the fact that the Army had established patrols in various parts of Oahu. No antitorpedo nets were available to draw around the ship.

The *Oklahoma* was moored outboard of and starboard side to the *Maryland*. Our bows were pointed toward the harbor entrance. Our mooring was right at the head of the stretch of water which extended down past the officers' club to the submarine base. The *Oklahoma* was the ideal target for the torpedo planes, which came in low over the submarine base, dropped their fish for a reasonable arming run, and hauled ass.

I did not have the duty, but I remained in the ship Saturday night. I was low on money and didn't have a date. I went to the movie on board, did some reading afterward, and listened to the big-band records being broadcast by a Honolulu radio station. Midnight came and went. I remember being surprised by the fact that the radio station did not sign off then. It usually did. In later years, I often wondered if it remained on the air that night, later than usual, to act as a beacon for the Japanese. Since I don't recall anyone else ever raising the question, I presume I must be in error about the station broadcasting later than usual. When I finally turned off the light, my cabinmate had not returned.

When the attack started, I was in my cabin, in my bunk, half-awake. The general alarm jerked me out of my dozing state. Its clamor was paralleled by an announcement over the general announcing system, "This is a real Jap air attack and no shit." I recognized the voice. It was Herb Rommel, a senior reserve ensign, who had grabbed the microphone on his way to his battle station in turret four. Only under the most unusual circumstances would an officer personally make an announcement in those days of formal battleship routine. And the use of obscene language by anyone over the general announcing system was just unheard of. So this had to be real; moreover, right after the last word of the announcement the whole ship shuddered. It was the first torpedo hitting our port side.

Before the general alarm sounded, several officers were eating breakfast in the wardroom. Ensigns Herb Rommel and Norman C. Hoffman were among them. Steward's Mate First Class Ralph M. Boudreaux ran in shouting, "The Japs are attacking—real bombs and torpedoes." The wardroom cleared in a hurry. As he went on deck, Herb looked in the eye of a torpedo bomber, rushed aft toward his turret and, on the way, sounded the warning over the general announcing system. Apparently, before the general alarm was pulled, the officer of the deck had had the bugler sound off with the call for "air attack" over the general announcing system. I don't remember hearing it, but I've no doubt about hearing Herb's warning.

My cabin was on the second deck, starboard side, outboard of the barbette of turret one. My cabinmate was a friend and classmate, Ensign Lewis Bailey Pride, Jr., of Madisonville, Kentucky. His battle station was in a director up the foremast. Across the alcove from the entrance to our cabin was another; in it, Marine Corps Second Lieutenant Harry Gaver was berthed. He too was a friend.

The general alarm and the announcement did not awaken Bailey. I had to shake him. We threw on some clothes. While doing so, we had a chance for a few words. We asked each other how in hell the Japs managed to get in without being detected by the PBYs. These were the big seaplanes based at Ford Island. Early every morning, these flying boats used to roar down the channel and stagger into the air for their daily surveillance patrol. When the battleships were in port, this very early takeoff was damned annoying. As the large planes applied full power down past Battleship Row, they awakened all the junior officers. (The senior officers didn't mind because they lived ashore.)

After the announcement of the air attack, further word was passed for all personnel not engaged in repelling air attack to take shelter below the armored deck, which was the second deck. When I left our cabin a few seconds after Bailey, I was stopped in the passageway by Lieutenant Lawrence H. Birthisel, Bailey's division officer. He had come down from the deck above where the more senior officers were berthed. He wanted to know if Bailey was awake and on his way. I assured him that he was. This took a few extra seconds, however, because Lieutenant Birthisel seemed dazed. I convinced him finally that Bailey was up and away and continued on to my battle station. The tragic part of the story is that Bailey Pride was killed that morning. Among those who survived, I was apparently the last one to see him alive.

I learned later that the officers of the 5-inch/51 battery had gone ashore together Saturday night.

They had reason to celebrate. During the immediately preceding at-sea period, the battery had completed a highly successful battle practice firing and collected a bunch of E's, the marks of excellence. But they carried on too long that Saturday night and missed the last boat back to the ship. As a consequence, they slept in their cars and caught the mail boat very early Sunday morning. This is why Lieutenant Birthisel seemed dazed—he was half asleep—and why he was so concerned about Bailey being awake and on his way.

In U.S. men-of-war there is a convention that for general emergencies, one goes forward and up on the starboard side and down and aft on the port side. As a consequence, I went around the barbette of turret one to the port side and started aft. I passed Second Lieutenant Gaver. He was on his knees, attempting to close a hatch on the port side, alongside the barbette. This hatch was part of the trunk which led from the main deck to the magazines and was used for striking down ammunition. There were men trying to come up from below at the time Harry was trying to close the hatch. No one who survived the attack saw Harry again. He too was killed that morning.

I continued aft on the port side until I got to the ladder which I knew led up to others which went directly to the signal bridge, my battle station. This ladder was just inboard of the damage control office. As I climbed the ladder to the main deck, I noticed the office was in disarray. There was a sailor in there on his hands and knees among a mess of papers and books. I don't believe he was wounded. Apparently a torpedo had detonated below and caused the damage.

On reaching the 01 deck, I went into the captain's cabin to see if his safe was locked. Special cryptological devices and plans were kept there. It was the responsibility of those of us in the communication department to jettison such devices in emergencies if we could. Because the captain was ashore, the cabin was empty. There were no stewards about. The safe was securely locked and far too big to try to move. I left the cabin and continued up the foremast on the way to the signal bridge.

Going from the main deck to the signal bridge, I was the first officer to pass the gun deck, where the 5-inch/25 antiaircraft mounts were located. The sailors there were not manning the guns. I asked why. It turned out that the boxes containing the ready ammunition were padlocked, and there was no compressed air for the rammers. The padlocks were broken and the ammunition was hand-rammed into the breeches. Then the gun crews discovered there were no firing locks on the breech blocks. They had been removed and were down in the armory

being cleaned for a scheduled admiral's inspection. As a result, not a shot was fired from these guns before the ship rolled over.

Afterward, I learned that the officer of the deck was required to keep the key to the ammunition ready boxes in his personal possession. A practice had arisen of hanging the key on a hook in the OOD shack. The senior watch officer objected to this and made the officer of the deck keep the key on a ring hung around his neck. On the morning of 7 December, the key was still around the neck of the officer who had stood the midwatch.

The gunnery officer, Lieutenant Commander Harry H. Henderson, wanted to keep a portion of the antiaircraft battery manned and ready while we were in port. He is reported to have been overrruled by the captain. Apparently, Captain Bode believed the threat of an attack was insignificant, and it was more important to get ready for the inspection which was scheduled for Monday. As part of our preparation for the inspection, some of our blisters were open when the attack took place. The manhole covers had been removed in some instances so that the blisters could be aired out for a later cleaning. Obviously, our resistance to flooding was minimal when the torpedoes hit. When the blisters dipped under, flooding had to be massive.

When I arrived at the signal bridge, I found that the watch had responded to the signals from the flagship and from the base signal tower. As I remember the signals flying were, "repel air attack" and "get under way and leave port."

One had a good view of the amidship and stern sections of the ship from the ladders which led from the gun deck to the signal bridge. The executive officer, Commander Jesse Kenworthy, was the acting commanding officer. He came and took his station on the starboard ladder. From there he could see not only what was happening to the *Oklahoma*, but he had a pretty good view of the harbor as well.

The *Arizona* blew up at about this time. A huge spout of flame and gray-black smoke shot skyward way above her foretop. The explosion sounded like many depth charges going off simultaneously. It was a sight and sound never to be forgotten. I found out later that the only *Arizona* officer forward of her stack to survive was Ensign Douglas Hein, a classmate of mine. Doug told me that he was with the admiral and captain on the flag bridge when the explosion occurred. When he regained consciousness, he was in the water, not knowing how he got there. He was badly burned on his back, head, and hands but otherwise he was intact. Doug recovered fully, but the tragedy is that he was lost later in an aircraft accident.

About the same time, the lines securing the *Okla-*

homa to the *Maryland* had started to pop as the list on the ship increased rapidly. The executive officer, watching all of this from his station on the ladder, gave the word to abandon ship. This word was picked up and passed along topside by shouts. I think that by this time power had been lost and the general announcing system was out. In retrospect, fewer lives might have been lost if those of us topside had made more effort to get the word to those below decks to abandon ship.

I can recollect distinctly only that first torpedo explosion that helped roust me out of my bunk, although there had been at least four or five hits by this time. Another friend, Ensign Norm Hoffman, who was the second division officer, counted five torpedo hits during the time he was running from the wardroom to his turret via its lower handling room and the climb up the center column to the turret booth. There were two more hits while he was in the booth testing telephones before William F. Greenaway, the leading boatswain's mate in the second division, put his head up the hatch in the

overhang and relayed Commander Kenworthy's order to abandon ship.

Before going over the side I remember seeing some of the *Maryland*'s guns firing with *Oklahoma* sailors helping to man them. Avoiding the torpedoes and the possibility of a quick rollover, I went over the high side, which was the starboard side. I can't remember climbing over a bulwark or going through the lifelines, but I do remember sliding down the side of the ship behind some members of the Marine detachment and ending up on the anti-torpedo blister. Once on the blister, I ran forward a few frames before going into the water between the ships. I remember thinking that I probably could not make the climb from the water to the *Maryland*'s blister, that there might be a boat tied up under the *Maryland*'s bow into which I could climb and, if not, Ford Island's shore wasn't that far away.

The water between the ships was covered with fuel oil (a smell I won't forget), but it was not burning as it was in other parts of the harbor. The swim

After Ensign Backus escaped from the capsizing *Oklahoma* (right), he took a boat from the *Maryland* (left) and helped to rescue others—after he and his companions were able to shake off the fog of war and remember how to start the boat's engine. (National Archives: 80-G-32706.)

up to and around the bow of the *Maryland* was uneventful. There *was* a *Maryland* motor whaleboat tied up directly under her huge starboard anchor. Two *Oklahoma* sailors, one a boatswain's mate second class, were already in the boat. Another joined us soon after I climbed in. I had a look at the engine and found it was a new diesel with which I was unfamiliar. I could not find the starter. All three sailors indicated that they, too, were strangers to the engine, so the four of us sat in the boat until there was a lull. I remember looking up at the gigantic anchor right over our heads and thinking that if a bomb hit the *Maryland*'s forecastle we would have had it. (I was told afterwards that a bomb had hit her forecastle but obviously it did not damage the chain stopper.) When the lull occurred, the boatswain's mate remembered where the starter switch was. I told him to take over as coxswain, I'd be the engineer, and the other two would help survivors out of the water. As we got under way, one of the seamen decided he wanted to be on the beach. He slipped over the side and swam to Ford Island.

We made at least two, possibly three or four, trips between the waters around the *Oklahoma* and the Ford Island fuel dock (just forward of where the *Oklahoma* and *Maryland* were moored). The memory is a jumble of snapshots. I am not sure of their order. A few bigger boats were in the area. There were quite a few people in the water. They were covered with fuel oil. Many were choking and spitting. The *Oklahoma*'s senior medical officer, Commander Fred M. Rohow, an older man, was in trouble. He was being held up by a young Marine. Dr. Rohow either had been wounded or had been hurt in getting off the ship. We got him and the Marine and some others aboard for one boatload. At one point while we were retrieving survivors, I realized the guns were roaring again. I looked up and could see what looked like bombers at high altitude. Even more nerve-wracking was the shrapnel from our own guns, which was splashing all around us. All of this was associated with the second wave of the Japanese attack.

Another snapshot is of either a Filipino or Chamoro steward whom we pulled out of the water. He had just come out of the porthole of a second-deck compartment on the starboard side. The porthole was by this time several feet under water, the ship having rolled all the way over to port. He was almost in a state of shock. He had had to fight his way out against the surging flood of water which was entering through the porthole. There were many others in the compartment for whom he did not have much hope. No others surfaced in the immediate vicinity during the next few minutes we were in the area.

On our last run by the overturned hull of the *Oklahoma*, I noticed an officer in dress whites, with spy glass and white gloves standing on the overturned hull near the stern. There were a couple of sailors with him in undress whites. As we swung in close aboard, I realized the officer was Ensign John "Dapper Dan" Davenport, a good friend and classmate. He was the junior officer of the deck and he was manning "the quarterdeck." As the ship rolled over, he and the sailors on watch with him just rotated their station to keep up with the roll. At that point, there was plenty of room in the boat for the three of them, but "Dapper Dan" refused to ride with us. The boat was filthy with oil and he would have nothing to do with us. He and his watch were taken off a short time later by, presumably, a much cleaner boat.

There were no more *Oklahoma* survivors evident in the water at this time. As a consequence, after we delivered our last load to the fuel dock, my crew left me when I indicated I wanted to go back out to help around the *California*. There seemed to be fires in the water alongside her and some swimmers in the water in the vicinity. Other boats were headed for them and, I believe, eventually pulled them out. In any event, we beached the *Maryland* whaleboat by the fuel dock and went ashore on Ford Island.

I am vague about what I did the rest of the day. I know I spent the night of 7 December, along with a lot of others, trying to sleep on the floor of the lounge of the Ford Island bachelor officers' quarters. "Dapper Dan" was alongside. Sometime during that night, some of our own planes came in and tried to land on Ford Island. Everyone was so trigger happy by then that everything cut loose. We in the BOQ had no idea of what really was happening. For a few moments, we thought it was another Japanese air raid. But the shooting stopped almost as quickly as it started, so it seemed unlikely that the enemy had returned.

There were all kinds of rumors making the rounds during those first twelve to twenty-four hours. For example, I remember someone telling me that the Japs were landing at Barbers Point. Someone else had them coming ashore at Kaneohe Bay. Equally groundless was an announcement made over the radio that the drinking water had been poisoned.

Whether it was because of these rumors or for other reasons that I never heard about, word went out to the survivors to report to the Ford Island armory. There each officer was issued a .45 automatic, clips, a holster and belt, and a pocketful of ammunition. The enlisted men were issued rifles, belts, and ammunition. Some effort was made to organize the sailors. Sentries were posted around what was left of the hangars, shops, and officers' quarters on Ford Island. Once it got dark, it was almost worth your life to go outside. What with the impact of the attack itself and the rumors, there were a lot of itchy trigger fingers around. In any event, one heard more than just a few rifle shots ring out on those first couple of nights after the attack.

One of the stories that went around had to do with the "Battle of the Tank Farm." Those familiar with Pearl will remember that there was a sizeable tank farm not far from the submarine base. The Marines, as the story goes, were responsible for security within the tank farm. The Army is said to have had the responsibility for the security of the perimeter. The Army sentries would hear the Marines patrolling in the tank farm and fire at the noise. The Marines are alleged to have shot back. This went on for a couple of nights before things got straightened out. I do not believe there were any casualties.

I cannot recall any specific effort that first day to organize the *Oklahoma* survivors. Some of us were milling about Ford Island, some were on board the *Maryland* and other ships, and some were casting about the landings at the naval base. Except for the watch, the senior officers were ashore when the attack started. It was reported later that when the captain got to the landing he was ordered to the ammunition depot at Lualualei.

Because the *Oklahoma* had capsized, there was a chance that some of her crew were alive, trapped in air pockets in the lower compartments. Either that first day, or early on the second, someone had thought of the possibility of cutting through the bottom of the hull to save them. I can remember members of the damage control repair parties, and people from the navy yard, I think, walking along the hull with blueprints, stopping to tap at likely places and then listening for a response. Holes were cut into the hull, and thirty-two crewmen were rescued. Some came out of pump rooms, and a large contingent of quartermasters was pulled out of steering aft. This was a huge compartment which included the auxiliary steering machinery and was where the propeller shafts pierced the hull. As the story goes, the quartermasters used clothes from the lockers to close off leaks through the ventilation ducts. I heard, also, that when the hole was cut into the hull to rescue them it was a race against time. Cutting the hole vented the air bubble in which the men were encapsulated and permitted the water to rise, but the cut was completed in time to get them all out safely.*

*For a vivid account by one of the thirty-two men, *see* Stephen Bower Young, "Out of the Darkness," *U.S. Naval Institute Proceedings*, December 1965, pp. 86–94. Editor.

Somehow the word was put out the morning after the attack for the *Oklahoma* survivors to move from Ford Island to the navy yard and assemble near the main gate. There the gun boss, Lieutenant Commander Henderson, took charge. At one point, while we were waiting there, an armed Marine went by with a prisoner marching in front of him. The prisoner appeared to be Japanese. As they tramped by, some ugly advice was given to the Marine by some of the crew. The mood was vicious. The memory of shipmates lost was both vivid and bitter. We spent that night on cots in the lounge of the submarine base officers' club. This, I think, is when I remember hearing rifle fire in the nearby tank farm.

Somewhere along the line, we were given either some credit or some money so we could acquire clothes and toilet articles. I'm afraid that quite a few of us survivors had used the Ford Island BOQ as a uniform shop. I, for example, "borrowed" a set of underwear and khaki shirt and trousers, socks, and a towel from one of the rooms. Like many of the other survivors, I was covered with oil, so a hot shower, shampoo, and change of clothes were great morale boosters. Nevertheless, we all came away from this raid with guilty consciences. When the occupants of the rooms returned, they must have thought a plague of locusts had swarmed through.

Being at the submarine base and being a communicator, I found a temporary job acting as a communication watch officer and a courier between submarine force headquarters and the submarines about to leave on patrol. This lasted, as I remember, for two, three, maybe four or five days. Then, our "permanent temporary" assignments came through. I was assigned to Patrol Wing 2 on Ford Island as assistant communications officer and communications division officer.

During this period of great uncertainty, the former commanding officer, Captain Foy, did a lot to boost the morale of the *Oklahoma*'s survivors. He visited them and had an open door for those who could come to see him. In some instances, he was able to reassure next-of-kin back on the mainland. I remember going to see him and seeking advice about my next assignment. Captain Foy's concern about his former crew was typical of the man.

On Ford Island, not far from the waterfront, there was a building with a small tower on it. This tower served as the site for a twenty-four-hour-a-day signal and lookout watch which we established for Patrol Wing 2. We revetted the tower with sandbags and from someplace we requisitioned a .50-caliber machine gun and mounted it. This "signal bridge" was manned at least partly by signalmen from the *Oklahoma*. Although posting this watch and mounting the machine gun were morale boosters, they were not very practical moves, so, as I remember, we secured the watch on the signal tower within a couple of weeks.

One of the good things about the signal tower was the view it gave us of ships entering and leaving Pearl Harbor. I'll never forget the stunned and shocked looks on the faces of the crews of the returning ships of the *Enterprise* task force. Fortunately, the carriers were at sea when the attack took place. Subsequently, they spent some time searching for the Japanese before returning to port several days later. As they entered the harbor, the crews obviously were having a hard time believing what they were seeing.

NOTHING is to be written on this side except to fill in the data specified. Sentences not required should be crossed out. IF ANYTHING ELSE IS ADDED THE POSTCARD WILL BE DESTROYED.

I am well (sick) -(Serious
I have been admitted to hospital as (wounded -(not serious
Am getting on well. Hope to return to duty soon.
I have received your (Letter dated *November 28*
(Telegram dated
(Parcel dated
Letter follows at first opportunity.
I have received no letter from you (for a long time (lately.

Signature *Brother (Paul H Backus)*
Date *December 9, 1941*
Subron 4 Standard Form No. F14   471-A—S/M Base, PH.—7-15-41—20M.

This is the postcard Ensign Backus sent to his sister in Connecticut in the wake of the attack on Pearl Harbor. (Courtesy of Commander Paul H. Backus, USN, Ret.)

One of the pressing problems after the attack was how to get word to one's family. Knowing that all the military circuits would be jammed for days with operational and logistic traffic, I telephoned Patricia Goepp, a girl I had been dating, and asked if she would try to get a cable out for me. She acted on faith, because I had no money at the time to give her. Also, from somewhere, I obtained a Navy issue postcard which I was allowed to mail and did so on 9 December. (If war was not expected immediately, why were these cards so readily available?) In the meantime, my family had been in touch with both our senator and congressman. They were working through the Navy Department, trying to find out if I had made it. Patty's cable got through about four days after the attack and before any word came via the members of Congress. The postcard arrived a few days later. My mother kept it, and I now have it.

There is a very sad parallel to this episode: about two weeks after the attack, I received a letter from Mrs. Pride, Bailey's mother. When she wrote the letter, she had only just heard of Bailey's death. I had not written her because I did not have and could not get Bailey's home address. She found my name through some frantic detective work. My mother had sent me a fruitcake for Christmas. It was in a large tin which was covered with several layers of brown wrapping paper. Bailey had used some of that paper to wrap a package of gifts which

Of all the ships sunk at Pearl Harbor, the *Oklahoma* was the most difficult to salvage. Because she had capsized, she could not be refloated until she had been rolled over by means of a system of winches and cables. (National Archives: 80-G-410524.)

he had mailed home. His package arrived in Kentucky about the time of the attack. That piece of wrapping paper had my mother's name and address on it as well as mine. Mrs. Pride telephoned my mother to ask if she had heard anything from me. By then, my mother had heard from me via Patty's cable. Shortly thereafter, Mrs. Pride had heard from the Navy Department of Bailey's death. She wrote to me to ask for whatever details I could give her. My reply must have seemed terribly inadequate.

My permanent change of duty orders to the commissioning crew of the battleship *South Dakota* came through about two months after the attack. I made it to the *South Dakota* in time to be hoisted aboard in the bucket of a crane just before she left the builder's yard at Camden, New Jersey, for fitting-out in the Philadelphia Navy Yard.

In 1944, following actions at Santa Cruz, Guadalcanal, the Norwegian Sea, and the Central Pacific, the *South Dakota* stopped at Pearl Harbor overnight to refuel. She had been hit during the Battle of the Philippine Sea and was on her way to the navy yard at Bremerton, Washington, for repairs and an overhaul. It was my first visit to Pearl since the *Oklahoma* had been "salvaged." Over the years since the attack, several of my shipmates, who also had been at Pearl on 7 December, had received official letters notifying them that certain of their personal effects had been recovered and placed in temporary storage awaiting their instructions for disposition. I had not received such a letter, so. when we arrived

at Pearl, I found out where the salvage office was and went there even though it was well after the close of working hours. There were a couple of very helpful people still there. They assured me, however, that if anything of mine had been identified and was salvageable, including my sword, they would have notified me. As I turned to leave, disappointed, but, nevertheless, eternally grateful that I survived, one of them pointed to a cane stand in a corner near the door and said that there were swords in it without names which had been removed from the *Oklahoma*. If I wished, I could look through them. I pulled out the first one which came to hand and rubbed the rust off where the name should have been. There it was—PAUL HUNTER BACKUS. Needless to say, it remains a poignant reminder of a dark day, of the loss of close friends and a lot of fine shipmates. We must never be caught by surprise again.

Since 1944, I have been back to Oahu just once, in 1972, for an all-too-short forty-eight-hour business visit. Nevertheless, there was time to get out to the *Arizona* memorial and up to the Punch Bowl Memorial Cemetery. At the Punch Bowl I found Bailey Pride's name, Harry Gaver's, those of two *Oklahoma* signalmen, Zvansky and Skaggs, and lots of others. I was struck by the simple but breathtaking beauty of this serene resting place. Arlington National Cemetery can't compare. The Punch Bowl setting again raises the question that no one, even the philosophers, has been able to answer satisfactorily, "Why them and not me?"

This shot, taken at Pearl Harbor in November 1944, shows how greatly generations of battleships changed. The huge USS *Wisconsin*, launched in 1943, is outboard of the refloated hull of the *Oklahoma*, launched in 1914. (Naval Historical Center: NH 78940.)

With Diamond Head for a backdrop, the National Memorial Cemetery of the Pacific (known as the Punch Bowl) sits in the crater of an extinct volcano. When he visited it following his retirement, Commander Backus wondered why he was spared when so many of his shipmates died in the attack on Pearl Harbor. (United Press International.)

Paul Hunter Backus (1917–   ) was graduated from the Naval Academy in 1941 and later received postgraduate education in ordnance engineering. He served in the *South Dakota* during much of World War II, and his later assignments included command of the destroyer *Isherwood* and a tour as assistant naval attaché in London. From 1956 until he retired from active duty in 1961, Commander Backus was simultaneously head of the Ballistic Missile Branch, Office of the Chief of Naval Operations, member of the Navy Ballistic Missile Committee, and member of the Steering Task Group of the Office of Special Projects. In 1959, his essay "Finite Deterrence, Controlled Retaliation" won the Naval Institute's General Prize Essay Contest. As a civilian, he has been active in defense and community affairs, working for Sanders Associates, the Mitre Corporation, and Analytical Systems Engineer Corporation. He now lives in Mont Vernon, New Hampshire, and is president of Trident Associates, Inc., defense consultants. (Courtesy of Commander Paul H. Backus, USN, Ret.)

Arizona Survivor

By Vice Admiral Kleber S. Masterson, U.S. Navy (Retired)

In the early spring of 1940, the fleet left the West Coast and went out to Hawaii for a ten-day trip. My wife Charlotte had always told me that she was going to follow me if she could, so she bundled up our two boys and went to Honolulu. She was going to stay there for the ten days. But the fleet didn't come back on schedule. It just remained out there.

About six months later, the *Arizona* returned to the West Coast for a short bottom-scraping visit to a shipyard. Charlotte came back long enough to turn in our rented house and store our furniture. Then she went back to Hawaii the same time I was going back out there in my ship.

During that period, the fleet generally operated out of Pearl Harbor and the anchorage at Lahaina Roads. We hadn't returned to the fleet base at Long Beach, because there was the danger of war coming along. The President wanted us that much closer to Japan. As a result, Charlotte and I lived all over Hawaii in the year and a half before the war. She was one of the few wives out there, and finding a place to stay was really hard because rents were high.

The trouble was that the Navy didn't send the wives out there at government expense. They were stuck on the West Coast or wherever they happened to be when the fleet left. Officially, the fleet was just out there temporarily during the whole time. It was never based at Hawaii. People in the armed services today just don't know how easy a time they've got in comparison with what the Navy was like then. The families had a rough time. It was expensive, but it was certainly worth every cent.

The expense was one problem, and another was the operating schedule. We'd rent a house in Honolulu, then the *Arizona* would go out on maneuvers and end up at Lahaina Roads. I'd give Charlotte a call, and she'd take the boys over to the Grand Hotel on Maui. So I'd get to see her a little bit of the time there. Many times I was the only officer leaving the *Arizona* to go ashore at night, because there wasn't another thing to do on the island unless you could see your family. It was a 20-mile trip over rough roads from Lahaina Roads to the hotel, but I'd get there one way or another.

The *Arizona* and the other battleships were engaged in a lot of training while we were in the Hawaiian waters. We'd come in port for a while, and then we'd go out and train. Just before the war started, the Navy Department ordered nearly all of our destroyers and some of the battleships to the East Coast to participate in the heightening activity that was going on in the Atlantic. We were stripped so far down in destroyers that just before the Japanese attack, the fleet commander was really worried about having us go out. We didn't have enough antisubmarine protection, and we were getting reports of submarines in the area all the time. I'm pretty sure that that was the primary thing back of the decision of the commander in chief, Admiral Husband E. Kimmel, to have us in port at the time of the attack.

Our attempts to stay ready for hostilities had an unexpected drawback. People had been crying "wolf" for two years, and you just can't keep anybody on the alert—especially when most of them can't be with their families—for two years without paying the price for it. Our price was probably a little bit of a lack of alertness at the last minute, when the Japanese finally came. Of course, that's one reason Admiral James O. Richardson was relieved. He protested leaving the fleet out there and exposed the way it was. But the President had the final say, and I'm sure it was President Franklin D. Roosevelt who made the decision that we were going to stay out there. He sent Admiral Kimmel out, and of course Admiral Kimmel bore the brunt of things.

When he was relieved of command, there were many more political motives than military ones. Because we were really well trained. Those ships were sharp. Our antiaircraft fire was terrible, because we didn't have proper antiaircraft directors. The newer ships, such as the fast battleships going into commission on the East Coast, had excellent fire-control equipment. But the ones like ours had the old Mark 19 antiaircraft director and coincidence range finders. We couldn't hit the side of a barn. Actually, though, we were more scared of submarine torpedoes at that time than we were of car-

rier air attack. Dumbly, we thought that our intelligence knew where the Japanese carriers were—within reason. But they fooled us. I really think the powers that be thought that when their carriers disappeared they were going to attack the Philippines rather than Pearl Harbor.

The only reason I'm alive today is that my wife was out in Hawaii. If she hadn't been there, I would have been on board ship. As it was, I was home on regular liberty Saturday night. I got the word by radio the next morning that Pearl Harbor was being attacked. I drove down to the harbor, and the Japanese planes were strafing the road ahead of me, behind me, but not where I was. I knew where the *Arizona* was moored, and I could see that she had definitely been sunk. It was a great shock to see her in that condition and to know that most of my shipmates were down inside of her.

I think one of the stirring things that came about after the air raid itself was the way yard workers

The *Arizona* and other ships of the Battle Force were based at Pearl Harbor from mid-1940 onward, even though their home ports were on the U.S. West Coast. It is only because he arranged for his family to live in Hawaii while his ship was there, that Masterson is alive today. (National Archives: 80-G-463589, and U.S. Navy: Naval Institute Collection.)

Probably the most dramatic moment in the attack on Pearl Harbor came when one of the *Arizona*'s powder magazines exploded, sending a column of smoke skyward. This frame is taken from motion picture footage of the explosion. The starboard side of the ship is nearest the camera; her maintop is visible to the left of the column of smoke; and the bow of the *Nevada* can be seen at the extreme left side of the picture. (National Archives: 80-G-6683.)

cut holes in the bottom of the *Oklahoma* and rescued some of the people who were trapped when she capsized. Of course, they didn't get anybody out of the *Arizona* after she was sunk, because she went straight down. Anybody who was down below was trapped underneath, and rescuers couldn't get to them. Besides, she didn't have enough watertight integrity to keep from flooding completely. We knew that.

I was finally able to get a boat at the landing, and I went over to Ford Island to see what I could do for the survivors of the *Arizona*. I was able to contact some of them over there. I thought I'd lend a hand at taking care of the burned people laid out there, but I soon found out that the little bit I knew about first aid wasn't going to help very much. So I went back and joined the *Arizona* people and started trying to get a muster of who was present. I wanted to try to find out where we should go to take part in the

fight that was still going on. We anticipated an invasion of the island or repeated air attacks. The Japanese had already knocked out practically all our airplanes. We didn't have anything to defend ourselves with except the guns that were left.

I did gather the firsthand information, from those who were on board, that the *Arizona* had sounded general quarters, and all her guns were trained out before she went down. The crew was shooting—not with the main battery but with the antiaircraft guns—when she blew up and sank. Flames engulfed the bridge, and Rear Admiral Isaac Kidd and Captain Franklin Van Valkenburgh were killed. Ensign Douglas Hein was the only man who got off the forward bridge area, and he was badly burned. The ones who were in the main top, however, did escape. Major Alan Shapley, head of the *Arizona*'s Marine detachment, was the spotter and main battery control officer. He and his people got away by climbing

The tattered American flag still flies from the fantail of the *Arizona* during the day of 7 December 1941. At sunset that evening, Lieutenant Masterson and a shipmate lowered it, and neither ever saw it again. (National Archives: 80-G-32591.)

down from the main top, going across the deck, and jumping off. Presumably, the flames hadn't reached that side of the ship, so they were able to swim ashore.

There weren't many survivors from the *Arizona*. Out of eighty-four men in my fire-control division, I think there were five survivors. Most of my men were in the plotting room at various fire-control stations. The only ones who weren't killed were the few who were away from the ship attending school and the men in the main top. I hated to lose so many shipmates, but I have never wished that I was on board during the bombing, because I couldn't have done a thing about it. I'd have been trapped in the plotting room. We didn't fight the antiaircraft battery on those ships from the plotting room, so I couldn't have helped in the battle. That's the only consolation I have.

Lieutenant Commander Sam Fuqua was the senior surviving officer from the ship. Before noon of that day, he had taken charge and started parceling us out. We had made arrangements where the var-

ious people would go, and I wound up in the *Maryland*. That evening, 7 December, I got a motor launch with Ensign Jim Dare, who had also come to that ship with me from the *Arizona*. We went over to the burning hulk of our ship, what was left of it, and hauled down the American flag. It was the big Sunday ensign flying from the stern, and it was dragging in the water and getting all messed up with oil. So, just at sunset, we took the flag down. At that time, we could still walk on the after deck, although within a few days, it gradually settled so that even the catapult was submerged.

We heard no noises, because there were, of course, no survivors under that little bit of deck we could walk on. After we hauled down the flag, we took the boat back to the ship that had become our temporary home. When I got back, I handed the flag over to the *Maryland*'s officer of the deck. I told him I hoped the ship would take charge of it and hang onto it. Somebody said later that the *Maryland* had it burned because it was so oily. But to this day, I don't know for sure what happened to that flag.

Kleber Sandlin Masterson (1908–   ) was graduated
from the Naval Academy in 1930 and served in the carrier
Lexington, on the staff of Commander Aircraft Battle
Force, and in the destroyers *Trever* and *Pruitt* before attending the Postgraduate School at Annapolis for ordnance instruction. He spent most of World War II in the
battleship *Pennsylvania* and the Bureau of Ordnance.
Assignments after the war included Commander Destroyer Division 102, commanding officer of the attack
transport *Lenawee*, the Armed Forces Special Weapons
project, and commanding officer of the *Boston*, the
world's first guided-missile cruiser. He was later Commander Cruiser Division 1, Chief of the Bureau of Naval
Weapons, Commander Second Fleet, and Director of the
Department of Defense Weapons Systems Evaluation
Group. He retired from active duty in 1969 and now lives
in Arlington, Virginia. His son, Rear Admiral Kleber S.
Masterson, Jr., is a member of the Naval Institute's board
of control. (Brooks Studio, Washington, D.C., courtesy of
Vice Admiral Kleber S. Masterson, USN, Ret.)

Last Man off the *California*

By Theodore C. Mason

Not all the memories of action at Pearl Harbor on 7 Dece٬ .ber are terrifying or glorious or bitter. I have the slight honor of being the last man off the battleship *California*. How it came about that a third class radioman achieved that distinction makes a rather amusing counterpoint to the nec-
٫sarily serious discussion of the day's events as a whole.

The night of 7 December found me crouched in a hastily excavated dugout on Ford Island, copying the fleet broadcast as dirt filtered through the chinks in the dugout roof onto my typewriter and me. When I was relieved, perhaps around 8:00 p.m., my communication officer was ordered, for reasons now obscure, to put a man back aboard the *California*. Lieutenant Proctor A. Sugg, an executive with one of the major radio networks in civilian life, chose me. With helmet, gas mask, Springfield rifle, and two-way portable radio, I was taken alongside by whaleboat and clambered to the top of number two turret for my lonely vigil.

On the slanting turret, my equipment and I kept sliding toward the sinister black waters to port. Around me the harbor periodically exploded into

As the *California* listed perilously to port on the frightening night of 7 December, Third Class Radioman Mason, who had been sent to keep watch aboard her, was relieved so that his radio gear would not be lost. (National Archives: 80-G-32456.)

sound and fury as nervous antiaircraft gunners let go at every aircraft alarm. The great ship, dark and lifeless, creaked and groaned as she shifted and settled deeper into the mud of the harbor bottom with her ninety-eight dead in their iron tomb.

After what seemed an interminable time, my earphones crackled with the cheerful voice of Lieutenant Sugg. "Mason," he said, "I'm going to send a boat over to take you off. We have reports the *California* is about to capsize, and I don't want to lose that valuable radio gear."

Theodore Charles Mason (1921–   ) enlisted in the Naval Reserve in 1939 and reported for active duty in 1940. After boot camp and radioman training, he joined the crew of the *California*, named for his native state. His experiences in the ship are detailed in a forthcoming Naval Institute Press book titled *Battleship Sailor*. After the *California* was sunk in the attack on Pearl Harbor, he spent part of 1942 in the Battle Force flag complement in the battleship *Pennsylvania*, then served on board the fleet tug *Pawnee* in the Solomon Islands and Central Pacific theater from late 1942 to 1945. After the war, he earned an A.B. degree in English from the University of Southern California. In the years since then, he has been a newspaperman, advertising agency executive, and freelance writer. He has written two technical books and numerous articles. Mr. Mason lives in Murrieta Hot Springs, California. (Courtesy of Theodore C. Mason.)

Refuge in *Detroit*

By John H. McGoran

For a while at least, the morning of 7 December began as any typical Sunday morning on board the USS *California*, in which I served as a signalman on Vice Admiral William S. Pye's Battle Force staff. After finishing breakfast, I took my dirty dishes to the scullery below. Funny, but that's the way peace ended. Just then, a sailor ran by, singing crazily, "The Japs are coming—hurrah, hurrah!" I don't remember the alarm that sounded general quarters. I only know that suddenly I joined in the rush to battle stations.

A few of us worked our way down a narrow passageway to "C" compartment, where an explosion had blown out our antiaircraft ammunition supply. At the end of the passageway, I saw the horror of countless bodies—my first realization that the game was for keeps. A seaman I remember as Smitty was supporting an almost lifeless sailor against a bulkhead. I helped pull the limp body back into the passageway, where I saw that this was an offensive, overbearing fellow I'd known since boot camp. If someone had asked me on 6

McGoran is the tall, helmeted figure wearing a white shirt as the motor launch in which he is riding approaches the port side of the burning *West Virginia*. He and his shipmates from the *California* were seeking antiaircraft ammunition. (National Archives: 80-G-19930.)

December to help him, I'd have said, "No way." But now, unconscious, he had no personality; he was just a life to be saved.

Later, I was in the wardroom helping the wounded when the word came to abandon ship. Whether or not this was an official order, I don't know, but the chief petty officer in charge was adamant in insisting that there would be no abandonment. Instead, he and a warrant officer formed a group to search for antiaircraft ammunition, since we could not reach our own supply. I became part of an ammunition search party which piled into a motor launch and headed in the direction of the USS *Maryland*. We tried to tell the crewmen on her forecastle what we wanted, but we could rouse no support. Their problems were far greater to them than whatever we idiots were shouting from our launch.

We headed for the dock, and once alongside, the remnants of our ammunition party broke up. I decided to wend my way toward the navy yard's water tower, which had a signal system on top. It must have been instinct prodding me to get back into a familiar environment. But once I reached the tower, I found that no additional personnel were allowed to go to the top because of the possibility that it might become a target.

I now headed toward the administration building, because I felt I should report to someone. Inside, I found other men in the same predicament as mine. Some were asking for hand guns to use against the attacking planes. There was a request for a working party, and I found myself at the disposition of the wife of the *West Virginia*'s gunnery officer. She assigned me to the Honolulu YMCA, where I would help women and children evacuated from the Pearl Harbor housing project. I rode with her the seven miles to Honolulu. "Good grief!" I thought. Would I, a sailor, have to say "sir" when reporting to this neat, completely feminine officer's wife? It wouldn't have mattered. If she needed the aura of military authority to help control the ref-

While McGoran and a few others were trying to scout up ammunition, burning oil compelled the captain of the *California* to order her crew to abandon ship. The men stream down lines on her starboard side. (U.S. Navy: Naval Institute Collection.)

ugee Navy dependents from Pearl Harbor, I would have given her a salute.

I was assigned to watch over a dormitory on the top floor of the "Y." Foldable canvas cots were set up in every available space to accommodate the 200 women and children who had arrived in groups during the last several hours. By 5:00 p.m., the dormitory was filled to capacity, and the distractions of settling in now gave way to an atmosphere of fear and tears. As night fell, we became aware that the city was under a blackout, a precaution against air attacks. It was one more thing for these shaken people to cope with. This blackout was strange to me, too. At sea, we had often practiced "darken ship," which meant no lights and no smoking in the open or weather decks, but we did have lights in our living quarters. So I shared in the general discomfort. Someone handed me a flashlight, which I saved for emergencies such as helping locate clean diapers in women's handbags. The dormitory was hot and stuffy. The odor of babies spitting up filled the room, and I knew it would be a long night.

All during the night, sporadic bursts of gunfire could be seen in the sky over Pearl Harbor. Later, the condition causing so much shooting was to be called "trigger-happiness," a reaction to fear. To feel it is to imagine the enemy lurking in every sound, in the sky, in the water. The sailors' trigger-happiness kept us awake and fretful. At 11:30 the next morning, we received word that the evacuees should return to their homes. My obligation, I felt, was now over.

I awoke with the sun on Tuesday morning and went over to a survivors' flat in an abandoned building for a breakfast of the lousiest coffee I had ever tasted. After that bilge water, they really did not deserve any work out of me, but I was assigned anyway to a five-man team collecting bedding throughout the base. On a return trip from the shipyard, we drove our stake truck through a parklike section of the base. As I rode the running board, the warm air felt nice against my face and I was beginning to enjoy the ride. In this relaxed mood I could hardly have guessed that feelings were so high against the Japanese. But suddenly, I was shocked into awareness.

The truck swerved to the right shoulder, and I resisted the force throwing me inside. "Kill him! Kill the dirty Jap!" cried a voice from inside. What was happening? I wondered. Then I felt my body flush with emotion as I glanced ahead. Our driver had taken it upon himself to seek and destroy "the enemy." He was trying to run down an Oriental, a short, middle-aged fellow who looked like a gardener for the area. Some in our group shrieked their

support. I was too far from the steering wheel to avert a tragedy, and I couldn't look at the man being hit. But I must have seen him, because I still remember the expression of pain on his face as he scampered clear of the charging truck. Laughter and regrets of failure bellowed from my co-workers, but I was secretly relieved to know that he was spared.

Although the *California*'s hull rested insecurely on the sloping bottom of Pearl Harbor, her superstructure leaned helplessly above water. Her crew had abandoned her, but a skeleton signal watch had returned, and a handful of signalmen tended her lines. It became my turn to stand watch. Three of us left the Ford Island hangar to relieve those on board. Like tightrope runners, we dashed across the cables restraining the ship by the quay. It was an electrifying sprint, because these cables were parting under the tension of holding the ship's slide into the channel. To this day, the thought of it is enough to raise the hair on my scalp.

All was deathly still, and we maintained just a token watch, rarely sighting our call letters. Most importantly, we watched and checked for changes in the inclinometer, and instrument for measuring the ship's list, because no sooner had we taken over the watch than we saw the *California* was slipping.

"Signalman!" cried an officer. "A message for CinCPac—operational priority—omit the heading. California's list dangerously increasing, request assistance." Omitting the heading, date, time, and number of words in the message considerably expedited the sending. The Commander in Chief Pacific Fleet immediately dispatched a large seagoing tug from the shipyard to aid us. The big tug groaned, her nose against the *California*'s port beam; rivers of water poured behind. Imperceptibly, the big battleship inched back from her agonizing roll. Seamen put out additional lines lashing the barbettes and the quays. For tension-packed hours, we checked and rechecked the inclinometer. Finally, it steadied, even indicated a slight leveling out. The crisis was over.

Wednesday was a happy day. The light cruiser *Detroit*, my brother's ship, steamed into Pearl Harbor. As soon as she was securely moored and activities on her bridge assumed a normal in-port calm, I signaled in semaphore with my outstretched arms: "C8 . . . C8," the call sign of the *Detroit*. One of her signalmen soon spotted me and answered, and I asked if he would check on Bob. Although PVTing—the sending of private messages—was strictly forbidden, he said he was "happy to accommodate." Bob, he soon reported, was on duty in number one engine room. When Bob heard I was

on shore, he came to the bridge, where the signal-man relayed our words back and forth. With great relief we assured each other we were safe and well.

Sunday, 14 December, marked a week since the attack. Now we learned that Admiral Pye was relieving Admiral Husband E. Kimmel as interim fleet commander in chief before Admiral Chester Nimitz took over. Consequently, Admiral Pye's flag personnel, which included me, would disband and be assigned to other duties. We were also told that the crew of the *California* would be reassigned. The thought of parting with my shipmates was saddening. The bond that can form among men on board ship has the strength of a family tie.

Then inspiration struck, and my spirits shot skyward. I would ask for duty on board the *Detroit*, my brother Bob's ship. Confidently, I marched up to the same concrete building I'd been in last Monday when I returned from the Honolulu YMCA. Approaching an officer, I blurted out my wish.

"What's holding you here?" he asked with blunt sarcasm. With a salute, I turned and went back to the boat landing, where I anxiously awaited a boat to take me to the *Detroit*.

Soon after I reported to the light cruiser, the gen-

After McGoran's staff duty on board the *California* ended, he arranged to serve in the light cruiser *Detroit* with his brother Bob. The picture of the two of them (Bob is the machinist's mate at right) was taken when the *Detroit* was at anchor in Tokyo Bay in September 1945 for the Japanese surrender ceremony. The cruiser was one of the few ships present both at Pearl Harbor, when World War II began, and in Tokyo Bay, when it ended. (U.S. Navy: Naval Institute Collection, and courtesy of John H. McGoran.)

eral quarters alarm sounded and I could hear the bugle sing the familiar tune—everyone to battle stations! I had no station yet, but like any good fire horse, I had to act fast. The crew of the *Detroit* moved with almost perfect precision—up starboard, down port. Something told me that I belonged on the signal bridge, where I would be at home. There, an officer was explaining why general quarters had sounded: "There's a midget submarine in the harbor." The "submarine's" periscope had been reported near the hospital ship *Solace*. This was my introduction to the *Detroit*, which was to be another "home" for almost four years. It was a curious beginning. The "periscope" near the *Solace* turned out to be a tin can, floating innocently past on the slow-moving currents of Pearl Harbor.

On one of my first nights on board the *Detroit*, I was stricken with an attack of claustrophobia. During working hours I had overheard the captain planning to spend the night ashore, so I decided to make use of his sea cabin in the tripod superstructure, just beneath the pilot house. Respecting the privacy of his bed, of course, I curled up in a deep pile rug to sleep on the deck. I was suddenly awakened from a dream by a door opening and was trying to brush the cobwebs away to collect my wits when I was stumbled upon.

"What in hell are you doing in here?" a stern voice demanded.

Without a word and taking full tactical advantage of the darkness, I slithered out and down a ladder to the safety of the decks below, leaving the captain sputtering to himself. If I had been recognized, it well could have been almost as much of a personal disaster as the attack on Pearl Harbor.

John Henry McGoran (1922–   ) enlisted in the Navy in 1940 and reported to the USS *California* in March 1941. He served in that ship until 14 December 1941 and then spent the remainder of the war in the light cruiser *Detroit*. He was discharged from the service in 1947 and returned to his hometown of Grand Rapids, Michigan. In 1953, he took a job as a correctional officer with the Alcatraz Federal Penitentiary at San Francisco. A year later, he married and went into business as owner of an automotive service station. After ten years, he sold the business and resumed his education. Between the College of Marin and the University of California at Berkeley, he earned a teaching credential. Circumstances prevented him from entering the teaching profession. Instead, he went into property management and maintenance, which now keeps him occupied. He lives in Corte Madera, California. (Courtesy of John H. McGoran.)

The "Lucky Lou"

By Commander A. L. Seton, U.S. Naval Reserve (Retired)

No account of the Pearl Harbor attack could be complete without a mention of the light cruiser *St. Louis* and the vital role she played that day.

That morning, when I saw a dark olive drab plane with a "meatball" insignia passing close aboard, astern of the *St. Louis* in the navy yard near Battleship Row, my first reaction was: "That stupid bastard! He'll be court-martialed for this!" I thought it was a lone, berserk Japanese pilot who somehow had gotten to Pearl and now would be in trouble with his navy and ours.

Dashing up the many ladders to my battle station in main battery control above the bridge, I saw the action develop fully. As the gunnery officer's talker on the 1JA command circuit, I heard a report that the sound-powered phones for the open antiaircraft stations were in the interior communication repair space deep down in the ship. Being nearest the hatch and familiar with all the ship's spaces, I handed my phones to the nearest lookout and rushed out to get and distribute the phones.

Since I had to make my way from the bottom of

The light cruiser *St. Louis* was one of the newest ships in Pearl Harbor when the Japanese attacked. She is shown here being commissioned at Norfolk, Virginia, on 19 May 1939. Her crew is lined up in ranks, waiting to board and to take along their seabags and hammocks, the light-colored bundles stacked behind them. (National Archives: 80-G-463405.)

Captain George A. Rood, commanding officer of the *St. Louis*, maneuvered his ship out through the narrow channel at the harbor entrance, despite the presence of enemy submarines. (U.S. Navy: Courtesy of USS *St. Louis* Association.)

the ship all the way up to sky control, which was above my station, I had a good look at what was happening on all levels. Our crew acted as though this was another drill except for outbursts of cheering every time a plane was hit within our very limited firing bearings.

But the observations and deeds of others, older and wiser, are more significant now. The captain, ex-submariner George A. Rood, recalled before he passed away in 1971 that no one gave the word to commence firing. "Our battery people," he said, "knew what was up, knew what to do and did it ... [they] took the initiative and opened fire with everything that would bear."

"Incidentally," he said in an aside, "I claimed six enemy planes shot down, and we were officially credited with three. . . . And, in the same way, our engineers knew what was required and commenced getting up steam on all boilers . . . so . . . we were able to get under way on reduced boiler power. . . . I knew that if any Jap submarines were present, they would be lying off the entrance ready to torpedo outgoing vessels and so we buckled on speed."

In the foremast structure "in a good position to observe the play" was Lieutenant Charles A. Curtze, on temporary duty for Commander Cruisers Battle Force. He recalls: "*St. Louis* put to sea through the

On her way toward the harbor entrance, the *St. Louis* steams past the *California*. The light cruiser was the first major U.S. warship to reach the open sea from Pearl Harbor on 7 December. (National Archives: 80-G-32446.)

narrow shallow entrance out through the reef making turns for about 25 knots but pushing or dragging her displacement in the water ahead or astern making good perhaps 10–12 knots. Torpedo evasion tactics were not possible."

An enemy submarine was waiting. The midget submarine fired two torpedoes on a perfect collision course. If the *St. Louis* had been sunk at this point, Pearl Harbor would have been bottled up for months. It was a crucial moment in the Pearl Harbor attack.

"The Jap got over-anxious," Captain Rood said, "and fired before we had cleared the dredged part of the channel."

Lieutenant Curtze, now a retired admiral, watched the torpedoes. The first "enroute to impact our starboard side abreast of turret three was apparently set too deep, struck a spit of coral and in exploding drenched us. A second torpedo running hot on a diverging track, a spread of about 10°, was countermined by the first or also hit a spit. . . . Captain Rood, with what seemed to me to be uncanny prescience and certainly with outstanding shiphandling, twisted the *St. Louis* past Waikiki just off the five-fathom curve and around Diamond Head where the *St. Louis* was attacked again. He swerved parallel to the torpedo track. . . . This may have been fired by an I-Class boat."

Throughout all this action, a teen-aged seaman, Daniel Patrick O'Connor, manned the wheel, standing his first watch as a special sea detail helmsman (the regular helmsman was ashore). O'Connor saw only the compass rose and the wheel indicator. But he was the proudest man on board when the captain came to him after it was all over and said, "Son, well done."

That night, at sea, most of the crew stayed up awaiting the now-late plan of the day for Monday, 8 December 1941. It contained a short but memorable message: "The Captain wishes to congratulate the entire ship's company for their splendid conduct during the trying Sunday's engagement."

From there, the *St. Louis* went on to earn eleven battle stars in every kind of enemy action, setting all kinds of gunnery records, and suffering a comparatively low loss of life. From the moment of Pearl Harbor until the end of World War II, she was known throughout the Pacific Fleet as "Lucky Lou."

Because of the surplus of warships following World War II, the *St. Louis* was decommissioned in June 1946 and placed in the Navy's reserve fleet at Philadelphia. In January 1951, she was transferred to Brazil and rechristened the *Almirante Tamandare* in that nation's navy. There was another quarter of a century of active service left in the former "Lucky Lou"; she wasn't decommissioned by Brazil until the mid-1970s. At that point, she was one of the last Pearl Harbor survivors still on duty.

Shortly after that, the USS *St. Louis* Association was formed by former crew members in an attempt to preserve our old ship as a museum—as an example of one of the finest cruisers the world has ever seen, one with a war record second to none. Our campaign resulted in a great deal of goodwill and generous amounts of recognition for the ship. Alas, we were not able to come up with sufficient financial support to get the ship back to the United States. The former *St. Louis* was thus sold to a Hong Kong firm to be scrapped. In August 1980, while being towed to Hong Kong, she managed to arrange another fate for herself. During a storm off South Africa, she sank—foiling the scrappers just as she had foiled the Japanese many years earlier.

Adolph Leonard Seton (1921–   ) enlisted in the Navy in 1939 and reported to the *St. Louis* in 1940. He became founding editor of the ship's newspaper *Hubble Bubble* in April 1942. He was commissioned an ensign in 1944 and later served in the destroyer *Borie*. After World War II, he left the Navy and was graduated from Duquesne University in 1948 and the Columbia University Graduate School of Journalism in 1949. He was recalled to active duty during the Korean War. In 1953, he joined the American Broadcasting Company and served in seven different positions before he retired. Following the decommissioning of the former *St. Louis* in Brazil, Commander Seton was the guiding force in the effort to save her. He now lives at 220 Otis Avenue, Staten Island, New York 10306, where he works as a public relations consultant and publishes the reborn *Hubble Bubble*. (Courtesy of Commander A. L. Seton, USNR, Ret.)

Like Swatting Bees in a Telephone Booth

By Commander Ted Hechler, Jr., U.S. Navy (Retired)

The customary prewar ways lasted right up to the time war started. I remember 6 December, the day before the Japanese attacked. Saturday morning inspections were an institution in the Navy before the war. On that particular day, the inspector was Rear Admiral H. Fairfax Leary, Commander Cruiser Division 9 and Commander Cruisers Battle Force. Leary had been in the job since early in 1941 when he relieved Admiral Husband E. Kimmel. I was then an ensign, serving in the new light cruiser *Phoenix*. The men were in their whites, lined up in rows for personnel inspection. When it came to the inspection of the ship herself, Leary had on his white gloves so he could check for dust. How irrelevant it would all seem twenty-four hours later.

The end of Saturday inspection was the traditional signal for liberty call, and I went ashore for the day and evening with two fellow ensigns, Garth Gilmore and Ellsworth Marcoe. We returned to the ship probably about 2:00 on Sunday morning, planning to sleep late. We were to be in leave status all day Sunday and planned to return ashore again on Sunday afternoon. In the meantime, the *Phoenix* would provide a free night's lodging, which was a consideration for some of us less affluent ensigns.

I was awakened at 7:55 by the loudspeaker, which was saying, "Set Condition III in the antiaircraft battery." This was an alert condition in which only the duty section was involved, and I was not planning to respond. Instead, I grumbled something to my roommate, who was the same Ensign Gilmore of the night before. I complained about yet another damned drill, and in Pearl Harbor on a Sunday morning, no less. In probably no more than ten or twenty seconds, this was all changed. I heard the sound of feet running on the deck overhead. Then came the sounds of the Klaxon horn and an announcement, "All hands, general quarters." This meant us, and we started to move out of our bunks. The voice on the loudspeaker now became shrill as the message changed to "All hands, general quarters! Man the antiaircraft battery. This is *not* a drill!" The words "this is not a drill" were repeated over and over, almost pleadingly.

If I needed anything further to accelerate me, it was the sound of our .50-caliber machine guns opening fire overhead. I quickly drew on my clothes and raced up the ladder to the main deck. I shall always remember the sight of our communication officer, Lieutenant William K. Parsons, attired in immaculate whites, standing there waving his arms at us. He held a batch of papers in his hand (he had evidently been on duty) and was shouting, "Come on, come on. It's war, it's war." By now, I was flying up three more decks to my station in sky forward, which controlled the four 5-inch/25 antiaircraft guns of the starboard battery. I was propelled on my journey by the sight of a torpedo plane that flew past the *Phoenix* at deck level. It carried a big red ball on the side. As I reached my station, our battery was already training out. The awnings which were still up from the admiral's inspection had to be taken down so the guns could train out. Locks were chopped off the ammunition boxes.

The *Phoenix* was moored that morning between two buoys in a berth known as C–6, located near the Aiea landing. She was 1,000 or so yards from the north end of Battleship Row along the east side of Ford Island. The *Nevada* was the nearest of the battleships to us. Also near the *Phoenix* was the hospital ship *Solace*. Because of the lack of high-level horizontal bombers—the kind of planes I was capable of directing fire at—during the initial phases of the attack, I found myself an unwilling occupant of a front-row seat from which to witness the proceedings. The sight that my eyes beheld from that perch at the forward part of the superstructure is difficult to believe, even today. The sky seemed filled with diving planes and the black bursts of exploding antiaircraft shells. Our batteries were among those firing shells in "local control," which meant that the fire was originated from the guns themselves. The Japanese planes were too close for us to take advantage of the more sophisticated automatic control which was normally provided by my station. In essence, the guns were laying out a pattern of steel in the hope that the Japanese planes would fly through it and be damaged in the process.

The only damage incurred by the *Phoenix* (indicated by arrow) during the Japanese attack came when she was struck by a machine-gun bullet. (Naval Historical Center: NH 50930.)

I have often described the experience as akin to trying to swat an angry swarm of bees in the confines of a telephone booth. To make matters worse, our shells were set with a minimum peacetime fuze setting which would not permit them to explode until they had reached a safe distance from the ship. In addition, some of the fuzes were defective, with the result that the unexploded projectiles were coming down ashore. Our best weapons under those conditions were the machine guns, which accounted for a number of enemy aircraft.

By shortly after 8:00 a.m., the harbor was a riot of explosions and gunfire. I looked at the battle line, from which huge plumes of black smoke were rising. As I watched, I saw the *Arizona* wracked by a tremendous explosion. Her foremast came crashing down into the inferno. Since I was in the corresponding station in my own ship, I naturally thought about what my own fate might be in the next few minutes. Bombs were exploding on the naval air station at Ford Island and the Army air base at Hickam Field. A Japanese torpedo plane came down our port side. It couldn't have been more than 150 feet above the water and looked as

if the pilot had throttled down, having just launched his torpedo at the battle line. He banked to the left as he got opposite us, as if to turn away. I could see .50-caliber tracer slugs going right out to the plane and passing through the fuselage at the wing joint. Suddenly, flames shot out from underneath, and he continued his turn and bank to the left until he had rolled over onto his back. A great cheer went up from our crew, because his demise was apparent. Unfortunately, he crashed onto the deck of the seaplane tender *Curtiss*, inflicting a number of casualties among her crew.

On our starboard side, the old repair ship *Vestal* was beached, her port side blackened by fire. Another plane came in, low over the water, toward our starboard quarter. This time, I saw a cross fire of tracers from the *Phoenix* and other ships. There was an explosion on the plane, and in the next instant there was nothing left but its debris descending to the water. Moments later, I heard the "zing" of a bullet whistling by. Later, we discovered a hole in the shield of a range finder below us. Of course, the air was so full of flying bullets and shrapnel by that time that it was impossible to tell the source,

The swarms of angry Japanese bees had left by the time Ensign Hechler, in his aerie in sky forward (arrow), viewed his ship's departure for the open sea. (National Archives: 80-G-32429.)

but that bullet constituted the total damage inflicted on the *Phoenix* that day.

The first wave of the attack seemed to end sometime around 8:25. About that time, the *Phoenix* attempted to get under way. We cast off and tried to go out around Ford Island, via the north channel. Signals from the naval base informed us that enemy submarines had been spotted and that the submarine nets at the entrance to the harbor were closed or being closed. So we were directed to return to our mooring. At about 8:40, the second wave hit us. Motorboats were making hurried runs across the harbor to return the officers and crewmen who had been ashore for the weekend. I can still see them making their way to our ship amidst the splashes of bullets and falling shrapnel. During this period our captain and executive officer returned aboard.

The second attack featured some high-level bombers, which brought my director into action. We fired numerous rounds at the aircraft, but much to my dismay, I did not see any flak bursts from our shells. We later replaced the ammunition, but I never learned the cause of the failures. The second

attack inflicted further damage on Pearl Harbor, but for some reason, the *Phoenix* did not come under attack. Perhaps it was because our ship's slim outline didn't present as attractive a target as other ships and because we were moored alone and thus harder to hit.

At any rate, shortly after 10:30, when the second attack was over, the *Phoenix* cast off and got under way. While our guns were still firing, we attempted to steam out the north channel. Once again, warning of submarines in the channel forced us to turn around and head back toward our berth. Then we went out the south channel. As we proceeded past the once-proud Battleship Row, we turned our binoculars on the terrible scene. We saw ship after ship in devastated condition, and the hangar on Ford Island was nothing but a skeleton of charred girders. Scores of ruined patrol planes lay in a heap on the runway. Flames were still licking up from Hickam Field. After another submarine warning and one last look back to the shipyard where the *Pennsylvania* lay in dry dock, apparently undamaged, we streaked for the open sea at 30 knots.

As we headed out, we could hear cheers from the

sailors on shore. One airman, astride the pontoon of his overturned floatplane, waved his clenched fist in the air as we passed through the harbor entrance. We finally made the open sea unscathed. Although we affectionately referred to our ship as the "Phoo Bird," she rightly deserved the nickname "Lucky *Phoenix*"—both that day and later in the war. Her name, although deriving from the city in Arizona, also comes from the bird in an ancient fable. When consumed by fire, it rose from its own ashes. Rather apt, in retrospect.

Theodore Hechler, Jr., (1916–   ) was graduated from the Naval Academy in 1940 and reported to the *Phoenix* in August of that year as assistant control officer of the forward antiaircraft director (sky forward). In 1942, he reported to flight training. Designated a naval aviator in June 1943, he received operational training and then became executive officer of VPB–92, a PBY flying-boat squadron operating in the Caribbean area. He earned a master's degree from the Massachusetts Institute of Technology in 1947 and spent the remainder of his twenty-year naval career in various engineering assignments in the field of guided missiles. Upon retirement from the Navy in 1960, Commander Hechler entered the aerospace field, first with the General Electric Company, then with the National Aeronautics and Space Administration, from which he retired in 1974. He was associated with the Discoverer and Apollo programs. Commander Hechler now lives in Annapolis, Maryland. (Courtesy of Commander Ted Hechler, USN, Ret.)

We Four Ensigns

By Captain Burdick H. Brittin, U.S. Navy (Retired)

On the night of 8 December 1941, I sat in my stateroom on board the destroyer *Aylwin* and put down on paper the events as I saw them during the preceding thirty-six hours. During the intervening years, my notes, half-forgotten, have gathered dust. Here they are; I have taken the liberty of adding comments because certain explanations are necessary.

"Today was a day of history for us at Pearl Harbor, for the United States, and I believe for the world. I am going to try to keep a running journal of these historic events and the small part I play in them. I am cognizant of the fact that being on a destroyer I will have to trust in God that both my ship and myself will see the end of hostilities."

A rather high degree of emotionalism runs through my notes; suffice it to say that I was extremely youthful at the time, had participated in a devastating event and was dog tired after the thirty-six hours of intense activity which immediately preceded my recording.

"Last night [Saturday] I went ashore with a friend of mine from the [destroyer tender] U.S.S. WHITNEY, and had a splendid time over some drinks and dinner. Thunder and the sharp crack of 5″ fire pulled me from my bed at 0800. My first reaction was one of disgust for I had planned to sleep in that morning."

Along with several other junior officers, I had planned to spend the night at Waikiki, for I did not have to report back aboard the *Aylwin* until Sunday evening. That Saturday night, I was a big spender, ran out of money—I believe unmarried ensigns were paid around 150 dollars a month in those days—and thus returned to the ship alone quite late that night.

"I looked out of my porthole and my heart must have stopped for I grabbed at the bulkhead to keep at a standing position. Right across from me the U.S.S. UTAH [old battleship target ship] was settling over on her side. On our starboard beam across the jetty the U.S.S. ARIZONA had just exploded and the sky was a mass of flames."

The *Aylwin* spent a day and a half at sea with no more than a skeleton crew on board. She left so hurriedly that the commodore, captain, and executive officer were all left ashore. Four ensigns, one of whom was the author, ran the ship. (National Archives: 19-N-26640.)

The *Aylwin* was moored to the X-ray buoys in Middle Loch. From that vantage point the heart of Pearl Harbor and Ford Island could be observed easily.

"I dressed partly, ran on deck and saw the orange sun of Japan painted on the bodies of planes passing overhead. That shocked me into activity and I ran to the bridge to my battle station. We were nested with the [destroyers] MONAGHAN, DALE, and FARRAGUT and it was magnificent how rapidly our entire batteries got into action. Needless to say we were all frightened because of the tremendous destruction around us and the apparent helplessness with which we were able to fight back. The Japanese had thoroughly bombed all of our air fields so they had complete mastery of the air. At approximately 0810 the AYLWIN received TBS [talk between ships—voice radio] orders to get underway. This we proceeded to do."

As I recall I put on dress whites which, in those days, were pretty much the uniform of the day. At this point in the attack, no surface ships were moving, the only planes in the air were Japanese, and our antiaircraft fire was sporadic and apparently not too effective. While at the time I was undoubtedly impressed by the speed with which we were able to commence firing, I doubt that it was controlled.

"It is of interest to note that there were only four officers aboard—all Ensigns—only two of whom were qualified to stand top watches (Anderson and Caplan). The total sea experience between the four of us was a little more than a year."

It was not unusual for senior officers of the fleet to spend their weekends at home, leaving a qualified officer of the deck as head of the duty section. In this case the officer of the deck was Ensign Stanley B. Caplan. Caplan and Ensign Hugo C. Anderson had been on board approximately six months, while the other officer and I had reported aboard for duty in early November. We were all products of Naval Reserve Training (the V–7 program).

"A bomb hit off our starboard bow hastened our cutting of the bow line and in a short time we were backing out into the channel. Another bomb sent our fantail against the anchor buoy and we could feel the ship vibrate signifying that we had damaged one of our screws."

Although this is pure speculation, I suspect that the Japanese pilots then considered they had completed their primary missions and therefore turned their attention to targets of opportunity, which included the destroyers and the tender *Whitney* moored in Middle Loch. Perhaps records will indicate otherwise, but it was our impression that we were the third ship out of the harbor.

"From then until we had cleared the channel I was nearer to death and yet lived than any other person I have ever spoken to. We were all in the hands of another being. The channel ahead of us was a mass of bomb explosions from high flying bombs, and at the time all the officers aboard were certain we would never get through. The U.S.S. MONAGHAN was the first in our column and did a splendid piece of work of ramming a submarine and dropping depth charges on her. We saw the sub get blown into the air and it brought cheers from the men."

I recall the action rather vividly, because the small two-man submarine surfaced before she was struck by the *Monaghan*. We passed close aboard and, up to that point, it was the only successful retaliatory action we had seen.

"I put on a steel helmet and went over the entire ship with the repair party stripping it for further action. It was not courage that led me about the unprotected deck—perhaps I was searching for something tangible to do. We were just passing the [seaplane tender] U.S.S. CURTISS when one of our gunners hit a low flying plane which crashed into the superstructure of the CURTISS and started a sickening blaze. How we succeeded in clearing the channel I will never know, but we did get outside and the marrow in our bones turned to water as we looked back on the smoke and flames that once was Pearl."

We continued firing our 5-inch/38 and .50-caliber machine gun as best we could until we had cleared the harbor. Afterward, I learned that our gunners rammed by hand because of the lack of high-pressure air and that no fuzes had been set because of mechanical problems. This makes suspect the subsequent official report that the *Aylwin* had been credited with probably shooting down three planes. Correspondingly, it appears logical that some of the *Aylwin*'s 5-inch shells landed in Honolulu, although the credit at the time went to the Japanese! Lastly, I am quite certain that it was our hit that caused one plane to crash into the *Curtiss*.

The midget submarine that tangled with the destroyer *Monaghan* assuredly came off second best in the encounter. Her tail section was knocked askew and her hull was heavily washboarded by depth charges. (U.S. Navy: Courtesy of Mrs. William Burford; also Naval Historical Center: NR&L (MOD) 26697.)

This photograph of pieces of a seaplane littering the broad fantail of the *Curtiss* shows the damage done to the tender. Both Ensign Brittin of the *Aylwin* and Ensign Hechler of the *Phoenix*, author of the preceding article, maintain steadfastly that their ships were responsible for shooting down a carrier plane that struck the ship. Maybe they are both right; then again, maybe they are not. (National Archives: 19-N-26297.)

We really stripped ship! I helped roll drums of nonessential lube oil over the side and personally cut free the beautiful mahogany accommodation ladder. Our whaleboat was left floating in the harbor.

"At about 1030 the last plane had gone and our division [Destroyer Division 2] patrolled the harbor entrance for submarines. Our Commodore [Ralph S. Riggs] and Captain [Robert H. Rodgers] tried to reach us at that time but our orders were to rendezvous with other units of the fleet so we four ensigns took the ship to meet some cruisers and the [aircraft carrier] U.S.S. ENTERPRISE. For the first time that day we saw our own planes in the air (one of our guns almost shot one down by mistake) and there was a feeling of temporary security and satisfaction as we took our station with the ENTERPRISE as her tremendous bulk cut rapidly through the seas."

Actually the reason we did not stop the ship to pick up the captain and commodore, who had followed us out of the harbor via small boat approximately one hour after our sortie, was not our orders to rendezvous with the *Enterprise*, but fear of submarines off Pearl. As destroyer after destroyer gained the sea, more and more contacts were reported, and depth charges were exploded with marked frequency. Whether there were many submarines present I still do not know; however, we considered it foolhardy to stop despite the fact that the captain's small boat tried to close us numerous times. The opportunity is rare indeed for an ensign to refuse his captain's request to come aboard, and further, to sail off with his ship. We did just that.

"I can not say enough for the men—they were just magnificent the way they held their battle stations. In the evening, steering south where five enemy aircraft carriers had been reported we started a search, and with our speed the men on the AYLWIN felt certain that we would catch them. How can I describe that night? A 3rd Class Quartermaster, [Charles E.] Wilcox, was the navigator; Caplan was the Captain; Anderson the Executive; [Ensign William K.] Reordan the gunnery officer; and I the torpedo officer. None of us slept, although complete exhaustion was not far off and our stomachs did not react to food. I remember my white uniform becoming filthy. I remember going around to the guns to cheer the men and I recall their grim looks of determination. I remember helping to shoulder the limp form of a man from the boiler room who had collapsed. I remember him mumbling something about his Mother. I remember going through the wardroom where exhausted men had fallen in a dead stupor and where the dead air of the passageway was so repelling that I reeled drunkenly out on deck to vomit bile. I remember men in the crew looking searchingly into my eyes and, like a damned hypocrite I remember smiling and joking."

I estimate that only a little over half the crew was on board, a disproportionate share of senior petty officers being left behind at Pearl. They, too, had planned the weekend with their families. I know there was but one signalman, one quartermaster, and two radiomen. The guns were manned by skeleton crews, and the engineers were spread so thin that none could leave their vital posts. We stayed at general quarters for thirty-six hours and, while we must have eaten something, I don't remember it.

"During the night we recorded a 47° roll! When the FARRAGUT loomed suddenly out of the darkness, I remember almost saying 'fire torpedoes!' I remember singing wild songs and talking to myself to stay awake and to enable me to keep my glasses on the water. And then I remember reality slowly coming back at dawn when the ENTERPRISE and her screen lay dead ahead."

That afternoon we received orders to form a scouting line—I believe the interval was ten miles—and proceed to the southwest at a speed of 30 knots. After dark we felt quite alone, for without lights or radar it seemed as though we were rushing through a tumultuous void to a rather uncertain fate. The seas were on the beam and the ship rolled and groaned throughout the night.

An error on our part almost produced a tragedy. Sometime during the night, a message came in directing the scouting line to break off the search and rendezvous with the *Enterprise* to the northeast. In our confused, shorthanded state, we did not recognize that the message was addressed to us; therefore, we did not decode it. Thus, roaring through the night we were unaware that the scouting line had turned, when we spotted a dark shape coming at us! We leveled our guns and trained the torpedo tubes. A light blinked, asking for identification. We responded and the dark shape identified herself as the *Farragut*, our sister ship! We relaxed and the light blinked again, "Where are you going?" We responded that we were proceeding on scouting-line duty and then, being dubious, asked where the *Farragut* was going. She reported she was proceeding to rendezvous and recommended that we follow suit. We reversed course and so ended up at the right time and place. The possible tragedy was narrowly averted and, much later when humor returned, a favorite speculation was where we would have been after our fuel had been exhausted had it not been for the chance encounter with our sister ship!

> "Our search had proven to be fruitless and lack of fuel sent us back to Pearl. At the harbor marker buoy we picked up the Commodore and our Captain who took the ship in. Never had it been so sweet to welcome the Captain aboard."

As was well documented by the Japanese after the war, the attack on Pearl came from north of the islands—not south. Our search was in the wrong direction. I recall that by the time we made our entry into Pearl after steaming all night at 30 knots our remaining fuel was down to around 5 per cent of capacity.

> "We were silent as we went in, for fires still burned and hangars and planes and homes were mere rubble. The [battleship] NEVADA had beached itself halfway through the channel to keep it clear after being hit by a torpedo. The water was up to her main deck and a good part of her topside was burned. Two of my close friends were aboard her. God grant that they lived. I vow that this all shall be avenged!"

Silence greeted us as we steamed in, and we responded in silence for there was nothing much to say. Even the captain's arrival by small boat was left in silence.

> "I remember now when I had been stripping ship on the way out of the harbor looking up and becoming paralyzed in position as a Japanese plane came right for me. I could not move—it must have passed not more than 200 feet overhead and its machine gun bullets splashed into the water alongside."

Anything but a conspicuous white uniform would have been instantly welcomed by me as that plane approached.

> "After we had gotten into port I fell exhausted into my bunk and was there for a few minutes when the general alarm rang. Drunk with sleep I ran blindly to my station where I heard the word that the Japs had made an attempted landing. A landing party was called for, but no confirmation report came through

so the Captain sent me by boat over to the PHELPS [flagship of Destroyer Squadron 1] for further orders. I carried my 45 in my hand and literally climbed up the side of the PHELPS. It had been a false report, so back to my ship and a sweet thing called bed."

Good fortune was ours that it was a false report, for many analysts subsequently felt that, had the Japanese come prepared for an amphibious landing, they probably would have been successful in gaining control of Hawaii.

Burdick Heinkel Brittin (1917–   ) was graduated from Union College in 1940 and commissioned in 1941 through the V–7 program. He spent eleven years at sea, mostly in destroyers, including service in World War II and the Korean War. He received his J.D. degree from George Washington University Law School in 1949, and from 1953 to 1956 was assigned to the International Law Division of the office of the Judge Advocate General, serving as adviser to the U.S. delegate to the International Law Commission in Geneva. He was secretary to the Chief of Naval Operations for Joint Chiefs of Staff matters from 1959 to 1961 and retired from active duty in 1963. He was later coordinator of ocean affairs for the Department of State. He is coauthor of earlier editions of the Naval Institute Press book *International Law for Seagoing Officers*, and sole author of the fourth edition, which was published earlier this year. Captain Brittin lives in Great Falls, Virginia. (Courtesy of Captain Burdick H. Brittin, USN, Ret.)

Encounters with a Midget

By Commander Earl D. Bronson, U.S. Navy (Retired)

On 7 December 1941, I was chief machinist's mate on board the submarine *Plunger*. We rounded Diamond Head on the surface about 7:30 that morning, heading for the barn after a three-month cruise to the West Coast. Needless to say, our plans for reunion with our families or a Waikiki liberty were rudely shattered when we were thoroughly strafed by planes with "fried-egg" emblems. We quickly dived and headed to the south submerged. Of course, we made no contact. Our boat entered Pearl on the morning of 9 December.

Early on 10 December, after fueling at the submarine base the day before, we—in anticipation of a renewed attack—moved away from the dock and moored to a buoy north of Ford Island to load stores and prepare for departure on our first war patrol.

At the next buoy, another submarine reported a sound contact. We manned our sound gear and between us pinpointed, by pinging, a submerged stationary object. We passed a grapnel and line to the 50-foot motor launch being used to provision us and it made a hookup. Since the object couldn't be moved by towing or lifting, it was assumed that we had pinged on some uncharted wreckage. We returned to the chores at hand and departed at daybreak on 11 December. This "dead" contact must have been one of the Japanese midget submarines used in the 7 December attack.

In 1952, while I was serving as first lieutenant of the Submarine Base, Pearl Harbor, I was again exposed to one of the midgets. In the process of im-

In 1941, Bronson was serving as a chief petty officer in the submarine *Plunger* when she made sonar contact with what was probably a Japanese midget submarine. Eleven years later, he made contact in a different way when a seawall construction project unearthed a midget which had been interred in 1942. (Courtesy of Mrs. William Burford, via Walter Lord.)

proving a dockside area, it was necessary to dredge out the previous fill material, drive sheet piling for retention, and refill to prevent further erosion of the parking area just inboard of the dock. This job was being done by a civilian contractor.

During the work, the contractor-operated dragline grabbed something too big to move; furthermore, the area was permeated by a distinctly disturbing odor. One of my crew members reported that he could smell chlorine gas in the area. When I arrived at the scene, it was apparent that the dragline operator had indeed made contact with more than he could handle. Further, the bucket teeth had penetrated and could not be readily extracted.

The foreman of the construction crew, informed of our suspicions that the dragline had run into a Japanese midget submarine interred during the original construction of the quay wall in 1942, then brought in a smaller rig and began cleaning the muck away from the area of the stuck bucket. Sure enough, there was the midget submarine which had been sunk by the destroyer *Monaghan* on the morning of 7 December and probably the same one we in the *Plunger* had pinged on soon afterward. The teeth of the dragline bucket stuck through the hull of the midget at a point that must have penetrated into the battery compartment and caused the leakage of chlorine gas. The area was not the most desirable place to work, so a couple of gas masks were provided, and my crew liberated the dragline-bucket by passing a line around it and pulling it free with a truck.

We decided that by excavating inboard and parallel to the hull, the boat could be rolled into the excavation and thus made to clear the space needed to continue the sheet piling on its planned line. The hull was reburied, and there it remains today—with the crew still inside.

Earl Dean Bronson (1913–   ) enlisted in the Navy in 1928 by falsifying his age. He reached the rating of chief machinist's mate before being promoted to warrant machinist in 1941 and ensign in 1942. Assignments throughout his career dealt almost exclusively with submarines—*Seagull, S-27, S-26, Barracuda, Plunger, Bang,* Submarine Division 202 staff, Submarine Division 52 staff, the submarine tender *Eurayle,* Mare Island Naval Shipyard, Hunters Point Naval Shipyard, officer in charge of the *Dentuda,* Submarine Division 11 staff, Submarine Base Pearl Harbor, Submarine Flotilla 1 staff, and Submarine Squadron 5 staff. In the 1950s, he was military government representative of the Bonin and Volcano islands. He retired from active duty in 1958, then worked for the Scripps Institution of Oceanography at San Diego as supervisor of the FLIP (floating instrument platform) program. He retired from that position in 1973 and now lives in Warner Springs, California. ("Cap" Crane, Vallejo, California, courtesy of Commander Earl D. Bronson, USN, Ret.)

Although the attacks on the ships of the Pacific Fleet in Pearl Harbor have quite naturally received the greatest share of attention in histories of the Japanese air raid, their effects were felt far beyond the harbor itself. In the next several articles, people who were ashore, both Navymen and civilians, recount their reactions—on 7 December 1941 and in the ensuing weeks and months.

Grandstand Seat

By Vice Admiral Lawson P. Ramage, U.S. Navy (Retired)

In early 1941, a former shipmate of mine was serving on the submarine detail desk in the Bureau of Navigation. He assured me that I would receive orders shortly to Submarine Squadron 5 in New London, Connecticut. I was looking forward to that with great anticipation, because that's where my family was. Then, all of a sudden, I got dispatch orders to the staff of Commander Submarines Scouting Force Pacific Fleet. He was Rear Admiral Thomas Withers, Jr., whose flagship was the light cruiser *Richmond*, based in Pearl Harbor. Fortunately, I was able to take leave to see my new-born son. I got to Connecticut for a three-week visit with my family, then flew out to the West Coast and sailed to Pearl Harbor on board a tanker. Arriving there, I reported to Admiral Withers's staff as the submarine force's communication, radio, and sound officer.

In due time, my wife picked up the whole family and flew them out to Hawaii. They arrived the first week in November, just a month before the blitz. We got located on the top of Pacific Heights, overlooking all of Honolulu and Pearl Harbor, and we were just settling into a very nice, peaceful existence. I must say, though, that the atmosphere was a little tense around headquarters, because Admiral Husband E. Kimmel, the Commander in Chief Pacific Fleet, had moved his staff over to the submarine base in Pearl Harbor. Admiral Withers and his staff had already moved there from the *Richmond* around the beginning of June. So we had been ashore for a few months when Admiral Kimmel and his people joined us.

Back around the first of October, Admiral Withers had decided that the situation was getting so tense that we should make some preparatory plans for the defense of Wake and Midway. He had dispatched two submarines to patrol off those islands, beginning about the middle of October. He told the skippers of the two boats before they left that we would be at war before they returned. However, they had completed their thirty days on station and had been relieved and returned to Pearl Harbor. That made it all the more likely that war would start before the next pair came back, because still more time had passed, and relations with Japan were continuing to deteriorate. Because of this at-

mosphere, no one can say that we weren't alerted to the possibility of war. But these were really the only concrete steps I know of that were taken in advance by the submarine force. The fleet as a whole had been divided into three task forces and was running maneuvers continuously.

My personal recollection of 6 December is still very vivid in my mind, because we had friends in playing poker that Saturday night, and we played on past midnight. We noticed in particular that the radio kept on playing after midnight, which was when it normally shut down. Some of the people with us said that the Hawaii stations always kept on broadcasting throughout the night, to serve as a sort of beacon, when there was a flight of planes coming out from the West Coast. That night, a group of B-17 bombers was en route.

I had the duty that Sunday morning, so I fully intended to go out to Pearl Harbor early. But my friend, Lieutenant Commander Ed Swinburne, who was our flag secretary, said that he would take the duty until ten o'clock, because he was a bachelor and in no rush to go home. Promptly at eight o'clock, our telephone rang, and I answered it. Ed said, "Get out here right away. The Japs are attacking Pearl Harbor."

Actually, I thought he was pulling my leg. So I said, "Oh yes, Ed, I know you can handle that situation. You can take care of it until I get there."

He said, "No, no. No fooling, this is the real thing."

"I know, Ed," I answered. "I don't know what's bothering you, but don't lose your balance."

And Ed just kept on insisting it was the real thing. About that time, there was an explosion right in the neighborhood. All of a sudden, some hysterical woman cut in on our telephone line and said, "Oh, something terrible has happened. What should I do? Who should I call? Who am I talking to?"

At that point, I told Ed I'd be down to the base to see him shortly. I walked to the front part of the house and looked out over Pearl Harbor. I could see that there was some smoke and could see some action out there. Then I turned the radio on, and there was a nice piece of church music wafting through the room. Someone interrupted the program to say that the Japanese were attacking Pearl Harbor.

That was about the extent of the announcement, and the station went right back to playing its beautiful hymns and so on.

I immediately got dressed and took off for Pearl Harbor. On the way down Pacific Heights, I passed fire engines that were on their way up to a house that had been hit in our neighborhood. I believe the damage was done by a shell from one of our own ships. The ship was firing at the Japanese planes, and the projectile went right straight through the house without exploding. It must have been very close to the first shot fired. The first wave of planes had passed over by the time I got to the naval base.

But on the way out there, every conceivable vehicle was loaded with sailors—buses, taxis, and everything else—rushing to get out there.

I drove up in front of the bachelor officers' quarters and, when I looked up, I saw the slowest moving planes I had ever seen. They were just kind of drifting around and circling, then making their dives. It was in no way comparable to what we are familiar with these days. The Japanese didn't have any opposition, so they were just taking their time. Of course, they swept down over the submarine base, heading straight toward Ford Island. When I got up to our office on the second deck of the

From his vantage point in the U-shaped headquarters building at the right-hand edge of the photo, Lieutenant Ramage had a grandstand seat from which to watch the Japanese attacks on nearby Battleship Row. In this picture, which was made in mid-October 1941, the submarine piers can be seen adjacent to the building that served as headquarters for both the submarine force and the Pacific Fleet. In order to provide better communications in the wake of the attack, wires were strung from the headquarters down into the radio equipment of the submarines. (National Archives: 80-G-411193.)

The oiler *Neosho* (center) backs away from her berth at Ford Island. Ahead of her is the battleship *California* and just astern of her is the hull of the overturned *Oklahoma*. Had the Japanese planes that bombed Battleship Row managed to hit the oiler, the fire and destruction around Ford Island would, in all likelihood, have been a good deal worse than was the case. The *California*'s halyards are filled with signal flags, transmitting orders from the Commander Battle Force to other ships in the harbor. (U.S. Navy: Naval Institute Collection.)

supply building, I looked out the windows and discovered that I had a grandstand seat for the whole performance. It was absolutely fantastic to see these planes just sliding right down to not more than 200 yards out in front of me. They were coming down and letting torpedoes go right into the battleships. It was just incredible to see the whole line of battleships engulfed in fire and thick black smoke.

It wasn't too long before most of the Pacific Fleet staff arrived. I remember Admiral Kimmel pacing back and forth there in front of us, his jaw stuck out. We were all just dumbfounded that this could happen. But there it was—not only in technicolor but with sound effects and all. In the midst of it, the thing that I think was most apparent was that none of us was at all concerned about his own safety. This is a funny thing, but it's typical of many combat operations. When you're in a dangerous situation, you figure something could happen to somebody else, but it's not going to happen to you. There might be terror if the danger is coming pretty close to you, but the Pearl Harbor attack was not

being directed at those of us in the headquarters building.

Even though we were only spectators, we were appalled at the horror of the whole thing—the dramatic shock of seeing our fleet going up. Just across the way was a repair base full of ships, and the Japanese were dropping bombs over there. But they apparently didn't hit anything except the dock and the old destroyer tender *Rigel*, which took several splinters. The thing that I think probably caused me more concern than anything was the oiler *Neosho*, which was heading for the Merry Point fuel piers. This was the slot where the Japanese planes were coming down to launch their torpedoes. If they had blown up the *Neosho*, that would have been the end of everything, but she got out of there safely.

The transformation that morning from peacetime—calm, everyday routine—to complete alert was really striking. I have never seen anything comparable happen so quickly in my life. When I wasn't watching our ships being attacked, I was busy trying to contact our submarines en route to Pearl Harbor. There were three P-boats, the *Pompano*,

At the time of the attack, headquarters for both Rear Admiral Thomas Withers, Commander Submarines Scouting Force, and Admiral Husband E. Kimmel, Commander in Chief Pacific Fleet, were in this building on the submarine base. The structure on top of the building, which was used for lookout training, was built during the war. The photograph was taken in 1945. (Naval Historical Center: NH 82373.)

Porpoise, and *Pollack.* They were about 200 miles east of Hawaii, just returning from overhaul on the West Coast. We had the *Gudgeon,* with "Joe" Grenfell in command, down at Lahaina Roads. Bill Anderson in the *Thresher* was coming in from Midway and was just about off Barbers Point on the island of Oahu.

I had had all the communications to myself there in the submarine base, but all of a sudden we found all our circuits, receivers, transmitters, and everything else preempted by the Commander in Chief Pacific Fleet. Commander "Germany" Curts was the fleet communication officer, and Lieutenant Commander Donald Beard was his radio officer. Don really rose to the occasion. They both did a magnificent job. Everybody did. Don managed to get reels of wire from all over; I don't know how he did it. I saw him running down the corridor with reels of wire from the positions up in the office on the second deck, down the stairs, out onto the docks, and into the submarines so he could use their transmitters and receivers. I've never seen so many things come on the line so fast.

Our submarines in the Hawaiian area weren't brought in. We told them to go south and lie low until the attack was over. We told everybody to stay clear. That was the primary thing at that point, not to make the situation any more complicated than

it was already. As soon as we could find out what had happened, we would bring them in. It was primarily for their own good to stay clear of that debacle.

We were up to our ears in all kinds of problems during the day. Then, when things finally started to calm down, people were coming in from the battleships. I remember some of the skippers coming in wearing their whites, and they had been in fuel oil up to their waists or even higher. They were white on the top and black on the bottom. I never saw such a sight—particularly the look of shock on their faces. They all had to be taken care of and billeted. So when I finally got relieved to go over to the bachelor officers' quarters, where I had a room for my duty nights, I couldn't walk more than about ten paces before someone from a security patrol would say, "Halt. Advance one at a time and be recognized." On the way to the BOQ, I think I was stopped about five or six times. Then, when I got up to my room, I found that I had about ten roommates. I had had the place all to myself before that.

During the next two or three weeks, I saw Admiral Kimmel frequently, because our offices weren't more than 30 feet apart. I didn't have any personal conversations with him, but I could see that he was tremendously shocked and upset. Naturally, he would be. Nobody had had the slightest inkling that the Japanese would be brassy enough to attack Pearl Harbor and our whole fleet there.

One of the things we did after the attack was put in censorship on all mail. I was absolutely amazed at the attitudes of the mothers telling their sons to get out there and kick you-know-what out of the Japanese. They were really belligerent, and they hadn't even seen the thing up close the way we had. I've never seen such language and such virulent hate, and these were letters from mothers to their sons. I never expected that something could stir up such emotion across the country. And I don't think the Japanese ever realized that they could touch off such a reaction either.

Lawson Paterson Ramage (1909–   ) was graduated from the Naval Academy in 1931 and served in three surface ships before reporting to submarine school in 1935. He was successively in the submarine *S-29*, in postgraduate training in communications, and in the destroyer *Sands*. In April 1942, he was detached from the submarine force staff, then served in the submarine *Grenadier* and commanded the *Trout*. As skipper of the *Parche*, he earned a Medal of Honor for a brilliant night surface attack against a Japanese convoy in July 1944. Postwar commands included Submarine Division 2, Submarine Squadron 6, and the attack cargo ship *Rankin*. As a flag officer, he had several tours in OpNav, commanded Cruiser Division 2 and the First Fleet, was Deputy Commander in Chief Pacific Fleet, and finally Commander Military Sea Transportation Service. Admiral Ramage retired from active duty in 1970 and now lives in Washington, D.C. (National Archives: 80-G-660184.)

A Patrol in the Wrong Direction

By Admiral Thomas H. Moorer, U.S. Navy (Retired)

In the years before World War II, naval aviation was not as specialized as it is today. Thus, I was transferred in mid–1939 from Fighting 6 in the USS *Enterprise* to Patrol Squadron 4, based at Pearl Harbor. VP-4, made up of twelve PBY flying boats, was soon redesignated VP-22, and it gave me the start of my patrol plane experience.

Under both Admiral James O. Richardson and Admiral Husband E. Kimmel, we were working hard—seven days a week—for many, many months before the war started. We had patrols nearly every day, and they lasted eighteen hours apiece. We'd go out in a wedge-shaped sector which looked like a thin piece of pie when you drew it on a chart. The idea was that the separation between your outbound and inbound tracks was double the distance of your visibility. If the visibility was 10 miles, you could have a 20-mile leg along the outer rim of the pie before you had to turn back to Pearl Harbor. If you didn't see anything as you looked out of the right side of the plane while heading away from the base, you were supposed to be able to spot it on the right side coming back. That meant the sector could

be about 9 or 10 degrees wide. If we had sought to provide coverage all the way around the compass, we would have needed somewhere between thirty-six and forty planes, and we didn't have that many. We usually had only about six available, and that meant we could do only about 60 degrees. The sectors for a given flight were picked at random.

For their time, the PBYs had a great deal of endurance, and their ability to go a long way between overhauls was the product of the superb enlisted crews we had in those days. Our men could make just about every repair themselves, and that's just what they did when I made a long flight with Lieutenant Commander Frank O'Beirne, commanding officer of the squadron. The decision had been made to send some Army B-17s to the Philippines, but there was no airstrip at Midway, Guam, or Wake that was suitable for them. So the only way they could get to the Philippines was to go from Hawaii down to Rabaul, then to Australia, and finally turn and go back north again to reach the Philippines. All this was a pretty roundabout route, and the whole thing was very, very secret. The military could still keep a secret in those days.

Frank and I went on ahead to survey the route and to make sure there would be enough fuel for the B-17s when they came along. There was a new fuel then, 100 octane, and it was quite scarce. It turned out that the Army planes were going to consume just about every gallon of it in all of Australia in order to get on through to the Philippines.

Because we didn't need runways the way B-17s did, our PBY was able to stop at a number of islands along the way—places such as Palmyra, Canton, Fiji, and New Caledonia. Interestingly, we were able to do so because of the network of support facilities built up by Pan American for its Clipper flights. There were no naval or military bases in some of these spots, and if it hadn't been for Pan American, we wouldn't have been able to operate. In the late 1930s and early 1940s, the Navy used the airline's facilities, its weather reports, and even traded spare parts. We could go to shops Pan Am had in these various places and get something as big as an engine. The government owes Pan American a fantastic debt.

Lieutenant (junior grade) Moorer (third from left) poses with his flight crew in front of a PBY of Patrol Squadron 22 shortly before the attack on Pearl Harbor. (Courtesy of *Naval Aviation News*.

Our trip around this circuit was quite an experience, done under complete radio silence and with all navigation by celestial methods. When we left Hawaii, we had the normal amount of spare parts, and we took along 600 pounds of canned goods to eat. We made the entire trip, which took about 120 flight hours, without any problems at all—and that's because our mechanics and radioman were so good. The radioman could listen to the radio, and if it wasn't working right, he knew almost by instinct that he should change such and such a vacuum tube—and that would fix it. Nowadays, the maintenance gets turned over to someone else, but these boys could repair anything right on the spot.

In fact, I had such a good crew that nearly every one of them was an officer within a year after the war started.

Along with the B-17s, the Philippines also got two squadrons of PBYs which comprised Patrol Wing 10. Some books about the Pacific war make it seem that all of us were oblivious of the fact that the Japanese existed. In fact, there was a tremendous amount of concern about them, and we were fairly certain that there was going to be a war. The only questions were when and how it would start. Based on U.S. intelligence sources, the main concern was that the ships at Pearl Harbor would be attacked by either sabotage or submarines. So the idea was

In the years preceding World War II, Pan American World Airways blazed a trail across the island outposts of the Pacific. By developing landing facilities, passenger terminals, and maintenance shops for its Clippers at places such as Wake Island (shown here), Pan Am created an infrastructure of which the Navy was able to take advantage. Japanese opposition to U.S. development of the Pacific island bases would probably have been a good deal greater in the prewar years if the Navy had done it. (Pan American World Airways.)

to get them inside the harbor behind nets. Of course, that was a mistake in one sense. On the other hand, if the ships had been out at sea, those that were sunk would have been gone forever. But we certainly weren't operating on a business-as-usual basis. I thought Admiral Kimmel took a very unfair rap, but I can see why President Roosevelt got rid of him the way he did in order to restore public confidence.

One of the things Admiral Kimmel was doing was beefing up the defenses of our outlying islands. The Marines had defense battalions on Wake, Midway, and Guam. A task force built around the *Enterprise*, with Vice Admiral William F. Halsey, Jr., in command, was sent to carry a squadron of Marine fighter planes to Wake. My patrol squadron had been located at Midway and operating from that island since early November. Suddenly, we were ordered to go to Wake, which was farther west. After we got there, we were given two assignments. One was to scout the operating area of the *Enterprise* to make sure she wouldn't be observed by the Japanese, and the other was to send one PBY to escort the Marine planes on their approach to Wake. The latter was my job. Because we were operating ahead of the *Enterprise*, I don't think she could have been discovered, but I believe Admiral Halsey would have attacked if we had encountered the Japanese. We were carrying bombs all the time. He was ready to go to war right then and there. That's how tense things were by early December.

Finally, after a month at Midway, we were relieved and sent back to Hawaii, arriving late on Friday night, 5 December. I had a brief chance to rest and visit my wife, who was just about to have our first child. My next regular flight was scheduled for Sunday. I was supposed to head southwest, toward the Japanese mandated islands. So I got dressed and was leaving for the naval base with my copilot, Ensign Jack Martin, when we saw the Japanese planes. We rushed out as hard as we could and arrived at the base while the first wave was striking Hickam Field and Pearl Harbor. We got a boat and rowed over to Ford Island, where our squadron was based. We had twelve planes, which were parked outside the hangars, and most of them were shot up quite severely. Virtually all of the damage to them was by strafing, because there was no bombing of any significance on the island itself.

I had a grandstand view of the attack. For instance, I saw the torpedo attack which was made on the battleships just a couple of hundred yards away. I saw both the *Pennsylvania* and the *Nevada* get hit, and I saw the *Arizona* go up in a tremendous explosion. Two destroyers, the *Cassin* and *Downes*,

were in dry dock, and I saw them get hit. I also had a good view of Japanese planes falling. This came mainly during the second attack wave, by which time the defenses on the island and the ships' gun crews had gotten organized. A good many Japanese planes were shot down by antiaircraft fire. As a matter of fact, it was so thick you could walk out on the parking area and scoop up shrapnel with your hands.

Naturally, those of us in the patrol planes felt very helpless while all this was going on, because we didn't have any aircraft that we could operate. Of course, everyone wanted to go out and retaliate. So, after the burning aircraft had been extinguished, we set about fixing the planes that were least damaged and inspecting control wires, hydraulic lines, and so forth, to make sure they still worked. By the next morning, two of the planes were flyable, and since one of them was mine, I had the first patrol after the attack. Admiral Kimmel felt that the most likely area in which we could find the Japanese was to the southwest—toward Kwajalein or Truk. Our instructions were to fly toward the islands all night long, then reverse course in daylight and head back to Pearl Harbor. We figured we were bound to see the Japanese attack force sometime during our patrol.

The takeoff was an eerie one, because there was a layer of heavy fuel oil on the surface of the harbor. It had come out of the torpedoed battleships, which were still burning and smoking. So we were trying to get up to flying speed with these damaged ships just off the plane's wing tips. Besides that, there were dozens of boats going back and forth, carrying the wounded and so forth. Their wakes splashed oily water up onto my windshield, with the result that I never did see anything until I was well clear of the island. It was a 100 per cent instrument takeoff after we got hit with the oil. I headed right for the hills around the harbor, then made a 130-degree turn and headed out to sea. Then we managed to get some gasoline and went out and cleaned off the windshield from the outside. Of course, you couldn't do that with modern airplanes, because you'd be going too fast. But in those days, you could stand up in the slipstream and get away with it. We went ahead and made our eighteen-hour patrol, out and back. Naturally, we didn't see the Japanese fleet, because the raid had come from the north instead of the south.

I've said that we were already preparing for war, even before the air raid hit, but still we had been admonished, over and over again, "Now don't do anything provocative." When we made the flight to Australia to prepare the way for the B-17s, we

The Ford Island Naval Air Station was adjacent to the berths of the battleships, which were the principal Japanese targets, and consequently came in for considerable damage. Note the detached PBY wings lying on the ground in both pictures. (National Archives: 80-G-19948 and 80-G-19944.)

were told both orally and in writing, "Don't do anything to provoke the Japanese. Don't get close to the islands. Don't use your radio." Now, all of a sudden, after 7 December, everything was changed. It took quite a bit of psychological adjustment to realize that the rules of only the day before no longer applied.

Finally, though, we had a focus for our efforts. In our prewar fleet exercises, for example, the man in the tail-gun position of a PBY had a pretty dull job, and it was difficult to keep him alert. But once the war started, the tail gunner in my plane would not even eat lunch. You couldn't get him away from his post. He was looking all the time.

Thomas Hinman Moorer (1912–   ) was in the Naval Academy class of 1933 and served in heavy cruisers before qualifying as a naval aviator in 1936. He was in fighter squadrons before reporting to PBYs. In early 1942, he survived being shot down and wounded near Australia. He continued in patrol aviation through much of the war and was on a number of staffs, then and later. He served in the carrier *Midway* and later commanded the seaplane tender *Salisbury Sound*. Among his flag assignments were Director of the Long-Range Objectives Group, Commander Carrier Division 6, Commander Seventh Fleet, Commander in Chief of the Pacific and Atlantic Fleets, Chief of Naval Operations, and Chairman of the Joint Chiefs of Staff. He retired from active duty in 1974. Admiral Moorer now lives in McLean, Virginia, and is with the Georgetown Center for Strategic and International Studies in Washington, D.C. (Courtesy of *Naval Aviation News*.)

Wipeout at Kaneohe

By Rear Admiral Arthur W. Price, Jr., U.S. Navy (Retired)

As the war clouds gathered over the Pacific in November 1941, we in Hawaii had plenty to keep us occupied. Early in the month, Saburo Kurusu, the special Japanese envoy to the United States, passed through on a Clipper flight to the mainland. Everybody went on double alert. Whatever we had been doing, we did it twice. If we normally had two planes up, we put up four. If we usually had one man on guard, we had two. Our alertness doubled.

Then, during the first week in December, we continued to be alert because of a peacetime exercise—our last in a long time—with the Army and the Army Air Forces. Though we didn't paint the planes that way, we called ourselves blue and the Army red. The exercise terminated on Friday, 5 December, and everything went back to normal for the weekend. Saturday night, we had a party, and I spent the night with friends in the enlisted housing area at Kaneohe, our new air station on the eastern shore of Oahu.

On Sunday morning, three PBYs from Patrol Squadron 14 (in which I served as an aviation metalsmith) had the duty off Pearl Harbor. It was one of those three, flown by Ensign William Tanner, that spotted a midget submarine outside the harbor. He dropped a smoke bomb to mark the position, and the submarine was soon attacked by the destroyer *Ward* near the harbor mouth. All three of the planes had been out since maybe four or five o'clock that morning, but unfortunately, none of them was patrolling to the north, which is the direction the Japanese carriers were coming in from. Tanner made his contact about 6:40, and it was an hour after that when I first knew anything was happening. I was awakened by enemy planes buzzing the housing area. There was an observation tower nearby, and to the Japanese it must have looked like an aircraft-control tower, because the first thing they did was strafe the tower. That woke us up.

My first reaction was, "I thought those maneuvers were over on Friday. What are they doing today? It must be the damned red Army again." The planes flew by, and then, all of a sudden, one of us said, "That's not a star. That's a red ball. The only thing that's got that is Japanese. What the hell is he doing here?"

At that point, we didn't see any bullets flying around or anything, even though the planes were pretty low. Then we heard the rat-a-tat-tat of strafing on the beach and knew this was for real. So we got in a car and drove to the squadron hangar, arriving just about the time everybody else was showing up from the barracks nearby.

The first wave of planes had strafed all the PBYs we had sitting out on the beaching ramp, and they were all burned. Our fire trucks were there, but they couldn't do much with burning aluminum. Even the planes out on the water were on fire. One of our boys who had been on watch in a plane out in the bay was strafed, but he had sense enough to crawl up onto the ramp. I went over and picked him up, but he was already dead. I put him in the back of the squadron truck—which, for some reason, I was driving by that time—and wrapped him in a cloth. There was nothing else I could do for him, so I just left him there.

Meanwhile, our men were setting up machine guns outside the VP-14 hangar. I went over to try to help out, and then somebody shouted, "Here comes a group of bombers." Our skipper said, "Let's get the hell out of here." So he and I and another man jumped into the truck, and we started heading over toward another hangar. When we got there, we looked up, and there came a formation of eight to twelve bombers, flying in a beautiful **V** formation at about 1,200 feet. As soon as we saw them approaching the hangar, we got out of the truck and dove under some construction material. The planes got right above us and let their bombs go. That was the end of our new hangar.

Those planes continued on, and as we were getting back into the truck, there was another group, also flying in a **V**. One of us expressed the thought that must have been in all of our minds, "What the hell are they going to bomb? There's nothing left." I guess the Japanese felt the same thing, because they kept on going. They flew over Kaneohe and went over to Bellows Field or Hickam Field; there was no more damage they could do to us. But our worries still weren't over.

About that time, a Zero fighter came down. We thought he was going to strafe us, because his guns were going, but evidently the pilot had been shot

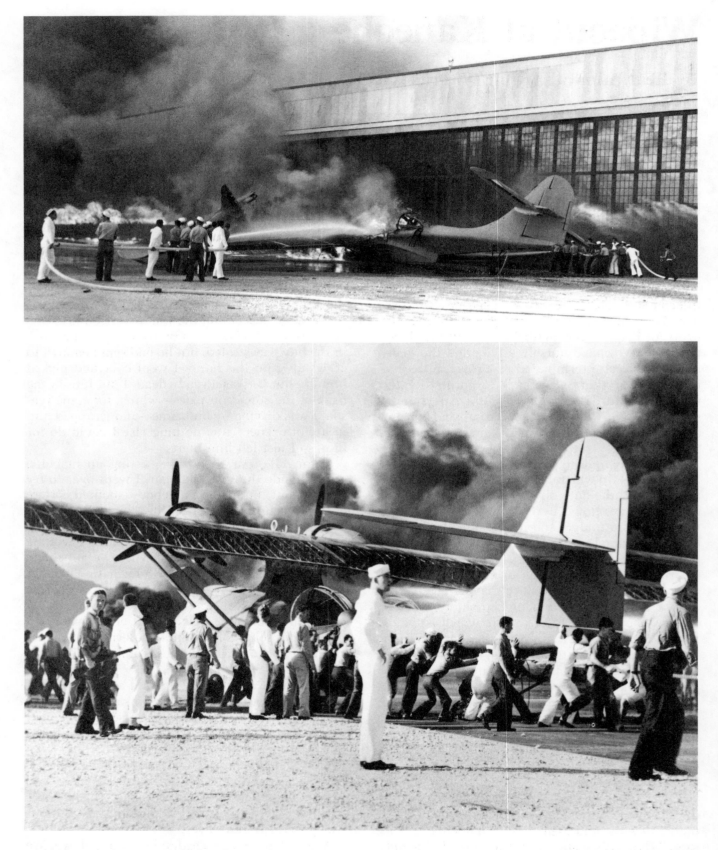

When the attack on Pearl Harbor began, thirty-six PBY patrol planes were stationed at the Kaneohe Bay Naval Air Station on the eastern side of Oahu. By the time the attack ended, thirty-three of them had been damaged or destroyed by the Japanese. The three survivors were away on patrol when the enemy struck Kaneohe. (National Archives: 80-G-32834 and 80-G-32837.)

already. He just flew straight into the ground right ahead of our truck, shooting the whole way. He hit the ground maybe 500 feet from us, and was thrown out of the plane. He was dead, of course, and all chopped up, so we threw him in the back of the truck. So here we were carrying the dead American from the seaplane ramp and the dead Japanese from the Zero.

We drove back to our hangar, and there we encountered Chief Aviation Ordnanceman John Finn, a man who was later awarded the Medal of Honor for his heroism that day. He was all shot up—looked as if he'd been peppered with the small stuff, .30-caliber machine guns. So it was back into the truck once more to take the chief to sick bay. He and the skipper and I were in the front, and the two corpses were in the back.

When we got to our destination, wounded men were flaked out all through the passageways because there were so many of them that there was no place to put them. I thought the medical people would keep Chief Finn there, he was in such bad shape. But he said, "No, I just want to get patched up." He wouldn't stay. Twenty minutes later, he was right back down at the skeleton of the hangar, getting the ordnance things organized.

By about nine o'clock, when things had died down, our three PBYs came back from patrol, and they didn't have a scratch on them. Those were the only planes we had left, because we lost thirty-three out of our thirty-six that morning. We knew the Japanese had hit us with carrier planes, so we took the depth charges off the PBYs and put on either bombs or torpedoes, I forget which, and sent the planes back out with new crews to look for the enemy carriers. Of course, the Japanese were long gone by then, and our pilots never did find anything. After the three of them had gotten airborne, the skipper had to take John Finn home to his quarters before he passed out.

After a while, even though we were generally in a state of shock, we began to get things sorted out. It turned out that the man I pulled off the ramp was the only one in our squadron who died that day. We did have a couple of men shot up pretty badly.

In addition to the Japanese pilot we picked up, we managed to recover some paperwork from his plane. Included was a map; everything on it was in Japanese, but we turned it over to naval intelligence and learned later that it indicated our water tank was a fuel farm. Those pilots had just peppered the hell out of that tank during the attack but couldn't set it on fire. I think that sort of confused them, but they sure weren't confused about what day to hit us.

Arthur Whyte Price, Jr. (1920–   ) enlisted in the Navy in 1939. After service in the *Wright*, Patrol Squadron 14, and Patrol Wing 2, he reported for enlisted flight training. Commissioned an ensign in 1944, he served in a number of training and operational billets, then studied at Marquette University and General Line School. Subsequent duties were in the *Floyds Bay*, Fleet Air Pacific staff, Naval Air Weapons School, and Naval Air Missile Test Center. After redesignation as an unrestricted line officer in 1956, he was executive officer of the *Stribling* and then commanded the *Liddle*, *Ashland*, *Duluth*, River Patrol Force (Task Force 116 in Vietnam), and Amphibious Squadron 11. As a flag officer, he was Commander U.S. Naval Forces Vietnam, Commander Amphibious Group Eastern Pacific, Commander Amphibious Force Seventh Fleet, and Deputy Commander Amphibious Force Pacific Fleet. He retired from active duty in 1975 and now lives in Coronado, California. (Courtesy of Rear Admiral Arthur W. Price, USN, Ret.)

Call Out the Marines

By Brigadier General Samuel R. Shaw, U.S. Marine Corps (Retired)

The attack itself was a surprise, but some defenses had been prepared beforehand on the premise that a surprise attack might occur. In these preparations, however, defense against air attack was only incidental to the basic plan of defense. It's odd to consider now, but the basic scheme was to defeat a commando type of attack mounted against the navy yard by hostile formations already ashore.

These preparations began shortly after the Japanese attacked and captured the French border defenses of what is now Vietnam in September 1940. That exposure of the urgency of their plans for the Greater East Asia Co-Prosperity Sphere was viewed by many as the opening phase of hostilities aimed at seizing the Philippines, the Dutch East Indies, Malaya, and Singapore. In order to operate in those far areas, the Japanese had made sure that this strategically important corner of Indochina could not provide bases for use by British, Dutch, or American forces.

In late 1940 and early 1941, a series of conferences was held among officers of the Fourteenth Naval District, the district and fleet intelligence offices, and the Marine Barracks. At that time, the defense of Oahu, including the fleet base, was an Army responsibility. The Army's intelligence estimate was that a sizeable number of local males of Japanese origin were organized and prepared to attack objectives on the island, especially the navy yard installations. Further, if such an attack occurred, it would be coordinated with other efforts such as shelling from submarines, air attacks by flying boats from the Marshalls, or perhaps some more powerful type of raid.

The Marines were never told what this estimate was based on, but in the event itself, of course, there was no single case of hostile action by any resident of Japanese descent. This is not to say that, at the time of those briefings and preparations, the Marines did not give the intelligence estimates full credence. It was easy to do. Some villages in the cane fields near Pearl Harbor, such as Aiea, right on top of the lower fresh-water pumping stations and through which we had to go to reach the upper pumping stations, were totally Japanese. Through open doors and windows, Japanese flags and pictures of Emperor Hirohito could clearly be seen in

many homes. There were a number of tall and fancy radio antennas, of the type associated with high-quality amateur radio stations. Many people believed these radios were part of a Japanese spy network. Frequent Marine reports of what they thought was highly suspicious activity finally brought information that the Federal Communications Commission and Army and Navy intelligence units kept watch on all of these amateur sending stations, and there was no sign of improper use.

The navy yard's internal sentry and patrol system was to function normally against saboteurs, arsonists or accidental fires, and unauthorized entry or observation. The Army was to take care of affairs outside the navy yard fence, and the Marines were to make the final defense of the yard if hostile units reached the wire fence on the perimeter or slipped inside it. There was not a surplus of people to get all this done. The 1st and 3rd Defense Battalions were then quartered in the navy yard but were already beginning to move out to their positions at Wake, Midway, Canton, and Christmas islands. The 2nd Engineers Battalion was beginning the construction of Camp Catlin in the cane fields halfway to Honolulu. These battalions would have their own tasks, such as antiaircraft defense. The plans provided that, in the event of necessity, such Fleet Marine Force units as were available would constitute additional units in reserve.

The perimeter defense line stretched from the main gate to the submarine base gate to the small bay at Aiea, where the outpost guarding the lower pumping station was quartered, and provided interlocking bands of machine-gun fire. Fortunately, the terrain made tactically sound positions fairly simple, except at the gates. Initially, these were to be open, dug in, and sandbagged emplacements. Eventually, they were to be replaced by reinforced-concrete gun positions. Those positions never got built, because it was decided that the sandbagged open holes would cause less comment and alarm on the part of the general population. There would be fewer questions as to why it was necessary to build defenses against ground attack coming from the interior of the island. Since, at the time, the belief seemed rather farfetched that the sites should also be capable of firing at aircraft, and the possibility of shelling appeared remote, the lack of overhead cover was of small concern.

However, to make the open machine-gun positions less obvious, ornamental concrete gate houses were built. They had raised parapets on their roofs, behind which the guns, ammunition, and water cans could be concealed. These were terrible sites for ground defense, because they did not permit grazing fire, but they turned out to be good for antiaircraft defense. Head-on shots could be fired at the torpedo planes passing over on their run at the ships in the harbor and strafing the sites en route.

The crews to man these weapons came from a rather unusual source. The two line companies, performing day-on-day-off guard duty, could not readily produce at any given moment of alarm the thoroughly trained gunners for specific gun-crew assignments. The permanently assigned men from "A" Company at the two gates could and did provide such crews, but the others came from the post's band. Usually the battle function of the band is as litter bearers. In this case, with a few additional men from the maintenance shops, they were trained as machine-gun crews, a principal element in the Marine Barracks plan for ground defense of the navy yard. When the Japanese came, these crews did a superb job in the only action they had, firing against enemy aircraft.

The guns at the main and submarine base gates were kept in fully ready condition; water jackets filled, hoses connected, and a couple of dozen ammunition boxes with belted ammunition. As each relief of the guard came on duty, it was required to check these weapon arrangements to be sure that all were in proper condition. The guns for the other positions were kept in a storage room in the basement of the main barracks building. These, too, were kept in fully ready condition except for filled water jackets, and they were checked daily by their crews. Periodic drills were held with designated truck drivers to practice breaking out all the gear and getting it to the prepared emplacements.

As 1941 slipped by, hostilities with Japan were clearly becoming more and more likely. As the tension mounted, everyone became more concerned about the security of important features within the navy yard. The European use of commandos, raiding units, and saboteurs showed what might happen to us. Particularly valuable were the sensitive oil-storage tanks within the yard itself, the power plants, several places where lengthy sections of pipes carrying the entire fresh-water supply for the navy yard were exposed, the dry-dock caissons, and a number of the then-scarce and classified repair shops, such as for radar and instruments. Some of them did not even have sentries guarding their exterior. The Marine Barracks was required to place sentries at many points not guarded before and to double the guard at many one-man posts. The additional men were found by the kindness of the two defense battalions who alternately reinforced the guard of the day from the barracks with enough men to fill all requirements. As time went on, the morning guard formations in front of the main building of the Marine Barracks grew to look like a Saturday morning parade.

That was the formation in ranks in front of the Marine Barracks that fine Sunday morning. The old and the new guard marched on and were standing at ease, waiting to begin the ceremony of morning colors. The men were equipped with M-1 rifles, and each man had three clips of ball ammunition. The men looked idly around as a column of planes, apparently guiding on the road from Honolulu, passed over the main gate area, flying at a suprisingly low altitude, headed toward the ships moored along the length of Ford Island.

The sergeant of the old guard, a man who had had a lot of time in Shanghai and seen much of the Japanese forces there, did a double take, a long and careful second look. He turned to the officer of the day and said, "Sir, those are Japanese war planes."

The officer in turn took a hard look and said, "By God, you're right! Music, sound 'Call to Arms!' " As the first notes from the bugle sounded, the harbor shook with the explosion of a torpedo in the side of one of our battleships. Without another command, the Marines in guard formation loaded their rifles, took aim, and began firing. The Marine Barracks, Navy Yard Pearl Harbor, had gone to war.

The explosions, fire, smoke, and zooming aircraft left no doubt in anyone's mind as to what was afoot. Marines poured out of the barracks, rifles in hand, most of them to the parade ground, where there was the clearest field of fire toward the aircraft attacking the ships. Noncoms supervised distribution of ammunition from the guard house and the nearby post armory. Within minutes, a hail of rifle bullets was pouring up at the Japanese war planes. Very soon, there was hardly a Marine around who was not shooting at the enemy aircraft.

The bandsmen broke out their machine guns and gear and took off for their positions as if it were a drill. The Marine gun crews at the gates later claimed that they opened fire before anyone else, before the first explosions from torpedoes and bombs. They were generally believed; after all, they were subjected to strafing fire as the enemy planes flew overhead toward their release points and had

Billowing smoke from ships burning in the harbor (above and right) provides a somber backdrop for these Marines on the parade ground of the Marine Barracks. (Naval Historical Center: NR&L (MOD) 26399, NR&L (MOD) 26398, and NR&L (MOD) 26402.)

a short jump on everyone else in learning that the war was on.

There are those, most of whom were not there, who later sneered at the idea that this small-arms fire of rifles and machine guns could have had any effect. During the first phase of the attack, this fire was a large part of the total delivered, and intercepts of voice radio transmissions by Japanese pilots returning to their carriers showed they had taken many hits. Until the 3rd Marine Defense Battalion departed for the Guadalcanal operation, they kept a dramatic proof of effectiveness in front of their headquarters—a wing from a Japanese plane downed within the yard. The wing was riddled by .30-caliber bullets.

An immediate task was to find out if this heavy air attack was accompanied by the expected ground attack on which our plans were based. With Japanese aircraft in every direction, and the horizon to the west blotted out by smoke from burning ships and aircraft, it suddenly seemed a quite reasonable expectation. Attempts to call by telephone to a number of sentry posts failed. Almost from the beginning, as a result of constant vibrations from heavy explosions, circuits through the navy yard switchboard were in only intermittent service. Probably, too, if they had a field of fire and visible enemy planes, the sentries were more interested in shooting than in answering a telephone. When it became evident that telephone reports could not be obtained, officers and senior noncoms were sent out to find out what was going on in the security system and whether anything like a ground attack was apparent. Nothing untoward developed within the navy yard, and there were no casualties among the sentries. Outside, in the vicinity of villages where the Japanese cane-field workers lived, primarily Aiea, the most noticeable thing was the absence of people.

Out of an early inspection visit came an incident that led to one of the bizarre touches in connection with the attack. An officer was sent to reestablish contact with the outposts at the upper and lower pumping stations above and below the village of Aiea. When he reached the lower station, he found all was well and that two radiomen had somehow come ashore there from the capsized *Oklahoma*. He told them he would take them back into the yard after he checked the upper pumping station. As the trio passed through an apparently abandoned Aiea, the large number and quality of radio antennas captured their attention. They all got out of the pickup truck and inspected some of the empty houses that obviously contained radios. The radiomen were much impressed with the high quality of the voice

sending-receiving sets they saw in these "poverty level" houses.

When they reached the upper pumping station, they found the outpost untouched. They were hypnotized, enthralled by the box-seat view they had of the spectacle laid out before them. The telephone was working—at least temporarily. After reporting the results of the patrol, the officer asked permission to bring in the radio sets, on the grounds that the lack of people in the village and the quality of the radios were evidence of something being out of order. Besides, the Marines from the barracks had never been happy with the technicians' determination that these radios were of no concern. The response was an enthusiastic affirmative, not only to have the radiomen see to the careful removal of the radios from the houses, but to have both sets and radiomen delivered to the Fourteenth Naval District intelligence office, where both would be put to immediate use.

Late that afternoon, we found out the purpose of these instructions. During the summer of 1941, as the likelihood of war became more visible, Marine language students in Tokyo were pulled out of Japan. If they had been trapped in Japan by war, they would have had no diplomatic immunity and would have been lost. They were brought to Oahu, placed on the Marine Barracks rolls for administration, and sent to study the Japanese language at the University of Hawaii under the supervision of the district intelligence office. These officers, like all servicemen, headed as fast as they could for their duty posts as soon as they knew the war was on. Most were living in bachelor officers' quarters. They very quickly reached the district intelligence office, where the immediate need was for information on the Japanese forces. The usefulness of the combination of these officers who knew the Japanese language and the fortunate "availability" of the voice radios that would be "requisitioned" from Aiea was recognized at once. Hence, the instructions to bring the radios posthaste into the navy yard.

The people in the Marine Barracks learned of this admirable arrangement about sundown when a number of the officers, with radios, showed up looking for working room. The space they were given in the administration building became too cramped and noisy with all that was going on. They were told to ask for room at the Marine Barracks. By that time, part of the headquarters staff of an Army antiaircraft battalion had been set up in the barracks basement. These people were squeezed over to make room and, for a couple of days, the Marine Barracks was equipped with what they came to regard as their own private communications intelligence station. Of course, the Japanese fleet soon retired out of listening range and the arrangement was ended. The officers were reassigned and the radios distributed within fleet intelligence.

As the second phase of the attack wound down near 10:00 a.m., no one knew what to expect. Would new waves of attacking aircraft suddenly appear? Would bombardment ships and transports come over the horizon to attempt a landing? Whatever was about to happen, it was necessary to get back to a more orderly operation.

The Marine riflemen on the parade ground were used to provide additional local security for a number of working areas in the navy yard. Officers commandeered their willing services to mount guard over things they believed deserved greater protection under the circumstances. This disrupted for a time the proper rotation of relief of the guard of the day. It took several days to get them all returned to their regular routine. Some, being fed and maintained in high style, were in no hurry to end the emergency detail.

The sentries who had been on post since four o'clock in the morning had to have food and water delivered to them while the guard of the day was being reorganized so that they could be relieved. The mess sergeant was instructed to prepare sandwiches and water to be sent out in trucks that would also carry replenishment ammunition. He at once explained that he would need some help. All his messmen and some of his cooks were still out on the parade ground with their rifles, as he said, "practicing being heroes, and to hell with the mess hall." He would need a search party to round up enough men to get the job done quickly. Since Sunday morning breakfast had been prepared for the on-going guard of the day, a hot breakfast was available in the mess hall, and those present could serve themselves. But quickly turning out a large number of sandwiches for absentees was another matter. Not to be forgotten either was the idea that breakfast ought not to be the only meal of the day.

The solution was readily at hand. The brig of the Marine Barracks was the "holding" brig, where all men in the fleet who had been convicted by general court-martial, usually of serious offenses and given relatively long sentences, were awaiting transportation to the mainland. There were about twenty of these men in the brig. They, and all the other brig prisoners, were marched to the mess hall, where they were told that they would be "prisoners-at-large" subject to the orders of the mess sergeant and his assistants and would not be returned to confinement until the emergency was over.

The scheme worked without a hitch. Not a single man took advantage of the circumstances to escape or make trouble. A number of them worked with such flat-out energy and intelligent initiative that recommendations were made that their sentences be commuted, subject to good behavior, and in every case that was done. It was the kind of thing that gave everyone involved a good feeling and pride in the whole affair. One of the prisoners said that he guessed it was a hell of a thing to say, but the Japanese attack had done some good for at least a few people. It was certainly so for some of them. Another prisoner was a Marine sentenced to a bad-conduct discharge, as an incorrigibly bad actor. Later in the war, I found this man a member of my battalion and had the pleasure of promoting him to staff sergeant.

Some time in mid-afternoon, a group of workmen from the navy yard came to the barracks with a problem. Many were wet, their clothes soaked in fuel oil, and all were dog tired and hungry. They were among the large number of workers on a night shift. When the attack came on, they joined in, fighting fires, controlling damage, doing whatever was indicated alongside the men in the fleet. Normally, they would have gone home at eight o'clock in the morning. The civilian cafeteria in the navy yard had not opened up. They needed food, for they expected to go back on the job. The Marine Barracks mess hall and those of the defense battalions went on a twenty-four-hour buffet style of operation. They fed anyone who came in the door. This lasted until some time on Tuesday.

There were other similar common-sense but outside-of-the-book approaches to problems that presented themselves. Many officers from the fleet were ashore with only the clothes they were wearing, and these were ruined, soaked in oil. The Fleet Marine Force Supply Depot and the post quartermaster held open house in their clothing-issue rooms. Any officer who showed up in oil-soaked khakis was handed a fresh set of skivvies, socks, khaki trousers, and a shirt, and pointed toward a head with showers where he could clean up and change into fresh clothes. Sailors were shunted down to the receiving barracks which had a stock of Navy uniforms and dungarees.

Shortly after noon, the naval hospital called, asking for the use of extra space. It was being flooded with casualties from the ships and aviation outfits on Ford Island and wanted to be able to farm out the less seriously injured who could survive with a minimum amount of care. The Marine Barracks found it could take quite a load. First, there was the post exchange, which had considerable space

On 8 December, the day after the attack, the author led a patrol through wooded Manana Canyon in search of spies and saboteurs. From left to right, the members of the patrol are First Lieutenant Dick Gard, Warrant Officer Ernie Saftig of naval intelligence, Captain Shaw, Marine Gunner Dick Hooker, and Captain John Earle. (Courtesy of Colonel Cornelius C. Smith, Jr., USMCR, Ret.)

that could be cleared readily. A very nice-sized beer hall and the staff noncommissioned officers' club were naturals; just move the tables and chairs outside. And finally, with a little more effort, the two-story wooden barracks which housed the 150-odd men of "A" Company could be made ready. This required crowding together the men of "B" Company and the barracks detachment in the main barracks building. Then the lockers and bunks of "A" Company were moved into the main barracks. As space was successively cleared, the hospital overflow, complete with bunks, linen, and blankets, was moved in. A few senior corpsmen had general supervision of these newly created wards. Before nightfall, with its prospect of a blackout and almost no place ashore equipped to be blacked out, these patients were fed from the mess hall, the crew of prisoners-at-large doing most of the work.

That night, exhausted, nervous men all over the navy yard, in the shock of a powerful surprise blow,

with death and destruction all around them, suffered a number of alarms and excursions, none of them caused by the actual presence of the enemy. There were some casualties. It is surprising that, under the circumstances, there were not more. Probably a major reason there were not is that it takes a great deal of careful training to teach people to shoot well with rifles in the darkness. There was no such training in those days, nor much more of it today.

One incident engendered an unfortunate frame of mind which was to plague us, and the island of Oahu, for weeks to come. Well after midnight, on an overcast night, the navy yard was pitch-black. Then someone threw the wrong switch. All the powerful floodlights for illuminating the lower fuel-tank farm came on. That end of the navy yard appeared more brilliantly lit up than a modern stadium during a night ball game. Someone in a building near the tank farm threw open a window and leaned out. In a voice so loud that it was heard at a great distance, a man screamed, "Shoot those lights out." Every man with a rifle, whether in range or not, joyfully responded. It was like Coney Island on the Fourth of July. As the lights succumbed to the instant fusillade, for a few seconds the sky was almost as brilliantly lit as before from the tracer bullets arcing through the night. Then all was black again.

For weeks thereafter, whenever a light showed in violation of blackout, many people felt licensed to fire a few rounds, at least in its general direction. It was a silly and dangerous practice that was difficult to stamp out. Finally, summary, if irregular, punishment was imposed on offenders. As sentries came off their posts, their weapons were inspected, and woe betide the man who had fired his rifle without a reason that an angry sergeant of the guard would accept as ironclad.

One night, some time later, the radars of the air defense system picked up a bogey over Oahu. When the searchlights cut on, they had in their beams a large flying boat. Later, there were garbled accounts indicating that it had set off photo flash bombs for night photography. No antiaircraft guns opened fire. All hands were determined to have no more trigger-happy misfortunes such as there had been immediately after the attack. By the time Army Air Forces authorities and naval aviation authorities had convinced air defense operations that this unidentified aircraft was not theirs, and thus had to be enemy, the airplane had disappeared from sight and from the radar screen. Shortly thereafter, the incident was repeated.

By happenstance, my wife, then a supervisor in the air defense command plotting room, was on duty on both occasions. She passed on the comic aspects (and the serious as well) of the spectacle of everybody following the Mongolian General Prudential Rule; "When in danger or in doubt, run in circles, scream and shout." Later, I was ribbing the Pacific Fleet's intelligence officer as to whether there was an exchange of immunity for each side's reconnaissance agents. It turned out that this was the first he had heard of the incidents. The reporting system had managed to avoid drawing CinCPac's attention to this embarrassing affair. But from then on, the problem of enemy reconnaissance aircraft got ample attention.

After the war, we learned that these flying boats had come from the Marshall Islands. The Japanese had perfected for themselves the U.S. Navy's "cruise control" technique for fuel economy in multi-engine aircraft and could make the round trip without refueling. But, at the time, the reaction was to es-

tablish a Marine detachment with two 4-inch naval guns at French Frigate Shoals in the hope that a hidden gun battery could scotch both submarines and planes. This "most distant outpost ever maintained by the Marine Barracks of a navy yard" lasted for about four months.

There was an odd sequel to this affair. Some nineteen years later, while I was on an official visit to the Japanese Self-Defense Forces, I was a guest at a lunch hosted by a Japanese admiral. Naturally, there was mutual comparing of wartime experiences. The host mentioned that, early in the war, he was with a patrol aircraft squadron stationed in the Marshalls. That led to a discussion of the above events. The admiral was much interested and, with a broad smile, said, "I remember the beginning of all that very well. I was the pilot of the flying boat both times."

Samuel Robert Shaw (1911–   ) was graduated from the Naval Academy in 1934. Before World War II, he studied at The Basic School, served in the cruiser *Tuscaloosa* and with 1st Battalion, 5th Marines, and studied at Marine Corps Schools. He commanded "A" Company, Marine Barracks, Pearl Harbor, from 1940 to 1943, then reported to the staff of Fleet Marine Force, Pacific. From 1944 to 1945, he commanded the Sixth Pioneer Battalion. He then held billets in research and planning before reporting to the staff of the 1st Marine Division in Korea in 1954. Before his retirement from active duty in 1962, he was at Headquarters, Marine Corps; Director of the Marine Corps Development Center at Quantico; and Commanding General, Landing Force Training Unit, Coronado, California. He then served on the staff of the Senate Armed Services Committee until 1972 and worked for the Selective Service System until 1976. General Shaw lives in Alexandria, Virginia. (Courtesy of Brigadier General Samuel R. Shaw, USMC, Ret.)

General Shaw wrote his recollections of events surrounding the attack many years after they occurred. In contrast, at least one Marine officer who was with him set down his observations virtually as things were taking place. Both the words and the drawings of Cornelius C. Smith, Jr., who was a first lieutenant at the time, depict the lives of the Marines at Pearl Harbor in December 1941.

"... A Hell of a Christmas"

By Colonel Cornelius C. Smith, Jr., U.S. Marine Corps Reserve (Retired)

This morning I was in the mess hall having a cup of coffee with Marine Gunner Floyd McCorkle. I had the desk yesterday and was just about to report in to the Colonel with the new O.D. [officer of the day]. At about 7:55, a sharp blast rocked the building, rattling the tableware and bouncing a big G.I. coffee cup onto the deck.

In about six seconds comes a second deafening roar. We jump to our feet and run out to the lanai for a look-see. From over Hickam Field, just in back of our barracks, comes a succession of attack planes, and you can see the Rising Sun on their wings and the bombs leaving the bellies.

For a moment we both stand there, speechless. Over near the drydock there is a terrific blast, and flames and smoke shoot hundreds of feet into the air. Now, men are stumbling out of the barracks, wide-eyed, dazed. Some are dressed. Some are lurching into pants and shirts, on the run; two or three are wrapped in towels.

Someone screams: "Get out of the building—take cover under the trees!" Someone else yells: "Get inside! Get inside! They're gonna strafe!" All of the time the bombs are falling. They whistle to earth, detonating with ear-shattering explosions. You can see the morning sunlight glisten on the bombs as they fall—silvery flashes, like trout or mackerel jumping out of the water. The bombs are falling a couple of hundred yards away, and you can hear the shrapnel whistling through the air.

Now, a few stray machine guns begin to bark, and a few riflemen aim their pieces skyward and let fly. God knows why. The attack is high-level, maybe 10,000 feet up. The men keep on firing, though. Well, at least they're doing something. Then the planes begin to dive. I've seen our own planes on training missions diving right where the Jap planes are diving now—right over Ford Island, Pearl City, and Waipio Peninsula. Who said the Japs were cross-eyed, second-rate pilots who couldn't hit the broad side of a barn door? Maybe so, but I'm standing on our Navy Yard parade ground looking up at them while they make a sandpile out of the Yard. They're kicking the hell out of Pearl Harbor, and it's enough to turn your stomach.

There goes the USS *Arizona*, smashed like a toy ship on a millpond. We don't know yet whether she was hit by bombs or torpedoes. Someone said a bomb went right down one of her stacks. But bombs or torpedoes—she's a goner. I wonder how many men went down with her? It was just a few days ago that our own Detachment Band was competing against the *Arizona*'s musicians in the Fleet "Battle of the Bands." Now, it seems a long time ago. [First Lieutenant] Don Merker says that two Jap midget subs have been spotted in the harbor.

There goes the *Oklahoma*. Six torpedoes slammed into her port side and she capsized in minutes. There goes the "Weavy" [the *West Virginia*]. Like the *Oklahoma*, she lists sharply and water rushes in everywhere. There goes the *Utah*. She rolls over like a celluloid duck in a bathtub, while men scramble out of port holes and climb over the keel to dive in the water. I stood JO [junior officer of the deck] watches on her bridge last year. Well, no one else ever will.

The Japs can't see—but they're making a beautiful mess of the *Oglala*. She gave my boys a rough time on the ball field, but we beat her. There were two teams we couldn't whip, though—the *Mississippi*, and the USS *Holland*. The "Pennsy" is tied up in drydock and the *Cassin* and *Downes* are on her bow. [First Lieutenant] Paul Becker just came up and said the two cans took a direct hit and are lost. The "Pennsy" suffered bow damage.

Now we are shooting back like crazy. There are .30s and .50s popping off everywhere. No coordination—just chaotic firing, with tracers streaking up like Roman candles. We have four .50s mounted on the barracks roof, and they are all working. So are guns from shore installations all around us, and from ships anchored in the stream.

Here come the strafers again, and bullets kick up dirt all around. There! Somebody got off a good burst at a Jap. His plane is over Captain Sammy Shaw's house now and in flames. It's like the old movies: "Hell's Angels," and "Dawn Patrol," but this is the real stuff. In several more seconds, that Roman candle of an airplane will smack into the Yard and explode in a ball of fire.

Their planes are everywhere—but where are ours from Ford Island? Wheeler? Hickam? Kaneohe? Ewa? By now, everyone who isn't shooting is watching. We are getting pasted, and only a few of the

Lieutenant Smith's talents as an artist enabled him to capture the feeling of the Pearl Harbor experience in this sketch and those that follow. As men from the stricken battleships sought refuge, Smith tried to find a friend who was serving in the *Oklahoma*. Only later did he learn that First Lieutenant Harry Gaver had perished in the attack. (Drawn by Colonel Cornelius C. Smith Jr., USMCR, Ret.; courtesy of Colonel Smith.)

enemy planes are hit. The AA [antiaircraft] guns have at last been set up and are slamming away.

I look at the colonel [Elmer Hall], and somehow I think both of us feel guilty. I look around at the men with the rifles in their hands and the bandoliers of ammo slung over the shoulder and they are shamefaced, too. Why? What did we have to do with this? Well, nothing, but there is still a plenty good reason. It's because we're all Marines, the best damned fighting outfit in the world—and we're taking a stiff hiding. Friends back home used to ask about the Japs. "Hell, we could blow them out of the water in three weeks!" But here we are with our pants down and the striking force of our Pacific Fleet is settling on the bottom of East Loch, Pearl Harbor. Who wouldn't be ashamed?

They've flown off now, but they've left their calling cards. Captain Sam Shaw sends me out with

sentries for Kuahua Island, and I have a chance to see the Yard. It's a mess. It's like an ant hill you've just teased with your toe. Men, like ants, are scurrying every which way. Traffic is tangled. Whistles screech. Men scream. And because there is a rumor of Jap landings, some trigger-happy people are shooting at anything that moves.

At Kuahua, we see men coming off the ships. They're dripping with oil, black and grotesque looking. Some are only oil-smeared, but many had to swim through fire and are hurt. We wade out chest-deep in the water to help the wounded ashore. A bunch of them are placed under a big tree. I post my sentries and return to the barracks. When I get there, rumors are flying thick and fast. They say the *Arizona* lost over 1,200 men, 800 in the *Oklahoma*. I wonder about Johnny Coursey, "Waz" Asmuth, and Harry Gaver [three Marine officers].

On the night of 7 December, tired Marines gather around their shortwave set to pick up broadcasts from Tokyo and elsewhere. The darkness so magnifies their sense of foreboding that the sound of a dropped bench resembles a rifle shot and the static of the radio sounds like machine-gun fire. (Drawn by Colonel Cornelius C. Smith, Jr., USMCR, Ret.; courtesy of Colonel Smith.)

It's night now, and the Yard is blacked out. In the messhall a bluelight lantern sputters feebly. I can't call [my wife] Katie in our place down near Kapiolani Park. I wonder if she thinks I'm dead? Surely she could hear all the firing today. Well, we'll just have to wait.

More rumors! The Japs have landed on Barbers Point. Parachute troops are coming down near Mt. Tantalus. Pearl has been bottled up. Midway has capitulated. Wake and Guam have fallen. Dispatch runners keep coming and going. Telephones keep ringing as the unbelievable rumors spread.

It's funny about the different noises. In peacetime and in daylight, they're just noises. Now we are at war, and this is the first night. A laundry cart rumbles across the asphalt patch out behind the bakery. With all of that weight and those tiny skate wheels, it sounds just like machine gun fire. A messman

drops a bench end on the concrete deck. A rifle shot. The short wave set crackles with static. More machine guns.

We sit around the radio in the O.D.'s office. [First Lieutenant] Dick Gard knows Japanese, but has trouble making sense out of the broadcast because of the interference. The haranguing is punctuated with Japanese martial music. Stirring, in a barbaric sort of way.

Suddenly the drone of motors is heard overhead. Are they back? Searchlights stab the sky and the AA guns begin again. Machine guns send up tracers. The dark sky lightens—just like it used to at home over the lake at Fairmount Park [in my home town of Riverside, California] when there were fireworks on the Fourth. But there's no music from the boathouse now and no kids fooling with sparklers. All through the night there's no sleep. We're all tense, expectant, waiting. Morning comes and men come into the messhall, their eyes puffy, faces drawn, unshaven, and dirty.

Monday, 8 December

Yesterday we had a parade ground and a ball diamond. Now the ball diamond is gone, on this rainy, grey Monday, and there are gun emplacements, trenches, and sandbags. In one day! Out where [Private] Maxie Stringer used to scoop 'em in at shortstop, there's an AA gun. There's another ack-ack where [Corporal] Johnny Dutra used to pull in the high ones in left field. This one is covered with chicken wire and little strings of gunny sacking.

We've been formed into task groups for "emergency jobs." I'm in Task Group 1 under Sammy Shaw. We will attend to Navy Yard security, providing guards, patrolling vital points and installations, escort and convoy ammo trains in and out of the yard. We double the guard at all posts; there are 65 separate posts now.

Colonel Hall thinks that Harry Gaver may have been pulled off the *Oklahoma* and may be in the hospital. I told the colonel I'd go see. I identify myself to the NCO on watch at the information desk, and explain my mission. He says that there are so many that no check list has been compiled. All the wards are full, and all the halls and corridors have mattresses placed side-by-side. All are taken. He says: "Just go on through and look, Lieutenant—I hope you find your friend."

I've never seen anything like this; the burn cases are charred, crisp skin like bacon rind, black and oozing. Many of the bed-ridden are under hooped sheets, and some have tubes inserted into the flesh to carry away poisons. Would I recognize Harry? Even the partially burned are covered with some sort of tannic acid, and all the patients are black with it. What can I say to Harry even if I do find him? And to the colonel? It seems only yesterday that Harry and Nancy Hall, and I and the others were dancing at the club in San Diego—and having those wonderful times together. And here I am looking for one of the old crew in this awful place.

No one speaks. Few can even move, but pathetic eyes follow me as I go through the wards. These men look so young, just kids, some of them. Probably some lied about their age to get into the Corps and the Navy. They ought to be back Stateside in high school—but here they are burned and broken and lying on the deck. I make some stupid remark about "not feeling so good" to one sailor. His voice is weak but he has courage. "No, sir." He's about 17. I mumble something about "staying with it"

and get out. I can't find Harry.* As I go outside, some sailors are loading boxes on a truck bed.

Tonight I went to Aiea to inspect 64 post. On the way back I noticed a house with two uncommonly tall antennae, and decided to take a look. The hunch paid off. Inside were 12 receiving sets and one large transmitter. The radios weren't Philcos, but expensive Nationals and Hallicrafters. The Japs in the house try to explain it away by saying that the owner is fixing up the sets for his friends. But there is other gear there also—two photo albums with pictures of Pearl—destroyers, cruisers, battle-wagons, the sub base, Aiea landing, and a lot more. The other album contained pictures of people the man had contacted by short-wave radio. He was a licensed ham operator, and there were pictures of people (and a log of their call-signs) from Omaha, Dallas, Vancouver, Sidney, and Melbourne. The book was filled with photos and notes from "hams" in Tokyo, Shimonoseki, Sasebo, Nagoya, and Hiroshima.

The interior of the place is plain. Several people occupy each room, and the rooms are dank and musty. There is a picture of Hirohito over the door in the dining room. The house may be cheap, but this gear isn't. I think the owner is some sort of intelligence agent. He may not be, but I'm going to turn him over to O.N.I. [Office of Naval Intelligence]; they can take it from there. He isn't here, but his brothers are.

"Where is he?"

"Not come back Waipahu since two days."

"Why?"

"Maybe scared got all this stuff."

I take his two brothers into custody and turn the whole shebang over to O.N.I. They seem glad to get it.

Tuesday, 9 December

Today I have orders from Colonel [Gilder D.] Jackson to go through Aiea with a fine-toothed comb. I am to take eight men and search every house having an aerial. There is a forest of aerials. At the first place I put two men in the rear, two in front, three in the street, and take one with me up to the door. There are three pairs of tabis on the porch. I knock.

A kid of about 13 answers. He is frightened and admits us without question. There is a radio, but no transmitter here. Still, one wonders about loyalty. These are the people delegate Sam King has called "100 per cent American," yet there is the

---

*Gaver was killed on 7 December. *See* article by Commander Backus on page 160. Editor.

As the Marines search Aiea for evidence of sabotage, they are struck by the antennas and the sophisticated radio sets that could well be links with Japan. (Drawn by Colonel Cornelius C. Smith, Jr., USMCR, Ret.; courtesy of Colonel Smith.)

ubiquitous picture of Hirohito on his white horse, and near it a photo of Admiral Togo—the old boy who routed the Russian Fleet at Tsushima in 1904. Also, there is a rising-sun flag on another wall and a small Shinto shrine in another room. I wonder if Sam King has been in these houses.

Of course this is a time of hysteria and "shooting from the hip." I remember stories of the Great 1918 War, stories about the German spies in Los Angeles and other Stateside cities. There were thousands of active agents, to be sure, but many innocent people were hurt by false accusations and prejudice. I suppose the Japs will get the same treatment this time.

And you can see why. Two days ago our Pacific Fleet was put out of commission by Jap carrier planes. Now here are these people, "100 per cent loyal," but are they? How powerful is the tie of blood? How strong that of adoption? Many of these people can't speak English. The women wear kimonos, and the kids go to Japanese language school

after their regular classes in territorial schools. The people kneel on pads and eat their meals from little tables, which stand about a foot above the floor.

In one room, a stocky middle-aged man was kneeling before a shrine in an attitude of meditation. The air was heavy with incense. We left him on his knees and went on out.

By the time we had searched eight or ten houses, the whole population was lining the streets. A sea of oriental faces—quiet, uncommunicative, impassive. We went next into a Filipino rooming house. They live like rats. "Rooms" are made by hanging musty blankets on ropes stretched across the open space. In these partitioned-off areas, six or eight men sleep on the floor; clothing, battered bags, and earthly possessions piled helter-skelter on the sad little mattresses. It is like a cave, an animal's lair. There were blocks of these warrens, but none had radio gear of any sort.

Up on the edge of the cane fields we find a transmitter, in a Jap house. Here is another amateur operator, known as K6PRU. We confiscate his equipment without delay, and give him a receipt.

No raids on Oahu today as forecast.

Wednesday, 10 December

No sleep last night. Several air raid alarms, false, but real enough to pile us all out of the sack and send us stumbling through the dark. They're bringing in some bodies at the Aiea landing. Those drowned on the 7th have been on the bottom long enough to float and bob to the surface. They've been dragging the bay, and the bodies are out there bobbing up and down like rubber dolls. The YTLs [small harbor tugs] are cruising around, and men are pulling in the bodies with gaffing hooks.

I hope Harry isn't one of these, but if he is, we may as well know. The colonel and I pile into a guard truck and go to the landing. There are about 200 crude coffins stacked there, and the stench is fearful. Four sailors are off-loading a corpse. It is grotesque. The torso, arms and legs are insanely out of proportion. The head is tiny, in comparison, like an afterthought attached to some macabre piece of sculpture. Water has sluffed away flesh and ID marks like tattoos are gone. The medics say that some skivvies still have laundry marks that are legible, and they are taking dental impressions also. All of the corpsmen [pharmacist's mates] are wearing rubber gloves that reach to the elbow. They say these dead are going to Nuuanu for burial.

Today we went over to the sub base to take a look at one of the midget submarines the Japs used. She's out of the water, resting on chocks, and doesn't look like much because she's so small. Still, she was able to get off a couple of torpedoes successfully. The conning tower is tiny, with room enough for one man to steer the craft. He's still in there. One of our ships rammed him, broadside, and he's caught, dead, with his legs still hanging out; I guess they'll have to cut him free with a blowtorch. I suppose the torpedoman inside is dead, too.

War has many faces. Today, shortly after noon, the NCO at the main gate called to say that a Filipino in a panel truck wanted to "see the general." I told the guard to escort the man to the barracks. Ushered into the room, he was grinning like a fox. Told the "general" was busy, he agreed to deal with me.

"Got four Japs in truck, no good man, I kill them!"

Just as he said, they were there, all right, dead as mackerel, throats slashed from ear to ear.

"Got six more under house, Wahiawa."

I called our post at Wahiawa, out near Schofield Barracks, telling the NCO in charge to check it out. Then we waited while the happy little Filipino chatted amiably about his "duty."

In 15 minutes or so, my man called back. "Yes, sir, they're there. What'll I do with them?" We called in the U.S. Marshal who sent out a couple of men and took our little warrior away. Probably he had lived with these Japanese as neighbors for years, and had had all kinds of disagreements, and so he took the direct approach.

Thursday, 11 December

Heard something interesting this morning. They say that the Jap pilot who crashed over by the hospital wore a McKinley High School ring. Lord knows how they ever found it. When we saw the wreckage, all that was left of him was a piece of his right heel in the torn shoe. Another pilot was reported to be in possession of a Honolulu street car token, another wore, not a Jap army uniform, but a Pearl Harbor Navy Yard workman's get-up—complete with badge! These things sound phony, but who knows? If true, when did these fliers leave Honolulu to join the attack squadrons that hit us? Three weeks ago? A year ago? One certainty is shaping up; there was Fifth Column work attending this raid—probably a lot of it.

Friday 12 December

Today, with the war five days old, I got a chance to see the civilian population at war. We've had our troubles out here in the Yard, and I guess they've had theirs. Soldiers abound downtown, and there are guards everywhere. The Hawaiian Gas and Electric Company on Kamehameha Boulevard, for example, is all sandbagged and protected with machine guns. The Matson docks are heavily guarded. The telephone company on Fort Street is alive with uniforms, and so are King Street, Beretania, Bishop, and the Ala Moana. All of the stores have butcher-tape on their windows. They are interesting. Some are strictly utilitarian in design; others are patterned works of art: geometric designs, floral patterns, "Vs" (for "Victory," I suppose), and so on. A marvelous thing is the human spirit.

Stores are closing at 3:30 p.m. now. There are only cash sales. Gasoline is rationed, ten gallons per month to each customer. In the Piggly Wiggly chain store the shelves were only half-filled. The town is under martial law, and the Army Provost Marshal has superseded the Territorial Judge. Blackout offenders and petty criminals are hit with a heavy hand. The blackout was novel for a day or two, but now it's a bore. You don't dare let any light show. Civilian defense people are roaming the streets at night shooting out lights in houses. Willful offenders may be fined $5,000 and jailed for five years. Early offenders (those being picked up now) are held on $100 bail. Most are poor and can't pay, but that is the way of it. There is no more liquor available, and the pubs are all padlocked. Lau Yee Chai's, Waikiki Tavern, The South Seas, Trader Vic's—all have bolted their doors and shuttered their windows. Pity.

Heard today that the Jap battleship *Haruna* was sunk off Luzon yesterday, and that the *Kongo* was badly damaged. Credit for sinking the *Haruna* is given to Captain Colin Kelly, U.S. Army Air Corps. I met him at a party given by [Second Lieutenant] Jack and Katie Farris at Hickam several months ago. I remember we played "Ask me another" from a quiz book. We chose sides and kept score as a matter of fact. He was good at it.

Germany and Italy declared war on us today. Well, now Hitler has succeeded in tying us up in the Pacific, which will give Germany relative freedom of movement in the Atlantic. In the long run, I don't see how Japan can profit from this war. Though we've taken a major setback here at Pearl, none of us has any doubt that we'll go on to victory. The Japs face eventual defeat by us and our Allies, or the humiliation of being a Nazi satellite. They lose either way. As for Italy—well, poor Italy.

Saturday 13 December

Have done a bunch of cartoons for the boys over the past few days—sketches of wartime barracks life, blackout gags, and so on. They get a kick out of them. The O.D.'s office has turned into something of a social circle. None of us can go "home" to Honolulu; we're all stuck out here on "day on, stay on," and so we gravitate to the desk, drink coffee, and swap rumors. I get dandy cartoon ideas in this lash-up. For instance: [Second Lieutenant] Ben Weatherwax came in this morning with the story (true) of meeting a wildly gesticulating soldier up near Salt Lake. He and his buddies had gas masks on and were using frantic sign language to Ben to put his on pronto. One soldier took off his mask long enough to shout that the enemy had just launched a gas attack. As it turned out, a pipe nearby had ruptured and a little chlorine gas got out. Well, maybe the "doggies" had something at that. I am standing duty every other day now. I have four junior officers in my crew: [Robert] Estes, [Colby] Howe, [John] Hefti, and [William] Muller.

Sunday, 14 December

We got a conscientious objector today from the Marine Air Station at Ewa, a staff sergeant. He is evidently a man of some education and sensitivity, and his statement was clear and somewhat convincing. I suppose each man must answer to his conscience in his own way, and surely the right of dissent is a cornerstone of our brand of political and moral philosophy. Still, this man, like his brothers who will fight this war, some dying, took an oath to defend his country, and bear arms for it in time of war. Now, while the bullets fly, his conscience supersedes his oath. He is awaiting general court-martial. I wonder how many times this will happen in this war?

Midway and Wake still hold out. When the 14th District contacted the boys on Midway and asked if they needed anything, the answer was: "Send us more Japs!" I wonder if [Second Lieutenant] Miles Barrett ever reached Guam? And I wonder about Dan Morgan, Marvin Starr, and "Harpo" Marx [Marine Corps officers] out on Guam. I hope they make out. I was talking to one of our language officers yesterday, and he told me how the Jap soldiers tortured captives in China in 1937. They insert the tips of fountain pens under the fingernails and squirt jets of ink into the wound. What really worries us is that Japan has been at war with China long enough now to overlook the niceties of conventional treatment of prisoners. I suppose that as the weeks pass, we'll hear all sorts of lurid tales about this. God grant that I may be wrong.

Wednesday, 17 December

Washington has informed the country that "one old battleship was sunk, one damaged, and two destroyers put out of commission." The item drew about 20 lines on the fourth page of the *Advertiser* here. Well, I suppose the Brass knows what it's doing, but the truth is bound to leak out sooner or later.

Admiral [Husband E.] Kimmel, General [Walter C.] Short, and General [Frederick L.] Martin were relieved of their commands today, pending inquiry and possible court-martial. This is a terrible thing for them, and I suppose that there will be controversy over this for years to come. Right or wrong, several points are clear. The Hawaiian garrison really wasn't ready for what happened. Because of miscalculation somewhere along the line, we lost capital ships and human lives. Nuuanu Cemetery speaks eloquently of overconfidence and apathy. Red Hill has scattered its dust over the graves of a thousand men because someone erred. Relief of command is tragic, but preventable holocaust is worse. Sometimes, men have to be replaced.

A new slogan is seen everywhere: "Remember Pearl Harbor!" It has a ring about it like, "Remember the Alamo!" "Remember the *Maine!*" I guess that years from now kids will see it in history books, and maybe some kid will raise his hand wildly, wanting to tell how his grandfather shot down a Jap plane, or got wounded, or caught a spy. And the teacher may be an unimaginative soul who will shut the kid up—but that all belongs to another day.

Wednesday, 24 December
Christmas Eve. "Peace on earth, goodwill to men." But where is the peace? Not here. Not anywhere, I guess. There's a blackout on, and only the bulky shadows of tall trees are etched obscurely against a silent sky. The same stars are there, but none light the way to goodwill among men. Here are only curses and damnation for the enemy. Last year I was home and we sang "Adeste Fideles" and "Silent Night." We opened the presents before a roaring fire and had Tom and Jerrys. Later, Mom, Alice, and Caroline went to Midnight Mass. A happy time. Out in the hallway someone just said: "This is a hell of a Christmas." He's right.

Cornelius Cole Smith, Jr. (1913–   ) was graduated from the University of Southern California in 1937 and commissioned a second lieutenant in the Marine Corps Reserve the same year. Between May 1941 and October 1945, he served overseas and had command at all levels from a platoon to a battalion. He left active duty in 1947 and worked as an architect for the Arabian-American Oil Company and as a museum curator for the Scripps Institution of Oceanography. He subsequently earned M.A. and Ph.D. degrees in history at Claremont Graduate School. During the 1950s, he was Chief, Historical Division, 15th Air Force, Strategic Air Command. Since 1967, he has devoted his time to writing, illustrating, painting, and sculpture. He has written nine books on the history of the Southwest and military history and has had numerous one-man shows of his paintings and wood carvings. Colonel Smith lives in Riverside, California. (Courtesy of Colonel Cornelius C. Smith, Jr., USMCR, Ret.)

The unexpected arrival of Japanese carrier planes compelled members of the Army, Navy, and Marine Corps ashore at Pearl Harbor into actions for which they had trained day in and day out. It led Tai Sing Loo into forsaking his usual role as a photographer and assuming several others for which he turned out to be also well suited. In his own charming brand of English, he provided an account that has since been widely reprinted.

How I Were at Pearl Harbor

By Tai Sing Loo

On the 6th of December, Saturday afternoon, I had made arrangement with [Platoon] Sergeant [Charles R.] Christenot to have all his Guard be at the Main Gate between 8:30 to 9:30 o'clock Sunday morning to have a group of picture taken in front of the new concrete entrance as a setting with the "Pearl Harbor" for Christmas card to send home to their family.

Sunday morning I left my home for Pearl Harbor after 7:00 o'clock. I was waiting for my bus at corner Wilder Avenue and Metcalf Street. Saw the sky full of antiaircraft gun firing up in the air, I call my friend to look up in sky, explain them how the Navy used their antiaircraft gun firing in practising, at that time I didn't realize we were in actual war. Our bus stop at Bishop and King Streets. We heard the alarm ringing from the third story building of the Lewers & Cooke, Ltd. Saw the window shattered. I walk up to Young Hotel corner and cross the street. Stop for a cup of coffee at Swanky and Franky. Suddenly all excitement arouse the Honolulu Fire Engine rush down Bishop Street and all directions. Taxi full load of sailor and marine dashing toward Pearl Harbor. I'm very much surprise what's all this excitement. I wave the taxi to stop and get on it to go back to Pearl Harbor. When I approach to Pearl Harbor surprise with great shock. Thought one of our oil tanks caught in fire, showing black velum of thick smoke in the air. I got off at the main gate of Pearl Harbor, met all the guards with arms and Machine Gun in placed. I was great shock with surprise the war are on. Watching many Japanese war planes attacked Pearl Harbor, dropping bombs right and left on dry docks and Ford Island. Suddenly terrific explosion. Fire broke out. I was very calm and waiting for the opportunity to get a ride to the Studio to get my camera. I was at the Main Gates standby with Marines. Guards at the Main Gates were bravery and cool headed to keep the by-standing away for safety and clear traffic. There were the young, fighting marines. We were under fire. The Japanese planes painted in aluminum, Red Ball under each wing, flew very low toward the Main Gates.

I wish my Graflex with me. I would had a wonderful close up shot of the Japese. Again the Japese flew around the Navy Housing Area and turn back,

Born in Hawaii of Chinese parents, Tai Sing Loo was a capable, established photographer, having worked at the navy yard since World War I. By the time World War II came, he had two trademarks, his helmet and the "put-put" three-wheeler in which he got around the navy yard. (Naval Institute Collection, and courtesy of Mrs. Evylyn Lee.)

During the course of the attack, Mr. Loo rendered invaluable assistance by helping to fight fires on board the ships in Dry Dock No. 1. In the foreground are the destroyers *Cassin* and *Downes*, and in the background is the fleet flagship *Pennsylvania*. Loo also helped get some of the Marines fed and even directed traffic for a while. Of his busy day on 7 December 1941, Loo wrote, "Every Kind Deeds its return many, many time Folds." (National Archives: 80-G-19943.)

head direct to Hickam Field, very low to drop a bomb to the Hangars, with terrific explosion, set fire the buildings. More planes flew direct the dry dock. Suddenly, I saw one plane had a hit. It flew direct toward West Locke Stream of smoke screen. Now this my opportunity to get in the Yard, one of the Leadingman of Machine Shop drove in his automobile. I hop in, he take me to the Studio and pick up my Graflex Camers to take some picture, second thought I change my mind, reason is because first place I didn't had no order, the second place I didn't had my famous Trade-Mark helmet on. I had a new English Helmet from Singapore, given by Admiral [Orin G.] Murfin a year ago, so I'm afraid some one will make a mistake me as a Jap and shot me down.

I went up to the Administration Building everythings OK. I met Mr. Wm. McIlhenny and Mr. W. C. Bohley at the stairway. We talk and both went toward the dry dock. I went to the Supply Dept. and saw many boy had a Steel Helmet on, so I went to see Lt. Cdr. Supply Officer for permission to hat one, the size are too large and heavy for me so I select one smaller size, painted green and white stripe. I went direct to the dry dock to help put out the fire on U.S.S. *Cassin* had the depth charges on her stern the U.S.S. *Pennsylvania* bow between *Cassin* and *Downes*. I knew it was very dangerous it may exploded damaged the dry docks and the U.S.S. *Pennsylvania*. We put our hoses directed the depth charges keeping wet. An Officer came near by said keep up the good work we had out hose right at it all the time, and I turn around and saw Lt. [William R.] Spear, order all men stand back, some things may happen, so I obey his order and ran back toward U.S.S. *Pennsylvania*, sudden really happen the terrific explosion came from the Destroyer few people were hurt and some fell down. I notice some large pieces of Steel Plates blew over the dry dock when I turn around and look, afterward I notice two extra hoses without nozzles, so I went to the Fire Station and brought back 2 volunteers pointed direct the depth charges, I call for more volunteers to help me clear and straighten up the hose around the First Street to clear for traffic at the same time purpose to gave the fire fighter a chance to extended the hose across over the bow of U.S.S. *Pennsylvania* to fight the fire at the *Downes* on Starboard side. Here come another Fire Engine from Submarine Base, I direct them to place their engine and connect this Hydrant #151 and direct them to the depth charges, so everythings are well done and successful accomplishment their service. A few words of my appreciation and vote of thanks

and successful credit to Lieut. Spear, in charge with his gallant spirit to kept his staff and volunteers calms, right at the job to see the depth charges were wet and kept away the fire. The Marines of the Fire Dept. of the Navy Yard, are the Heroes of the Day of Dec. 7, 1941 that save the *Cassin* and *Downes* and U.S.S. *Pennsylvania* in Dry Dock No. 1.

I saw the crew threw out empty 5″ shell on the dock, I gether up in Piles with some sailors so I met Chief [Machinist's Mate Armand J.] LeTendre to help me order some hose from Supply Dept. to place in this Hydrant No. 151, corner Avenue D and First Street. I also request Lt. [Milton M.] Foster to order me more hoses, with in half an hour and hour the Chief brought back 6 new hoses and other load from Lt. Foster and other Chief which I have about 12 length of hose to stand by. Why I order this hoses for? The Answer—for emergency something may happen I will be there with readiness, reason why, the magazines were taking out from the U.S.S. *Pennsylvania*, and many casing and empty shell, at the same time were under fired the Jap Airplanes flew over head where up in the clouds. The U.S.S. *Pennsylvania* antiair-craft crews were in full action, I wasn't excited and very calm about Street to protect the 2 new hoses, I were little worry because I have no nails and lumber to nail between the two planks separated while the heavy traffic going by with Emergency Cases to the Naval Hospital without crushing the hoses. I met Captain [Charles D.] Swain passing by I had his permission to have the Carpenter of the BoatShop to help me nail this planks together. He went to telephone, within few minutes four men marching down with nails and lumber. I were very happy, here comes the Carpenters ready to started nailing suddenly the roaring Anti Air Craft Guns in action, I call my men to dodging for safety, after the Enemy Planes disappear we all returns to our duty, the four men didn't came back at all left the hammers, nails and lumber, so I was very fortunely for two of our local boys passing by and helping me to finish the job, it were very thankful to volunteers their service to stand by with me during the Emergency, I had two men standing by the Hydrant #119 locate Corner Ave E and First Street near the head of Dry Dock No. 1, four men guarding the two hoses in emergency for readiness in case of fire broke out from the Magazine Casing.

I was self volunteer to be Traffic Police and directing the Traffic during the rushing hours of Emergency, I get a big piece of Maroon cloth to signaling the ambulance to look at those planks easily passing over, to save my hose and other word to give the wounded patients rest easily from rough crossing on the heavy plank I directed all four hours to kept the First Street clear of right away to the Naval Hospital. Many heavy Contractor Trucks passing by with all Defenders and Emergency Call Employee, to report to the Shop for standby. I direct all this group of trucks turn up to Avenue E and unloaded the Employees. Everythings were successfully executing. I enjoyed my duty and a word of appreciation to my volunteers friends of their bravery and courageous to their service, during the emergency and Under Fired. Everythinks were under control and we all secure and roll up the hoses and returns to the Supply Dept. We were hungry no lunch so I brought each one a Box Ice Cream for lunch and we all dismissed about 3:30 p.m.

One of the Marine Patrol approaching toward me, if I will do the boys a great service of the Marine Guards and Sailor, which their have no lunch and some without breakfast, so I went to the garage to take my Red PutPut to the 3rd Defense Fleet Marine Mess Hall to see my friend Tech. Sergt. [Joseph A.] Newland for help, I told the story regards the Post Guard have been neglected to release for lunch. Tech-Sergt. Newland were very kind and his Cook to prepared some sandwiches ham and chicken, fruit all I can delivery to the Post. You should hear what were their saying. Charles, you are one life saver. I have been riding round and round the dry dock until every one had a sandwiches on every post except the Fuel Oil Farms. I send 50 chicken and hams sandwiches apples and oranges and buns with ham to the shops supt. office. After I returns the Mess Sergt. report no breads be served and water are being poison. I serving some civilians and the Post and Guards Hot Tacks, apples and orange. The water is poison. At the Dry Dock all the workman have no lunch and hungry, working on the U.S.S. *Downes* and U.S.S. *Cassin*, I ran short of everything about 6:00 p.m. I told the men go to the Mess Hall of the 3rd Defense to have their meal without charges and drink tomatoes juice and fruit. About 7:00 p.m. I went to the garage to have them take me to the Main Gates.

At the last though I have the driver drove me to the Mess Hall, the Mess Sergy. gave me 3 gals. can iced cold tomatoes juice and 3 dozen oranges and bag full of Hot Tacks, I gave the driver to take back to Garage night force. I left the Navy Yard at 7:30 p.m. at Main Gates. I was very fortunely an automobile pass by. Kady invited me to take me back to town, she just drive off the Ferry boat from Ford Island. She left me off the Hawaiian Electric Co. It was a black out night, I walk across the Army and Navy Y.M.C.A. to the Beretania Street to walk direct to the Thomas Square and stopped for a rest.

I ask the soldier guard on patrol, with appreciated very kindly if he will halt an automobile to take me home, if convenience on their way home. I told him I came back from Pearl Harbor, I'm Chinese. He shake my hand and glad to be of service, to the Chinese friend. An automobile approach and stop, the soldier request the owner if he will help to take me home to the University. Happening the driver knew me very well, he heard my voice, so he invited me in his car and drove me to my home at the front door, I extend my appreciation and thanks him very kindly to see safe home. My wife and four children were happy and thankful I were safely at home.

As the Confucious say, "Every Kind Deeds its return many, many time Folds."

Tai Sing Loo (1886–1971) was born in Honolulu and became one of Hawaii's best-known photographers. After working for the *Honolulu Star-Bulletin* for a number of years, he went to work in the Pearl Harbor Navy Yard around the end of World War I. In 1919, he climbed a 760-foot radio tower to take a panoramic photograph of the harbor. The picture so impressed the officers of the navy yard that he was made official photographer, an assignment he kept until 1949. He did outside commercial work as well; for example, in 1926 he photographed an eruption of Mauna Loa Volcano. Mr. Loo wrote his account of his experiences during the Japanese attack shortly after the event, but the Navy Department did not release it for several months. After he retired from the Pearl Harbor naval base, he continued to do photographic work until the day he died. (Courtesy of Mrs. Evelyn Lee.)

A Navy Bride Learns to Cope

By Peggy Hughes Ryan

Until the Japanese struck in December 1941, I was like most young Navy wives in Hawaii—taking the tropical pleasures for granted. I was no stranger to the islands, having lived there twenty years before when my father, an Army officer, was stationed at Schofield Barracks. One of my childhood memories was that of Father's artillery battery going out on maneuvers to Kole Kole Pass to oppose a simulated amphibious landing by the Japanese. Perhaps because of this childhood exposure to a threat that never materialized—plus the fact that my generation had grown up in an era of international crises (Spain, Manchuria, Ethiopia, the *Panay* incident, to name a few)—by 1941, I was too conditioned to war scares to give them much thought. I think my contemporaries felt similarly.

On my return to the islands in April 1941, this time as a bride, I found that Honolulu had not changed greatly. The Royal Hawaiian, Moana, and Halekulani were still the main hotels at Waikiki. The beach was uncrowded. There was no excessive crush of tourists. Most of them still came by ship, although the Pan American China Clippers were now flying. Ginger or pikake leis cost fifty cents or a dollar and were sold by buxom Hawaiian women operating from ancient Ford trucks.

My husband Paul, a lieutenant (junior grade), was attached to a submarine at Pearl Harbor. After some searching in the area following our arrival, he and I were able to find a house in a congenial neighborhood. It was a small cul-de-sac of ten houses just beneath the Punch Bowl in Honolulu. All ten were rented to young Navy couples. The rent was sixty dollars a month—with gardener. Honolulu seemed a paradise indeed.

That summer, our way of life did suffer some changes, which should have given us an early warning. For instance, one day in August, my husband left for his usual working day at the submarine base, but at noon I learned that he was departing on a long voyage—date of return not known. This was the beginning of a new program of war patrols instituted by Rear Admiral Thomas Withers, Jr., who commanded twenty-one Pacific Fleet submarines. I learned later that Paul's boat, the USS *Dolphin*, had sailed for Midway, more than 1,200 miles to

Peggy Hughes and Paul Ryan were married at Norfolk on 2 April 1941, just before leaving for Hawaii. The bridesmaid is the bride's sister, Betty Hughes Van Every, and the best man is Lieutenant Salem A. Van Every, Jr., a naval aviator. To the consternation of their father, a graduate of West Point and career Army officer, both sisters married Annapolis men. (Courtesy of Mrs. Peggy Hughes Ryan.)

During part of 1941, the Ryans lived in this guest cottage on a private estate. Included in the fifty-dollar-a-month rent was the use of the estate's secluded beach. (Courtesy of Mrs. Peggy Hughes Ryan.)

Among off-duty pleasures in the summer of 1941 was this beach picnic near the Army's Bellows Field. From left to right are Winifred "Wink" Middleton, Lieutenant (junior grade) John Middleton, torpedo officer of the submarine *Dolphin*, Peggy Hughes Ryan, and Lieutenant (junior grade) Paul Ryan, communication officer and assistant engineer of the *Dolphin*. (Courtesy of Mrs. Peggy Hughes Ryan.)

the northwest. Upon his return, my husband left in October for a patrol to Wake Island.

There were other indications that trouble was brewing. In October, my father passed through Honolulu en route to the Philippines, where he was to command a regiment. My mother was not allowed to accompany him, which was understandable now that service wives were arriving from the Philippines, having been summarily evacuated because of worsening developments. In November, we were mildly surprised to see Hawaiian Territorial Guards manning machine-gun emplacements on the roofs of the municipal power plant and the telephone exchange. This was at the time of Special Envoy Saburo Kurusu's "last proposals" mission to Washington. Yet such was our unquenchable optimism that we took the visible presence of the Guardsmen as only a precautionary measure—not cause for alarm for the safety of Hawaii. Instead, we presumed that any trouble would first break out in the Philippines.

On 3 December, my husband returned from a forty-seven-day patrol and was scheduled for a ten-day leave. We spent Saturday evening, 6 December, at a movie at Fort DeRussy, an old Army post at Waikiki. The next morning, we were awakened by what we thought was artillery fire. Sleep being out of the question, we cursed the Army for conducting practice at such an ungodly hour, but we were suf-

ficiently aroused to turn on the radio. The excited announcer kept repeating that the city was under attack and that all military personnel should report to their stations. Ridiculous as it sounds, in between his spot reports he continued his program of organ music. Hoping prayerfully that the "attack" was actually a realistic practice, I soon sensed that those explosions were real bombs.

I ran outside dressed in my robe while Paul quickly donned his khaki uniform. In the sky above the city and over Pearl Harbor 8 miles away I could see diving planes and black puffs of smoke from antiaircraft fire. More ominous were great clouds of smoke over Pearl Harbor and Hickam Field, adjacent to the base. By now, my husband had jumped into our convertible (with the top still down—to my unreasoning dismay) and with three of our officer-neighbors went tearing off to the naval base.

In a few minutes, a small crowd of young Navy wives and small children, still in nightclothes, had gathered in our lane looking wonderingly at the sky and at each other. Probably we were in a state of shock, but no one panicked. Tied together by a common danger, we soon assembled at one of the homes for mutual comfort and a sharing of speculations.

During the day, our anxiety grew as we suffered from lack of information. I am sure that each of us was plagued by secret fears, not only for ourselves but for those we loved. There were so many uncertainties. Was the original attack to be followed by others? Would there be an amphibious landing? Or a bombardment by battleships? Being familiar with the possibilities of naval attack we were, as a group, perhaps more apprehensive than the average citizen of Oahu. But during that long day, we felt a complete sense of confidence in the ability of our armed forces to prove their superiority, and not once did I see or hear a note of pessimism. In fact, by tacit consent we tried to retain our sense of humor and use a light approach to keep ourselves cheerful.

For the next two days following the attack, all of us magnified the specter of follow-up strikes beyond all reason. The sound of antiaircraft artillery disturbed the night silence as trigger-happy gunners fired at nonexistent targets. The two radio stations, KGU and KGMB, were understandably short of information on damage reports because of the tight censorship. The city, jammed with defense workers and military dependents evacuated from Army posts and the naval base, was full of sensational rumors—mostly false. Two Japanese carriers had been sunk offshore! The U.S. Fleet was engaged in a sea battle off the islands! Probably the news generating the most alarm was that parachutists had landed on country club fairways and that Japanese saboteurs had been sighted on the northern coasts of Oahu. They had been positively identified by the "red disks" on the shoulders. Hypervigilance became the order of the day. During the next few days, a series of air-raid sirens kept us dashing about. My reaction, and I wasn't alone in this, was to run for the nearest closet with a frying pan over my head for a helmet.

The uncertainty, mixed with apprehension, was not lost on the small children in our neighborhood, and I remember one mother's successful effort to assure her little family that she would use "Daddy's dress sword to strike down any Jap who tried to enter the house!" So convincing was she that the children promptly went to sleep happily ignorant of the fact that an officer's dress sword is about as lethal as a stick and can hardly cut a wedding cake, as I had discovered some months earlier.

The question of safe drinking water became a problem. Fearful of bombs or sabotage which might damage the water mains, the Board of Water Supply directed that we immediately fill tubs and pots with water. On the afternoon of 7 December, another radio announcement warned that the water supply may have been poisoned; soon after, we were informed that the water would be safe for drinking if it were boiled. Twenty-four hours later, the city engineers assured us that tests now proved the water to be pure, with no need to boil it before drinking.

Blackouts went into effect when Lieutenant General Walter C. Short, the Army commander, declared a state of martial law only hours after the attack. Block wardens were quickly recruited, and in their haste to fill these posts, the authorities probably made some questionable choices.

Our particular block warden was an elderly retired pipefitter, who, impressed by his sudden rise in importance, became something of a minor dictator in enforcement of the regulations. Peering through our windows in the dark, he would distinguish the glow of cigarettes or the radio tubes. At once he would startle us by pounding on the house and shouting "Put those lights out!" Frantically we would throw a blanket over the radio and crush the offending cigarettes while our zealous warden threatened fines and jail sentences.

The wardens even could be a physical danger to each other, as was sadly demonstrated on the night of 8 December, when a sixty-year-old Hawaiian-Chinese warden suddenly came upon two of his fellow wardens. Although they were his friends, they failed to recognize him in the dark. Jittery to the point of terror, they mistook him for a Japanese parachutist and beat him to insensibility. He died the next day at Queens Hospital, his skull fractured by blows from a heavy flashlight. The tragedy provided a strong incentive for people to remain indoors at night, whether they were authorized to be out or not.

Wearying of spending each night in blackness, with no entertainment except for listening to the radio, and with no seeming alternative but to cover the windows, doors, and cracks with blankets and towels—which made any such room an oven—I devised an air conditioner of sorts. This was a small box frame covered with chicken wire. After filling it with excelsior and wetting it down, I fitted this contraption to the window, stuffed the cracks with paper, and set an electric fan just inside the window. This drew in outside air which was cooled by passing through the wet excelsior. We now had a comfortable lighted room—and without any harassment from the block warden.

The fear of espionage by enemy agents was a constant worry to the authorities. As a security measure, the Army provost marshal forbade the sale of potential spy devices such as photographic and radio equipment. All ham radio operators were told to turn in their sets. One luckless ham found himself in trouble because the police had found three Japanese ham station exchange cards in his house.

But problems of illegal possession of spy gear were minor when compared with the question of what to do with the 158,000 Japanese comprising 37 per cent of Hawaii's population. We already knew that Secretary of War Henry Stimson had authorized the rounding up of all West Coast Japanese, whether they were U.S. citizens or not. General Douglas MacArthur in Manila had placed 25,000 Japanese in confinement. As it turned out, Admiral Chester Nimitz, newly in command of the Pacific Fleet, subsequently dissuaded Secretary of the Navy Frank Knox and others who wished to incarcerate Hawaii's Japanese. His reason was simple and one that may not be well known: most of the "Japanese" agricultural employees in the islands were Okinawans. Further, little would be gained by locking up thousands of loyal workers in giant concentration camps. To do so would mean that Hawaii's economy—especially on the plantations—would halt, if one-third of the population were suddenly removed.

The decision to not imprison "our" Japanese was a particularly fortunate one in the case of my cleaning woman, Hatsuyo. She was a diminutive creature of uncertain age who had been born in Japan and spoke little English. Once a week, she made my small house immaculate for $1.25 a day, the going wage in an era when the base pay of my husband was $175 a month. Besides being a quiet, diligent worker, Hatsuyo never failed to bring or buy from the itinerant peddler fresh flowers which she helped me arrange in true Japanese style. So great was our mutual regard that I was truly distressed when after the attack she failed to appear on the usual day. At the end of two weeks, the thought crossed my mind that she might have been planted in our home by Japanese to collect possible submarine intelligence, and now that we were at war her usefulness presumably was ended.

On the third week, when Hatsuyo finally appeared, I was mildly shocked at her appearance—woebegone, abject and tearful. In her pidgin English she tried to convey her shame for the attack, saying that she did not have the courage to face me until now. I reassured her that she was in no way to blame and she continued to be a valued worker until my departure.

In its determination not to be caught napping by an enemy gas attack, the Army had ordered everyone to carry a gas mask, and on 10 December each of us was issued one at the nearest defense headquarters. It was a cumbersome thing in a canvas khaki case—about the size of a leg of lamb. Then came another requirement that every resident dig a splinter shelter in his yard large enough for the home's occupants. Our landlady had her gardener dig a community shelter large enough for all her tenants. But because this cool, damp spot was soon taken over by scorpions and the huge island toads known as "buffos," we absolutely refused to go there during air-raid warnings, preferring bombs to crawling, jumping things.

The outbreak of hostilities meant that many of the merchant ships plying between the West Coast and Honolulu were diverted to the war effort. Consequently, imports to Hawaii fell to a trickle. We particularly felt the lack of canned goods, paper products, toiletries, and other household items we had taken for granted. Fresh fruit and sugar we had in abundance. As for beef, the huge Parker ranch on the big island of Hawaii supplied the other islands, some shipments of meat being flown over in the small inter-island passenger planes. After an initial period of shortages, the navy yard commissary gradually improved its selections although many non-basic items remained unprocurable, even after the supply line from the States began to operate with wartime efficiency.

Possibly Hawaii's delegate to Congress, Sam King, helped to ease our shortage problem by issuing stern statements disclosing that before the blitz a penny-pinching Budget Bureau had turned down a congressional plan to designate 3.4 million dollars for a six-month emergency food supply for Hawaii. We all agreed that this had been a poor decision by the government.

If there were certain shortages in consumer items, there was a veritable glut of sales in second-hand furniture and autos in the few weeks left in December. Some early-departing families panicked at the rumor that these items could not be guaranteed shipment back to the States, and many took a large financial loss. One officer friend, who was leaving immediately for distant duty, sold his car to the first comer for $35. My husband and I were offered a large lot in Manoa Valley for the ridiculously low price of $1,000. We turned it down, to our everlasting regret. Surprisingly, in view of the shortages, prices in the stores remained stable—for a while. Liberty House offered sport shirts for $2.00 and slips for $1.25. The hoarders soon moved in, and supplies in the shops quickly gave out.

But shortages were a minor irritation compared with the discouraging battle reports in the press and on the radio. The disaster at Clark Field in the Philippines just after Pearl Harbor affected me personally. My father, with his troops on Luzon, now seemed to me to be in real danger, and although I had no way of knowing it, his capture on Bataan was only weeks away. (He was rescued by Russian troops in Manchuria in 1945 and returned to active duty.) The fall of Guam and Wake Island meant that some of our service friends faced a most uncertain future. Worse, the terrible toll of our 2,403 killed and some 1,178 wounded on Oahu was beginning to filter out.

In spite of the discouraging news from the war front, those in our little cul-de-sac were determined to celebrate Christmas as much as possible in the traditional way. Few husbands would be present, because most of them had departed on operational missions. The absence of any Christmas trees posed a problem. In past years, these had been brought in from Seattle or San Francisco, but with cargo space at a premium, none could be expected this year. However, our thoughtful landlady supplied the need by furnishing us branches from ironwood trees, which have a bushy appearance not unlike an evergreen. These we wired to a broom handle, producing a passable Christmas tree, at least in the eyes of the little children. For the adults, I contributed our last bottle of whiskey to the communal celebration.

Our liquor shortage stemmed from the military governor's ban on the sale of all liquor, wine, and beer effective the afternoon of 7 December. Inevitably, the absence of the evening cocktail prompted the inventive among us to experiment with weird recipes for fermenting pineapple juice—which we had in abundance. Regrettably these concoctions were largely undrinkable, so we became resigned to abstinence. On one occasion, the drought was temporarily ended when one of the husbands appeared with a quart of grain alcohol, vaguely accounted for as "surveyed from the ship's binnacle." It made a potent punch when mixed with fruit juice and ice, and turned the afternoon into something of a block party.

The number of my friends being evacuated from Honolulu continued to grow. The first to go were those who had lost husbands; next came mothers with babies, and last, pregnant women. We had been warned by the military authorities that we would receive only twenty-four hours' notice of departure, so we lived from day to day out of suitcases, never sure when our call would come.

By mid-April, our group had dwindled to the few who either had husbands based on shore duty or held defense jobs, such as that of mail censor. But I was unemployed and, worse in the eyes of the Army, pregnant. Moreover, my husband was now absent on longer patrols. One reason I had been able to remain until now could be traced to the yeoman in the transportation office who had previously served with my husband; by request he replaced my card on the bottom whenever my name came up in the pile of evacuees' cards. Eventually, the stack grew too small to hide my name, and I received my call on 20 April.

My preparations were brief; our few household goods, mainly wedding presents, had been shipped several months before, and I had only to close my trunk and suitcases. The transportation office clerk informed me that the sailing was to be kept secret, but how does one conceal a departure with so much baggage in evidence? Friends drove me to the pier where the leave-taking was subdued. No bands, flower leis, and paper streamers—so customary in prewar years. Instead there was a mixed group, nearly all women and children, with the unmistakable look of refugees. Quite a few were of Oriental descent, and many going to the States for the first time, some to live with their in-laws. I thought of the problems sure to arise for all concerned.

The shabby transport *H. F. Alexander* to which I had been assigned was, to my amazement, the same ship which had taken my family and me from Seattle to Honolulu in 1920. At that time she was the U.S. Army transport *Great Northern*, and I remembered well how she had rolled in a rough sea because of her narrow beam.

By noon on 22 April, we got under way to join a

Mrs. Ryan interrupts her packing to pose in her husband's naval jacket and fore-and-aft hat. (Courtesy of Mrs. Peggy Hughes Ryan.)

convoy off the Pearl Harbor channel. Planes were circling overhead, and harbor craft patrolled around us as we were shepherded into formation. It was a distinct contrast to our arrival in Honolulu a year before in the SS *Matsonia*.

The stateroom, which I shared with two other women, was very small, and made even more so by the installation of three tiers of wooden bunks. I chose a bottom berth, but found it took some practice to even turn over because of the narrow clearance. My delicate condition and the uncomfortable rolling of the ship persuaded me to spend much of the eight-day voyage in my bunk.

My roommates were Army wives, and we made a congenial group. But the fact that "there was a war on" became soon apparent. For instance, when I rang for our stewardess, a shopworn-looking blonde appeared with a cigarette in her mouth demanding to know "Whatsa matter with you, honey?" Later, we were to learn that she was one of a group of civilian evacuees, some of whom had lived on the fringes of the economy along Hotel Street, and had been offered free passageway if they would work their way across.

The return to the mainland was a dreary trip in the British-manned liner *H. F. Alexander* which, as the Army transport *Great Northern*, took Mrs. Ryan and her family to Honolulu in 1920. (Naval Historical Center: NR&L (MOD) 15505.)

Shipboard life was austere. There were no recreational facilities such as shuffleboard, a lounge, movies, or card room. The meals were adequate if not appealing, the chefs relying heavily on mutton, beef, potatoes, cabbage, and turnips. The usual dessert was pudding or cake—both rubbery—or canned fruit. The bread was a type of hard roll which had been taken aboard in Australia, some weeks before. Our limited social life was further curtailed on the fourth day out when the captain forbade anyone to appear outside of her particular passageway after the dinner hour. Apparently some of the more restless women had been—to put it charitably—fraternizing with the crew. So the captain's order was a prudent one in view of the youthfulness of the seamen and the presence of bored or commercially minded females.

The ship's company was an unusual one. Most of the officers, who wore the conventional merchant marine uniform, were overage for active service; most, in fact, had been brought back from retirement. The crew members were predominantly boys in their teens. They wore a motley assortment of clothing, usually bell-bottomed trousers with jerseys or singlets, and many were barefooted. When I suggested to an officer that the crew looked inexperienced, he assured me that all had survived at least one sinking. He added that the Royal Navy, desperate for manpower, had stripped the merchant marine of all the more able seamen, leaving only the boys and older men.

In our convoy were ten ships—six naval vessels and four merchantmen. We were formed into two columns, the *H. F. Alexander* being the second ship in the port column. In the starboard column we recognized the damaged battleship *Nevada*, which had been patched up and was undoubtedly headed for one of the navy yards. The cruiser *San Francisco* steamed ahead of the convoy while the destroyers *Case* and *Reid* ranged back and forth on the flanks. We zigzagged constantly during the day and even at night when the moon was bright. The weather was usually very windy and squally, and quite rough.

We passed much of our time watching the naval ships perform maneuvers. Every morning the *San Francisco* would catapult a seaplane for antisubmarine patrol. Then, three hours later, a second plane was shot off, after which the first one would land alongside the cruiser to be hoisted aboard by a crane. Then there was the day when the *Nevada* and the transport *Henderson* held a firing practice with their 5-inch guns aiming at a target spar towed by the *Pyro*. When told that the *Pyro* was an ammunition ship, we could only hope that the aim of the gunners was accurate.

Our greatest concern was a submarine attack. Daily, when we woke in the morning our first move was to look out the port to check the presence of our escorts. One night, we were nearly thrown out of our bunks as the ship made a sudden turn to port. We immediately surmised that a submarine was after us; not until morning did we learn that the *Chaumont* had fired a red flare signalling a submarine contact, later reported to be false. Incidents like this kept us a shipload of nervous women.

One outstanding feature of the *H. F. Alexander* which proved that we were sailing with professional mariners was the marked consideration shown for the safety of the passengers. Not only were we required to muster every day at our assigned lifeboats, but we were briefed on the location of the boat's water flasks and rations. We practiced wearing and adjusting our life jackets, which had to be within arm's reach at all times, no matter where we were. Every morning an officer made the rounds of the outboard cabins to dog down our porthole cover. But unfortunately, the room at once became stifling, so in defiance of safety regulations, we reopened the port with a sturdy coathanger, first being sure to turn out all lights. With the wisdom of age, I now recognize that if we had started to sink, the open port would have reduced the floatability of the ship. But at the time, for us it was the question of dying of suffocation or opening the port.

On the seventh day out, the purser announced that an entertainment would take place that evening in the dining room. After dinner, stewards pushed tables together to form a makeshift stage.

Our master of ceremonies was a retired vaudevillian whose wife served as the pianist. By any standards, the show was a true amateur hour. But if the harmonica players, magicians, jugglers, and singers were undistinguished, the show also provided the most unforgettable incident of the voyage. It came when one of the very youngest of the crew began to sing old Irish ballads in a beautiful tenor. He evoked such a feeling of nostalgia that the entire audience became affected, and most of the women were teary-eyed. There was not one person listening who did not share his longing for home, whether it was faraway Ireland or some special place each of us had left behind. We had been uprooted, and the young Irish boy had suddenly and poignantly made us realize it.

On the afternoon of 28 April, we suspected we were nearing the West Coast when a destroyer, the USS *Laffey*, came steaming over the horizon and came alongside the *Nevada* to deliver a package. Promptly, the battleship left the formation and headed north in company with the *Laffey*. The next day, we sighted a scouting blimp on antisubmarine patrol. These next were anxious hours, for according to our rumor experts, enemy submarines always lurked off busy ship channels. Happily, there were no alerts and early in the morning of 30 April the sight of the Golden Gate generated a mass feeling of relief at reaching safety in the beautiful city of San Francisco.

Forty years later, as I look back on my Pearl Harbor experience, I remain convinced that most young Navy wives who were there did what they had to do—adjusted to the unusual and accustomed themselves to the unexpected. Which, after all, is what a service wife must do in any era.

Peggy Hughes Ryan (1916-   ) was one of four children and spent her growing-up years moving from Army post to Army post in Hawaii, Oklahoma, Texas, and California. Her two brothers were graduated from West Point, and she received a bachelor's degree from the University of Southern California in 1939. To the consternation of their father, both she and her sister married naval officers. During World War II, Mrs. Ryan and her baby daughter were ship-followers. In the postwar years of "active co-service" with her husband, Mrs. Ryan lived in Washington, D.C., several times and California frequently. Two most demanding tours of duty were in Havana, Cuba, and Ottawa, Canada, in both of which her husband was naval attaché. Their active naval years ended in 1972, and they now live in northern California, where they enjoy the pleasures of being grandparents. (Courtesy of Mrs. Peggy Hughes Ryan.)

Did the Japs Win?

By Evelyn W. Guthrie

Perhaps I should start out by saying that I am a Navy junior; my father was Rear Admiral Yancey S. Williams. My husband was Harry A. Guthrie. Hal was graduated with the Naval Academy class of 1921. By February 1941, he was a commander on the staff of Rear Admiral John H. Newton, Commander Cruisers Scouting Force. The flagship was the USS *Chicago*, based at Pearl Harbor. The fleet was often at sea, so when the Honolulu Red Cross Motor Corps asked for volunteers, I jumped at the chance to keep busy. Having recently returned from our embassy in Berlin, where my husband was naval attaché, I was well aware of the world diplomatic situation. American wives were being evacuated from the Far East, so I thought I might avoid future evacuation from Honolulu if I joined the Red Cross.

I was in a class attended by service wives and local residents. We all passed the first aid, but when it came to the course in mechanics, the local bigwigs of the chapter decided not to include the service wives. Fortunately, one of our members was the daughter of a Navy captain and arranged for us to take the mechanical course at Pearl Harbor. Our teachers were a couple of hard-boiled, old-time machinists. From their initial attitude, we gathered they were really out to give us the works. Thanks to our sense of humor, we prevailed. As our lessons progressed and we emerged greasy and grimy from contact with our car engines, the machinists gradually began treating us with great respect. We all passed the examination, which included changing a tire on a heavy truck, with flying colors and the congratulations of our instructors.

By early December, my husband and I were expecting war to break out at any time. On 5 December, we considered conditions so precarious that we went to a lawyer's office and signed our will. I drove him to Pearl Harbor, and his ship left port on 6 December as part of a task force taking planes to the Marines at Midway. At the time, I had no idea where the *Chicago* was headed or how long she would be out of port.

On the morning of 7 December, I was up early and writing a note to Hal when I heard antiaircraft firing. I jokingly added in my note that the Army was certainly up early on a Sunday. I then found

While her husband's ship was based at Pearl Harbor, Mrs. Guthrie served as a volunteer worker with the Hawaii chapter of the Red Cross Motor Corps. In the group photo, she is the third from right in the fourth row. (Courtesy of Mrs. Evelyn W. Guthrie.)

my newspaper had not been delivered, and when I tried to phone there was no sign of life on the line. Since we did not have any programs from the mainland before nine o'clock on Sunday mornings, I never thought of turning on my radio. I decided to walk out to the drugstore, mail my letter, and pick up a Sunday paper. As I was leaving our apartment, the landlady called to me and excitedly announced that Pearl Harbor was under attack. It never occurred to me to doubt her word.

I ran back to the apartment, quickly changed into my uniform, grabbed my first-aid kit, and dashed down the back way to my car, a heavy Buick. About that time, two naval officers who lived in the same apartment house came running out, understandably excited about getting back to their ships. They leaped at my offer to take them to Pearl Harbor, and one of them asked if I would also go around the block to the next street to collect his division commander. With my three passengers, I stepped on the gas for Pearl Harbor, but the roads quickly became clogged with traffic. About the time I got to the Oahu Prison, I found I could not make much headway. We had been taught in our course always to leave enough room to turn a car around, so I did and headed for Red Hill Road. This was a back way to Pearl Harbor and gave us a clear track to the naval base.

I pulled up to the old officers' club landing to drop off two of my passengers. A scene of unbelievable horror greeted us. Several of the battleships were afire. Men were jumping overboard and trying to swim through the fiery oil on the surface of the water. I confess that I felt tears streaming down my face at this nightmarish spectacle. But there was no time to stop for tears or thoughts. There was still one passenger in my car, and he asked me to take him to Ten Ten Dock. This dock was opposite the naval air station on Ford Island. It was very wide and had rails on which a large traveling crane was operated. My passenger, Lieutenant Johnny Andrews, was an old friend of my husband's and mine. He told me his ship was docked there and had no fuel, ammunition, or stores on board. As he left, I wished him luck, and he thanked me politely for the ride.

I started back along the dock just as a Japanese plane made a dive-bombing attack on the battleship *Pennsylvania* in Dry Dock No. 1. Her antiaircraft fire drove off the attacker, but not before the plane dropped its bomb on one of the two destroyers docked forward of the battleship. I had the impression that the bomb blew off the destroyer's bow. It created a terrific blast and repercussion that enveloped my car and made it careen back and forth across the dock. I did not hit anything, nor did the

During the height of the Japanese attack, Mrs. Guthrie drove an officer to Ten Ten Dock, where his ship was. The dock is shown here with the light cruiser *Helena* moored alongside. A bomb blast sent her car careening wildly along the dock, but she managed to regain control of it. (U.S. Navy: Naval Institute Collection.)

As a result of the damage done in the vicinity of Ten Ten Dock on 7 December, the *Helena* was moved into Dry Dock No. 2, which had not been completed when this photo was taken on 10 December. Alongside in Dry Dock No. 1 are the battleship *Pennsylvania* and the destroyers *Cassin* and *Downes*. On the other side, the shattered hull of the destroyer *Shaw* has floated partway out of the dry dock she was in at the time of the attack. (National Archives: 80-G-387577.)

car receive a scratch. When I got it under control, I pressed down the accelerator and drove quickly to the Red Cross headquarters in town. I must have been numb from the experience, because I don't recall anything else.

Things were rather confused at the Red Cross. There was no one there to give orders. Finally, four of us decided to go to civilian defense headquarters to volunteer our services. A supervisor swiftly dispatched us to Tripler Army Hospital. Piling into my car, we dashed to Tripler and reported to the duty officer. The scene there was a bloody one. A stream of ambulances and vehicles of all types was converging on the hospital. As the wounded were brought in on stretchers, we cut their clothing from the area of their injuries, and after that they were taken directly to an operating room. We then split up, and each of us was sent to a hospital ward to help with the casualties.

These men were all from Hickam Field ground crews who had tried to get some planes airborne. In their vain attempts, they were badly wounded. At infrequent periods, a nurse or a doctor of the regular hospital staff would arrive to give them some attention, but there was little that could be done for them. All of those who had lost an arm or a leg died that day. From about ten o'clock in the morning, when I arrived in the ward, until late in the afternoon, when some real nurses arrived, I was alone and felt helpless. I could only hold the hand of a dying man, give him a drink, or help the wrought-up hospital corpsman who was busy wiping up blood from the floor so no one would slip.

About 4:00 p.m., a doctor arrived and told me to return to my headquarters, because Tripler had had an unusually good response from volunteers. I collected the other three women who had come with me, and we returned to our Red Cross office. A supervisor took a good look at our disheveled appearance and told us to go home for a rest and clean clothes. We must have been a sight. Our uniforms were wrinkled and soiled with blood. We probably looked as if we had emerged from a battlefield, which in a sense we had. Someone handed me a tin cup and told me to drink up. It was straight whiskey and almost removed my tonsils. But it gave me the lift I needed to drive home.

In the next few days, we all plunged into activity. We were busy at the Red Cross headquarters and also involved in the urgent business of delivering surgical dressings to the naval hospital and to Tripler. During the course of one of my trips, I picked up several enlisted men at the Pearl Harbor gate and gave them a ride to town. They told me their ship had just come into port, having missed the attack. As we drove along a stretch of road which went past cane fields and the airport, there were armed Hawaii National Guardsmen posted at intervals. They were of Japanese descent, and I could see the look of consternation on the faces of my passengers. A chief petty officer with four gold hash marks had the courage to speak up, "Gosh, Ma'am, did the Japs win?"

I didn't think I could ever laugh again, but we all did when I explained the identity of the guards.

Evelyn Williams Guthrie (1898–   ) was born in Boston and educated at Notre Dame Academy, Girls' Latin School, and Radcliffe College (B.A. in English and psychology, 1919). She later studied German at Berlin University while her husband was assistant naval attaché from 1935 to 1938. In the 1920s, she was a secretary with Metropolitan Life Insurance Company. During World War II, she was a secretary at the Mare Island Navy Yard and was also a censor at the Honolulu post office. Following Rear Admiral Guthrie's retirement from active duty in 1950, Mrs. Guthrie acted as his secretary while he was West Coast representative of Wallace Press of Chicago. Since his death in 1971, she has traveled extensively and has worked as a travel agent in recent years. Mrs. Guthrie has written an unpublished book titled *Home is Where You Hang Your Hat*, which describes her experiences as a Navy wife. She now lives in San Mateo, California. (Courtesy of Mrs. Evelyn W. Guthrie.)

For Americans in Hawaii, torpedoes, bombs, fires, explosions, and strafing provided vivid evidence that they had suddenly been thrust into war. After that, it was a matter of adjusting and getting on with it. For Americans in Tokyo, the evidence was not as dramatic but just as certain. Members of the embassy staff were made virtual prisoners. The military personnel among them had no chance to get on with the war—at least not until they were freed from their captivity by repatriation. Henri Smith-Hutton, then a commander, was the U.S. naval attaché at the embassy. Like two other contributors to this volume, Edwin T. Layton and Arthur H. McCollum, Smith-Hutton had undergone Japanese-language and intelligence training. The luck of the draw made it inevitable that at least one of the Navy's experienced Japanese-speaking intelligence officers would get caught in Japan when the war broke out. The author of the following memoir is one of those who did.

American Prisoners in Japan

By Captain Henri Smith-Hutton, U.S. Navy (Retired)

In January 1941, U.S. Ambassador Joseph C. Grew heard the rumor circulating in Tokyo that in the event of a break between the United States and Japan, the Japanese would make an all-out surprise attack on Pearl Harbor. He talked to me about it and said he understood that one of the main sources of the rumor was the Peruvian minister in Japan. I said that rumors like this had circulated from time to time, but I hadn't heard this one. When he said he was reporting it to the State Department, I understood why, even though it was impossible to verify the story. I added that with all the talk of war, there was always speculation among diplomats and newsmen about what each country might do.

I told the ambassador that while I thought this was just a rumor—since it was most unlikely that the Japanese planners would let their real plans get out of the secret category—it was logical for them to concentrate an attack on our fleet, no matter where it was. I told him that the Japanese had a history of making surprise attacks, so our commanders should be very vigilant.

In July, Admiral Teijiro Toyoda became the Foreign Minister in Prince Fumimaro Konoye's cabinet. I knew him quite well. He was a soft-spoken officer who spoke English well, having been in England as assistant naval attaché and as naval attaché. He was one of the group of senior naval officers, including Admiral Kichisaburo Nomura and Admiral Mitsumasa Yonai, who were pro-Anglo-Saxon, not pro-German. He was well known in Tokyo for his moderation. So when he became Foreign Minister, we were all very pleased. I think Ambassador Grew found him pleasant and straightforward to work with.

Then, when the Konoye cabinet fell, Admiral Toyoda was forced to resign. He was put on the inactive list of the Navy, as his good friend Admiral Nomura had been earlier. Nomura had been sent as ambassador to the United States by Prince Konoye and was continued after General Hideki Tojo became Prime Minister. Nomura and Toyoda were of a kind. There was no question of disgrace in being placed on inactive duty since they were subject to recall to serve in the Navy.

Joseph C. Grew, U.S. Ambassador to Japan at the time of the attack on Pearl Harbor, provided strong leadership during the embassy staff's internment. (National Archives: 208-FS-3850-2.)

On 8 December, by the Japanese calendar, I got up a little earlier than usual and went downstairs to have breakfast in our dining room, where we had a good short-wave radio. The day before, we'd had some unusual reports from the United States and also from the south. I'd heard on San Francisco radio the news that Ambassador Grew was getting a message to be delivered to the Emperor, and I'd also heard that Japanese ships had been sighted heading south along the coast of Malaya. I conferred briefly with the British naval attaché and with the counselor of the British Embassy. About ten o'clock on Sunday night, I called the code room at our embassy and found that the message the ambassador was supposed to deliver had just been received from the Japanese telegraph office, so he hadn't yet had a chance to take it to the Emperor. That morning, I was wondering whether anything had happened during the night.

In May 1940, Admiral Osami Nagano gave a luncheon at the Tokyo naval club for foreign attachés and their assistants. At this time, Admiral Nagano (front row, center), who played a key role in the decision to attack Pearl Harbor, was Chief of the Japanese Naval General Staff. Third from left in the front row is Rear Admiral Nobutake Kondo, who was in command of forces in the battles of Midway and Guadalcanal. Third from right is Lieutenant Commander Smith-Hutton. (Naval Historical Center: NH 79962).

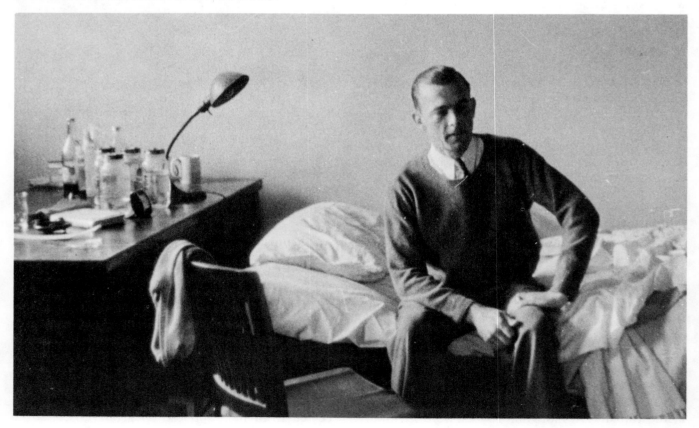

Lieutenant Commander Martin R. Stone became assistant naval attaché in June 1941, in time to be interned with the rest of the American embassy's staff. During the internment he slept in this bed in his office. (Courtesy of Mrs. Henri Smith-Hutton.)

I had discussed the situation with my wife Jane, and we had decided that we weren't going to send our daughter to school that morning, which was Monday. I couldn't get San Francisco on my radio because of static, so I shifted to Shanghai radio, which came in clearly. The announcer was just saying that Americans were asked by the consul general in Shanghai to stay off the streets and not to be excited. The consul general would inform them of events later in the day, and in the meantime they should remain as calm as possible. I told Jane, who was just getting up, that apparently something unusual had happened in Shanghai. I didn't know what it was, because the radio report was indefinite, but if she'd hurry we might get to the embassy to see whether we could learn more there.

This was just before eight o'clock. She came down very soon. It was a two-minute walk, a short distance down the street and then about 50 feet to the entrance to the embassy garage. There was a police kiosk there that had been put up a few months before. The policeman on duty usually smiled and said "Good Morning," but on this day he didn't pay any attention to us. We walked in and headed toward my office. Before we got there, we passed the office of Lieutenant Commander Martin R. "Mert" Stone, assistant naval attaché, and saw that it was full of people, listening to the office radio. When my friends saw me, they asked, "Have you heard? San Francisco radio says the Japanese have at-

tacked Pearl Harbor!" I went to my office to telephone the ambassador. He was incredulous, so I had to repeat the report. He said he had left Foreign Minister Shigenori Togo about fifteen minutes earlier, and Mr. Togo hadn't mentioned an attack.

The ambassador told me to go to the Japanese Navy Ministry to find out if there was any truth in the report and, if so, when he could expect official notice of the declaration of war. Although it was after 8:00 a.m., the streets were deserted. At the Navy Ministry, which was only about four blocks away, I asked for Rear Admiral Ryozo Nakamura, the senior aide to the Navy Minister. When he appeared, Nakamura looked sad, because I think he was really a friend of the United States. He said the report was true. He had just learned about it himself, and he could verify it. As to the declaration of war, he couldn't say, because that would have to come from the Foreign Office, not the Navy Ministry. After we talked a while, I said this might be the last time I would see him. I hoped he would survive the war. He said he hoped the same for me. He usually said "Good-bye" in this room, but on the morning of 8 December, he came down the staircase and saw me to my car.

I got back to the embassy and told Ambassador Grew that Admiral Nakamura had confirmed the attack. The ambassador had already given instructions to burn all classified papers and codes, and the officers in the embassy were soon busily en-

This photograph shows the U.S. embassy in Tokyo. The chancery (office building) is at the center, and on either side are apartments for the embassy staff. Visible beyond the chancery roof is the top of the Japanese Diet building. (Courtesy of Mrs. Henri Smith-Hutton.)

gaged in burning. By the time I got to my office, the electricity in the embassy had been shut off, so we couldn't operate the radio. The police soon arrived and confiscated the radio sets in the embassy. So there we were, in a darkened building with no contact to the outside world. The staff was busy burning papers in large trash cans, dousing the papers with kerosene. The embassy was a smoky, dirty place—and that was how Pearl Harbor day started for me.

The conditions of our internment in Tokyo were not bad. We were crowded but not mistreated. Certainly, there was no comparison, though, to the treatment of the Japanese in Washington who were sent to a luxurious hotel in Hot Springs, Virginia. Ambassador Grew took firm charge of the situation within the compound, and in my opinion he showed remarkable leadership. For example, within the first few days he firmly stopped our police guard and kept them from making a real prison camp out of the compound. One evening, we found that a policeman was hidden in the window curtains, listening to us. About six of us rushed at him and in very rough Japanese told him to get out. He did, and the next day the ambassador sent a stiff note to the Japanese Government (through the Swiss minister) to protest this violation of our diplomatic status. After that, the police were more circumspect.

During the internment, there were about sixty-five of us. Because Japan had been at war with China for several years, many food items were hard to get. As a result, the staff had sent a large food order to a San Francisco wholesale grocer in September, and the order was delivered in November. We got coffee, canned hams, meats, fish, and vegetables since those items were almost impossible to get in Japan. Unfortunately, we used up our provisions faster than we might have if we had realized that we were going to be interned for a long time. In 1914, the German Embassy staff left Tokyo a week after the declaration of war. It was the middle of June in 1942 before we left.

Christmas celebration was certainly one of the highlights of our stay. The ladies did a wonderful job. They made pretty decorations out of very little, and we still had a supply of good food and enjoyed that. Also a group of ladies practiced in secret, and on the night before Christmas about ten of them appeared out of nowhere singing carols. There wasn't a dry eye among us after that. Much to the dismay of some in the embassy, we cut down one of the spruce trees in the garden. It was a perfect Christmas tree. Many who found out where it came

Jane and Henri Smith-Hutton dressed to attend the ceremony held by the Emperor every New Year's Day for members of the diplomatic corps. This one was in 1940; the couple was not invited by Hirohito in 1942. (Courtesy of Mrs. Henri Smith-Hutton.)

from objected, but it was Christmas, and we had a tree.

The Jimmy Doolittle raid was certainly another of the highlights during our stay. On 17 April, it was announced that there were going to be air-raid drills. They started in the afternoon and lasted three days. We used our blackout curtains in the embassy. Up to then, the drills had not been very interesting, but this one was. On 18 April, the day after the drills started, air-raid sirens were tested in the morning, and there were a few fighter planes flying about. About 12:30 p.m., we heard several explosions, and the sirens sounded again. An Army officer who was on the roof of one of the apartment buildings called to me to say that the drill was certainly one of the most realistic ever held. He could see smoke from two or three fires, apparently caused by explosions.

On our way to lunch, my wife and I encountered the Swiss minister, who had been to see Ambassador Grew. We asked him whether there was any possibility that this was a real raid. He said he didn't think so. Shortly after that, we all gathered for lunch. It was a beautiful sunny day, warm and pleasant, so the dining room was open into the garden. The residence is on a hill, and we could see the smoke in the distance. Suddenly, we heard another loud explosion. When this happened, my wife and Ned Crocker, first secretary of the embassy, rushed out into the garden. Just as they got there, they got a glimpse of a plane flying a little above the tree-tops. It passed out of sight in a few seconds, so the rest of us didn't get a look at it.

We resumed our lunch, and there was a warm discussion of the events of the morning. Half our group thought it was a genuine air raid, but no one could be sure of the nationality of the planes. We had not the faintest idea where they came from. However, that night Tokyo radio announced that there had been a raid by ten aircraft which came in from the north of Japan. The nationality was not mentioned. The radio said that the planes had dropped bombs but had damaged mostly hospitals and schools. The radio reported also that all planes had been shot down. It wasn't until much later that we heard from the Swiss a few more details about the famous Doolittle raid. (By that time, we were able to listen to local broadcasts in Japanese, because our captors had returned one of our small radios.)

In the more than six months we were held, we played bridge and poker every day. The poker game went on without interruption every day of the internment. Some of the people played for rather high stakes, and several of them won or lost $2,000–3,000. That was more than I cared to risk. I did win first prize in our bridge tournament. It was a silver plate, donated by Ambassador Grew, engraved to the champion of the "Greater East Asia Bridge Meet." I still have the plate and cherish it.

We also played badminton, and Mert Stone laid out a very ingenious nine-hole golf course around the apartments and swimming pool. There were three or four good golf tournaments. I am not an enthusiastic golfer and played only occasionally, but many played almost every day. We were all organized as far as sports and recreation were concerned. I advanced in the badminton meet and was defeated in the semifinals. There was keen competition and a good place to play in the embassy garage. So we had plenty of things to do, even though it was too cold to swim.

Our rations got skimpier as time went on. We ran out of liquor about the first of February. The tobacco lasted a little longer, but in the end we were smoking coffee grounds in our pipes. The Japanese arranged for us to get ration cards for cigarettes after a certain period, and we got the "Cherry"

Golf provides a diversion for the captive staff of the embassy. At center, Ambassador Grew follows through on a shot, while Ned Crocker, first secretary of the embassy, watches. At left, with his back to the camera, is Charles "Chip" Bohlen, a career diplomat who was later U.S. Ambassador to Russia and France. (Courtesy of Mrs. Henri Smith-Hutton.)

brand since they were much like American cigarettes. The winter was rather severe for Tokyo, but my wife and other ladies who could sew made clothing out of drapes and curtains. We used much of our limited allowance of fuel oil to have hot water for several hours every evening before dinner. That way, we could all have warm baths and keep our clothes clean.

Finally, about the first week in May, the Swiss minister told us that the Japanese Foreign Office had proposed that Lourenço Marques in Portuguese East Africa would be the exchange point. The liner *Asama Maru* would take Americans from Japan, Hong Kong, Saigon, and Singapore. The *Conde Verde*, an Italian liner caught in the Far East, would take North and South Americans from other places in China. The State Department accepted the plan after some discussion, and 10 July was set as the target date when we would be exchanged for Japanese internees coming home.

On 17 June, we left the embassy to go to Tokyo Station. Curiously enough, the few Japanese at the embassy (those who were made to stay at first but who finally seemed to welcome staying)—the janitors, cooks, one or two maids, and caretakers—all lined up to wave good-bye as we drove out of the embassy compound. They were really rather emotional about it. We shouted farewell and then drove through the streets to the station.

The police had cleared all the streets, so they were completely deserted. The station was almost deserted also. When we got there, we encountered a number of officials on the platforms. Among them was Rear Admiral Nakamura from the Navy Ministry who had come down to say "Good-bye" to Commander Stone and me. We went on the short trip to Yokohama—about 20 miles—and straight to the dock where the *Asama Maru* was moored. We arrived without incident.

After we got aboard, the ship moved out and anchored in the harbor, and there were a number of delays. It wasn't until 25 June, more than a week later, that we finally sailed. I think the delay was largely because of changes in routing instructions and questions of clearances. Some of the civilians who joined the ship felt that the negotiations might have fallen through. Some of them, including the newspapermen and managers of the large oil companies, had been very badly treated. I found out later that they were very much worried. One of them told the ambassador that rather than go back to the internment camp and brutal police treatment, he would commit suicide. Others felt they could not stand any more, because they were rather

elderly, and they had been roughly treated by the Japanese police. The police had tried hard to make them confess that they had been spying on Japan, which of course was not the case.

It was a considerable relief when the *Asama Maru* weighed anchor and we were able to begin our long journey toward home.

Henri Harold Smith-Hutton (1901-1977) was graduated from the Naval Academy in 1922 and served in the *Huron*, *Black Hawk*, *Peary*, and *Idaho* before undertaking three years of study of the Japanese language. He later served in the Office of Naval Intelligence, had two tours as intelligence officer on the staff of Commander in Chief Asiatic Fleet, and was executive officer of the *Lawrence*. He also had two tours of duty as naval attaché in Tokyo. After being repatriated from Japan at the beginning of the war, he was intelligence officer on the staff of Admiral Ernest J. King, CominCh. From 1944 to 1945, he commanded Destroyer Squadron 15, later redesignated Mine Squadron 21. After the war, he served on the Pacific Fleet staff and as commanding officer of the light cruiser *Little Rock*. After duty on the staff of the Chief of Naval Operations, he was naval attaché to France and Switzerland until his retirement from active naval service in 1952. (Courtesy of Mrs. Henri Smith-Hutton.)

In June 1941, having been retired from the regular Navy five years earlier because of physical disability, "Jasper" Holmes was recalled to active duty. He was assigned to the intelligence staff of the Fourteenth Naval District at Pearl Harbor, even though he had neither training nor experience in intelligence. Until soon after the Japanese attack, his chore was to keep track of the positions of noncombatant ships at sea in the Eastern Pacific, but thereafter he became involved in much more vital work. Though he was not one of the Navy's codebreakers, he certainly contributed to their success. His duties in the underground office where he worked were on behalf of the Communications Intelligence Unit headed by Commander Joseph J. Rochefort, who is discussed in this book by Rear Admiral Edwin T. Layton. Rochefort's subterranean group used the cover name of Combat Intelligence Unit. In the following article, Holmes tells of the changes that the outbreak of war visited upon the codebreakers and the island of Oahu.

Pearl Harbor Aftermath

By Captain Wilfred J. Holmes, U.S. Navy (Retired)

Sunday, 7 December 1941, was a watershed in the lives of nearly everyone in Hawaii. Monday dawned on a different world with different problems, different objectives, and schedules whose orientation was different from what it was before Sunday's sunrise. The Combat Intelligence Unit was no exception to changes in a changing world.

Information on the positions of merchant vessels dried up as ships at sea clamped down a tight radio silence, so our efforts were more and more directed toward keeping track of Japanese submarines. However, we continued to plot the courses of ships we had been tracking until we were sure they had reached port. This proved well worth the effort.

A week before the attack on Pearl Harbor, the SS *Steel Voyager* set out from Panama for the long haul to Honolulu. When news of the attack shattered the peace of the Pacific, she was closer to Honolulu than to any other port of refuge. We guessed that she would keep quiet and keep plugging along to her destination. One night, radio direction finders fixed the position of a Japanese submarine on the great-circle track of the lone freighter and dead ahead of her estimated position. The port director sent out a blind broadcast message to the *Steel Voyager*, directing her around the danger. Our estimate of her position proved correct. Her captain made a radical change of course to avoid the submarine. A few days later, he safely made port, maintaining that he had been saved by the warning message.

Another incident involved the *William Ward Burrows*, a naval transport under the command of Captain Ross A. Dierdorff. She departed from Pearl Harbor before 7 December on a supply mission to Johnston Island, a small atoll 700 miles southwest of Oahu. On the night of 15 December, Johnston Island was shelled by a Japanese force thought to be a cruiser and a destroyer, but which was actually two submarines, the *I-16* and *I-22*. The *William Ward Burrows* had completed her mission and left the island a few hours before the bombardment. Dierdorff proposed to return to it and render assistance, but the Commandant Fourteenth Naval District, having received information that there were no casualties on the island, directed the ship to return to Pearl Harbor.

I remember that night very well. There was a

Commander Joseph J. Rochefort (Courtesy of Mrs. Janet Rochefort Elerding.)

voice tube between my plotting table and the district operations office two floors above, but over it had come few requests for information. Suddenly I received a peremptory demand for the position of the *William Ward Burrows*. It required only a minute to prick it off on the chart, and I answered "17–10 N, 168–40 W."

A moment later the voice tube rumbled with the command, "Check that position."

I recognized the irate voice of a captain who was noted for his antagonism to the whole Combat Intelligence Unit, so I carefully checked my data before confirming my first answer, and explained that my estimate was based on the assumption that the

William Ward Burrows was carrying out her assigned schedule on time. In answer, the voice tube roared orders for me to report immediately to the operations office with my charts.

While collecting my charts and notes, I realized that if a mistake had been made my hide would be nailed to the wall, but as I started for the door I encountered a grim-faced Rochefort, adjusting his tie and straightening his hat, preparatory to leaving the basement. "I will answer that call," he told me, and relieving me of the charts, he marched up the stairs to face the challenge.

Ten minutes later, he returned, barely suppressing a grin. A green and flustered watch officer in the operations office had forgotten that the 180th meridian ran down between Johnston and Wake, dividing west longitude from east. He had plotted the position I gave in east longitude, putting the *William Ward Burrows* in a precarious spot between Wake Island and the Marshall Islands. Rochefort immediately spotted the error and delivered a cynical lecture on elementary geography to the red-faced operations watch.

Rochefort was amused, but I was not. I was impressed with his instant assumption of complete responsibility for his organization, and his readiness to stand between one of his junior officers and wrath from without. It was an example of the leadership that inspired into our outfit an ironclad morale that knit us forever into a unit.

From traffic intelligence we were able to determine the positions of Japanese submarines quickly and accurately, but there were few U. S. antisubmarine vessels available for inshore patrol. A Japanese submarine could bob up to the surface, send a quick radio message, and submerge again to safety before an antisubmarine patrol could be directed to the spot. Many depth charges were dropped on phantom targets, and there were many frustrations.

One night, an Army observation post on Kahala beach, just east of Diamond Head, reported that a submarine was lying just outside the reef, charging her batteries. Less than a block from where I lived on Black Point, a battery of two coast-defense guns looked down on Kahala Reef. Maybe the submarine was close inshore to communicate with spies; but whatever her mission, the Black Point battery then had the opportunity to be the first coast-defense battery to fire at a real enemy target since the Civil War.

The battery had been there for many years. Its two 8-inch guns were ancient and short-ranged, but they were well placed to defend the beaches at Diamond Head and Kahala. During the years the guns

had been there, Black Point had developed as a beach colony, occupied mainly by artists and submarine officers' families. When word came down the line that night to "open fire on a surfaced submarine in grid position Helen seven five," the battery was ready. The two big guns were swung around to the proper bearing, and the gunpointers found that they were looking right into the windows of the house we knew as "George Hunter's old house," not 50 yards away. Moreover, ranged down the slope to the water's edge, under the muzzles of the guns, were twenty other houses where families were sleeping in blissful ignorance of what was happening on the other side of the chain-link fence that divided the Army from the civilian area.

Quite properly, Fort Ruger's commanding officer decided that, submarine or no submarine, he had to evacuate the area before he could open fire. By the time that was done, the submarine had completed her business off Kahala beach and was long gone from there. The next morning the Army tore down "George Hunter's old house," but the other inhabitants slowly filtered back to their abandoned homes.

Considering the trauma of the sudden transition from peace and security to war and disaster, Hawaii's civilians and the equally green military and naval personnel cooperated very well. Two or three times a week, air-raid alerts were conducted. When the siren sounded, my wife Isabelle would put on her steel helmet, snatch up her gas mask and her air-raid warden's flashlight, and dash off to "man" the Kahala civil-defense center. Most of the alerts were false alarms.

Early one morning, the most probable hour for an air raid, while I was on my way to Pearl Harbor, the warning sounded. At the siren's scream, all cars except those heading for action stations were required to pull over to the side of the road and stop until the all-clear signal was given. Since I was en route to Combat Intelligence, I stepped on the accelerator, sped into the navy yard, and dashed down into the basement to arrive at the crux of the crisis.

Rear Admiral Claude C. Bloch, Commandant Fourteenth Naval District, was there, with steel helmet, gas mask, and pistol, conferring with Rochefort over the charts of Oahu. Combat reports were pouring in from the operations office above. A formation of three enemy cruisers was reported on the horizon off Oahu's northern shore. Shore defenses reported coming under fire, with heavy shells falling on the beaches. Shore batteries reported taking landing craft under fire. Fighter planes were locked in desperate battle over Ewa Plain, just west of Pearl Harbor.

Rear Admiral Claude C. Bloch, Commandant of the Fourteenth Naval District, makes a point with Secretary of the Navy Frank Knox. (Naval Historical Center: NH 57377.)

Then, suddenly, it all died down. The enemy cruisers turned out to be three small converted seaplane tenders en route from California to the Naval Air Station at Pearl Harbor. Their attempts to identify themselves by signal searchlight had been mistaken for gun flashes from enemy ships. The defending shore batteries had opened up on phantom landing craft in the surf. Splashes from the shore batteries' short salvos explained the reports of heavy shells falling on the beach. Pilots of fighter planes, scrambling from both Army and Navy airfields, tested their guns by firing a few bursts as soon as they reached altitude, and the chatter of their machine guns had been reported as an air battle over Ewa Plain. Everybody felt silly after it was all over, but nobody had been hurt and everybody profited to some extent by the realistic battle practice.

The naval air station had enjoyed a great deal of independence in scheduling its operations, and it had failed to report the anticipated arrival of its seaplane tenders to either the fleet operations office or to the Fourteenth Naval District's Combat Intelligence Unit. The ships, approaching from the eastward, had inadvertently circumvented the short-legged air search in that sector and had rashly made

landfall on Oahu at the most sensitive hour of dawn. After this experience, the naval air station cooperated enthusiastically with Combat Intelligence.

When the joint Army-Navy Defense Center of the Hawaiian Sea Frontier was established in the tunnels under Red Hill, the plot moved up there, where it could be better coordinated with the air searches and with the port director's plot of convoy routes. I stayed behind in the basement with William Dunbar, the yeoman who was my assistant. The Communications Intelligence Unit had suddenly developed an insatiable need for manpower. We were already working on its fringes and were irresistibly drawn into deeper and deeper involvement.

The reason for all this activity I did not know, or need to know in order to be useful. There was a great deal of ordinary administrative work to be accomplished. No one, other than the regulars, was allowed behind the steel doors, so the organization had to be self-supporting. Chief Yeoman Durwood G. Rorie, an old-timer in communications intelligence, supervised the work assignments, security, janitorial service, and supplies. No one questioned his authority inside the basement, but we had to have a commissioned officer to work with the navy yard, the Submarine Force, the Pacific Fleet staff, and other outside agencies. Lieutenant Jack S. Holtwick, who already had charge of the mysterious machine room into which I never intruded, handled this additional duty. As the volume of work increased, however, the entire attention of this wiry, quick, and energetic young officer was required to program and supervise the business machines and the very secret coding machine. The more routine chores fell on me. Also, as the organization grew, so grew the demands of the cryptanalysts for odd bits of information: place-names; charts and maps; positions of our own forces, especially submarines; news reports; and other information whose relevance I could only conjecture.

The demand for trained people greatly exceeded the supply. Admiral Bloch offered the band of the battleship *California* as trainees, and Rochefort promptly accepted. The *California* was resting on the bottom of Pearl Harbor, her main deck under water. Her band had survived, but their instruments had not, so they were among the technologically unemployed. Many of these musicians turned out to be such competent cryptanalysts after a short period of instruction that a theory was advanced that there must be a psychological connection between music and cryptanalysis.

Very early in December, a messenger from the district intelligence office had delivered to Rochefort a package of encrypted messages. Of course, I did not know about this until later, and I doubt that Rochefort knew then how the messages had been obtained. Captain Irving H. Mayfield, the district intelligence officer, had long been quietly trying to circumvent the Federal Communications Act of 1934 to get at the protected communications between the Japanese consul general in Hawaii and the Foreign Office in Tokyo. The act forbade commercial communications companies from disclosing to anyone, other than addressees, the contents of messages filed with the companies for transmission. The previous summer, by trying to pick up ships' weather reports at a commercial radio station, I had bulled into his delicate negotiations. Mayfield had tapped the Japanese consul's telephone line, but that yielded no useful information. The encrypted messages filed with the local communications company remained sacred until some time in November, when David Sarnoff, president of Radio Corporation of America, visited Honolulu. Admiral Bloch persuaded Sarnoff to authorize the delivery of RCA file copies of Japanese messages to Captain Mayfield. The first batch came in less than a week before the attack on Pearl Harbor.

These messages were in diplomatic cipher. The Combat Intelligence Unit was assigned to work on naval codes and was not prepared to work on the consular messages. However, Farnsley C. Woodward, a chief radioman in the cipher section, had had experience with diplomatic messages. He recognized that the messages were in two different ciphers. One of them was too complicated for him to tackle alone, but the other one he would be able to break, given time and a sufficient number of messages. Woodward and Marine Corps Major Alva B. Lasswell worked night and day deciphering and translating the consular messages, but before the morning of 7 December they found only dull and useless ones about routine consular business.

After the Japanese attack, the district intelligence office and the Honolulu police raided the Japanese consulate before all its files had been burned, and managed to seize some messages that yielded interesting information. Among them were those of Takeo Yoshikawa, who had made frequent reports on torpedo nets and the arrival, departure, and berthing assignments of ships at Pearl Harbor. One message reported on the harbor's air defense and remarked on the absence of barrage balloons.

About 10 December, the cryptanalysts discovered another interesting message. It had been sent by Consul General Nagao Kita on 6 December, but of course there was no way for the cryptanalysts to read it, or even identify it as important, until the code had been at least partially broken. This mes-

sage revealed that Otto Kuehn, a German national who had been residing in Honolulu for several years, was a Japanese intelligence agent. Anticipating the loss of radio and cable communications between the consul general and Tokyo, Kuehn had devised a bizarre system of communication. He proposed to inform Japanese submarines off Hawaii of U. S. ship movements in and out of Pearl Harbor by arrangements of lights in windows at night, and of drying sheets on a clothesline near his house in Kailua by day. He planned to transmit other information to Japan or to Japanese ships at sea by coded paid advertisements in radio broadcasts. Kita had to transmit the proposed schedule to Tokyo in a vulnerable cipher because the more secure diplomatic code had already been burned.

I do not remember how or why I learned about this message, but I had met Kuehn, and his wife and daughter, on several occasions. Unfortunately for Kuehn, his avid interest in things naval and military and his unconcealed Nazi connections had attracted the FBI and both Navy and Army intel-

Admiral Husband E. Kimmel was Commander in Chief Pacific Fleet at the time of the attack. Holmes writes: "There were many inconsequential omissions in the defenses of Pearl Harbor, but in more than thirty years of postmortems no one has proposed a course of action Kimmel could have taken that would have greatly changed the situation for the better." (Naval Historical Center: NH 48588.)

ligence to him. He was picked up within hours of the attack. I doubt that his proposed means of communicating got through to the Japanese, although the submarine loitering off the beach at Kahala might have been at the wrong beach and looking for signal lights in windows.

Admiral Bloch showed the message to Secretary of the Navy Frank Knox, who was then at Pearl Harbor. The secretary directed that it should be shown only to Mayfield and Admiral Husband E. Kimmel, Commander in Chief Pacific Fleet. Communications Intelligence would far rather have a spy go free than reveal that we could read Japanese coded messages. Several times, provost marshal agents came down to our basement to confer with Rochefort, but I have no idea how much he revealed to them. Kuehn was tried by a military court and sentenced to death, although no cryptographer testified at his trial.

This incident had an interesting sequel. Kuehn's death sentence was commuted to life imprisonment and he was shipped off to the U. S. mainland for confinement. When the war ended, he was returned to Germany and released there. After he died, his widow came to the United States and petitioned to recover the value of the house they had bought in Kailua and which had been confiscated. Some twenty years after the war, I visited Japan and made the acquaintance of several Japanese ex-naval officers who had been engaged in planning and intelligence. Captain Toshikazu Ohmae remarked to me one day that he was on the last voyage of a Japanese merchant ship to Honolulu just before the war broke out. His mission was the delivery of 25,000 dollars to Kuehn to pay for the Kailua house. I asked him if Japan had ever received anything for the money, and he ruefully admitted that it had not. If Mrs. Kuehn ever received compensation for the Kailua house, she should reimburse the Japanese Government. It was their money.

In the meantime, Hawaii and the Pacific Fleet were settling down for a long war. Despite our confusion, frustration, and shortage of antisubmarine vessels, the Japanese submarines swarming around Hawaii accomplished relatively little. The Japanese awarded high posthumous honors to the crews of the five two-man submarines, all of which were sunk or captured on the first day of the war without having inflicted any significant damage. The twenty-five large submarines involved in the Hawaii operation did little better. They sank the *Cynthia Olsen* and the *Lahaina*, both small freighters, about midway between Honolulu and the mainland and, in the first month of the war, sank two other freighters closer to Honolulu. An observation plane from the

I-7 successfully reconnoitered Pearl Harbor on 17 December and furnished Tokyo with accurate information on the results of the Japanese air attack. The *I-70* was sunk north of Oahu by planes from the *Enterprise*, and the other blockading submarines were so frequently bombed and harassed that they were unable to torpedo any combat ships. For this happy immunity, Communications Intelligence deserved some of the credit.

The Pacific Fleet staff had difficulty pulling itself together. In prewar planning, Admiral Kimmel had anticipated that a Japanese attack on Wake Island might present an opportunity for naval action. On 16 December, after many delays, a complicated operation involving three separate carrier task forces got under way to relieve Wake. The next day, President Franklin D. Roosevelt removed Kimmel from all duty, more than a week before Admiral Chester W. Nimitz arrived to take over. Thus, the expedition to relieve Wake, already handicapped by inadequate logistic support and poor leadership afloat, was further burdened by lack of decisive direction from the interim Commander in Chief Pacific Fleet and his staff at Pearl Harbor. The opportunity to attack the Japanese invasion forces was lost. Wake Island surrendered to the Japanese on 23 December. That date, rather than 7 December, was the nadir of morale for the Pacific Fleet. It was a high price to pay to provide a scapegoat for the Pearl Harbor disaster.

There were many inconsequential omissions in the defenses of Pearl Harbor but, in more than thirty years of postmortems, no one has proposed a course of action Kimmel could have taken that would have greatly changed the situation for the better. At the beginning of a war, all leaders are untested and, if one is knocked out of the box in the first inning, it may be good policy to try another. A decision to relieve a defeated commander is not a question of justice. There is no justice in a war that sends one man to safe duty in a basement while thousands of his comrades are dying in desperate battle within a mile of where he sits. Kimmel should have been relieved, but not in disgrace; and the decision to relieve him at that particularly critical moment was an error in judgment greater than any Kimmel ever committed. That Nimitz was the one chosen to replace him was the great good fortune of the United States.

It was a miserable Christmas. Luckier than most of my fellows, I had a few hours to spend with my family before I had to be back on duty at sunset. I spent most of my time blacking out my tiny "study" by sealing its windows with heavy building paper so there would be one place in the house where we could have a light at night. Nervous patrols were apt to shoot at any light that showed after dark. Many of our friends were at sea, in submarines and in the task forces, and their families expected to be evacuated momentarily to the mainland. For some of the latter, our house on Black Point was a comfortable refuge. Izzy and my son Eric were permanent residents of Hawaii and not on the evacuation list. I dreaded having to make the decision if an opportunity should come for them to leave. Izzy would have refused to go if she had an option, but it would be selfish of me to let her stay.

There were many indications that life in Hawaii would be harsh for everybody. Japanese submarines had begun shelling the beaches in surprise night attacks. So far they had not shelled Oahu, and none of their bombardments had caused much damage. Japanese submarine commanders apparently liked to expend their deck-gun ammunition before leaving their area at the end of a patrol, and this habit helped us anticipate when an area would be clear of submarines. But a hit from a wild shell fired at random was just as deadly as any other, and Black Point was backed up against a myriad of legitimate military targets. On the other hand, evacuation to the mainland meant a long slow voyage in a convoy through seas infested with hostile submarines. There was little peace on earth or good will to men that Christmas.

Light was just around the corner. Nimitz arrived on Christmas Day to take over command of the Pacific Fleet. I met him one morning in the corridor at CinCPac headquarters, which was then on the second floor of the submarine base's supply building. He greeted me by name, and evidently knew that I had been retired for physical disability and recalled to active duty. He had little reason to remember me. I was engineering officer of the *Barracuda* when he was Commander of Submarine Division 20. The only other occasion I could remember when I had talked to him was when Izzy and I made our white-gloved social call on the division commander and Mrs. Nimitz in Coronado eleven years before. Just seeing him at Pearl Harbor gave me the feeling that we had turned the corner.

The aura of calm confidence that radiated from Admiral Nimitz renewed everyone's morale, but it must have been a heavy burden for him to maintain. Many years after the war, when Izzy and I visited Admiral and Mrs. Nimitz at Berkeley, California, he told me what his arrival at Pearl Harbor was like. Two years before that, he had commanded a division of battleships in traditional spit, polish, and punctilio. That Christmas morning, the motor

Because Holmes and his wife Izzy were permanent residents of Hawaii before Pearl Harbor was attacked, they were able to remain there throughout the war. (Courtesy of Captain Wilfred J. Holmes, USN, Ret.)

whaleboat that transported him across the harbor afforded him a depressing view of five battered, capsized, and sunken battleships, still unable to move from where they had been blasted. As he passed an inlet crowded with ships' boats, a staff officer explained that those boats were loaded with dead sailors. When Vice Admiral William S. Pye, who had commanded the Battle Force, succeeded to interim command of the fleet, he brought with him many of his Battle Force staff, without relieving Kimmel's old CinCPac staff. The result was confusion superimposed upon disaster. Admiral Nimitz told me that the fleet surgeon was dosing many of the staff with whatever they used for tranquilizers in those days. Kimmel was still in Honolulu, appearing before the Roberts Commission, which

The Roberts Commission investigated the attack, beginning in late December 1941. Commission members, left to right, are Brigadier General Joseph T. McNarney, Admiral William H. Standley, Supreme Court Justice Owen J. Roberts, Rear Admiral Joseph M. Reeves, Major General Frank B. McCoy, and Walter B. Howe. (United Press International [Acme].)

was there to investigate the defeat at Pearl Harbor. Who could have foreseen that, within six months, the black despair of disaster and defeat would be dispelled by a brilliant victory?

One afternoon in the last few days of 1941, three members of the Roberts Commission, Admiral William H. Standley, Admiral Joseph M. Reeves, and Justice Owen J. Roberts, came down into the basement. The two admirals engaged Rochefort in a close conference, but Justice Roberts asked to see the charts and logs we kept during the attack. The Roberts Commission had been instructed to avoid talking to people about communications intelligence, and Roberts probably disassociated himself from the two admirals in meticulous observance of the limits of his jurisdiction. I was unaware of all this, so while I was showing him the charts, I mentioned some of the relevant information we had gained since the attack by decrypting Japanese consular messages.

Had we intercepted the Japanese consul general's communications earlier, we might have deduced that Pearl Harbor would be one of the first Japanese air targets and been forewarned. Like nearly everyone else, including the Roberts Commission, I then believed that only two Japanese aircraft carriers had taken part in the Pearl Harbor strike and, had we not been surprised, we might have defeated the attack. This hypothesis was disproved by information we acquired later, but I believed it then, and lamented our timidity in respecting the sanc-

tions of the Communications Act of 1934 that protected the Japanese consul general's communications.

Justice Roberts remarked that if naval officers in their zeal to defend the United States could disregard its laws, we would already have lost much of the liberty we were trying to defend. I was deeply impressed by the magnanimity of his arguments, which I interpreted to mean that those who made the laws that had handicapped Pearl Harbor's defenders shared with them the responsibility for the disaster. Years later, when I read the complete Roberts Report, I realized that I had misconstrued his meaning.

In Justice Roberts's authoritative opinion, nearly all communications intelligence activity was illegal, and presumably should have been stopped when the Communications Act became law. Had that happened, surely Midway would have been a Japanese victory, and Hawaii probably would have been invaded by the Japanese in the fall of 1942. The maintenance of a balance between privacy and freedom on one hand and safety and survival on the other has been a difficult problem throughout all our history.

When the Roberts Commission departed, we could put the past behind us and face a difficult future. The new year began with Nimitz firmly in the saddle. Rochefort summed it up when he exclaimed, "Forget Pearl Harbor and get on with the war!"

Wilfred Jay Holmes (1900-   ) was graduated from the
Naval Academy in 1922 and served in the battleship *Ne-
vada* before undergoing submarine training. He then
served in a number of submarines and commanded the
S–30 before being retired for arthritis of the spine in 1936.
He soon embarked on a civilian career as instructor of
engineering at the University of Hawaii and, under the
pen name of Alec Hudson, wrote naval fiction for *The
Saturday Evening Post*. Recalled to active duty, he worked
with the Communications Intelligence Unit throughout
World War II. In 1946, he returned to the University of
Hawaii and held a number of posts, including dean of
engineering, before he retired from the university in 1965.
Holmes Hall at the university is named for him. Captain
Holmes lives in Honolulu. This article is an excerpt from
his book *Double-Edged Secrets*, which was published by
the Naval Institute Press in 1979. (Courtesy of Mrs. Her-
bert Knowles.)

In discussing the transfer of command of the Pacific Fleet from Husband
E. Kimmel to William S. Pye to Chester W. Nimitz, it is useful to digress
and return briefly to Washington, D.C. Here is the beginning of the process
for that last transfer, as viewed by the aide to the incoming commander in
chief.

Replacing the Commander in Chief

By H. Arthur Lamar, former Commander, U.S. Naval Reserve

In November and December 1941, the Arlington Annex to the Bureau of Navigation was being completed. Some people had moved into their offices already, but Rear Admiral Nimitz, the chief of the bureau, was still located at the Navy Department building on Constitution Avenue.

At the time, one of the duties of the aide to the chief of the Bureau of Navigation was to serve as ex officio secretary of the Navy Uniform Board. Admiral Ernest J. King, Commander in Chief of the Atlantic Fleet, had us trying out a number of fancy new uniform ideas, so I had been a clothes horse for several months. Whenever Admiral King got a

wild idea for a new uniform, the uniform shop in the Brooklyn Navy Yard would make up an outfit, and I would have to put it on and appear somewhere in public. On 6 December, I was wearing blue trousers and a white top—Russian style—at the Army Navy Country Club. I stayed out quite late and didn't get home to Falls Church until early the following morning. I got a call sometime before lunch, and my half sister said, "Somebody wants you from the Navy Department."

I thought it was just one of the routine calls I often received from BuNav duty officers on weekends. So I said, "Well, I'll call him back shortly."

On 31 December 1941, three and one-half weeks after the Japanese attack, Admiral Chester W. Nimitz assumed command of the Pacific Fleet. From right to left in this photo are Admiral Husband E. Kimmel, Nimitz, Vice Admiral William S. Pye, Lieutenant General Delos C. Emmons (Army), Rear Admiral Claude C. Bloch, Rear Admiral William F. Furlong (profile extending under Bloch's chin), Rear Admiral John H. Newton, Rear Admiral Thomas Withers, Rear Admiral Milo F. Draemel, and Rear Admiral William L. Calhoun. (Naval Historical Center: NR&L (MOD) 27134.)

But then she came running back and said, "It's Admiral Nimitz, and he says to get into uniform and get in there, but fast." I didn't know what was happening until I got into my car and heard the radio report as I started down Arlington Boulevard.

I think Admiral Nimitz was just as surprised by the attack as I was. Mrs. Nimitz drove him down to the Navy Department. She took along one thermos of coffee and one of soup, and that's what we lived on that day and night. As a matter of fact, we stayed there for three nights, sleeping in the old Navy building, and Mrs. Nimitz fed us.

During the day on Sunday, Admiral Nimitz was involved in meetings in Admiral Harold Stark's office, Secretary Frank Knox's office, and in his own. His first reaction was that he wanted the Navy Department to appear ready for duty the following morning. So I spent all afternoon on the telephone, calling up all the naval tailors I could muster and asking them to open their places of business. You never saw such a mess on Monday morning when people came to the Navy Department in uniforms that didn't button. We had been wearing civilian clothes on duty up to then, and some of these people had gotten fat during their years of shore duty. And others just didn't have all of their uniform items. Rear Admiral John Wainwright, one of my favorite admirals, was evidently missing his raincoat and overcoat. He had on his admiral's cap, and below it was a very loud Scottish tweed coat. I remember watching him out of a window.

Around 16 or 17 December, I picked up the telephone, and a deep voice said, "May I speak to Chester?" I was quite insulted that anyone should be calling my admiral by his first name, and then a deep voice said, "This is the President. Put him on the phone."

So the admiral talked to President Franklin Roosevelt, then came rushing out of the door and said, "Where is my car? I've got to go to the White House." Two hours later, he came back and told me what he had learned from Knox before he left to meet the President, "I am going to the Pacific."

On Friday, 19 December, Admiral Nimitz and I went to Union Station to catch a train to the West Coast; from there, the admiral would fly on to Hawaii. At the suggestion of the White House and the Office of Naval Intelligence, we were traveling under assumed names and in civilian clothes. As we were leaving the Navy Department for the railroad station, there were three senior officers to see us off: Admiral Stark, Admiral James O. Richardson, and Captain John F. Shafroth, Jr. Captain Shafroth was Admiral Nimitz's assistant bureau chief. Admiral Stark gave me a little canvas bag and said, "Don't let this out of your possession, and do not open it until you are well along the way outside of Chicago. Then show Admiral Nimitz what's inside."

There was also something that Admiral Richardson was very insistent on. He had me take along two quarts of Old Granddad, and he said, "Every night, before dinner, make sure the admiral gets two good slugs, because he's got to get some rest."

So we took the Baltimore and Ohio Railroad out to Chicago, and from there we went on the Santa Fe Superchief to Los Angeles. Up to the time of the trip, Admiral Nimitz had not been informed of the extent of the damage to the fleet. So once we were on the Superchief, I opened up the canvas sack, and the contents were simply ghastly. It was full of photographs of the battleships damaged and turned over—the complete havoc that was Pearl Harbor.

I always felt in my dealings with Admiral Nimitz that he thought Admiral Husband Kimmel had not been given a fair shake in the thing. I could well understand that feeling when I remembered his reaction to seeing those photographs for the first time. He said, "It could have happened to me."

Howell Arthur Lamar (1911-   ) was graduated from Washington and Lee University in 1933 with a degree in business administration and worked as an investment trust analyst for the Washington Loan and Trust Company before being commissioned as a Naval Reserve officer in 1937 through the "specialist" program. He was ordered to active duty in May 1940 on the congressional desk in the Bureau of Navigation and appointed aide to the chief of the bureau in February 1941. After accompanying Admiral Nimitz to the West Coast, he returned to Washington to become aide to the Chief of Naval Personnel, Rear Admiral Randall Jacobs. Commander Lamar rejoined Admiral Nimitz as flag lieutenant in August 1942 and remained in that billet through November 1945. He was released from active duty in 1951 and resumed his civilian career as an executive with the Singer Company. He is now retired and lives in Titusville, Florida. (U.S. Navy, courtesy of H. Arthur Lamar.)

In his reflections on the Pearl Harbor attack, Admiral Nimitz not only concluded that the disaster might have befallen an officer other than Admiral Kimmel, but he shared the view held by a good many people that things might have turned out much worse for the United States than they did. He expresses that view in the following extract from a letter he wrote to Admiral David L. McDonald, then Chief of Naval Operations, on 3 April 1965. Toward the end of the passage, when he speaks of Admiral Isoroku Yamamoto, Commander in Chief of the Japanese Combined Fleet, Admiral Nimitz is probably confusing the attack on Pearl Harbor with the Battle of Midway six months later. In both cases, Vice Admiral Chuichi Nagumo commanded the carrier striking force. In the drive toward Midway, Yamamoto was indeed following along with a force of heavy ships, including his flagship *Yamato*. During the Pearl Harbor operation, however, Yamamoto was in the battleship *Nagato*, then his flagship, and she was in an anchorage at Hashirajima, Hiroshima Bay, in the Inland Sea of Japan. Even without Yamamoto's ships in reserve, the Japanese attack force for Pearl Harbor still possessed an overwhelming preponderance of carriers and thus probably would have fought the U.S. Pacific Fleet at ranges too great for battleship guns to come into play.

God's Divine Will

By Fleet Admiral Chester W. Nimitz, U.S. Navy

Several times in recent weeks I have been quoted—correctly—that "as bad as our losses were at Pearl Harbor on 7 December 1941—they could have been devastatingly worse"—had the Japanese returned for more strikes against our naval installations, surface oil storage and our submarine base installations. Such attacks could have been made with impunity as we had little left to oppose them. Furthermore—I have been correctly quoted in saying that it was God's divine will that Kimmel did not have his fleet at sea to intercept the Japanese Carrier Task Force that attacked P. H. on 7 December 1941. That task force had a fleet speed at least 2 knots superior to our speed—and Kimmel could not have brought the Japanese to a gun action *unless* they wanted it. We might have had one carrier but I doubt if the LEXINGTON could have joined in time—Picture if you can—6 Japanese carriers working on our old ships which would be without air cover—or—had the Japanese wanted to avoid American air attacks from shore—they could have delayed the action until out of range of shore based air. Instead of having our ships sunk in the shallow protected waters of P. H. they could have been sunk in deep water—and we could have lost *all* of our trained men instead of the 3800 approx. lost at P. H. There would have been few trained men to form the nucleus of the crews for the new ships nearing completion. Not only were the ships of the enemy task force faster—they were more modern—and the Japanese main fleet under Yamamoto was in the rear—in support—if needed. Nagumo—the Commander of the P. H. Attack Force—missed a great chance by not following up his attack. . . .

Admiral Nimitz assumes command of the Pacific Fleet, 31 December 1941, on board the submarine *Grayling* at Pearl Harbor. The flag officer at right, with his head bowed, is Rear Admiral Thomas Withers, Jr., Commander Submarines Scouting Force. (Naval Historical Center: NR&L (MOD) 27151.)

Chester William Nimitz (1885–1966) was graduated from the Naval Academy in 1905 and served in several surface ships before going to submarine training in 1909. He subsequently commanded submarines before helping develop diesel engines and serving in the tanker *Maumee*. He was executive officer of the *South Carolina* and later had staff duty with Admiral Samuel S. Robison, Commander in Chief Battle Fleet. Nimitz's involvement with submarines continued in the 1920s and 1930s and was interspersed with a tour in command of the NROTC unit at the University of California at Berkeley. He commanded the heavy cruiser *Augusta*, Cruiser Division 2, and Battleship Division 1 before becoming Chief of the Bureau of Navigation. As Commander in Chief Pacific Fleet and Pacific Ocean Areas, Admiral Nimitz was instrumental in the victory over the Japanese. He was Chief of Naval Operations from 1945 to 1947 and later a goodwill ambassador to the United Nations. (Naval Historical Center: NR&L [MOD] 24727.)

A War Correspondent's Odyssey

By Joseph C. Harsch

My wife Anne and I left San Francisco on board the SS *Lurline* in late November 1941, headed for Honolulu. My assignment from Charles Gratke, overseas news editor of *The Christian Science Monitor,* was to spend the mid-winter months in Japan and China and then head for Moscow through Iran—provided the Soviets were still in the war by spring. At the time I left Boston, the Germans were still pushing hard to take Moscow before winter closed in.

I had been in Berlin from mid-October 1939 to the end of January 1941. I had come out then because reporting from Berlin—which was easy until President Roosevelt beat Wendell Willkie in the 1940 election—became much more difficult the moment the Germans knew Roosevelt had won. They had hoped until then that the United States would keep out of the war. After the election, they made it drastically more difficult for us to travel, talk to people, and learn what was going on. To the Germans, we were future enemies. Several of us pulled out together at that time. I returned to Boston, wrote a series for the *Monitor,* turned the series into a book for Doubleday (*Pattern of Conquest*), covered the Army's summer maneuvers in Louisiana (where I was briefed on Lieutenant General

Walter Krueger's operations by his chief of staff, Colonel Dwight D. Eisenhower), then took a holiday in California. My wife was going with me as far as Honolulu, leaving our son William with my parents in La Jolla. I was scheduled to fly out of Honolulu on a Pan American Clipper on 7 December.

The *Lurline* landed in Hawaii on 3 December, and we went to the Halekulani Hotel, where we had rooms in one of its detached cottages. We were assigned a table in the dining room next to Rear Admiral and Mrs. H. Fairfax Leary, whom we knew from Jamestown, Rhode Island. Vice Admiral and Mrs. William Pye were at another table near us. Some time that day or the next, I checked in at the Navy public relations office in Honolulu and found there were two young officers in charge. Through that office, I put in a request to meet Admiral Husband E. Kimmel. I was told to be at his office at eight o'clock the morning of 6 December. I had rented a car for the duration of our stay in Hawaii, so on Saturday morning, my wife and I rose early, drove to Pearl, and parked in front of the Pacific Fleet headquarters. Anne stayed in the car reading. I had arrived about five minutes early and was taken into Admiral Kimmel's office right on schedule. He was surrounded by his staff. Lieutenant

The Matson liner *Lurline* steams off Diamond Head. She left the Harsches at Honolulu shortly before the war started and took Mrs. Harsch back to the West Coast soon thereafter. (U.S. Navy: Naval Institute Collection.)

Commander Waldo Drake, the staff public relations officer, opened the conversation by mentioning that I had been in Berlin for the first year and a half of the war. The admiral and members of the staff immediately began asking me questions about the German Army, its morale, quality of equipment, etc., and about the general public attitude toward the war. This must have gone on for about half an hour. They seemed intensely interested. Perhaps I was the first person through there for some time who had actually been in Germany in the beginning phases of the war. After I had answered everything I could, I took the initiative. The conversation, as I recall it, went as follows:

Harsch: "Admiral, it's my turn now to ask a question."

Kimmel: "All right, go ahead."

Harsch: "I know nothing about the situation out here in the Pacific theater. I'll ask the obvious question. Is there going to be a war out here?"

Kimmel: "No."

Harsch: "Would you please explain why you seem so confident that there won't be a war?"

Kimmel: "Yes. Since you have been traveling over recent days, you probably do not know that the Germans have announced that they are going into winter quarters in front of Moscow. That means that Moscow is not going to fall this winter. That means that the Russians will still be in the war in the spring. That means that the Japanese cannot attack us in the Pacific without running the risk of a two-front war. The Japanese are too smart to run that risk."

I do not remember any further conversation. I suppose it went on for a while. But my memory does not carry anything beyond his positive assertion of no war for the United States in the Pacific and his reason for that assertion. I have often wondered since then how confident he actually was—whether he really believed what he said or whether it was his stance for public consumption.

When I woke up in our hotel room the next morning, I heard a lot of banging sounds. I woke Anne and said, "Listen to this, dear. You have often asked me what an air raid sounds like. This is a good imitation."

She listened and remarked, "Oh, is that what it sounds like?" Then we both fell asleep again. Later, she woke me and suggested that it was time for our morning swim. We donned bathing clothes, went to the beach, had a swim, and started back in. At the shore, another bather was looking toward Pearl Harbor. We looked, too, and noticed several columns of black smoke rising.

"What's going on?" I asked.

He replied, "They have been having some kind of an exercise, but I guess it's all over now."

We then went to our room, got dressed, and went into the dining room for breakfast. It was full of people, mostly naval officers and their wives. Mrs. Fairfax Leary was at her table. No one seemed aware of any untoward happening. While we were eating, Anne pointed to a ship out on the near horizon and said, "What is it doing?" The ship seemed to be dodging around, and there were splashes nearby. I replied that I supposed it was another war game. A little later, she asked, "Where is that ship?" Whether sunk or steamed away, the vessel was by then gone.

Before we had time to wonder more about the missing merchant ship, a woman came into the dining room in semi-hysterical condition saying such things as, "The battleships are burning," "I saw red balls under the wings," "They were shooting at our car," "I was taking my husband down to his ship." Someone who knew her had at first tried to be reassuring, saying it was only an exercise, but her repeated statements finally seemed to get through. All around the room, officers got up, shook themselves, and headed for the door. The idea that it was not an exercise but the real thing spread around the room—not suddenly, but slowly. When the realization finally got to my head, my first thought was that I was a war correspondent but with no credentials. So I told Anne I would have to go to town and get some. She watched me leave with a look of some anxiety on her face.

I went first to the downtown Navy public relations office where I was given a Navy war correspondent card. Then I went to the intelligence office at Fort Shafter. A cavalry colonel in riding britches and boots was in charge. While he was making out an Army credential for me, a typical Army sergeant's voice came on the intercom. It was announcing such things as "paratroopers landing on Diamond Head," "troop transports and cruisers approaching Kailua Beach," "two battleships off Barbers Point." The colonel reached for his holster belt, strapped it on, and strode out the door and down the steps, presumably heading for the enemy. I pocketed my second credential, headed for a point overlooking Pearl Harbor, and then saw the wreckage. From there I headed for the cable office where I wrote out a quick account of what I had seen and handed it to the clerk. But at that moment someone came out of the back room and stated that a total blackout had been ordered; no cables would be sent.

Soon after the attack, one of the naval officers at the downtown public relations office invited Anne and me to join him and his wife at their house. We settled into a routine there. I did what reporting I could about what had happened, and about what was continuing to happen. I ran down as best I could all the many rumors about Japanese sabotage—poisoned wells, cables cut, water supply sabotaged, etc. I was unable to find any confirmation of hostile action by Japanese on the island—other than that sergeant-type voice on the intercom during what must have been the final wave of the attack. I wrote out a cable every day as though I had been able to file to my newspaper. I handed it in each day so that the collection of reports would go out whenever the communication ban was lifted. We usually gathered on Waikiki Beach in the afternoons.

One day, while I was sitting there comfortably wondering what was going on in the big outside world, the horizon filled up with ships. The four Matson liners soon appeared, surrounded by a swarm of destroyers and cruisers. Within a short time, the liners had discharged a reinforcement division plus about thirty war correspondents. The correspondents promptly interviewed the usual taxi drivers. The communication ban was lifted that night, and my stories went through. So did the lurid accounts of the new arrivals—full of poisoned wells and sabotage of every conceivable description. Also, we were informed that all civilians who wished to do so could go back on board the four liners on their return journey to the West Coast. Anne went back on board the *Lurline*.

By that time, I had become friends with Red Knickerbocker and Ed Angley of the *Chicago Sun-Times*. All of us had made our way to the Pacific Fleet headquarters and were by then well acquainted with Waldo Drake. One day shortly after Anne had headed for home, Waldo called and asked me, "Would you like a trip?" To where, I asked him. He said that he couldn't tell me anything but that there would be a trip. I wanted to be sure that it would not be going in the wrong direction for me. I had been told by my editors to get to Singapore if I could. Waldo knew that. Finally, after much discussion about whether we should go on a cruise to "nowhere," Red Knickerbocker and I agreed to go.

The following morning, which was 11 January 1942, we took all our gear with us and reported to the carrier *Enterprise* at Pearl Harbor. Soon after we had boarded and the ship was under way, an officer asked if we would like to meet the admiral on board. "Yes, please," we said. He took us to the front of the flight deck, where we were presented to Vice Admiral William Halsey. There were tears in his eyes—whether from the wind whipping in

On the flight deck of the *Enterprise* in January 1942 are, left to right, "Red" Knickerbocker of the *Chicago Sun-Times*, Commander Alvin I. Malstrom, air officer of the carrier, and Joseph C. Harsch of *The Christian Science Monitor*. (Courtesy of Joseph C. Harsch.)

over the lip of the deck or from depth of feeling was an unanswered question. He spoke about "getting those yellow bastards." He sounded the very model of a fighting admiral.

After that, we settled into the routine of shipboard life. Red and I were assigned "battle stations" in the fighting top above the bridge. We learned about the routine of a big carrier at sea in time of war. After a week or so, we were summoned to the admiral's cabin where Halsey informed us that he was heading toward the Gilbert and Marshall islands for a strike at the Japanese there. He also told us he had a message from Admiral Chester Nimitz, the new Pacific Fleet Commander in Chief, telling him that both of us wanted to get to Singapore and that he had authority to help us on our way if he could do so without interfering with his own operations. He told us that a destroyer would be coming alongside shortly to refuel. If we wished, he would put us over in a breeches-buoy and we would at least get to Samoa. We agreed to go since the alternative would be to head back to Pearl after the attack on the islands. Soon thereafter, we found ourselves aboard the USS *Lamson*, a fine destroyer fitted out as a squadron leader, and we made the acquaintance of the skipper, Lieutenant Commander Preston V. Mercer.

He took us into Pago Pago and to the local naval station. He then took his ship out to sea. A day or so later, the horizon was again filling with ships, and soon we made out the now-familiar outlines of the four Matson liners with suitable escort, including the *Lamson*. They came into the harbor and unloaded a division of Marines with full equipment. Then, one by one, the liners headed out to sea again. We were offered a chance to go back with them to California. We debated the idea. Red insisted that we were halfway across the Pacific and we should stay where we were, even though no one could tell how we might expect to get from there to the far side of the ocean. So we concluded that there was no point in starting all over again. The next day, we were rewarded. In came the *Lamson*, and Lieutenant Commander Mercer sent for us and asked if we wanted another ride. We asked where he was heading, and he answered, "I can't tell you, but I would be happy to have your company. If you want a ride be at the pier at 0800 hours in the morning." We were there. The *Lamson* took us aboard and headed to sea. As we rounded the outer point of the harbor, we were summoned to the bridge where Lieutenant Commander Mercer asked, "Would you like to know where you are going?" We practically went to our knees. He laughed and told us—New Zealand. He then explained that he had just been assigned to the new Southwest Pacific Command and that Admiral Leary was to be its commander. At that very moment, he told us, Admiral Leary was leaving Pearl Harbor by Clipper. Until we got to New Zealand, the admiral would have no ship under his command from which to fly his flag, so we would try to beat the flying boat to our mutual destination. It was a fast run indeed, at full speed the entire way. And it was a most comfortable run, because Mercer liked to have his wardroom run properly. There were freshly laundered napkins for every meal and something close to gourmet food. The Navy knows how to live well.

Skipper Mercer summoned his crew to the fantail as we entered the channel to the harbor at Wellington. He told his crew that we were the first U.S. ship to reach the Southwest Pacific since the Pearl Harbor attack; therefore, it was up to us to make the best possible impression on the locals. He took us in through the long and very irregular channel at high speed, so fast that he almost made a nervous wreck of the executive officer who was doing the navigating. As we approached our destination, we

Rear Admiral H. Fairfax Leary. (Naval Historical Center: NH 48267.)

saw the big cruiser *Australia* ahead of us. Lieutenant Commander Mercer took us alongside at high speed, threw the *Lamson* into reverse at the last possible moment, and brought her up against the cruiser as though we had been in a rowboat. It was beautifully done. The Aussies looked down at us with obvious admiration.

Red and I made our farewells, went across the *Australia*, walked out of the navy yard, hailed a taxi, and told the driver to take us to the best hotel. As we were going up the steps, a man approached us and asked: "Are you Messrs. Harsch and Knickerbocker?" We said we were, and then he asked, "Would you like to meet the Prime Minister?"

We answered, "Yes, we would be delighted, but could we please check into the hotel first?" He permitted that, somewhat grudgingly. He then rushed us off to the office of Peter Fraser, the Prime Minister. Fraser's first question was, "How long are you planning to stay here?" We replied that we wanted to leave as soon as we could get a plane or ship for Australia or Java and asked if he could help us. He said he would be delighted to and was most relieved to hear that we wanted to go elsewhere. He confided that he had been afraid we intended to stay there on the assumption that the war might soon reach New Zealand. He telephoned the airline office and informed us that we had seats on the first plane from there to Sydney.

Red and I left the Prime Minister's office and returned to the hotel, where Admiral Leary was already installed with his staff. We asked him what we would be allowed to write about our travels. He gave us instructions and told us to hand our copy to his intelligence officer when we had finished writing. We then went to our separate rooms to write what we each thought was in order. The intelligence officer passed both our pieces, which were then filed at the cable office. Then Red and I handed each other our respective writings and learned that we had interpreted the admiral's instructions differently. Knickerbocker wrote a lovely color piece describing the landing of a division of Marines on a tropical island, location unstated. I wrote that the link between America and the Allies in the Southwest Pacific had been forged and was open to Allied forces. Back home, our respective newspapers gave our stories to the Associated Press which twinned them for general use—leading to the erroneous impression that U.S. Marines in force had landed in New Zealand. It must have puzzled the hell out of the Japanese.

Joseph Close Harsch (1905–   ) was graduated from Williams College in 1927 and earned an additional A.B. degree from England's Cambridge University in 1929. That same year, he joined the staff of *The Christian Science Monitor*, an affiliation which has continued almost unbroken ever since—as Washington correspondent, Rome and Berlin correspondent, war correspondent, foreign affairs columnist, chief editorial writer, and since 1974 as roving correspondent. In 1939, he was given temporary leave from the *Monitor* to serve in Washington as assistant director of the Inter-Governmental Committee on Political Refugees. As a result of his book about Germany, Mr. Harsch joined CBS news as a commentator and remained with the network until 1949. He was later with both NBC and ABC. In the 1950s and 1960s, he was NBC's senior European correspondent and diplomatic correspondent. His book *The Curtain Isn't Iron* was published in 1950. Mr. Harsch lives in Jamestown, Rhode Island. (Courtesy of Joseph C. Harsch.)

Mr. Harsch displayed remarkable timing. He had been in Germany as that nation's military forces scored devastating successes in western Europe. He was in Hawaii for the attack on Pearl Harbor. After his stop in New Zealand, he went on to Java and was there when the Japanese invaded that island. Thence he went to Australia, where he was just in time to report the arrival of General Douglas MacArthur after his evacuation from Bataan.

Another long-time newsman who wound up at Pearl Harbor at the time of the Japanese attack was Waldo Drake, whom Harsch mentions in his article. The principal difference is that Drake was Admiral Husband E. Kimmel's public relations officer and, as such, wore a naval uniform. He and Harsch attended the same interview with Admiral Kimmel on 6 December. While his recollections of that meeting are not identical with those of Harsch, they are similar in substance. Both men remember the admiral saying that the Japanese were not about to make war on the United States.

"I Don't Think They'd Be Such Damned Fools"

By Rear Admiral William Waldo Drake, U.S. Naval Reserve (Retired)

I'm a former waterfront reporter with the *Los Angeles Times*, and I was in the Naval Reserve from the time it was reorganized in 1926. I covered the Pacific Fleet as part of my beat on the San Pedro waterfront. Before the war started, in early 1940, I was called to active duty in the office of the assistant commandant of the Eleventh Naval District, based in San Pedro. Then, early in 1941, I was ordered to the staff of Admiral Husband E. Kimmel, whom I had never met, as his public relations officer.

We had a lot of visitors, newspapermen and correspondents. I remember especially vividly an incident just before the attack on Pearl Harbor. We had a visit from Joseph Harsch, who was a correspondent for *The Christian Science Monitor* and had been covering the war in the Mediterranean, particularly the campaign in Greece. He expressed an anxiety to have a talk with Admiral Kimmel. Well, Admiral Kimmel was a tremendously fine naval officer, but he wasn't too enthusiastic about the working press. So, I was quite surprised when the admiral said, "Sure, have him come out." Harsch came on 6 December, the day before the attack. Admiral Kimmel, who was rather nonchalant in his treatment of correspondents, put his white shoes on the desk and answered Joe Harsch's questions with complete truthfulness.

Joe asked him, "Admiral, now that the Japanese have moved into Indochina and occupied the Camranh Bay area, what do you think they'll do next?"

The admiral said, "I don't know. What do you think?"

Harsch then asked, "Well, do you think they're going to attack us?"

And Kimmel answered him, "No, young man, I don't think they'd be such damned fools."

That afternoon, the admiral called me back and said, "I like that young fellow. Why don't you show him around Wheeler Field and the Army areas over the hill?" So I drove Joe all around the back country of Oahu—Schofield Barracks and Wheeler Field—and took him back to his hotel. The next morning, the Japanese attacked Pearl Harbor. The interview with the admiral was off the record at the time and,

Vice Admiral William S. Pye was Nimitz's choice to become Commander in Chief Pacific Fleet, but Admiral Nimitz got the job instead. (Naval Historical Center: NH 47253.)

as far as I know, Joe Harsch never mentioned, either in publication or to his friends, what Admiral Kimmel told him that day.

After that, of course, Vice Admiral William S. Pye relieved Admiral Kimmel, and then on Christmas morning, Admiral Chester W. Nimitz arrived at Pearl Harbor to try to pull the fleet out of the low state in which he found it. Just after he stepped ashore at the submarine base, he called his staff together in Admiral Kimmel's old office. Admiral Pye, the temporary commander in chief, was there also. In a very few minutes, speaking softly, Admiral Nimitz convinced all hands of his ability to lead us out of the wilderness. He began by describing the meetings in Washington that led to his selection. He emphasized that he had urged the appointment of Admiral Pye, "but such," he said, "was not to be." And he said it with Admiral Pye sitting alongside him. As to the fleet staff, he said there were going to be no changes: "I know most of you here, and I have complete confidence in your ability and judgment. We've taken a whale of a wallop, but I have no doubt of the ultimate outcome."

William Waldo Drake (1897–1977) worked for the *Los Angeles Times* for forty years, taking time out for World War II. During his tenure as public relations officer for the Pacific Fleet, he often went to forward areas for combat operations. He was wounded during the landing at Eniwetok in February 1944. At the end of the war, he was on the staff of Edwin Pauley, President Harry S. Truman's representative on the Allied Reparations Commission. From 1945 to 1949, Drake was Asian correspondent for the *Times*, covering the war between Chinese Nationalist and Chinese Communist forces. In 1949, he moved to Europe as bureau chief. While covering the Hungarian uprising in 1956, he and his wife were detained for a time in East Germany by Soviet officials. From his European base, he also covered the Middle East and Africa. He retired from the newspaper in 1962 and in later years was active in civic affairs in Orange County, California. (Courtesy of John Drake.)

Alone among the naval officers who might be considered culpable for the overwhelming surprise achieved by the Japanese, Husband E. Kimmel did not get a chance to redeem himself. Admiral Harold R. Stark commanded U.S. Naval Forces in Europe during much of the war and performed valuable diplomatic services in relations with the British. Rear Admiral Richmond Kelly Turner, chief of the War Plans Division of the Navy Department, won justifiable acclaim for his genius at amphibious warfare in the campaign in the central Pacific. Captain Theodore S. Wilkinson, Director of Naval Intelligence in late 1941, became a distinguished flag officer who also played a major role in the amphibious successes against the Japanese.

Admiral Kimmel was not given a second chance. He was forced into early retirement and spent the remaining years of his life in a bitter and frustrating attempt to vindicate himself. His fleet intelligence officer during the months leading up to the attack on Pearl Harbor was Lieutenant Commander Edwin T. Layton. In the memoir that follows, Layton, whose shrewd predictions helped lead to the stunning U.S. victory at Midway in 1942, tells more than just the story of Admiral Kimmel and the politically motivated investigations in the years following the attack: he puts U.S.-Japanese relations into perspective by taking the reader back to the early 1920s.

Admiral Kimmel Deserved a Better Fate

By Rear Admiral Edwin T. Layton, U.S. Navy (Retired)

The first ship I reported to after my graduation from the Naval Academy in 1924 was the *West Virginia*, then the newest battleship in the fleet. During the first week of 1925, she and two other battleships were sent to San Francisco to be host ships for the Japanese Midshipman Training Squadron. There were three Japanese ships: the old armored cruisers *Asama*, *Yakumo*, and *Izumo*. The most junior ensigns of the U.S. ships were detailed as escorts for Japanese midshipmen. The visitors had completed their course at the Japanese Imperial Naval Academy at Etajima and would be commissioned as ensigns following the cruise. I was the boarding officer for our ship and also made a call on our "opposite number," the *Asama*.

During the time we spent with the midshipmen, I found them very eager to be friendly and was surprised that they spoke fine English. Half of them spoke perfect English; the other half spoke excellent French. The ones who had taken English could speak colloquially—not just in textbook fashion—and could converse with ease and fluency. The real kicker for me was that there was not one U.S. naval officer present who could speak a word of Japanese. For the first time, I learned what "losing face" was. I felt ashamed for the United States. But that didn't prevent me from having a good time with the Japanese midshipman who became my companion for the duration of the stay. We had lots of fun. In fact, my opposite number wanted to visit an American speakeasy and a nightclub, so I took him to one of each.

After the Japanese ships left San Francisco, I wrote an official letter to the Navy Department. I said that during the midshipmen's visit, we should have had somebody present to speak Japanese. If we didn't have a policy of doing such things, I said, we should have one, and I volunteered to learn the Japanese language. I got a standard form letter acknowledging receipt and pointing out the requirements for foreign-language instruction. One of the provisions was completion of five years of sea duty. I continued to show my interest, and after the necessary five years, I received the assignment. In the

In 1929, Lieutenant Joe Rochefort (above) and Lieutenant (junior grade) Layton sailed together for the Orient and Japanese-language training. Thirteen years later, their combined intelligence efforts enabled the U.S. Pacific Fleet to win the Battle of Midway. (Naval Historical Center: NH 64844.)

summer of 1929, I sailed from San Francisco to Japan on board the liner *President Adams*. Also on board during the voyage were Lieutenant Joseph J. Rochefort and his wife and young son. Thirteen years later, Joe Rochefort's brilliant codebreaking ability helped us have a U.S. task force stationed off Midway Island when the Japanese came to attack.

During my language training, it was most difficult to try to live on a junior lieutenant's salary. Living in Japan was very, very expensive. Since I couldn't afford to ride taxis, I walked where I was going, and that was fortunate, because it put me in touch with shopkeepers and others. Mr. Naoe Naganuma, our instructor, had instituted a new course when Rochefort and I arrived. Instead of using Japanese primary school texts, he taught us Japanese the way a child learns it. First, we picked up the

This street scene shows the Matsuzakaya department store in Tokyo at the time Layton was in Japan for language training. (U.S. Navy: Naval Institute Collection.)

During their stay in Japan, Rochefort and Layton got out among the people, rather than confining themselves to classroom instruction in Tokyo. Note the rickshaws on this street in Yokohama. (U.S. Navy: Naval Institute Collection.)

conversational language and only then did we start instruction in reading and writing. After we had a basic grasp of the language, we were sent out "into the country"—away from Tokyo and English usage. That forced us to use Japanese twenty-four hours a day. We kept in correspondence with our instructor in Tokyo and also picked up lessons from retired college professors we encountered elsewhere.

My "country instructor" was a retired gentleman of culture, a student of Chinese classics and of Oriental history and art. One day, when we were discussing Japan and its people, he said, "You must never forget the Japanese capacity for revenge. . . . [It] is the central theme of our drama, the central theme in much of our history and poetry, in old novels, and in today's movie scripts. . . . It is the strongest motivating influence in our life." He also said, "Never forget that we Japanese cannot forget, nor forgive, the United States for having classed us as second-class or third-class citizens when it barred Japanese immigration in 1924, along with [and here his face contorted with hate and scorn] Indians, Chinese, Koreans, Indonesians, and scum like that. Always remember that in the Japanese mind we are a superior race. Being excluded from America was an insult but being included by the United States with the Koreans and Chinese was a stain on our honor that call for revenge." I recalled those words when I reached my office in Pearl Harbor around 8:35 or 8:40 on the morning of 7 December 1941—as the second wave of Japanese bombing was in progress and the *Arizona*, the *Cassin*, and the *Downes* were exploding.

During the time we were taking our language training—and the practice continued up through World War II—Japan had a mania about spies and security. For example, the Japanese had large geographical areas called "fortified zones" in which even Japanese people were frequently arrested for sketching, painting, or even carrying a camera. The monument to American Commodore Matthew C. Perry in Uraga (near Yokosuka) was in a fortified zone. Right alongside the monument was a very badly done sign in what we called "Jap-lish" saying "Photography no because here." If we asked for a reason, we were told that a picture of the monument would include the water behind it and could be used for intelligence purposes in planning an amphibious landing.

After my language training, I had an assignment for four months in 1932–1933 as assistant naval attaché at the American Legation in Peiping (Peking), and that brought me further contact with the Japanese who, by then, had started their campaign in China. I didn't get back to the United States until

February 1933 and then spent five months in the Office of Naval Intelligence in Washington for a major debriefing. I also started the plotting of strategic industry, power grids, and so forth in Japan. As it turned out, the information was later used for World War II bombing targets.

Because I had been away from the fleet for a long time, I was then ordered to the USS *Pennsylvania* as officer of turret one and first division officer. A year later, I switched to turret four and made it the first E (for excellent) turret the *Pennsylvania* had had in many years. It was during this assignment that my path again crossed that of Joe Rochefort. The *Pennsylvania* was the flagship of the Commander in Chief U.S. Fleet, Admiral Joseph M. Reeves, and Rochefort was the fleet intelligence officer. In the fall of 1934, while we were in port at San Pedro, California, Joe sent for me and said, "There's a man ashore here who works with the Eleventh Naval District. He's a doctor who works with ONI's undercover organization ashore that keeps track of what's going on in the Japanese community. He's just discovered, through his contacts, that the Japanese naval tanker which came in today has some special Japanese film which they intend to show to the Japanese association ashore tomorrow night. We believe that this film is subversive, and we'd like to have you help the undercover boys ashore in this matter."

The Japanese Citizens Patriotic Society had rented an auditorium from Shell Oil and had the right to deny entry to any nonmember—namely, me. Following the suggestion of a naval intelligence agent, I posed as a fire insurance inspector, taking along a fire extinguisher to say that I was there to enforce regulations against smoking during the showing of the film. I even provided myself with some false credentials, saying that I was there to protect the insurance interests of Shell Oil. When I got to the meeting, I showed the Japanese chairman of the local group my fake credentials and pretended not to know any Japanese. They discussed it among themselves for a while and then told me, in English, that I could leave. So I brought out my paper and said, "Me no here, no movies." By this time, there were 200 or 300 people there, and I was going around telling people to put out their cigarettes.

The movie itself was pretty corny, but this was their way of telling people that the emperor system was best and that democracy was no good. One scene was typical; an animated cartoon showed financier J.P. Morgan pushing a wheelbarrow full of money over the bodies of the poor and downcast. It was quite unpleasant. During the course of the evening, a curious Japanese sailor turned my fire

In the mid-1930s, Layton got involved in counterintelligence when a Japanese naval tanker brought a propaganda film to San Pedro, California, for showing to the Japanese community there. Posing as an inspector for a fire insurance company, Layton infiltrated the meeting at which the film was presented. Moored at the pier opposite are the Navy transport *Henderson*, center, and Vincent Astor's yacht *Nourmahal*, right. (Stanley A. Wheeler, San Pedro, California.)

extinguisher upside down and got a faceful of foam for his trouble. He also got foam all over the floor, making quite a mess. Because I had to clean it up and made quite a commotion about it, the Japanese chairman came over after the show and gave me five dollars for my trouble. When the meeting was over, I got together with the doctor and the professional ONI agent in a Long Beach bar, and there we sat and drank up most of the five dollars, celebrating the success of our operation.

I wrote up a report of the affair for Joe, and he in turn put together a report for Admiral Reeves and ONI. So that worked out pretty well. It may have been what led to my next assignment, as a counterspy. A year later, in 1935, by which time I had worked up to become the *Pennsylvania*'s senior watch officer, Joe again sent for me—this time while the ship was en route to San Francisco as

part of a fleet maneuver. Once he had closed the door in the staff area, Joe gave me my instructions. When we got to Hunters Point Navy Yard, I was to take a train to Bremerton, Washington, and there board the Navy tanker *Brazos*, which was sailing for Dutch Harbor, Alaska. He said that there was a Japanese spy in the Dutch Harbor area. The fleet commander in chief wanted the spy out of the way so he wouldn't be able to observe and report on our ships when they got there as part of Fleet Problem XVI.

The *Brazos* got to Dutch Harbor early one morning, and I went ashore in civilian clothes to see what I could do. I went to the local postmaster, who was also the federal judge in the area. I gave him a letter of introduction from an aerologist who had been stationed there, and I asked to talk to the postmaster in private, saying that I was on highly confidential business of the United States. He closed the post office window and invited me into an adjacent office. There I told him that I was on orders from the commander in chief of the fleet to come to Dutch Harbor and see to it that a Japanese spy was put out of circulation. I asked him for his help in the matter, and he replied, "Ah, we've only got one Japanese here. He is Mr. Shimizu from Seattle, but he's not a spy, is he?"

I told him that I presumed that since he was the only Japanese there, he must be the man I was sent to take care of. Thereupon, the postmaster recommended I go see his friend George, the federal marshal for the territory of Alaska. He explained that George was half-Aleut, a graduate of the University of Washington, and thoroughly trustworthy. After getting directions, I walked up an unpaved road to George's house, which also contained his office and the federal jail for the area. After I told him of my mission, he thought it over for a short time and then replied, "From what I hear, this Jap Shimizu has been in violation of the law here for some time by bootlegging, but I have to have a complaint and evidence. Why don't you go down and buy a bottle of booze from him, bring it back to me and file a complaint, and I'll take him into custody? Then we'll take him down to the federal judge [the postmaster] who can handle the matter as the law provides."

I got directions to Shimizu's place, which was back of the only street in town, and knocked on the door. When a Japanese man opened it, I said, "I understand you've got some booze here for me, and I need it very badly. I just got in on the boat."

He looked at me and said, "That'll be two dollars." He handed me over the bottle, and I gave him the money and walked down to the corner where the marshal was waiting for me. I handed him the stuff, and he told me I'd better taste it to be sure it was alcoholic. I took a taste, and it was alcoholic all right—like shellac! He then marched up and arrested Shimizu for violation of federal law—possession of untaxed alcoholic beverage. We then took him down to the post office where the postmaster took us to a room bearing the sign "Federal District Court" and announced, "Court's open."

Shimizu pleaded guilty to the charge, and the judge/postmaster sentenced him to thirty days in jail. I thanked the marshal for his quick action on behalf of the commander in chief and for safeguarding the national interest. He then told me there was still another angle to the problem—that Shimizu had a gal downtown, the town whore. She might be his assistant and ready to help him report what the fleet would be doing. He suggested that she may

have been planted to gather information from sailors. So perhaps she should be put in jail too. I asked him how we might accomplish that, and he offered to get her out of the way if he had proof of her prostitution.

I told him that the ship's mail orderly was down at the dock waiting for me, so I went back to him and gave him the story. I told him that if he would go to this whore and pay her two dollars (which I would give him), then come and testify concerning her prostitution, the marshal would throw her in jail. It worked out just as we had planned. That evening, the whore asked the female jailer to pass a note to Shimizu. She didn't know that this jailer was the marshal's Aleut wife, so the note went right to the marshal. He sent word for me and showed me the note. I suggested that he copy it and pass the original on to Shimizu. They passed notes to each other thereafter, and then Shimizu asked for stationery and an envelope so he could write a letter "to his parents." It was in Japanese, addressed to the Tokai Trading Company in Seattle. Again, the marshal sent for me and showed me the letter, which was on his desk. I asked him if it had been placed in a U.S. mailbox yet, and he said it hadn't. I asked him to be a witness to the fact that I was not violating the postal regulations when I opened that letter. The report was in Japanese and told the intended recipients that he had been arrested and was sorry that he wouldn't be able to do what was expected of him. Furthermore, his friend, who had helped him by "contacts," was in jail also. In the meantime, I had sent a message, through the *Brazos*, to the fleet flagship: "For Joe—Mission accomplished." I learned later that Shimizu and the whore were released, then declared undesirables and deported from Alaska. I'm sure that it wouldn't be possible today to pull off such an effective counterintelligence mission for a mere four dollars.

In June 1936, after three years on board the *Pennsylvania*, I was detached with orders to report to Washington. I had previously indicated that I wanted to be assigned as assistant naval attaché in Tokyo, so I could continue to use my Japanese in a practical way. But I learned that the job had already been committed to someone else. So I wound up in Op-20G, the communications intelligence section of the Division of Naval Communications. In a sense, I was working for both the Office of Naval Intelligence and the Communications Division of Naval Operations. I was assigned to the translation section, and my immediate task, in addition to translating anything that might be available currently, was to conduct recovery and research on the

Japanese Navy's "blue code." It was not the current code then, but the idea was to fill in the blanks in past messages, because they might be of value later. As an example, one of the messages I chose to research dealt with the battleship *Hiei*. She was listed in *Jane's Fighting Ships* (and officially by the Japanese) as a training ship with a top speed of less than 20 knots. But when I finished breaking a certain message and translating it, it said that the *Hiei* had just finished making more than 30 knots on her official speed trials following overhaul and modernization. Information such as this was then filed away in a sealed envelope in an ONI safe until needed. Up to World War II, our naval intelligence publications carried the *Hiei* as having an "official" top speed of 20 knots, but then the publications were "updated" just before the war to reflect the more authentic data. Officers who had studied their intelligence publications were thus not surprised when the *Hiei* made high-speed runs to bombard Guadalcanal in the autumn of 1942.

My tour in Op-20G was a short one, only about seven months, and in 1937 I got my chance to go to Tokyo as assistant naval attaché. By that time, there was no doubt of a military buildup in Japan. For example, when I came in by train from my little seaside place in Hayama each morning, I saw Japanese troop trains assembled in yards and flatcars loaded with artillery and motor transport. Also, whenever I walked by the Imperial guard barracks to get to the U.S. embassy, I had to be wary because the sentries stood guard with fixed bayonets and had a nasty habit of charging at foreigners, yelling loudly, and forcing us into the street. I saw them drive women and children off the sidewalk; I suppose it was just to show that they were rough, tough military people.

During the course of my tour there, the embassy received a message from the Chief of Naval Operations, saying that Amelia Earhart, the famous aviatrix, had been lost somewhere in the Pacific. The attaché was directed to approach the Japanese and ask if they had any ships which might be able to join in the search. The request was then translated into formal Japanese, and I made an appointment to deliver it to the Japanese Navy Ministry. There I presented the request to Admiral Isoroku Yamamoto, then the Vice Minister of the Navy. The request was acknowledged, and the Japanese reported later that the only ship they had in the area of their mandated islands was the *Kamoi*. They told us the seaplane tender had searched the area in which she was operating but had found no trace of the missing plane.

While I was in Tokyo, I naturally formed impressions of the Japanese officers whom I encountered, including, of course, Admiral Yamamoto. As I have always told people who asked about him, I viewed him as a very human, very real, and very sincere man. Many Japanese are hard to "get to." They are quite reserved, sometimes to the point of being aloof. One sometimes has the impression that they are like actors in a drama, wearing false faces or masks to suit their roles. With Yamamoto, I got to feel that on social occasions he did not wear his false face. He was my host once at a theater party, another time at a duck hunt, and another time at a geisha party. He could be quite relaxed with people and made it a point to go around and talk to each of his guests. He was also quite skillful at games such as poker and bridge. He was a Japanese champion at the games of "go" and "shogi," which are something like chess and checkers. He was hard-working and devoted to his profession.

In a sense, I was involved with Admiral Yamamoto again several years later, in 1943, when I took the original intelligence to Admiral Nimitz which resulted in Admiral Yamamoto being shot down in the South Pacific. In this regard, Admiral Nimitz asked, "Do you think we ought to?" I told him I thought so, and later I drafted the dispatch which authorized and directed our fighter planes to go after him. Nimitz read it over carefully and then wrote a postscript on the dispatch, "Best of luck and good hunting." I had known Yamamoto before, but now he was the enemy. Admiral Nimitz had asked me if there was anyone who could take his place. I replied, "Absolutely none. Absolutely none." And that's when Admiral Nimitz decided to go ahead.

There were many other interesting aspects of my stay in Tokyo, including a cat-and-mouse game over Italian reports that the Japanese were building super battleships with 18-inch guns. We went to the Japanese and asked them about it. The reply was a masterpiece of circumlocution. It didn't tell us whether they were or were not, in fact, building such ships—only that the Italians had no basis for such statements. The report turned out to be true, although there were a number of similar ones that proved groundless.

In April 1939, I was detached and returned to the United States to take command of the destroyer *Boggs*. I bring this up mainly to point out that even an officer such as myself with a specialty in intelligence and the Japanese language was still considered a general line officer back in those days and expected to follow the normal sea-shore rotation patterns. It was a pattern that would be broken in my own case with the coming of the war.

I was detached from my destroyer command at Pearl Harbor on Saturday, 7 December 1940, a year to the day before the war broke out. I reported immediately to the battleship *New Mexico*, then the flagship of Admiral James O. Richardson, Commander in Chief U.S. Fleet. I was assigned as the fleet intelligence officer. Shortly after I reported aboard, Admiral Kichisaburo Nomura passed through Honolulu en route to Washington as Japan's new ambassador to the United States. I had known him years before, so Admiral Richardson ordered me to meet Admiral Nomura's ship at the dock when it came in and to act as his naval aide during his stay in Hawaii. I accompanied him on official calls, receptions, and to a big dinner in his honor given by the Japanese in the Hawaiian Islands. I was the only non-Japanese on hand, and they obviously didn't expect me there. After being introduced, Admiral Nomura made a speech in Japanese, and in it he said, "I won't have to have this talk interpreted, because 'Leftenant' Commander Layton understands Japanese perfectly. I want you to know that he's an old friend of mine. He's here as my personal guest and my friend. I am going as ambassador to Washington; I am going there to make friends and straighten out any problems our

Lieutenant Commander Layton (right) serves as naval aide to Admiral Kichisaburo Nomura (civilian suit and glasses) during the latter's stopover in Hawaii. Nomura was traveling to Washington to be Japanese Ambassador to the United States, where he sought to reassure his audiences concerning friendship between the two nations. (Courtesy of Rear Admiral Edwin T. Layton, USN, Ret.)

nations may have. I want my friend 'Leftenant' Commander Layton here to be present during all my conversations and all speeches I make here, because I have nothing to hide from anyone, and I want him to know and assure his government that I am sincere and honest." I saw Admiral Nomura several times in Tokyo before he died there in 1964. Speaking of his days as ambassador, he'd say, "You know, in America they'll never understand or believe that I never knew about Pearl Harbor [beforehand]."

In the autumn of 1940, Admiral Richardson had gone to Washington to see the President and the Chief of Naval Operations. At the time, I didn't know why he was going, although I do recall that there was a Drew Pearson kind of a story out of Washington saying that he had differed with President Roosevelt. I saw several dispatches in which he wanted to send ships back to the West Coast so they could have some leave, liberty, recreation, overhauls, and so forth. He indicated that Pearl Harbor was not a good place to keep the fleet and that it was very bad for morale. This viewpoint was counter to what the President wanted, and Admiral Richardson wound up being detached rather summarily by Roosevelt. Admiral Husband E. Kimmel then took command of the Pacific Fleet on 1 February 1941.

Admiral Kimmel was a very forthright officer. He could sometimes be a little starchy, but he was more starchy with senior officers who were lax than with junior officers. He was demanding in devotion to duty, setting in his own performance an outstanding example. He had little tolerance for laziness or indecision. He had an infectious, warm smile when pleased by something and a frosty demeanor if displeased.

After he had assumed command, he sent for me to review the current intelligence and to discuss the activities and dispositions of the Japanese Navy. He wanted a full briefing on intelligence, how much we knew and how much we didn't. I told him everything I knew, without reservation. He wanted to know if I thought we would continue to get significant decrypts of intercepted Japanese messages. I told him: "I don't know where we are right now with regard to progress. I have not had any information other than what I picked up by talking to Rochefort [who by then was on the staff of Rear Admiral Claude C. Bloch, Commandant of the Fourteenth Naval District in Hawaii], but he's not working on any system now; his unit works in accordance with orders from Washington. We are not receiving anything now; Washington may have

The last prewar change of command of the fleet took place on 1 February 1941 on board the flagship *Pennsylvania*. Admiral Husband E. Kimmel, new commander in chief, is at the microphone shaking hands with his predecessor, Admiral James O. Richardson. Compare this scene of spit-and-polish formality with the much less resplendent scene (page 261) when Admiral Nimitz assumed command of the fleet on board the submarine *Grayling* eleven months later. (Tai Sing Loo photo; courtesy of Mrs. Evelyn Lee.)

great quantities of information, holding it to furnish us when the time comes." Rochefort and his people had been assigned by Op-20G to do cipher and code recovery for a naval system, and they were furnishing Admiral Kimmel with a daily Japanese radio traffic analysis, but they were not given access to diplomatic intercepts, the famous "Magic" messages referred to throughout the Pearl Harbor hearings. Admiral Thomas C. Hart and General Douglas MacArthur were getting "Magic" in the Philippines, and the British had a "Magic" machine as well, but Rochefort didn't. The machine was supposed to have been furnished to Rochefort's unit in Pearl Harbor but went to the British instead. I've heard this was on President Roosevelt's initiative after a meeting with Churchill.

A few months later, I gave Admiral Kimmel a translation of part of a book, written in Japanese, titled *Shall America and Japan Fight?* I had read the whole book and had translated significant chapters that dealt with "questions in the mind of the U.S.

Commander in Chief Pacific Fleet." These questions were the following: "On declaration of war, will he move the fleet from its West Coast bases at San Pedro and San Diego to Pearl Harbor? Will Japanese submarines contest the fleet's passage there? Will he have enough escorts? While the fleet is in Pearl Harbor, what is the chance of a Japanese raiding squadron, centered around a couple of *Akagi*-class carriers, some speedy battleships, such as the *Haruna* and the *Kongo*, and some heavy cruisers of the *Nachi* class, making a raid on Pearl Harbor? Will a raiding force strike the United States in the Aleutians, or even occupy strategic places up there?"

I gave this summary to Admiral Kimmel to read. When he returned it, we discussed, in a general way, the various points made by the author. In discussing the author's idea of a Japanese carrier task force raid on Pearl Harbor, Admiral Kimmel asked me if I thought the author was writing from any official or semiofficial point of view. I said that, in view of the Japanese mania for secrecy, I doubted that he

The USS *Pennsylvania*. (Tai Sing Loo photo; courtesy of Mrs. Evelyn Lee.)

was reflecting an official position. He asked me if I thought they would take such a risk, and I told him that taking such a risk would be possible, particularly if they thought they could get away with it, because they were not entirely orthodox in their methods. Kimmel then sent for Captain Charles H. McMorris, his head of war plans, and I can still almost quote what he said: "Soc [McMorris's nickname, short for Socrates], Layton here and I have been discussing the chances of the Japanese making an attack on us here."

And McMorris replied, "What's that?"

"We were discussing something that was written in Japanese about a Japanese carrier task force making a strike on Pearl Harbor. Do you think there would be a chance of that?"

McMorris answered him, "Well, maybe they would; maybe they would, but I don't think so. Nope. Based on my studies, it is my considered opinion that there are too many risks involved for the Japanese to involve themselves in this kind of an operation."

So, with that, we sort of put the book out of our minds and went about our business. We did con-

Admiral Kimmel (front row, center) and his staff gather on board the flagship *Pennsylvania* in the summer of 1941. Lieutenant Commander Layton is third from right in the middle row. Lieutenant Commander Waldo Drake, author of another article in this book, is fifth from left in the same row. (Courtesy of Rear Admiral Edwin T. Layton, USN, Ret.)

tinue to be concerned as to whether we were getting sufficient information from Washington. As a result, I wrote to my opposite number in the Office of Naval Intelligence, Commander Arthur H. McCollum. I told him that Admiral Kimmel and I had been discussing intelligence—what we had, what we didn't have, and what we would like to be assured of receiving. I referred specifically to the "Dip," or diplomatic decrypts. We didn't then know specifically about "Magic." My letter stated that we hadn't been receiving any, and the situation was getting tense. We thought we ought to be receiving some and wondered if there was a blackout—that is, had they lost their ability to read the Japanese coded traffic?

McCollum's reply, which is in the record of the Pearl Harbor investigation, was to the effect that they couldn't furnish us the material because of security. In addition, if we were to receive all the material they received, we'd have to have as big an organization as they did in order to analyze it. His letter concluded by stating that we had to depend on those in the Office of Naval Intelligence to go through all the material, sift it out, and furnish us with anything that would affect the mission of Admiral Kimmel's command. I was disappointed in McCollum's description of the ONI position. I showed the letter to Admiral Kimmel and voiced my concern. He then wrote to Admiral Stark to request assurance of intelligence support, and Stark wrote him a letter similar to the one McCollum had sent me. Even so, there were still those who said afterward that Kimmel "got all the information" and therefore was at fault for the Japanese success in the Pearl Harbor attack. The fact is that he didn't get the intelligence and wasn't at fault.

The ONI manual (ONI 11) that was then in effect, clearly set forth the duties and responsibilities of the Chief of Naval Operations (through his Director of Naval Intelligence) to keep the commander in chief of a fleet fully apprised of all intelligence pertinent to that fleet command. Some years later—in late 1944, I think it was—the registered publications officer on the Pacific Fleet staff came around one day and said he had some changes to make in the ONI manual in my safe. He took custody of it and returned after making the changes. I was busy at the time and put it back into the safe without examining it. I happened to open it some time later and found that the entire section having to do with the duties and responsibilities of the Chief of Naval Operations (through ONI) and the fleet commanders in chief (through fleet intelligence officers) had been removed, and no replacement pages were furnished. I then sent the custo-

dian around to see if there were any ships in port that might not have entered the changes, because I wanted to save a copy of the regulations in force as of 1941. But if any ship's officers hadn't made the changes, they wouldn't admit it. Later, during the congressional investigation of Pearl Harbor, when I wanted to refer to the ONI instructions, I could not, because those instructions had by then become a series of blank pages.

In any event, McCollum's assurance that we would get important information from Washington probably helped give us a false sense of security. One example came when the Japanese moved into Indochina. The CNO sent us two messages which were obviously decrypts of Japanese dispatches which said that Carrier Division 2 was operating off Indochina to back up what was virtually a Japanese ultimatum to Vichy France. The receipt of these messages made us feel that when something important came, we would get it, particularly any messages that had a relationship to the mission of the Pacific Fleet. Later, shortly before Pearl Harbor was attacked, we were furnished a few more messages by Admiral Stark. When we got a few (of the many the CNO had), it was really worse than giving us none at all.

Among the messages we did get from Washington were one or two saying the Japanese were burning their codes in Batavia, Singapore, Manila, and other such places, none of which indicated anything other than possible trouble in Southeast Asia. The CNO did not send Kimmel the decrypts which ordered the Japanese consul in Honolulu to divide Pearl Harbor into zones in order to facilitate reporting the locations of U.S. naval vessels there. Nor did we get the orders to the consul to report each day thereafter, and whether there were any departures or arrivals in the harbor. Decrypts such as that, which should have directed the CNO's eyes toward Pearl Harbor, were never sent to Kimmel. They had this material back in Op-20G. It was circulated in Washington and should have been sent to the Commander in Chief of the Pacific Fleet. Admiral Kimmel was absolutely not kept well advised. That's been proven time and again. It's just beyond my understanding. That is why I feel that Admiral Kimmel was so badly used, so badly treated.

Had we had a "Magic" machine in Hawaii, I think things would have turned out differently. We at Pearl Harbor were the ones who had first seen the militarization of the mandated islands early in 1941 when ONI hadn't made that deduction on the basis of the same information. I'm sure that had we seen messages that had to do with Pearl Harbor, then there would have been a different evaluation of those items of intelligence. There's an old Indian saying that the snake in your corner is the largest. This is true in intelligence. If you receive intelligence that has to do with where you are, you give it greater significance. In the late autumn of 1941, Washington was too involved with the shipping war in the Atlantic to take proper notice of intelligence that related to the Pacific. Had "Magic" decrypts been available to us, they would have at least alerted us to the possibility of an attack on Pearl Harbor.

We did still have Joe Rochefort's daily analysis of Japanese radio traffic. From mid-November onward, Joe's reports reflected the formation of various task forces. Since these were composite forces, Admiral Kimmel told me on the first of December that he wanted to have a report setting forth the locations of the Japanese fleet units. Previously, Joe's traffic analysis had given good general information on the movement of forces, but the Japanese Navy had changed call signs on 1 November and again on 1 December. This tended to obscure the information, although we could still get some fairly good indications. At that time, many fleet units were changing their locations, as seen by traffic patterns. By the time I'd prepared the report for Admiral Kimmel, Joe phoned to say that more changes were being made and that he would like to postpone the report one more day to reflect the latest locations.

I told Admiral Kimmel's aide, Lieutenant Ernie Blake, of Joe's request because of the constantly changing information, and the reply was in the affirmative. So I told Joe to work all night if necessary and get the report to me the first thing in the morning so I could review it before passing it on to the admiral. Even as I was reviewing it early on the second of December, Joe called with new changes. I made the alterations in pencil but did not list Carrier Divisions 1, 2, 3, 4, or 5, because there was no radio traffic to or from the carriers or their commander, nor were they information addressees on any messages except a supply-type message to the *Akagi*. Before taking the location sheet to the admiral, I called Joe again, and he said there hadn't been any information on carriers for a long time. He didn't know where they were, but he believed they were probably in home waters in Japan. So I wrote down "Unknown—home waters?" and took it to the admiral. He read the report through very carefully, then said, "What? You don't know where the carriers are?"

"No, Sir," I replied.

"You haven't any idea where they are?"

"No, Sir. That's why I have home waters down there with a question mark. I don't know."

"You mean to say that you are the intelligence officer of the Pacific Fleet and you don't know where the carriers are?"

"No, Sir, I don't."

He then said, "For all you know, they could be coming around Diamond Head, and you wouldn't know it?"

I answered, "Yes, Sir, but I hope they'd have been sighted by now."

He kind of smiled and said, "Yes, I understand." His manner during this exchange was jocular, in that he was impressing me with the fact that I didn't know where the Japanese carriers were. Since I didn't know, they could be almost anywhere—even rounding Diamond Head. In the years since then, I've worn a hole in the seat of my trousers from kicking myself so often. When the admiral made that remark about Diamond Head, how I wish I had thought back to the book which came out earlier in the year and said that one possibility was a Japanese attack on Pearl Harbor!

On the Saturday a week before the attack, 29 November, I arrived late at the staff mess which was ashore at the Pearl Harbor submarine base. During lunch, someone asked me for my opinion of "the situation," and I told him that I thought I'd be back in my office the following day. They doubted that things were that serious, but I repeated my conviction. At lunch on Monday, 1 December, there was a great "Ha, ha, ha. What happened to your crisis, Layton? Layton and his Sunday crisis."

The next Saturday, 6 December, I was again late for lunch. Admiral Kimmel had sent me out to see Vice Admiral William Pye, Commander Battle Force, on board his flagship *California*. I took with me a dispatch reporting sightings of a concentration of transports and warships, including submarines, heading south of Camranh Bay and some other Japanese ships headed toward the Gulf of Siam. Admiral Pye and his acting chief of staff, Captain Allan E. Smith, were on the quarterdeck. I handed them the message, saying that Admiral Kimmel would appreciate Admiral Pye's comments, if any. They both read it over and said that the Japanese were probably going to occupy a position in the Gulf of Siam as an advance base and operate from there, probably against the Burma Road. They asked me what fleet intelligence thought of it. I replied that I didn't believe they'd stop there, although part of their operations might be against the Burma Road. I said I thought that they probably had objectives farther south, the Dutch oil, because we had cut off our oil to Japan. I added that I didn't think the Japanese would leave the Philippines on their flank. Since the Japanese never left their flank exposed, they'd attack the Philippines, and we'd be at war.

Both of them said, "Oh, no, the Japanese won't attack us. We're too strong and powerful."

On returning, I reported to Admiral Kimmel and related their remarks. Admiral Kimmel got me to repeat it all, then he looked at me in a way he could look at people—straight through them—and he snorted, as if disappointed in their reply. So I went to the staff mess for lunch and apologized to Commander Willard A. Kitts, the senior officer present, for being late, and I explained why. I passed on the significance of my conversations on board the *California*, and Commander Kitts said, "Ah, Layton and his Saturday crisis."

The following morning, when I came rushing into the headquarters building during the attack by the second wave of carrier planes, the first person I encountered was Commander Bill Kitts. He said, "Here's the guy we should have listened to more often." Later that morning, Captain McMorris sent for me, and I went into his office in the war plans section. He said, "Layton, if it's any satisfaction, you were right and I was wrong." I told him I didn't find any satisfaction in it.

As I've said earlier, I got to my office a little past 8:30. My yeoman, who had had the duty, gave me an intelligence log sheet, a recording of the events and times, up to the minute. It included a list of the ships that had been hit, those that were sinking, those that were asking for assistance, etc. It made me physically ill. The phone rang, and it was Lieutenant Commander "Ham" Wright, over in Joe Rochefort's outfit, saying they'd just got a direction finder bearing—a two-way reading which meant that the Japanese radio transmissions could be coming either from the north or the south. About this time, Admiral Kimmel came out and looked at the operations plot. I had gone down there and laid down the two bearings. Admiral Kimmel was understandably a little testy because of the reciprocal bearings rather than just one. He felt (and correctly, too) that intelligence should be able to tell him where the enemy was. At about that time, a radio message was received from one of our ships reporting that two carriers were to the south of Pearl Harbor. Actually, the report was of two cruisers. They were actually our own, but the report was garbled, and it came out as two carriers south of Pearl. We knew we didn't have any carriers there, and it wasn't until late afternoon, when we recovered a plot board from the Japanese pilot who

had crashed into the *Curtiss*, that we found out that the navigation sheet for his return flight indicated that he was to go back to the north.

There was another item of interest, which came in a telephone message from Rochefort shortly after Ham Wright gave me the "bilateral" bearings. "The *Akagi*, the flagship of the carrier force, is out here," Joe told me.

"How do you know it's the *Akagi*?" I asked.

"That same ham-fisted warrant officer that uses the transmitter key as if he is kicking it with his foot is on the key now, sending a message to Tokyo."

In late morning, around eleven o'clock, some officers arrived in the operations section of our headquarters at the submarine base. When I went there to look at the operations plot, I saw a short, slightly heavyset vice admiral, still wearing his life jacket. His white uniform was spotted with fuel oil, and his face was blackened by smoke or soot. His eyes were almost shut, and he looked dazed as he stared off into space, not saying a word. This was Admiral Pye, who twenty-four hours earlier had assured me that the Japanese would not attack us because we were "too strong and powerful."

People were rushing in and out of the headquarters that day, but Admiral Kimmel remained surprisingly calm. Certainly he was shocked, and he was mad—mad at the Japs. He looked sad too, because a lot of men had been killed. The admiral stayed in his office until that night. The attack which had so devastated him in the larger sense had also struck him in a personal way. During the second attack wave, while he was standing at his window looking out over Pearl Harbor, he was hit with a spent machine-gun bullet that cut through his white uniform and raised a welt on his chest. I wasn't present, but later Admiral Kimmel showed it to me and asked, "I'm supposed to turn in all captured enemy material to fleet intelligence according to our instructions, am I not?" I told him that he was, but he said, "I'd like to keep this, if I may." And he did.

About a week or so after that, an official dispatch came in from Washington ordering Admiral Kimmel relieved of duty as Commander in Chief Pacific Fleet. Admiral Pye was given temporary command until Admiral Kimmel's replacement arrived. I saw a copy of that dispatch and went to Admiral Kimmel's office to see him, but no one was there except the Marine orderly. He would tell me only that Admiral Kimmel had "retired to his quarters." I'll have to say that the relief was not totally unexpected. Losing baseball teams have their managers fired. I was very sorry when he left, but I realized that this was his fate. But I never had any idea at that time that he would get the dirty deal he eventually received.

While Admiral Pye was acting commander in chief, he used the war plans section of Kimmel's staff, but he relied on his own operations people. Of course, the relief of Wake Island had been planned by Kimmel and Kimmel's staff, and the forces allocated for the relief of that island had been started forward by Kimmel before Pye took over. Maybe the shock of Pearl Harbor affected Pye's self-confidence. Maybe the responsibility, the chance of having our relief force attacked and defeated overwhelmed him. It seemed that the minute he had an excuse to call it back, he did so.

We believed there were some Japanese carriers around Wake in support of the landing there. Traffic analysis suggested that Carrier Division 2 may have been detached from the Pearl Harbor strike force to go and assist in an assault on Wake. Had Pye been successful and caught those carriers as we did with the ones at Midway the following year, it would have been a real blow to the Japanese. It would have been their second failure at Wake and would have taken some of their Pearl Harbor glory away. It would have been a great morale lifter for the United States. Some said we couldn't afford to lose any carriers; we couldn't afford to lose the *Saratoga*, which had Marine squadrons on board to fly to Wake and be based there. Lieutenant (junior grade) "Butch" O'Hare, the fighter pilot who later won the Medal of Honor, told me after the ship returned to Pearl Harbor that the Marine fliers who had been scheduled to join their fellow Marines on Wake were nearly mutinous after they learned of Admiral Pye's orders to cancel the operation. Some of them threatened to get into their planes and fly to the island anyway.

Morale was really low at that point. To lose to an enemy that fought you, and fought you well, is one thing. But to lose because your own admiral was a "nervous Nellie" was another.

Right at the end of December, Admiral Nimitz came in to take command of the fleet. As soon as I had a chance to talk to him, I asked to be detached. I told him that I wanted to go to sea, in command of a destroyer if possible, and kill Japanese. He told me that he wanted me to stay on—that he had confidence in me and that I could kill more Japanese sitting in my chair than I ever would commanding a destroyer. And that's how I wound up staying in Pearl Harbor through much of the rest of the war. Naturally, there's no way of knowing what would have happened if I had gone back to sea, but the staff duty did give Rochefort and me a big opportunity a few months later. This time, we were able

to follow the Japanese carriers, and that's what enabled Nimitz to spring a trap and win the Battle of Midway.

In the meantime, Admiral Kimmel had reverted to rear admiral and had succumbed to pressure to retire from active duty. As a followup to the blow we'd taken at Pearl Harbor, Admiral Ernest J. King, the new Chief of Naval Operations, ordered a one-man official investigation by Admiral Hart, who was then retired. This was followed in 1944 by an official Navy court of inquiry, the highest investigative tool available to the naval service. It was headed by three admirals—Orin G. Murfin, Edward C. Kalbfus, and Adolphus A. Andrews—all of them experienced in fleet-operations. All individuals who were considered as possibly guilty of an infraction, inaction, or incorrect action were named as "interested parties." They were allowed to attend all the hearings, listen to all the testimony, have their own counsel present, and cross-examine all the witnesses. The court held its hearings, then deliberated and arrived at its findings—that Admiral Kimmel was not guilty of any dereliction of duty or neglect of duty. The court found, as did its Army counterpart, that if there was any neglect or dereliction, it was in Washington, because Stark and General George C. Marshall, the Army Chief of Staff, had not furnished their respective commanders with the vital intelligence necessary for execution of their missions.

Since Washington had already publicly blamed Admiral Kimmel and Lieutenant General Walter C. Short, the Army commander in Hawaii at the time of the attack, it couldn't let these findings

The Navy's court of inquiry called to investigate the attack on Pearl Harbor convenes in July 1944. Left to right, the members are Admiral Edward C. Kalbfus, Admiral Orin G. Murfin, and Vice Admiral Adolphus A. Andrews. (U.S. Navy: Naval Institute Collection.)

stand. Having the blame placed in Washington, where it belonged, would involve the prestige and position of the President of the United States. So, to cover up, the Chief of Naval Operations and the Chief of Staff of the Army applied identical but highly unusual solutions to their quandaries. One-man investigations were usually tools for minor administrative inquiries involving unimportant matters. But some legal shark discovered that a one-man investigation did not have any provision for the rights of an "interested party" (accused) being present to hear all testimony, or being represented by counsel, or having the right to cross-examine witnesses. The one-man "investigation" thus became the vehicle for the CNO and Army Chief of Staff to conduct a "star-chamber" inquiry without any of the usual safeguards guaranteed by civil or military law.

So Admiral King ordered Admiral H. Kent Hewitt to be the one-man investigating board for the Navy. Lieutenant Commander John F. Sonnett, a Naval Reserve lawyer, was given orders to act as "counsel" (prosecuting attorney) for Admiral Hewitt. Sonnett was a clever and crack lawyer in the Department of Justice. (After the war, when he was Assistant Attorney General of the United States, he successfully prosecuted union leader John L. Lewis.) During the Hewitt investigation, which began in May 1945 and lasted until July of that year, Sonnett conducted all the questioning. As far as I was concerned, the only thing Admiral Hewitt did was administer the oath. It soon became apparent that Sonnett's questions were a lawyer's "trick" questions, in which he'd ask for a "yes-or-no answer" to a long, involved question of many parts, some not directly related. After repeatedly saying that I couldn't answer such involved questions with a simple "yes" or "no," Sonnett would continue to repeat the question, as if he'd not heard my protest. I appealed to Admiral Hewitt to have his counsel phrase his questions into simple interrogatories and stop using such trick legal questions. I protested to the admiral that these questions were like the famous "Is it true you've stopped beating your wife?" Any answer is incriminating: "yes" means you did beat your wife but you've stopped it, and "no" means you are still beating her!

Sonnett asked questions something like this:

"Now, isn't it true that, the circumstances being X plus Y equalling Z, and also in view of the fact that A plus B minus C equals D, that so and so came about, without regard to this and that. Please answer yes or no." The fact was that neither "yes" nor "no" would truthfully answer the question. I never got a chance to explain. He'd take my "yes"

Admiral H. Kent Hewitt. (Naval Historical Center: NH 49142.)

John F. Sonnett. (United Press International [Acme].)

or "no" (either would serve his purposes), then go on to another trap question. After I had objected to Admiral Hewitt several times, he asked the lawyer to rephrase the question, but after a simple question or two, Sonnett would shift back to the same, long, involved "trap" question. I refused to answer because the question couldn't be answered in that form. I saw Sonnett in Washington after the war was over, and he came to me and apologized at great length for being so rough on me. I told him that I could not let an apology remove the sense of unfairness I felt over his type of questions. He said something about "having to do my duty."

I did state, several times, that I wanted the record to show that I had objected to those questions, to the fact that they were "trick" questions, and to the fact that they were designed to entrap me. I specifically appealed to Admiral Hewitt that the record show my objections and my reasons for not being able to respond to such questions. He said, "So be it," but my complaints never appeared in the printed record. The first time I saw the record was when the congressional investigation of Pearl Harbor commenced in December 1945.

It was officially announced that the purpose of the Hewitt investigation was to examine further matters that had not been fully covered by the Navy court of inquiry, or ones which were not entirely clear. The "interested parties" to the court of inquiry objected to the one-man investigation when they discovered that they could not be present, nor have counsel present, nor cross-examine witnesses. Their objections, even though perfectly proper, were ignored! These "one-man" Army and Navy investigations were merely legal frauds with which to overturn the findings of the courts of inquiry. This was the dirtiest trick imaginable. The way they treated Admiral Kimmel was disgraceful; to think the Navy would do this to one of its own. Admiral King may have been a great naval officer, but in my opinion he was less than "great" when he found it politically expedient to follow the President's wishes to "whitewash Washington" for the disaster and to make a scapegoat of Admiral Kimmel through such shoddy legal manuevers. That action destroyed a lot of my faith in the Navy. I just couldn't believe that such a dishonest thing could happen. This is why my sympathies are strongly with Admiral Kimmel and very bitter toward those in Washington who acted in so base a manner.

As the Chief of Naval Operations and CominCh at the time, Admiral King signed the final "verdict" of guilt on Admiral Kimmel. As the person responsible for that miscarriage of justice, he killed Kimmel. Kimmel died of a broken heart.

Edwin Thomas Layton (1903–   ) served as Pacific Fleet combat intelligence officer throughout World War II. From 1946 to 1948, he commanded the Naval Net Depot at Tiburon, California, then served until 1950 as director of the Naval Intelligence School, Washington, D.C. He was Fourteenth Naval District intelligence officer for several months in 1950, including the period when the Korean War broke out. From 1951 to 1953, he was Pacific Fleet intelligence officer and assistant chief of staff to Commander in Chief Pacific. In 1953, he ws promoted to rear admiral and then served in intelligence billets with the Joint Chiefs of Staff. He was later assistant chief of staff to Commander in Chief Pacific Fleet and again director of the Naval Intelligence School in Washington. Admiral Layton retired from active duty in 1959 and later worked in Japan several years for Northrop Aircraft Corporation. He now lives in Carmel, California. (Courtesy of Rear Admiral Edwin T. Layton, USN, Ret.)

Sources of Articles

"I Led the Air Attack on Pearl Harbor," published in *U.S. Naval Institute Proceedings*, September 1952, pp. 939–952.

"Aircraft Battle Force," pp. 78–83 of unpublished autobiographical manuscript. Published with the permission of Mrs. Arthur W. Radford. The complete manuscript is on file at the Hoover Institution on War, Revolution, and Peace, Stanford, California, and at the Naval Historical Center, Washington, D.C.

"Evolution of Aircraft Carrier Tactics of the Imperial Japanese Navy," adapted from a paper written for the use of Clark G. Reynolds in preparation of his book *The Fast Carriers: The Forging of an Air Navy* (New York: McGraw-Hill, 1968). Published through the courtesy of Dr. Reynolds and with the permission of General Genda.

"Aerial Attacks on Fleets at Anchor," published in *U.S. Naval Institute Proceedings*, August 1937, pp. 1126–1132.

"Air Raid, Pearl Harbor. This Is No Drill," published in *Hearings before the Joint Committee on the Investigation of the Pearl Harbor Attack*, 79th Congress (Washington, D.C.: U.S. Government Printing Office, 1946), Part 32, p. 444.

"Stepping-Stones to War," published in *U.S. Naval Institute Proceedings*, September 1951, pp. 927–931.

"My God, They Can't Do That to Me," adapted from Naval Institute oral history interviews of Admiral Dyer by Dr. John T. Mason, Jr., 19 June and 13 November 1969, pp. 186–216. The complete transcript of Admiral Dyer's oral history is on file at the U.S. Naval Institute; Nimitz Library, U.S. Naval Academy; and the Operational Archives Branch, Naval Historical Center, Washington, D.C. This edited version is published with the permission of Admiral Dyer.

"The Navy Was Not Ready for War," published in "Barometer," *Naval War College Review*, September-October 1980, pp. 82–83. Published with the permission of the Naval War College.

"The Last Months of Peace at Pearl Harbor," published as "The Last Days of Peace in Pearl Harbor," *U.S. Naval Institute Proceedings*, December 1971, pp. 85–88.

"Hawaii Operation," published in *U.S. Naval Institute Proceedings*, December 1955, pp. 1315–1331.

"The Taranto Lesson," adapted from Naval Institute oral history interview of Admiral Ansel by Dr. John T. Mason, Jr., 15 September 1970, pp. 79–89. The complete transcript of Admiral Ansel's oral history is on file at the U.S. Naval Institute; Nimitz Library, U.S. Naval Academy; and the Operational Archives Branch, Naval Historical Center, Washington, D.C. This edited version is published with the permission of Mrs. Walter C. Ansel.

"Unheeded Warnings," adapted from Naval Institute oral history interviews of Admiral McCollum by Dr. John T. Mason, Jr., 2 February, 17 February, and 17 March 1971, various pages. The complete transcript of Admiral McCollum's oral history is on file at the U.S. Naval Institute; Nimitz Library, U.S. Naval Academy; and the Operational Archives Branch, Naval Historical Center, Washington, D.C. This edited version is published with the permission of Commander Arthur H. McCollum, Jr., U.S. Navy (Retired).

"Aide to Admiral Stark," adapted from Naval Institute oral history interview of Admiral Smedberg by Dr. John T. Mason, Jr., 2 October 1975, pp. 141–184. The complete transcript of Admiral Smedberg's oral history is on file at the U.S. Naval Institute; Nimitz Library, U.S. Naval Academy; and the Operational Archives Branch, Naval Historical Center, Washington, D.C. This edited version is published with the permission of Admiral Smedberg.

"The Fog of War," adapted from Naval Institute oral history interviews of Admiral Wellborn by Dr. John T. Mason, Jr., 4 January and 8 February 1972, pp. 124–147. The complete transcript of Admiral Wellborn's oral history is on file at the U.S. Naval Institute; Nimitz Library, U.S. Naval Academy; and the Operational Archives Branch, Naval Historical Center, Washington, D.C. This edited version is published with the permission of Admiral Wellborn.

"War Plans Under My Mattress," adapted from an interview of Admiral McCrea by Paul Stillwell, 29 August 1980, and from McCrea's trip notes dated 5 February 1941.

"Cutting the Red Tape," adapted from an interview of Admiral Holloway by Paul Stillwell, 12 September 1980.

"This Is a War We Could Lose," adapted from Naval Institute oral history interviews of Mr. Baldwin by Dr. John T. Mason, Jr., 21 April and 16 June 1975, pp. 307–315, 333–337. The complete transcript of Mr. Baldwin's oral history is on file at the U.S. Naval Institute; Nimitz Library, U.S. Naval Academy; and the Operational Archives Branch, Naval Historical Center, Washington, D.C. This edited version is published with the permission of Mr. Baldwin.

"The President Faces War," adapted from *The Reminiscences of Frances Perkins*, Volume VIII (1955), pp. 35–98, in the Oral History Collection of Columbia University. Published with the permission of the Oral History Research Office, Columbia University.

"The Strange Assignment of the USS *Lanikai*," excerpted from "The Strange Assignment of USS *Lanikai*, *U.S. Naval Institute Proceedings*, September 1962, pp. 70–83.

"Worse Than Dante's Inferno," adapted from Columbia University oral history interview of Admiral Anderson by Dr. John T. Mason, Jr., 23 March 1962, pp. 234–251. The complete transcript of Admiral Anderson's oral history is on file at Columbia University; Nimitz Library, U.S. Naval Academy; and the Operational Archives Branch, Naval Historical Center, Washington, D.C. Published with the permission of the Oral History Research Office, Columbia University.

"A Tactical View of Pearl Harbor," adapted from "I Remember Pearl Harbor," *U.S. Naval Institute Proceedings*, December 1972, pp. 18–24.

"The Value of Gold Braid," adapted from Naval Institute oral history interview of Captain Merdinger by Dr. John T. Mason, Jr., 28 December 1971, pp. 32–41. The complete transcript of Captain Merdinger's oral history is on file at the U.S. Naval Institute; Nimitz Library, U.S. Naval Academy; and the Operational Archives Branch, Naval Historical Center, Washington, D.C. Also published as "Under Water at Pearl Harbor," *U.S. Naval Institute Proceedings*, December 1976, pp. 48–49. Published with the permission of Captain Merdinger.

"The Cheer-Up Ship," published in "Comment and Discussion," *U.S. Naval Institute Proceedings*, September 1973, pp. 97–98.

"The Raising and Salvaging of the *Nevada*," excerpted from "Rejuvenation at Pearl Harbor," *U.S. Naval Institute Proceedings*, December 1946, pp. 1521–1547.

"The Silver Mine," written expressly for *Air Raid: Pearl Harbor!* by Captain Buckley. A related item was published in "Comment and Discussion," *U.S. Naval Institute Proceedings*, January 1974, p. 80.

"Why Them and Not Me?" written expressly for *Air Raid: Pearl Harbor!* by Commander Backus. Also published in *U.S. Naval Institute Proceedings*, September 1981.

"*Arizona* Survivor," adapted from Naval Institute oral history interview of Admiral Masterson by Dr. John T. Mason, Jr., 6 December 1972, pp. 81–90. The complete transcript of Admiral Masterson's oral history is on file at the U.S. Naval Institute; Nimitz Library, U.S. Naval Academy; and the Operational Archives Branch, Naval Historical Center, Washington, D.C. This edited version is published with the permission of Admiral Masterson.

"Last Man off the *California*, published in *U.S. Naval Institute Proceedings*, June 1978, p. 97.

"Refuge in *Detroit*," published as "I Remember It Well," *U.S. Naval Institute Proceedings*, December 1979, pp. 64–66.

"The 'Lucky Lou,' " updated from version published in "Comment and Discussion," *U.S. Naval Institute Proceedings*, January 1977, p. 84.

"Like Swatting Bees in a Telephone Booth," published in *U.S. Naval Institute Proceedings*, December 1980, pp. 72–74.

"We Four Ensigns," published in *U.S. Naval Institute Proceedings*, December 1966, pp. 106–109.

"Encounters with a Midget," published in "Comment and Discussion," *U.S. Naval Institute Proceedings*, April 1975, p. 87.

"Grandstand Seat," adapted from Naval Institute oral history interview of Admiral Ramage by Dr. John T. Mason, Jr., 27 August 1973, pp. 38–59. The complete transcript of Admiral Ramage's oral history is on file at the U.S. Naval Institute; Nimitz Library, U.S. Naval

Academy; and the Operational Archives Branch, Naval Historical Center, Washington, D.C. This edited version is published with the permission of Admiral Ramage.

"A Patrol in the Wrong Direction," adapted from Naval Institute oral history interview of Admiral Moorer by Dr. John T. Mason, Jr., 10 March 1975, pp. 91–112. The complete transcript of Admiral Moorer's oral history is on file at the U.S. Naval Institute; Nimitz Library, U.S. Naval Academy; and the Operational Archives Branch, Naval Historical Center, Washington, D.C. This edited version is published with the permission of Admiral Moorer.

"Wipeout at Kaneohe," adapted from Naval Institute oral history interview of Admiral Price by Commander Etta Belle Kitchen, U.S. Navy (Retired), 13 May 1978, pp. 47–56. The complete transcript of Admiral Price's oral history is on file at the U.S. Naval Institute; Nimitz Library, U.S. Naval Academy; and the Operational Archives Branch, Naval Historical Center, Washington, D.C. This edited version is published with the permission of Admiral Price.

"Call Out the Marines," published as "Marine Barracks, Navy Yard Pearl Harbor: December 1941," in *Shipmate*, December 1973, pp. 16–20. Published with the permission of the U.S. Naval Academy Alumni Association, Inc.

". . . A Hell of a Christmas," published in *U.S. Naval Institute Proceedings*, December 1968, pp. 63–71.

"How I Were at Pearl Harbor," published as "How Happen I Were at Pearl Harbor," *U.S. Naval Institute Proceedings*, December 1962, pp. 156–158.

"A Navy Bride Learns to Cope," published as "From the Distaff Side," *Shipmate*, December 1974, pp. 15–21. Published with the permission of the U.S. Naval Academy Alumni Association, Inc.

"Did the Japs Win?" adapted from interview of Mrs. Guthrie by Captain Paul B. Ryan, U.S. Navy (Retired), published as "A Navy Wife at Pearl Harbor," *Shipmate*, December 1975, pp. 21–23. This edited version is published with the permission of the U.S. Naval Academy Alumni Association, Inc.

"American Prisoners in Japan," adapted from Naval Institute oral history interviews of Captain Smith-Hutton by Captain Paul B. Ryan, U.S. Navy (Retired), 18 July and 25 July 1974, pp. 323–351. The complete transcript of Captain Smith-Hutton's oral history is on file at the U.S. Naval Institute; Nimitz Library, U.S. Naval Academy; and the Operational Archives Branch, Naval Historical Center, Washington, D.C. This edited version is published with the permission of Mrs. Henri Smith-Hutton.

"Pearl Harbor Aftermath," published in *U.S. Naval Institute Proceedings*, December 1978, pp. 68–75, and in *Double-Edged Secrets: U.S. Naval Intelligence Operations in the Pacific during World War II* (Annapolis: Naval Institute Press, 1979), pp. 30–43.

"Replacing the Commander in Chief," adapted from Naval Institute oral history interview of Mr. Lamar by Dr. John T. Mason, Jr., 3 May 1970, pp. 1–11. The complete transcript of Mr. Lamar's oral history is on file at the

U.S. Naval Institute; Nimitz Library, U.S. Naval Academy; and the Operational Archives Branch, Naval Historical Center, Washington, D.C. This edited version is published with the permission of Mr. Lamar.

"God's Divine Will," published as "Pearl Harbor Postscript," *U.S. Naval Institute Proceedings,* December 1966, p. 126.

"A War Correspondent's Odyssey," written expressly for *Air Raid: Pearl Harbor!* by Mr. Harsch.

"I Don't Think They'd Be Such Damned Fools," adapted from Naval Institute oral history interview of Admiral Drake by Commander Etta Belle Kitchen, U.S. Navy (Retired), 15 June 1969, pp. 1–5. The complete transcript of Admiral Drake's oral history is on file at the U.S. Naval Institute; Nimitz Library, U.S. Naval Academy; and the Operational Archives Branch, Naval Historical Center, Washington, D.C. This edited version is published with the permission of Mr. John Drake.

"Admiral Kimmel Deserved a Better Fate," adapted from Naval Institute oral history interview of Admiral Layton by Commander Etta Belle Kitchen, U.S. Navy (Retired), 30 May 1970, various pages. Access to the complete transcript requires the specific permission of Admiral Layton. This edited version is published with the permission of Admiral Layton.

Index